you so much

GYA-AAH!

for supporting this hapless alligator

for so long!

KOYOHARU GOTOUGE

Hi, I'm Gotouge! It makes me sad to say it, but this is the final volume of *Demon Slayer: Kimetsu no Yaiba*. Thank you to everyone who has cheered me on and was involved with the series. All the encouragement and support I received from the people who read my work meant so much to me, so no amount of thanks I can offer would ever be enough. Your kindness cheered me on the whole time and from all sides. Thank you so much for reading this manga. I worked hard on it, so I'm really happy. Truly, I'm blessed to have been able to present *Demon Slayer* to the world. I look forward to the day when we can all meet again!

Tales from hundreds of years ago exist in the present, and after the passage of decades and centuries the events of today will become stories of the past. Grandfathers and grandmothers, fathers and mothers—everyone experiences a time of childhood, a time that leads to the present. You yourself are part of that great flow, and as you overcome times of hardship, the years pass by. The very moment that you think all is lost is the moment when you must stand firm and not stray from the path. I hope you will be strong in difficult situations and harsh circumstances. But it's also not good to push yourself too hard, so take things at a reasonable pace. Keep your eyes fixed forward and find your own bliss.

DEMON SLAYER:
KIMETSU NO YAIBA
VOLUME 23
Shonen Jump Edition

Story and Art by
KOYOHARU GOTOUGE

TRANSLATION John Werry
ENGLISH ADAPTATION Stan!
TOUCH-UP ART & LETTERING John Hunt
DESIGN Jimmy Presler
EDITOR Mike Montesa

Printed in the U.S.A.

Published by VIZ Media, LLC
P.O. Box 77010
San Francisco, CA 94107

10 9 8 7 6 5 4 3 2 1
First printing, August 2021

RATED T TEEN
ratings.viz.com

PARENTAL ADVISORY
DEMON SLAYER: KIMETSU NO YAIBA is rated T for Teen and recommended for ages 13 and up. This volume contains realistic and fantasy violence.

VIZ MEDIA
viz.com

SHONEN JUMP

DEMON SLAYER

KIMETSU NO YAIBA

23

LIFE SHINING ACROSS THE YEARS

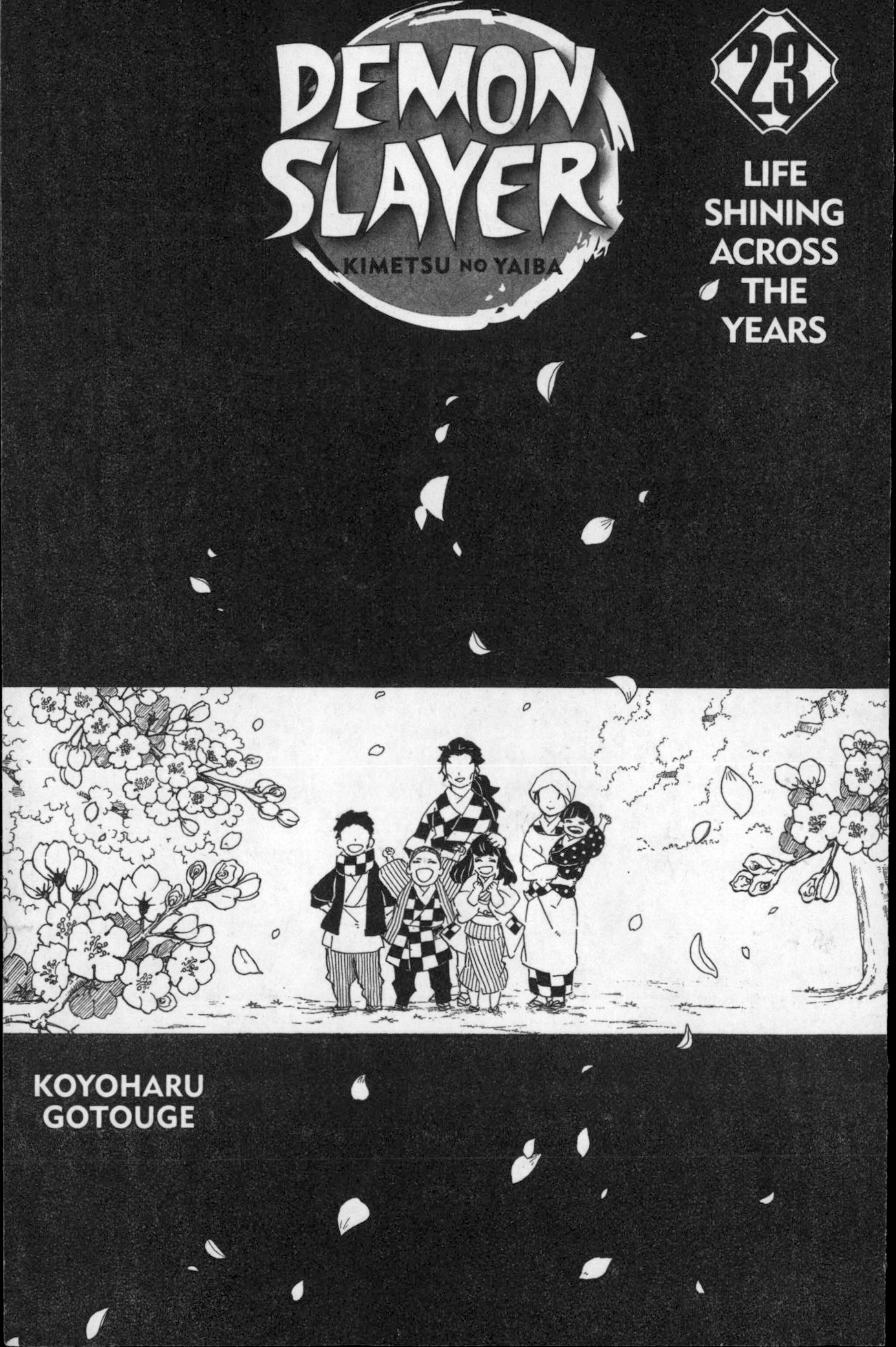

KOYOHARU GOTOUGE

CHARACTERS

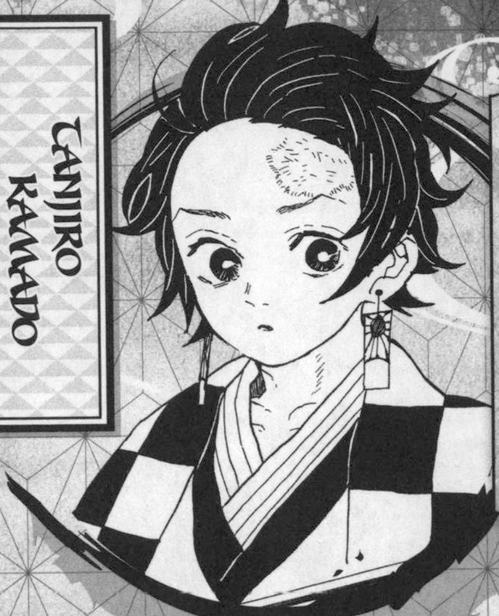

TANJIRO KAMADO

A kind boy who saved his sister and now aims to avenge his family. He can smell the scent of demons and an opponent's weakness.

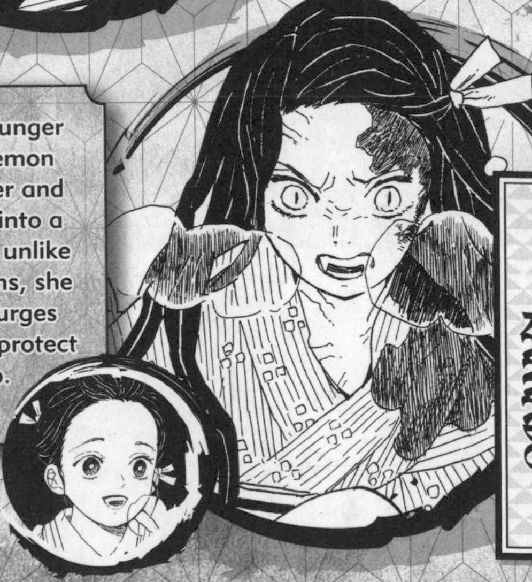

NEZUKO KAMADO

Tanjiro's younger sister. A demon attacked her and turned her into a demon. But unlike other demons, she fights her urges and tries to protect Tanjiro.

STORY

In Taisho-era Japan, young Tanjiro makes a living selling charcoal. One day, demons kill his family and turn his younger sister Nezuko into a demon. Tanjiro and Nezuko set out to find a way to return Nezuko to human form and defeat Kibutsuji, the demon who killed their family!

After joining the Demon Slayer Corps, Tanjiro meets Tamayo and Yushiro—demons who oppose Kibutsuji—who provide a clue to how Nezuko may be turned back into a human. Nezuko manifests the ability to withstand sunlight, so Kibutsuji attacks Ubuyashiki Mansion. The Demon Slayers suffer many losses, but they kill all the Upper Rank demons and eventually find Kibutsuji! As Tamayo's poison makes him grow weaker, will they be able to deliver the final blow? It all comes down to this desperate clash, but how will it end?!

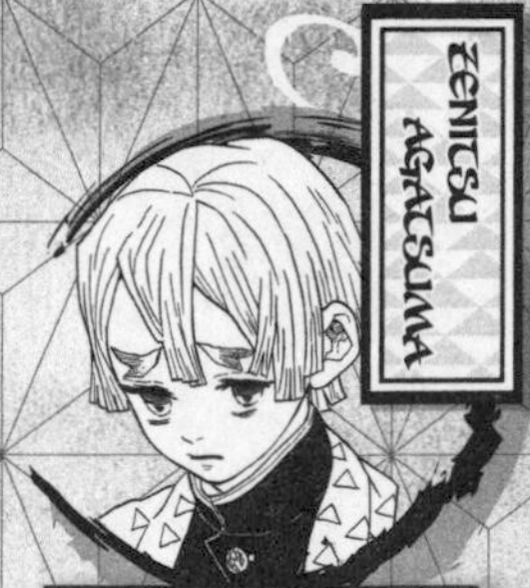
ZENITSU AGATSUMA

He went through Final Selection at the same time as Tanjiro. He's usually cowardly, but when he falls asleep, his true power comes out.

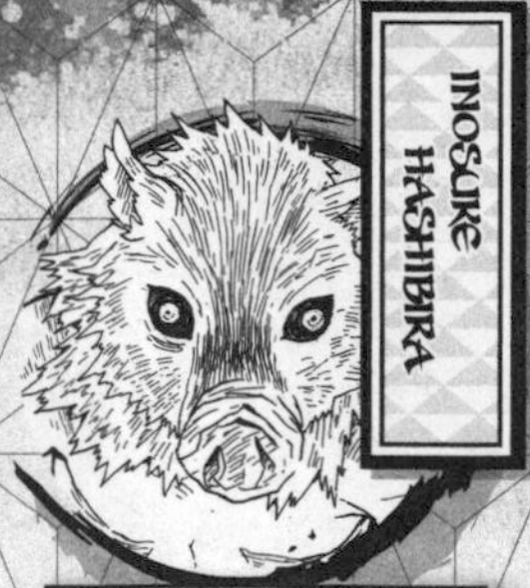
INOSUKE HASHIBIRA

He also went through Final Selection at the same time as Tanjiro. He wears the pelt of a wild boar and is very belligerent.

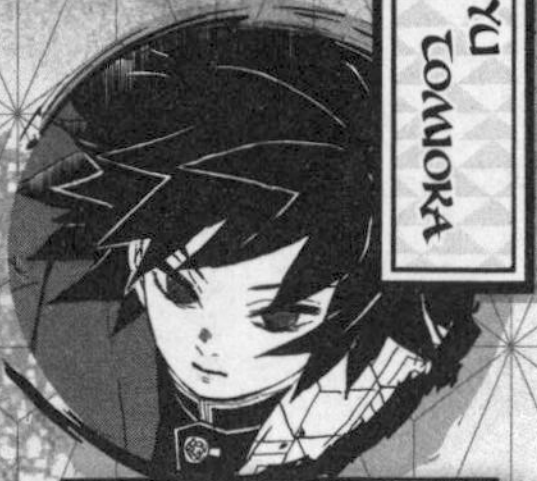
GIYU TOMIOKA

The Hashira who invited Tanjiro to join the Demon Slayer Corps. He has always cared about Tanjiro.

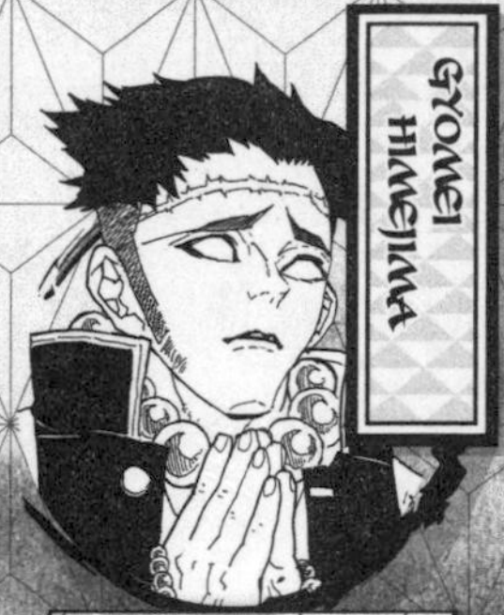
GYOMEI HIMEJIMA

Stone Hashira in the Demon Slayer Corps. He is always clasping a rosary and reciting a Buddhist prayer.

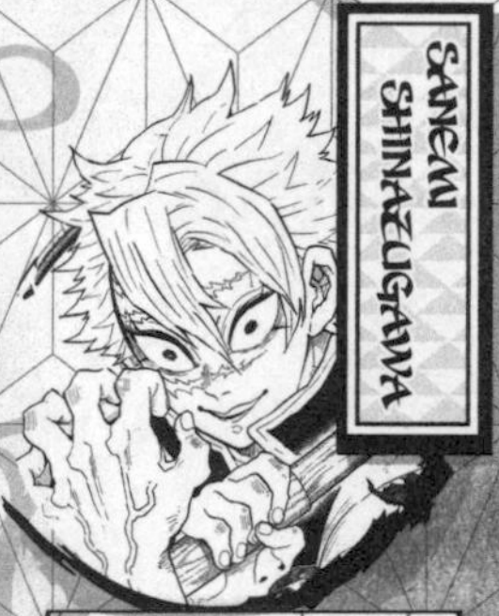
SANEMI SHINAZUGAWA

Wind Hashira in the Demon Slayer Corps. He has a harsh attitude toward his younger brother Genya.

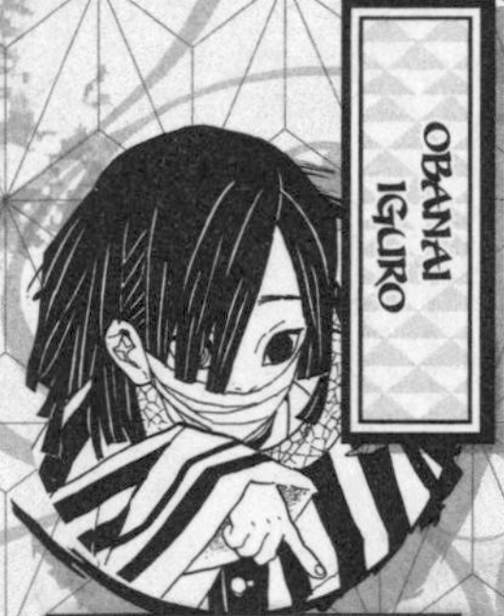
OBANAI IGURO

Serpent Hashira in the Demon Slayer Corps. He's always in the company of his snake Kaburamaru.

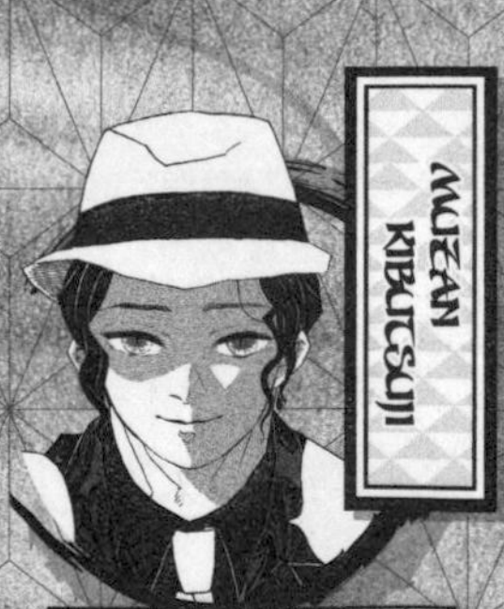
MUZAN KIBUTSUJI

Kibutsuji turned Nezuko into a demon. He is Tanjiro's enemy and hides his nature in order to live among human beings.

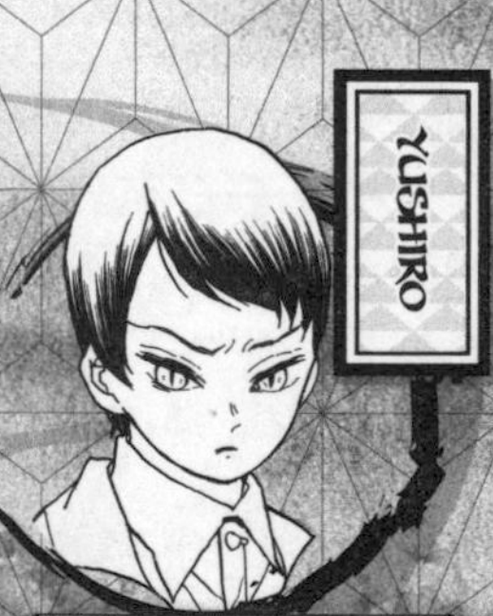
YUSHIRO

A young boy who is a demon. He is devoted to Tamayo and possesses a Blood Demon Art called Eyeblind. He is pretending to be human so he can work alongside the Demon Slayers.

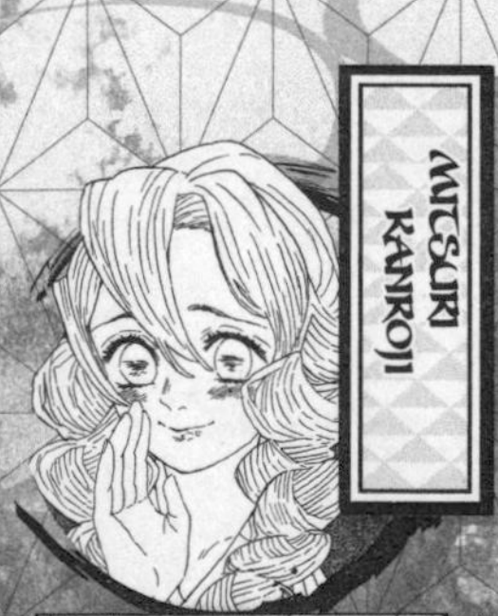
MITSURI KANROJI

Love Hashira in the Demon Slayer Corps. She joined the Demon Slayer Corps to find a man to marry.

CONTENTS

DEMON SLAYER

KIMETSU NO YAIBA

23

LIFE SHINING ACROSS THE YEARS

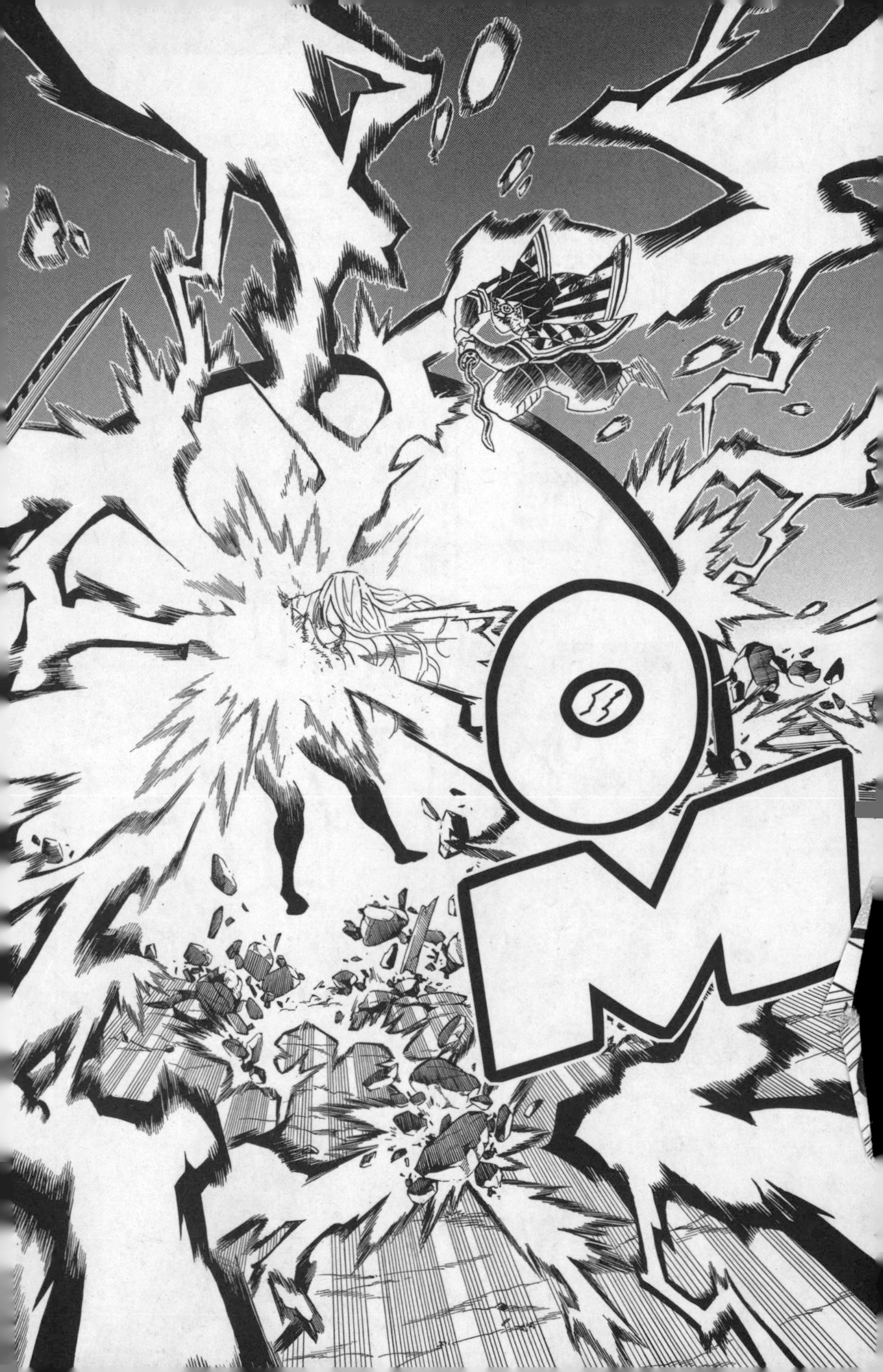
OM

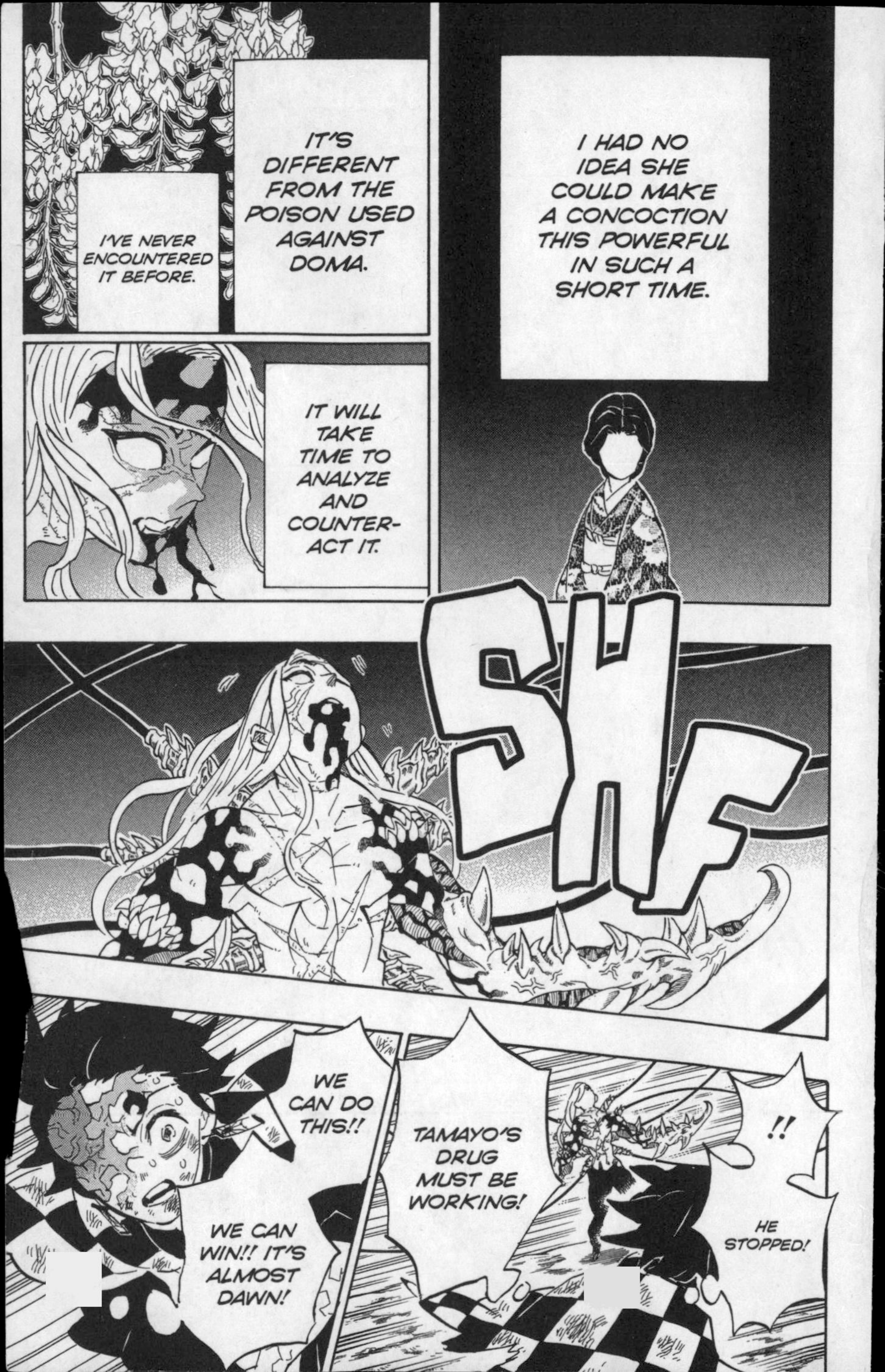
I HAD NO IDEA SHE COULD MAKE A CONCOCTION THIS POWERFUL IN SUCH A SHORT TIME.
IT'S DIFFERENT FROM THE POISON USED AGAINST DOMA.
I'VE NEVER ENCOUNTERED IT BEFORE.
IT WILL TAKE TIME TO ANALYZE AND COUNTER-ACT IT.
SHF
!!
HE STOPPED!
TAMAYO'S DRUG MUST BE WORKING!
WE CAN DO THIS!!
WE CAN WIN!! IT'S ALMOST DAWN!

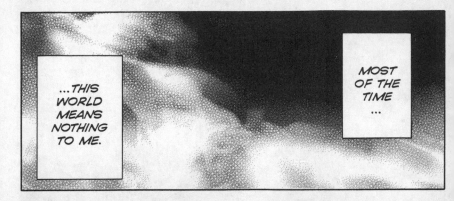

MOST OF THE TIME ...
...THIS WORLD MEANS NOTHING TO ME.
ATTACKS AND DAMAGE FROM BRIGHT-RED BLADES SHOULDN'T WORK ON ME.
THE BRIGHT-RED BLADES OF THESE DEMON SLAYERS PALE IN COMPARISON TO HIS.
AND REGENERATING SHOULDN'T EXHAUST ME.
HOWEVER, THE FOUR DRUGS IN MY SYSTEM HAVE TURNED ORDINARILY INEFFECTIVE ATTACKS...
...INTO EXTREMELY EFFECTIVE ONES THAT ARE TAKING A PHYSICAL TOLL ON ME.

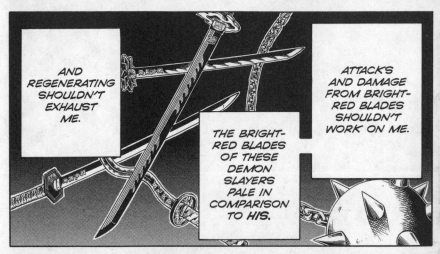

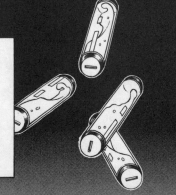

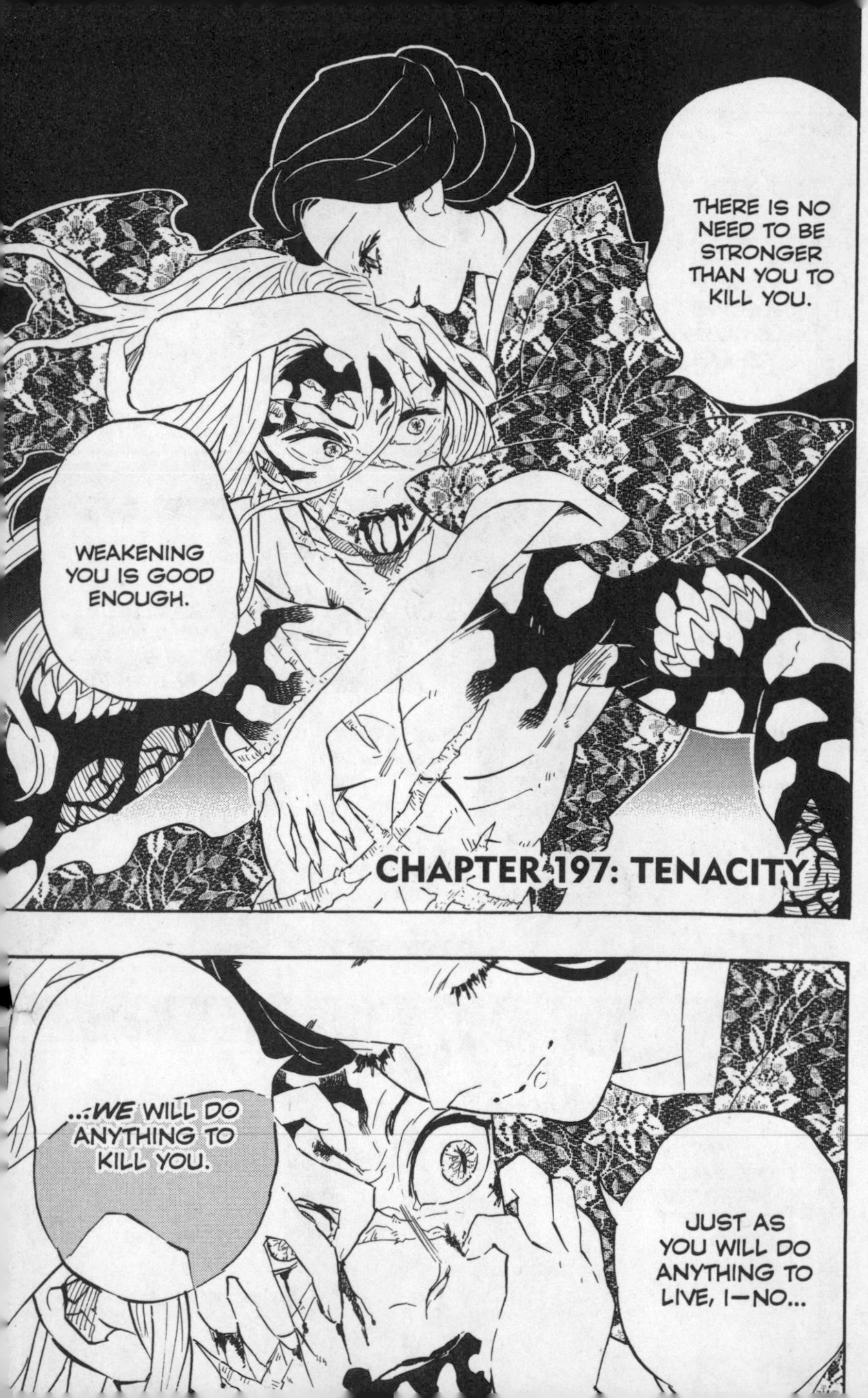
THERE IS NO NEED TO BE STRONGER THAN YOU TO KILL YOU.
WEAKENING YOU IS GOOD ENOUGH.
CHAPTER 197: TENACITY
JUST AS YOU WILL DO ANYTHING TO LIVE, I—NO...
...WE WILL DO ANYTHING TO KILL YOU.

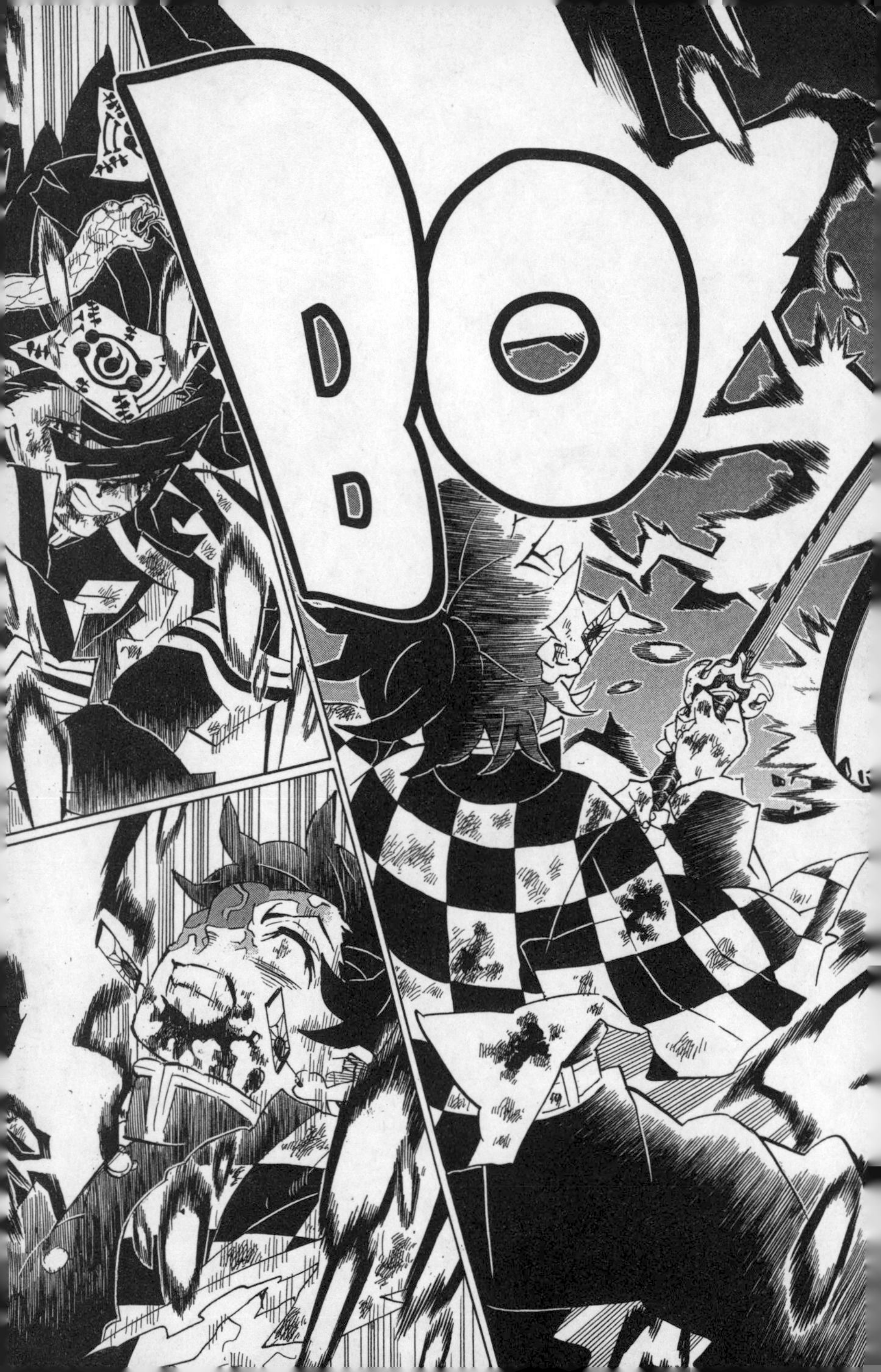

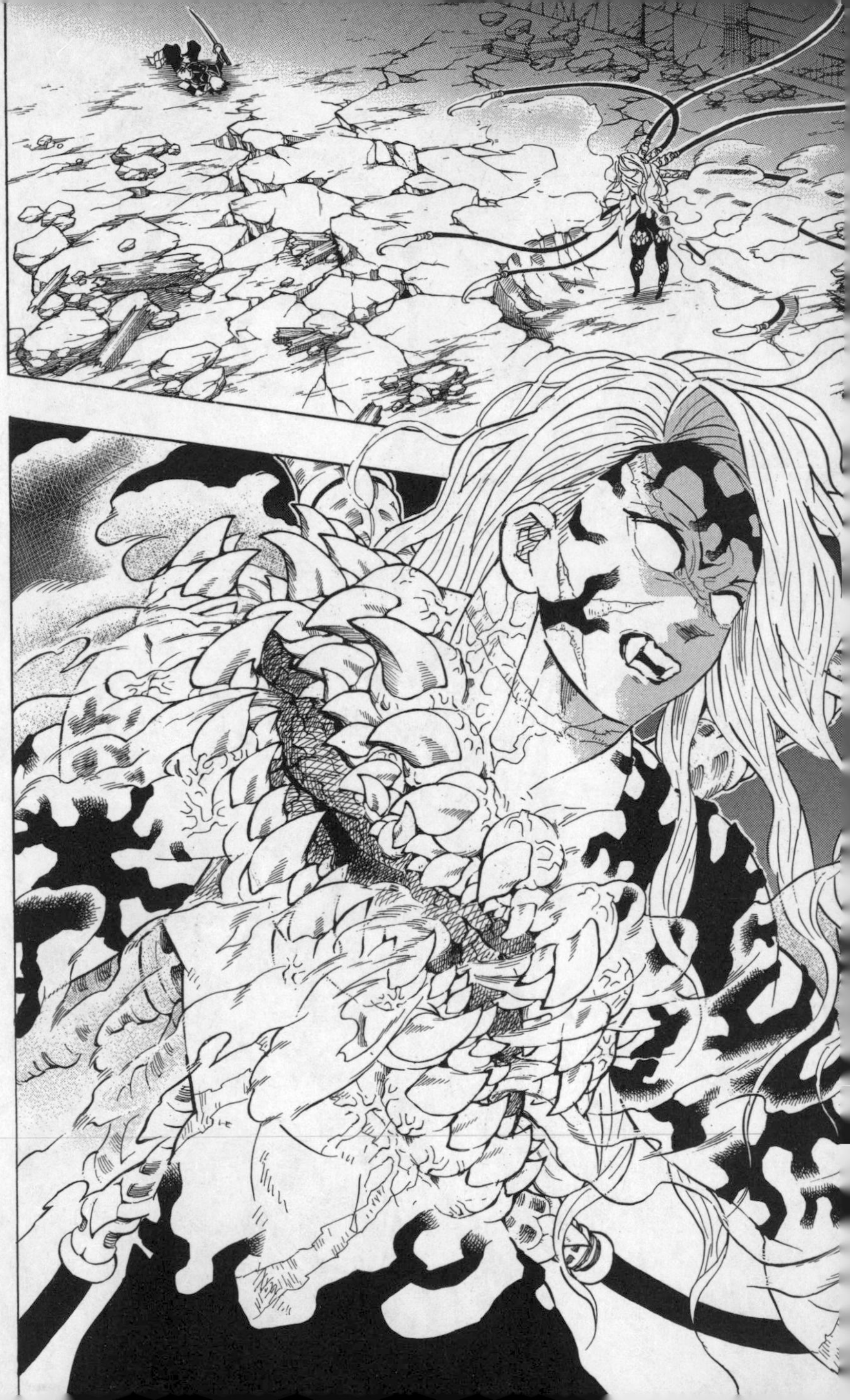

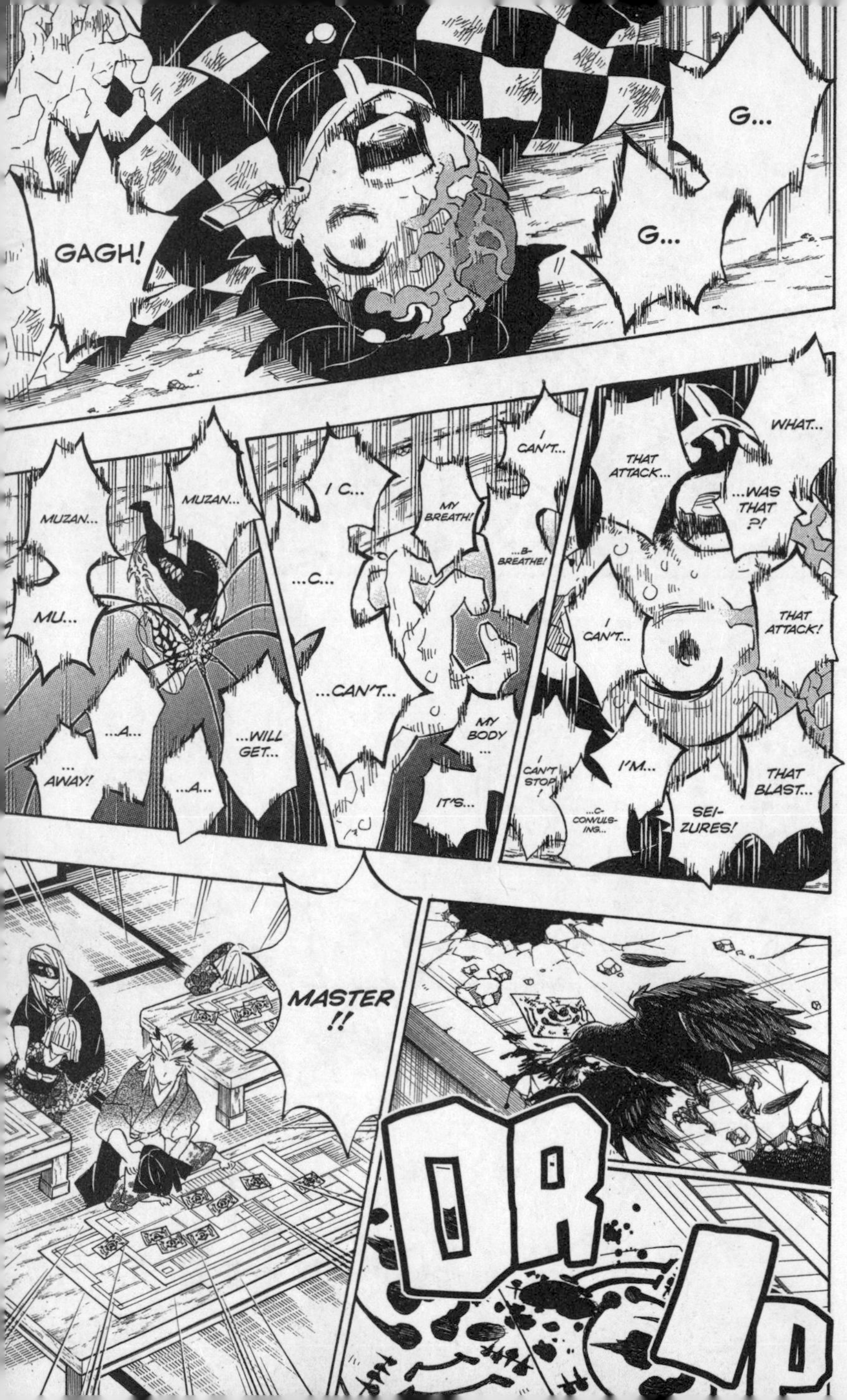
G...
G...
GAGH!
WHAT...
...WAS THAT?!
THAT ATTACK...
THAT ATTACK!
I CAN'T...
THAT BLAST...
I'M...
SEI-ZURES!
I CAN'T STOP!
...C-CONVULSING...
I CAN'T...
MY BREATH!
...B-BREATHE!
I C...
...C...
...CAN'T...
MY BODY...
IT'S...
MUZAN...
MUZAN...
MU...
...WILL GET...
...A...
...A...
...AWAY!
DR
MASTER!!

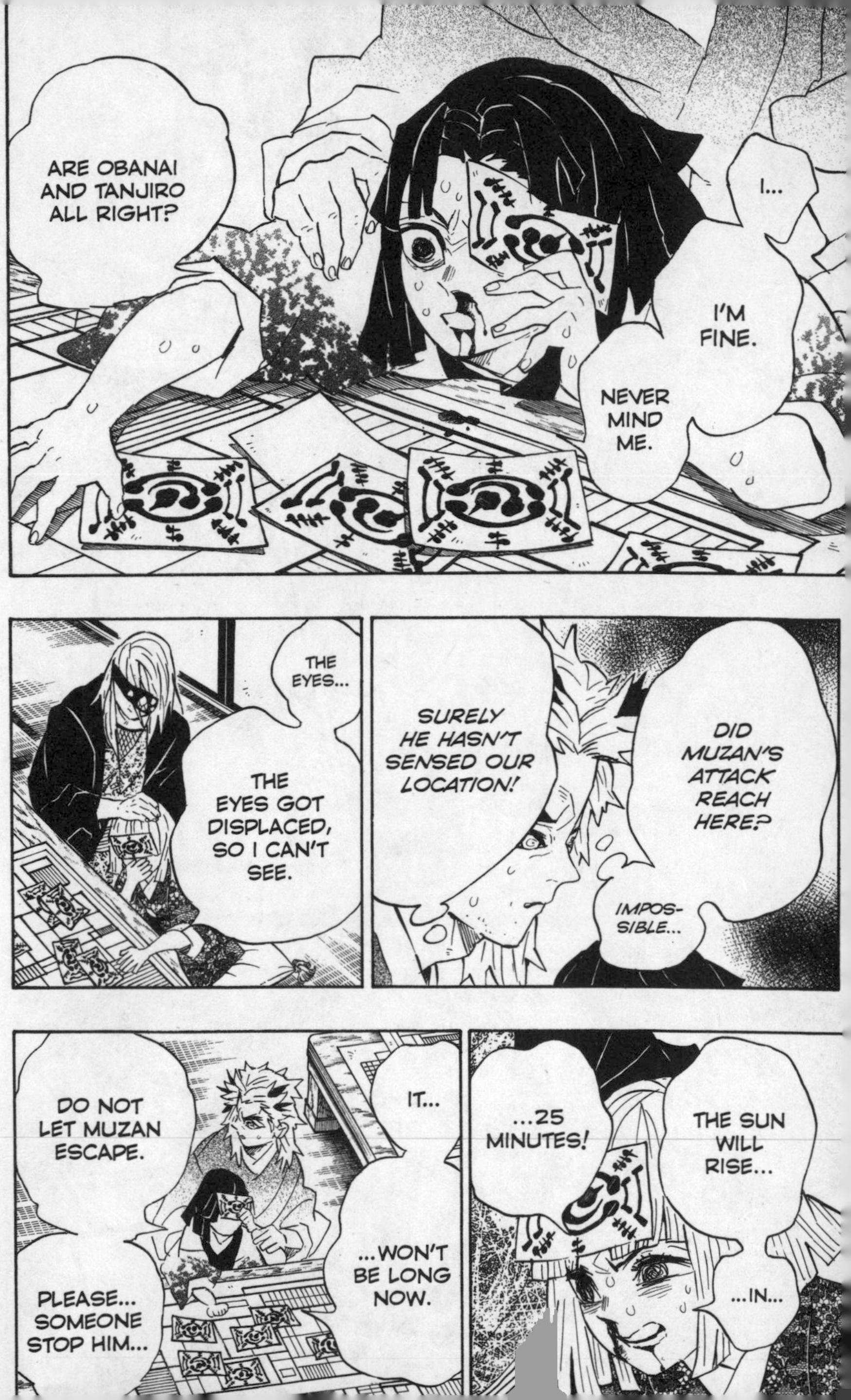

I...
I'M FINE.
NEVER MIND ME.
ARE OBANAI AND TANJIRO ALL RIGHT?
DID MUZAN'S ATTACK REACH HERE?
IMPOSSIBLE...
SURELY HE HASN'T SENSED OUR LOCATION!
THE EYES...
THE EYES GOT DISPLACED, SO I CAN'T SEE.
THE SUN WILL RISE...
...IN...
...25 MINUTES!
IT...
...WON'T BE LONG NOW.
DO NOT LET MUZAN ESCAPE.
PLEASE... SOMEONE STOP HIM...

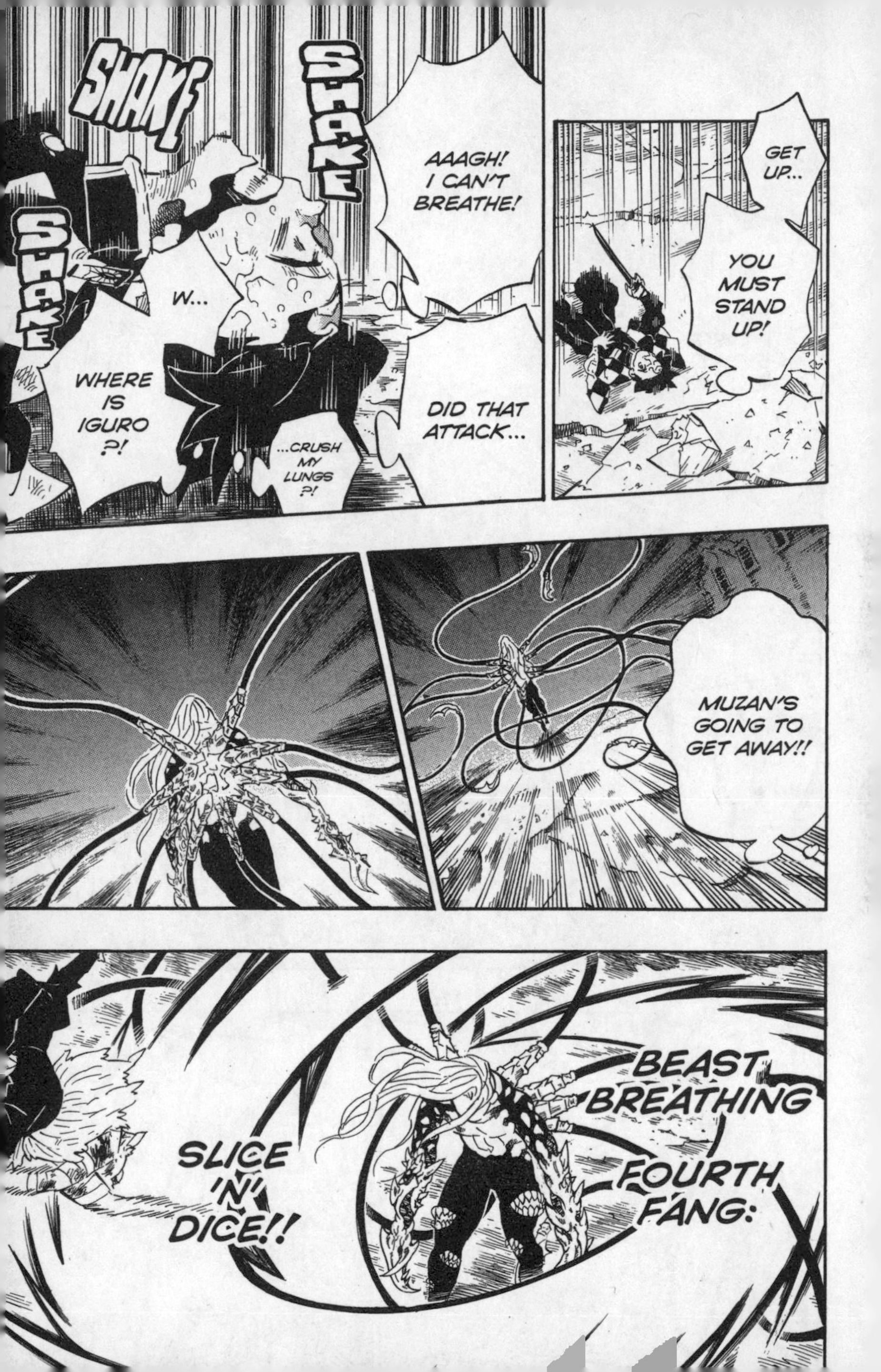
GET UP...
YOU MUST STAND UP!
SHAKE
AAAGH! I CAN'T BREATHE!
SHAKE
DID THAT ATTACK...
...CRUSH MY LUNGS ?!
W...
SHAKE
WHERE IS IGURO ?!
MUZAN'S GOING TO GET AWAY!!
BEAST BREATHING
FOURTH FANG:
SLICE 'N' DICE!!

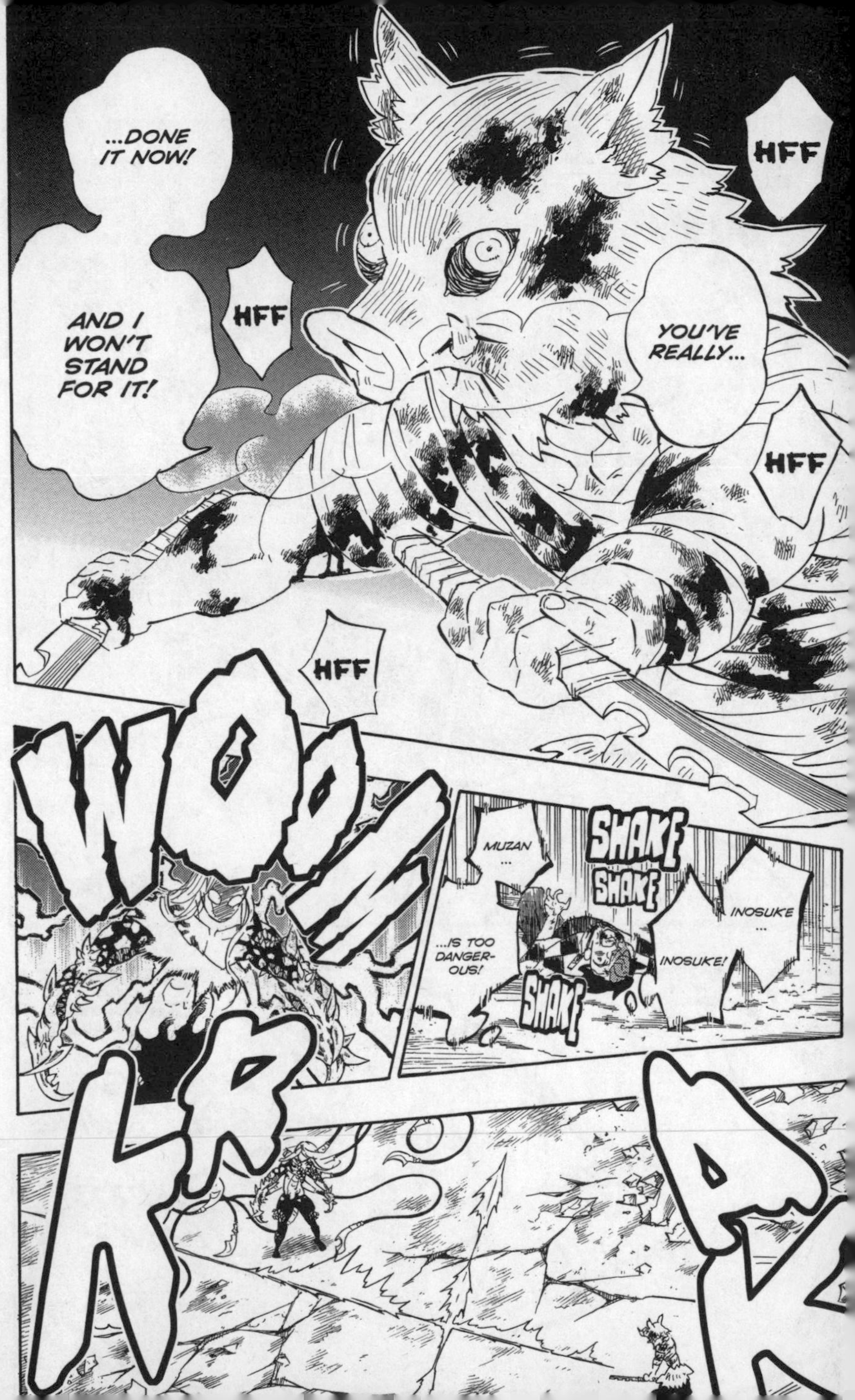
HFF
YOU'VE REALLY...
...DONE IT NOW!
HFF
HFF
AND I WON'T STAND FOR IT!
HFF
INOSUKE ...
INOSUKE!
SHAKE
SHAKE
MUZAN ...
...IS TOO DANGER-OUS!
SHAKE
WOOM

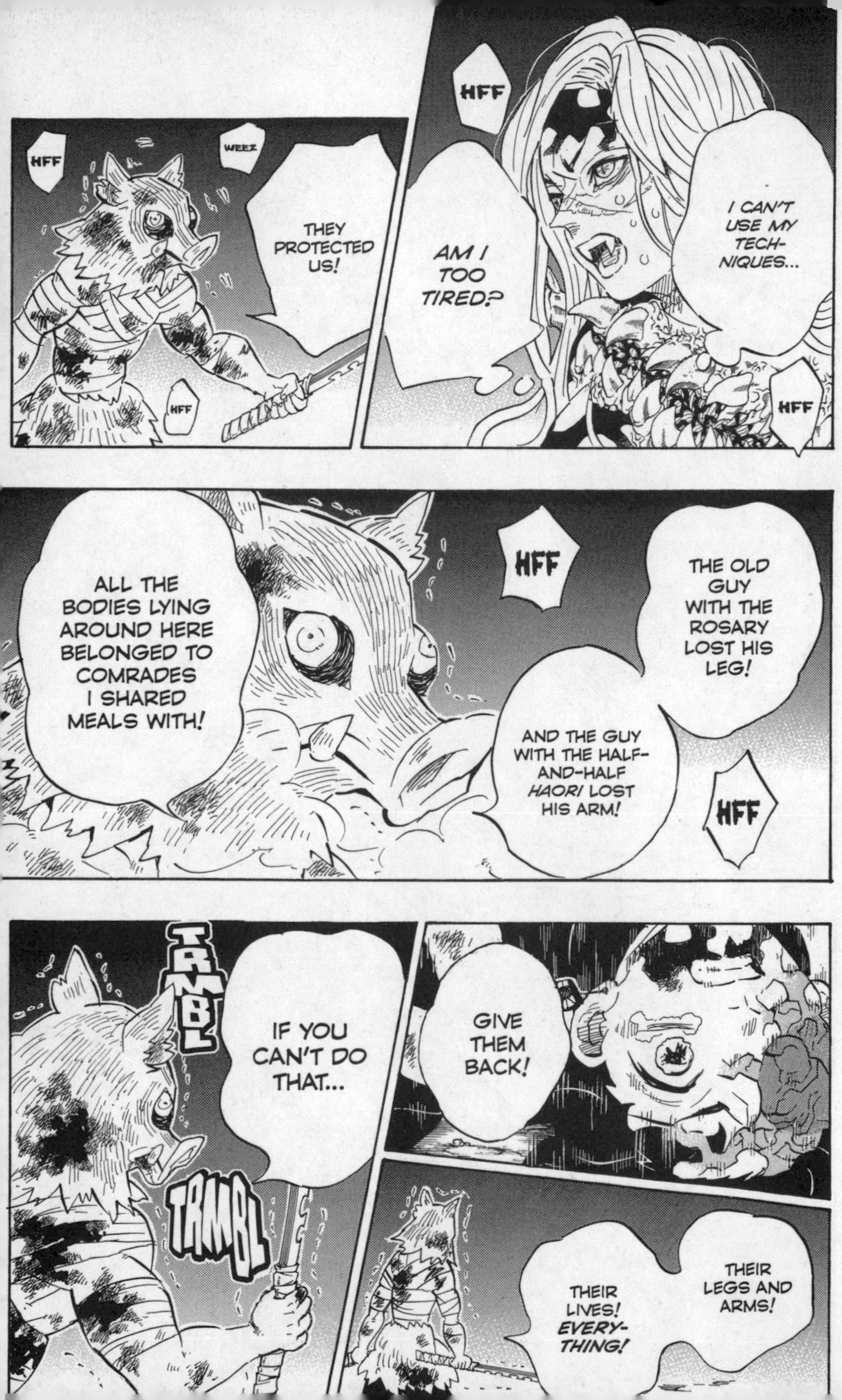
HFF
I CAN'T USE MY TECH-NIQUES...
AM I TOO TIRED?
HFF
WEEZ
THEY PROTECTED US!
HFF
HFF
HFF
THE OLD GUY WITH THE ROSARY LOST HIS LEG!
AND THE GUY WITH THE HALF-AND-HALF *HAORI* LOST HIS ARM!
HFF
ALL THE BODIES LYING AROUND HERE BELONGED TO COMRADES I SHARED MEALS WITH!
GIVE THEM BACK!
THEIR LEGS AND ARMS!
THEIR LIVES! *EVERY-THING!*
TRMBL
IF YOU CAN'T DO THAT...
TRMBL

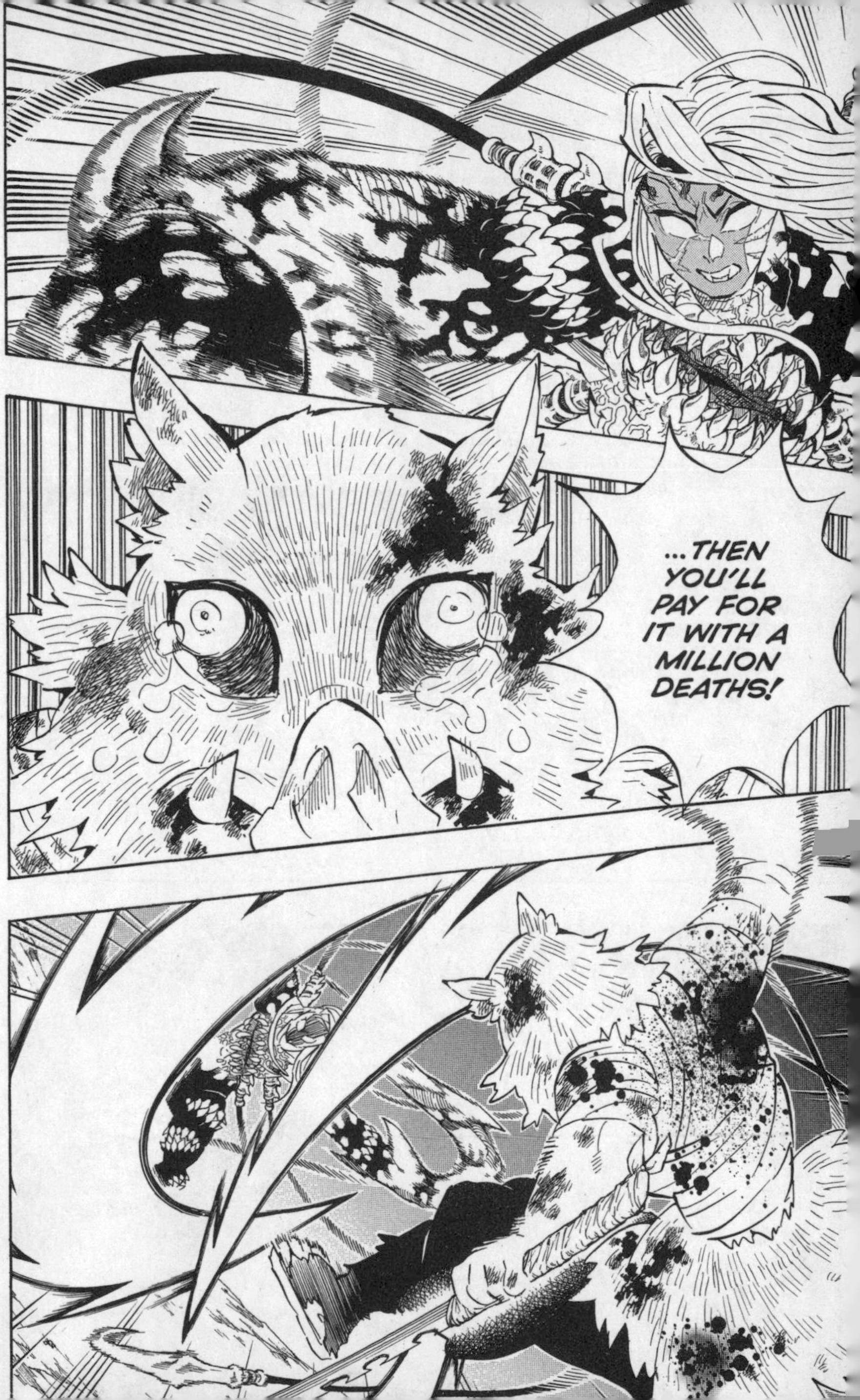
...THEN YOU'LL PAY FOR IT WITH A MILLION DEATHS!

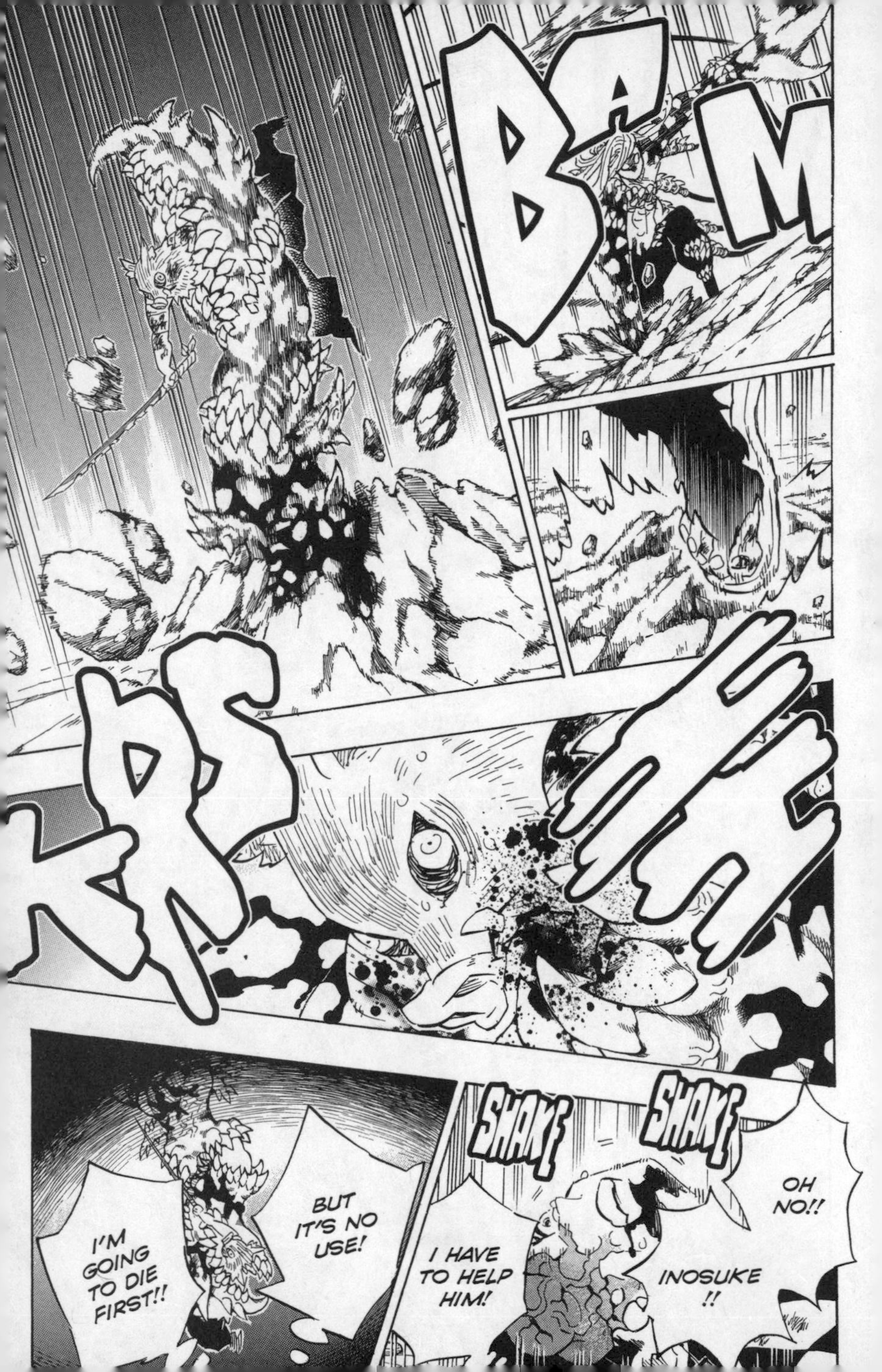
BAM
SHAKE
SHAKE
OH NO!!
INOSUKE!!
I HAVE TO HELP HIM!
BUT IT'S NO USE!
I'M GOING TO DIE FIRST!!

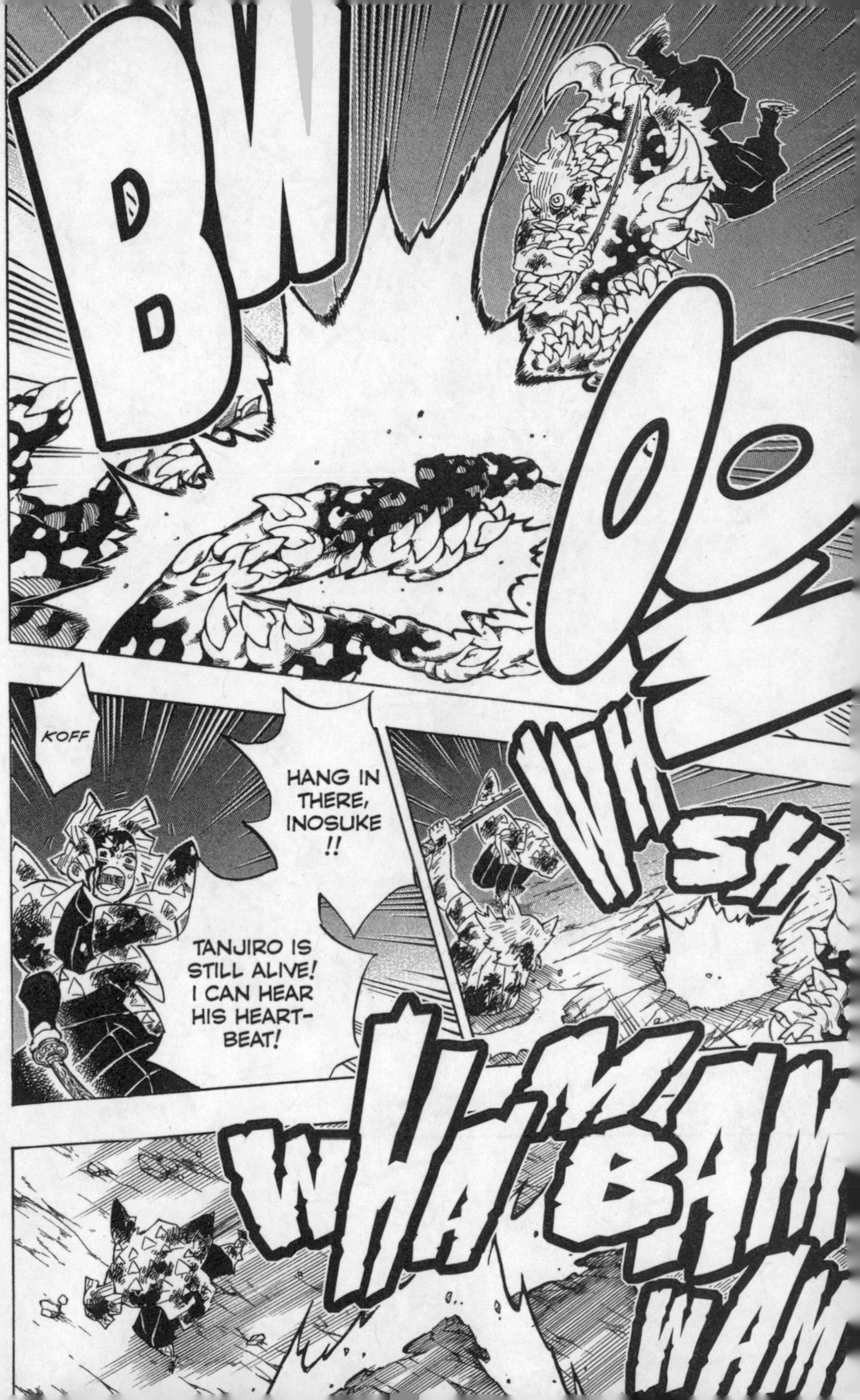
BWOO
WHSH
HANG IN THERE, INOSUKE!!
KOFF
TANJIRO IS STILL ALIVE! I CAN HEAR HIS HEART-BEAT!
WHAM
BAM
WAM

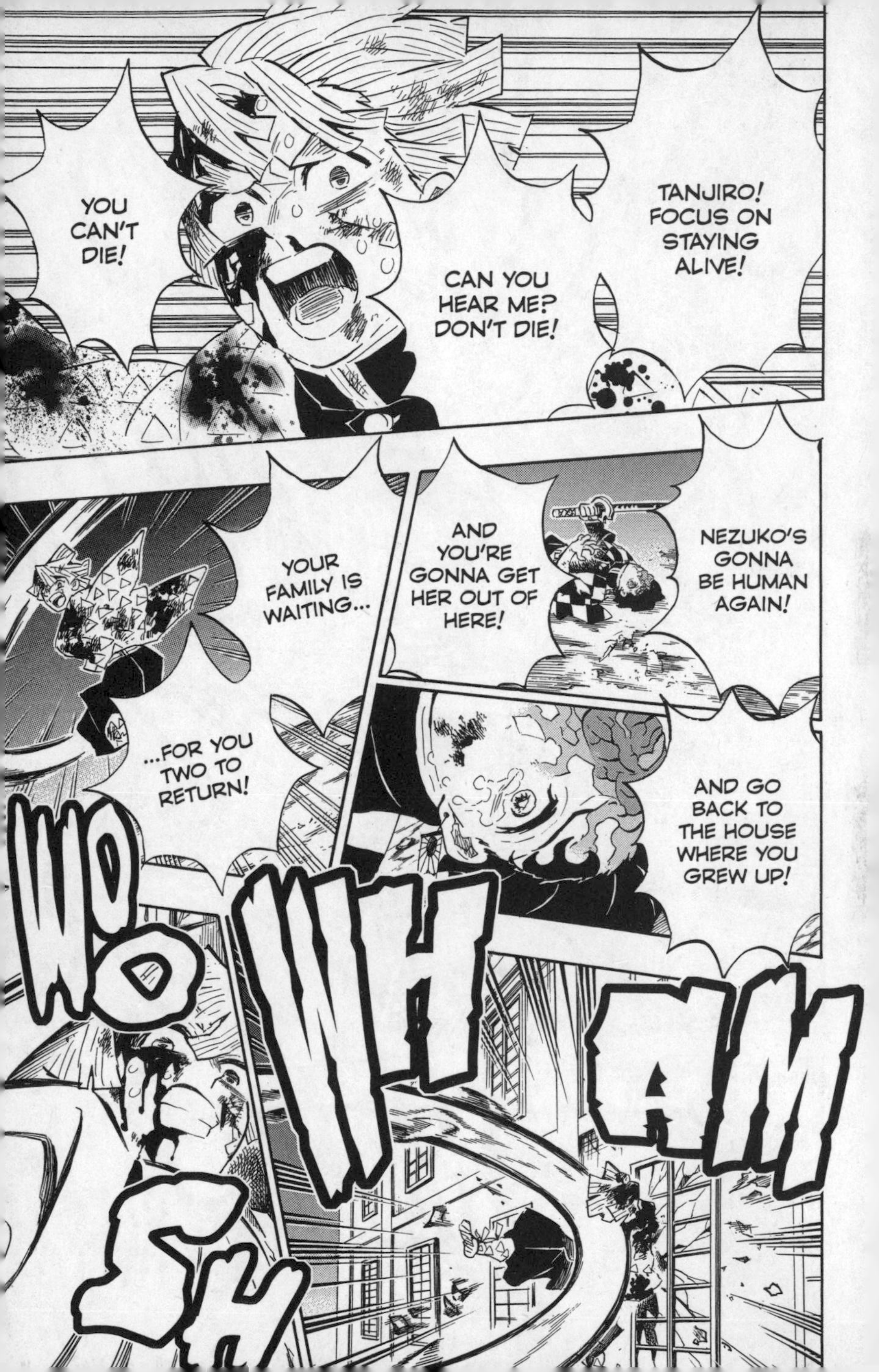
TANJIRO! FOCUS ON STAYING ALIVE!
CAN YOU HEAR ME? DON'T DIE!
YOU CAN'T DIE!
NEZUKO'S GONNA BE HUMAN AGAIN!
AND YOU'RE GONNA GET HER OUT OF HERE!
AND GO BACK TO THE HOUSE WHERE YOU GREW UP!
YOUR FAMILY IS WAITING...
...FOR YOU TWO TO RETURN!
WHAM
WHOOSH

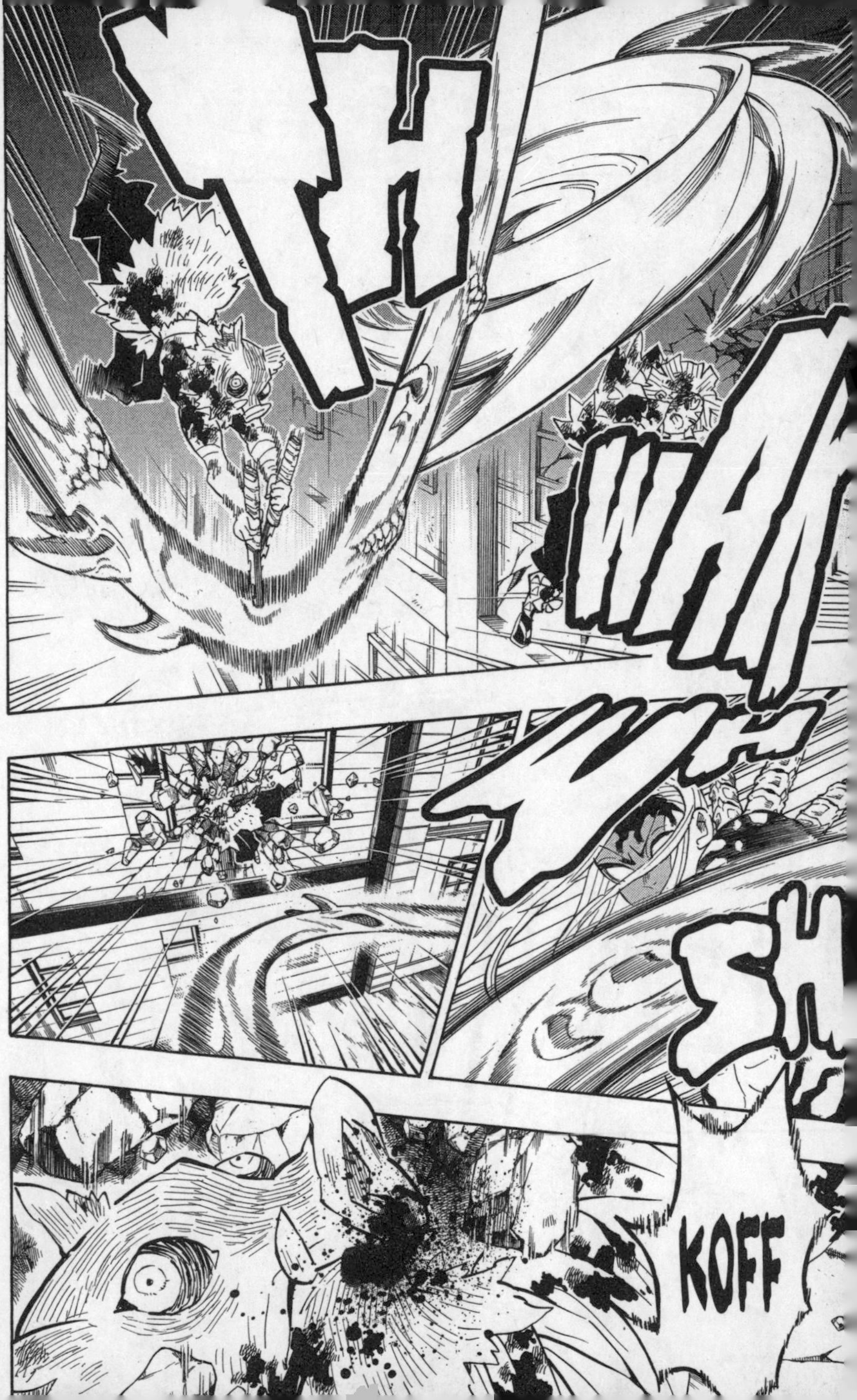
KOFF

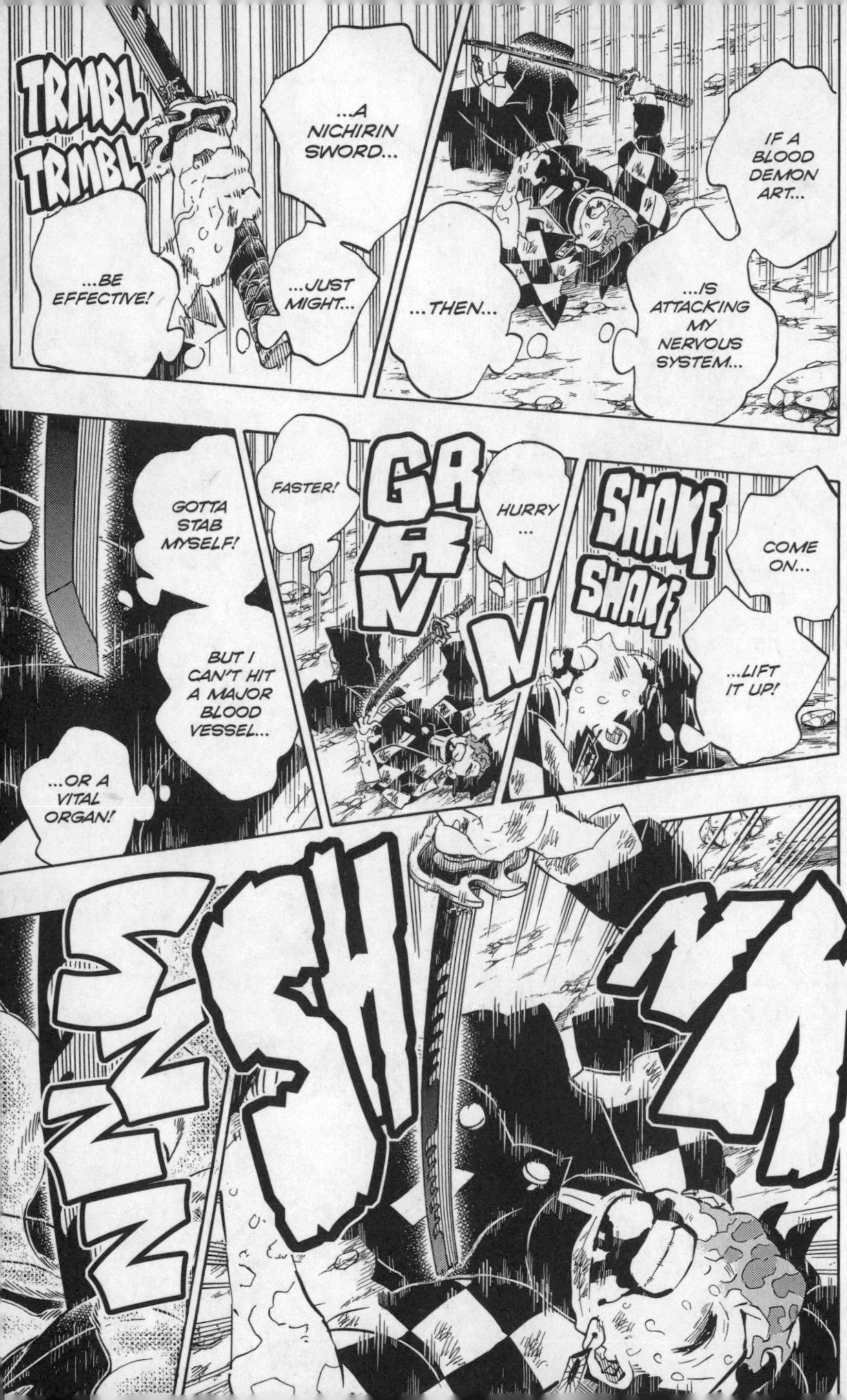
IF A BLOOD DEMON ART...
...IS ATTACKING MY NERVOUS SYSTEM...
...THEN...
...A NICHIRIN SWORD...
...JUST MIGHT...
...BE EFFECTIVE!
TRMBL TRMBL
SHAKE SHAKE
COME ON...
...LIFT IT UP!
HURRY...
FASTER!
GOTTA STAB MYSELF!
BUT I CAN'T HIT A MAJOR BLOOD VESSEL...
...OR A VITAL ORGAN!

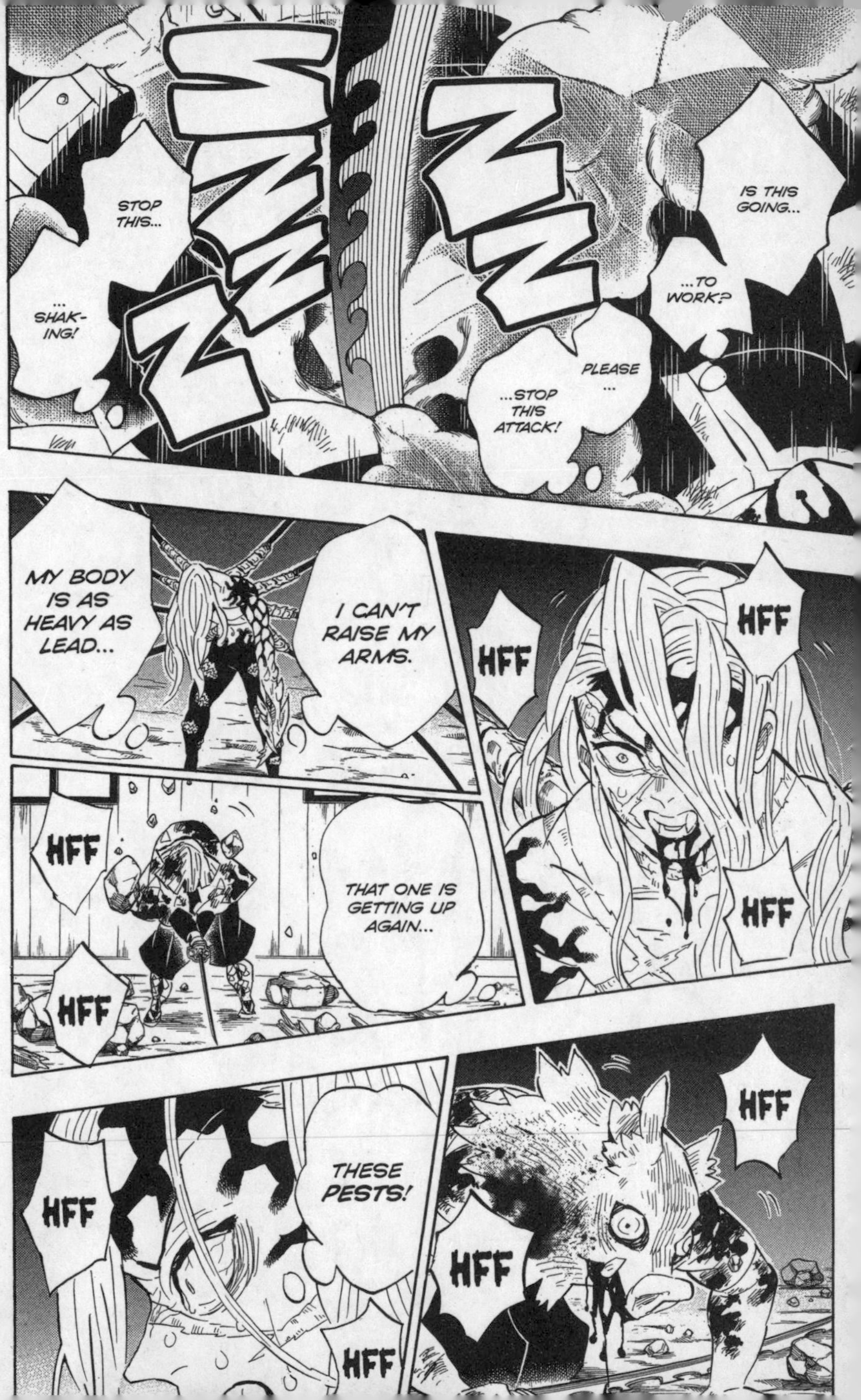
IS THIS GOING...
...TO WORK?
PLEASE...
...STOP THIS ATTACK!
STOP THIS...
...SHAKING!
HFF
HFF
HFF
MY BODY IS AS HEAVY AS LEAD...
I CAN'T RAISE MY ARMS.
THAT ONE IS GETTING UP AGAIN...
HFF
HFF
HFF
HFF
THESE PESTS!
HFF
HFF

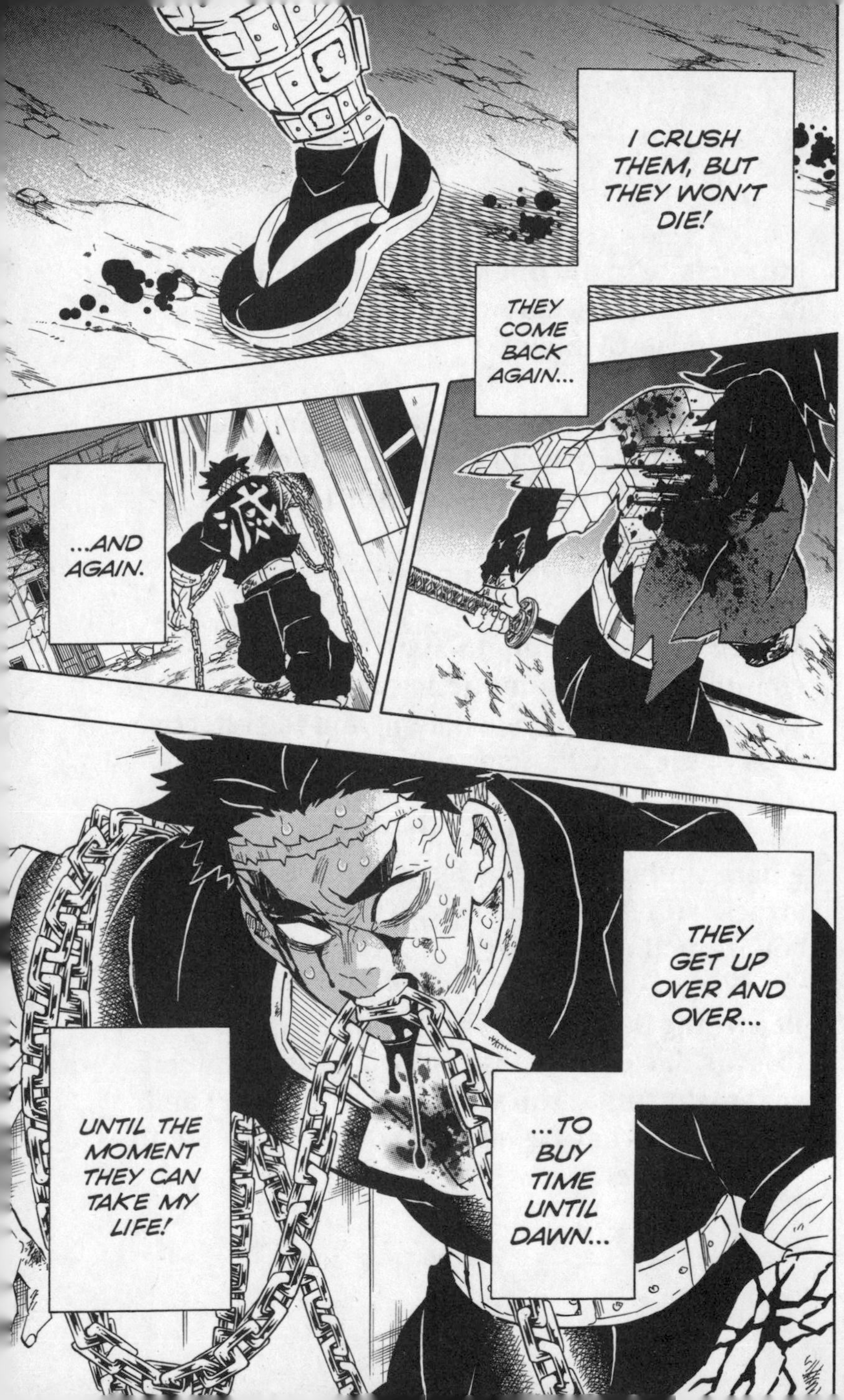
I CRUSH THEM, BUT THEY WON'T DIE!
THEY COME BACK AGAIN...
...AND AGAIN.
THEY GET UP OVER AND OVER...
...TO BUY TIME UNTIL DAWN...
UNTIL THE MOMENT THEY CAN TAKE MY LIFE!

Muzan is so invincible that only the sun can kill him. Here's the Demon Slayers' strategy for surviving until dawn:

Kagaya Ubuyashi agitates Muzan, then launches a preemptive strike to create an opportunity for Tamayo to administer the poison.
↓
Tamayo's poison weakens Muzan.
↓
Muzan expends strength analyzing and counteracting the four active agents in the drug. The drug slows his movement, and the effectiveness of the attacks against him increases.
↓
The corps members hold Muzan somewhere where sunlight will strike, and they continue to attack with ferocity so he can't concentrate on counteracting the drug.

Regarding Nakime and her abilities, Kagaya Ubuyashiki analyzed the information obtained so far (the unnatural way demons appear) and determined that Yushiro was the most suited to combating her.

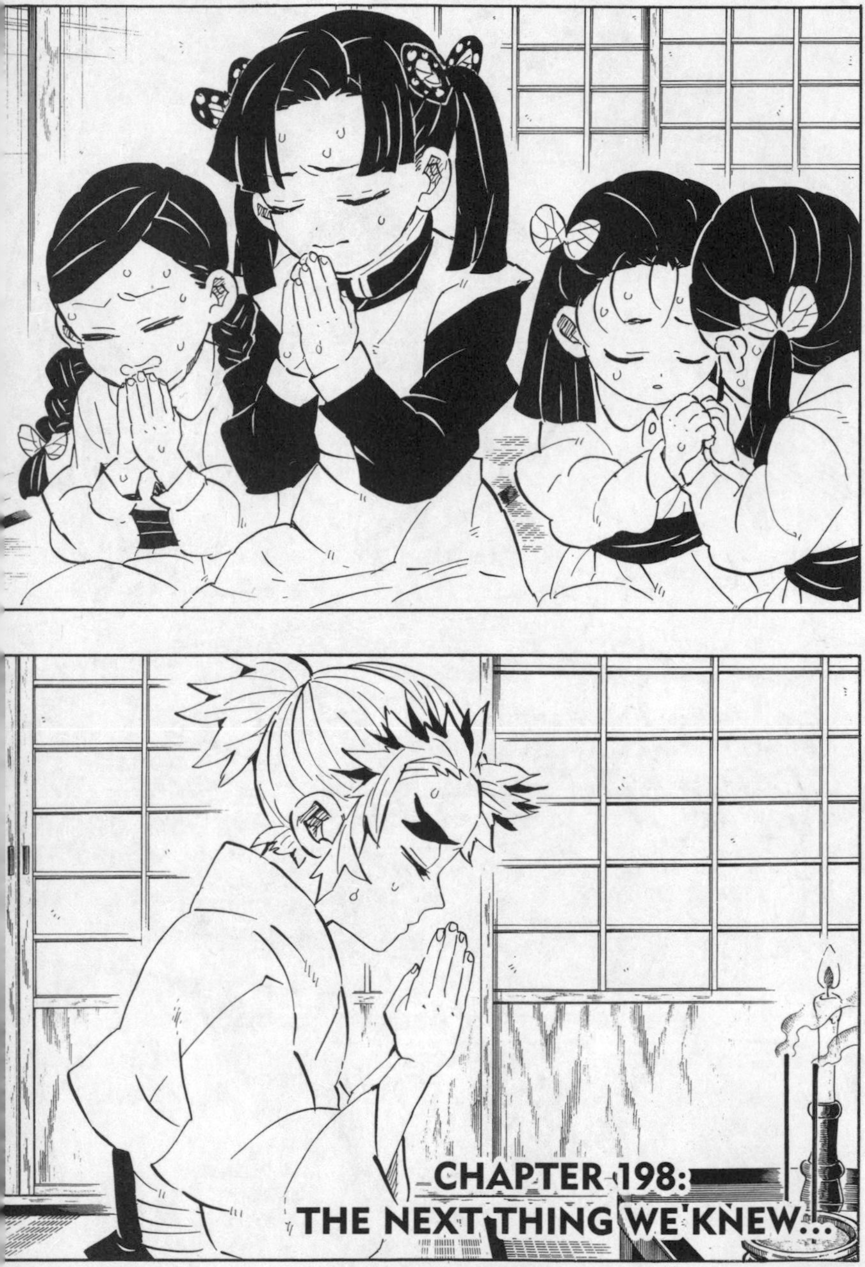
CHAPTER 198:
THE NEXT THING WE KNEW...

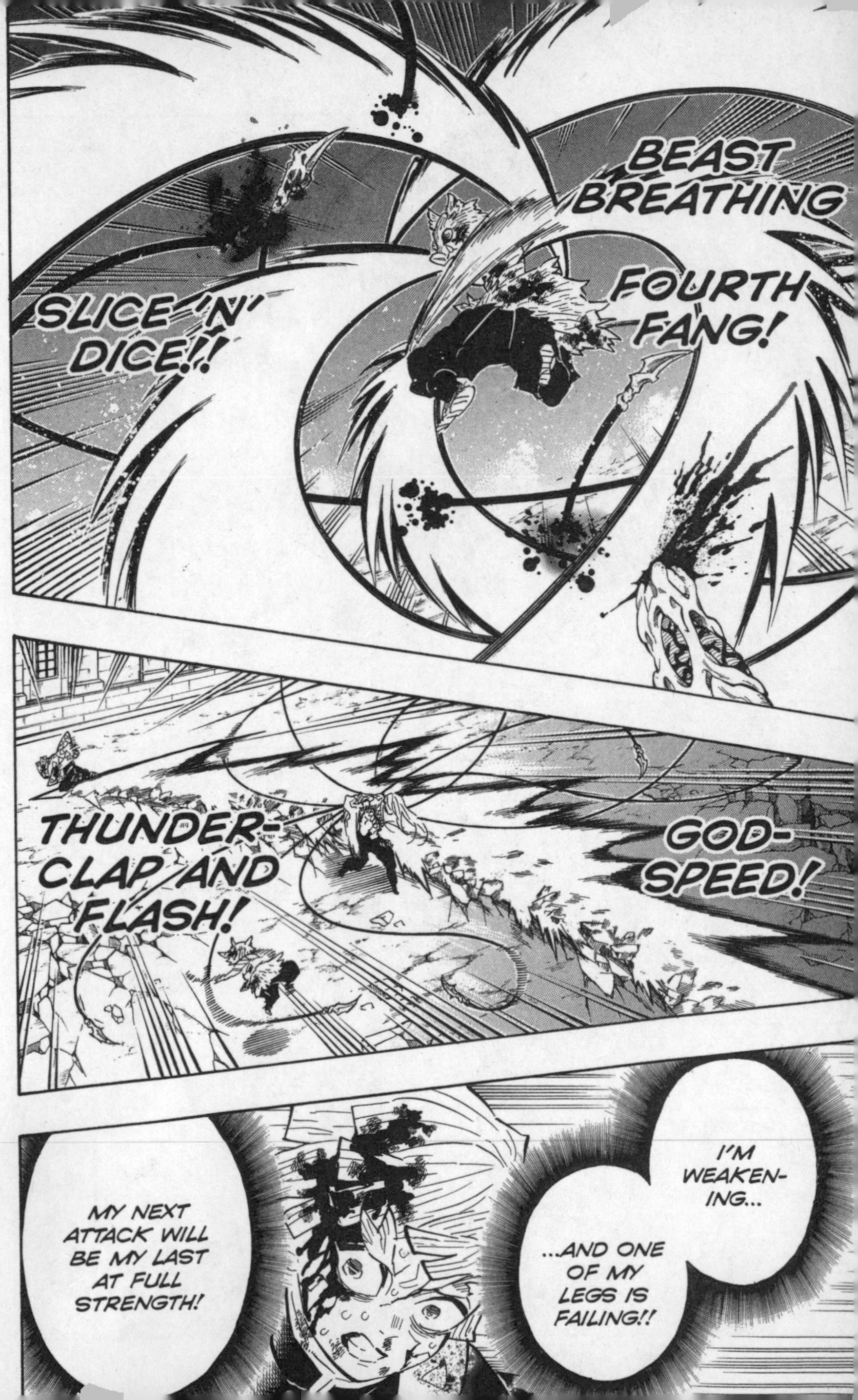
BEAST BREATHING
FOURTH FANG!
SLICE 'N' DICE!!
GOD-SPEED!
THUNDER-CLAP AND FLASH!
I'M WEAKEN-ING...
...AND ONE OF MY LEGS IS FAILING!!
MY NEXT ATTACK WILL BE MY LAST AT FULL STRENGTH!

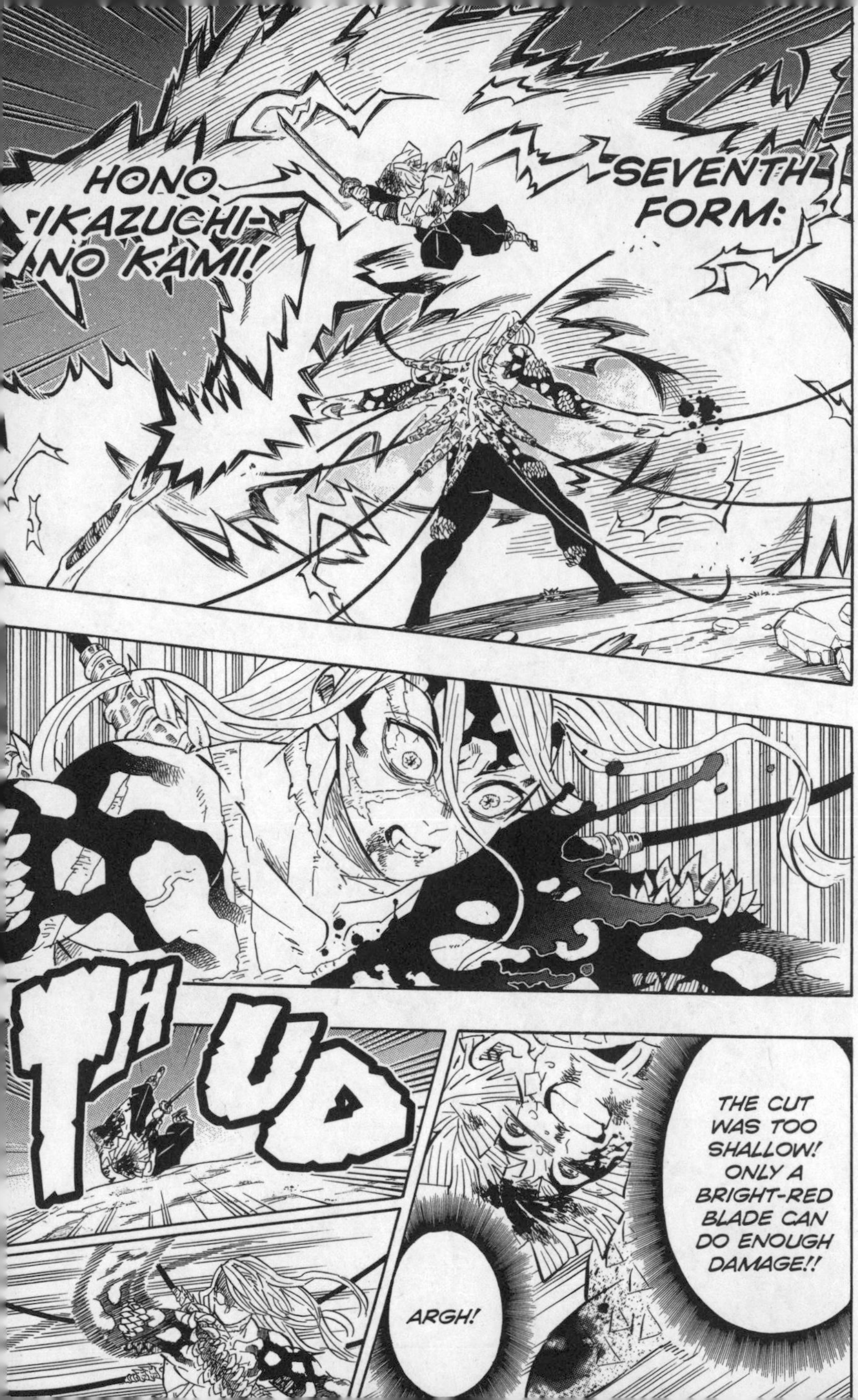
SEVENTH FORM:
HONO-IKAZUCHI-NO KAMI!
THE CUT WAS TOO SHALLOW! ONLY A BRIGHT-RED BLADE CAN DO ENOUGH DAMAGE!!
ARGH!
TH'UD

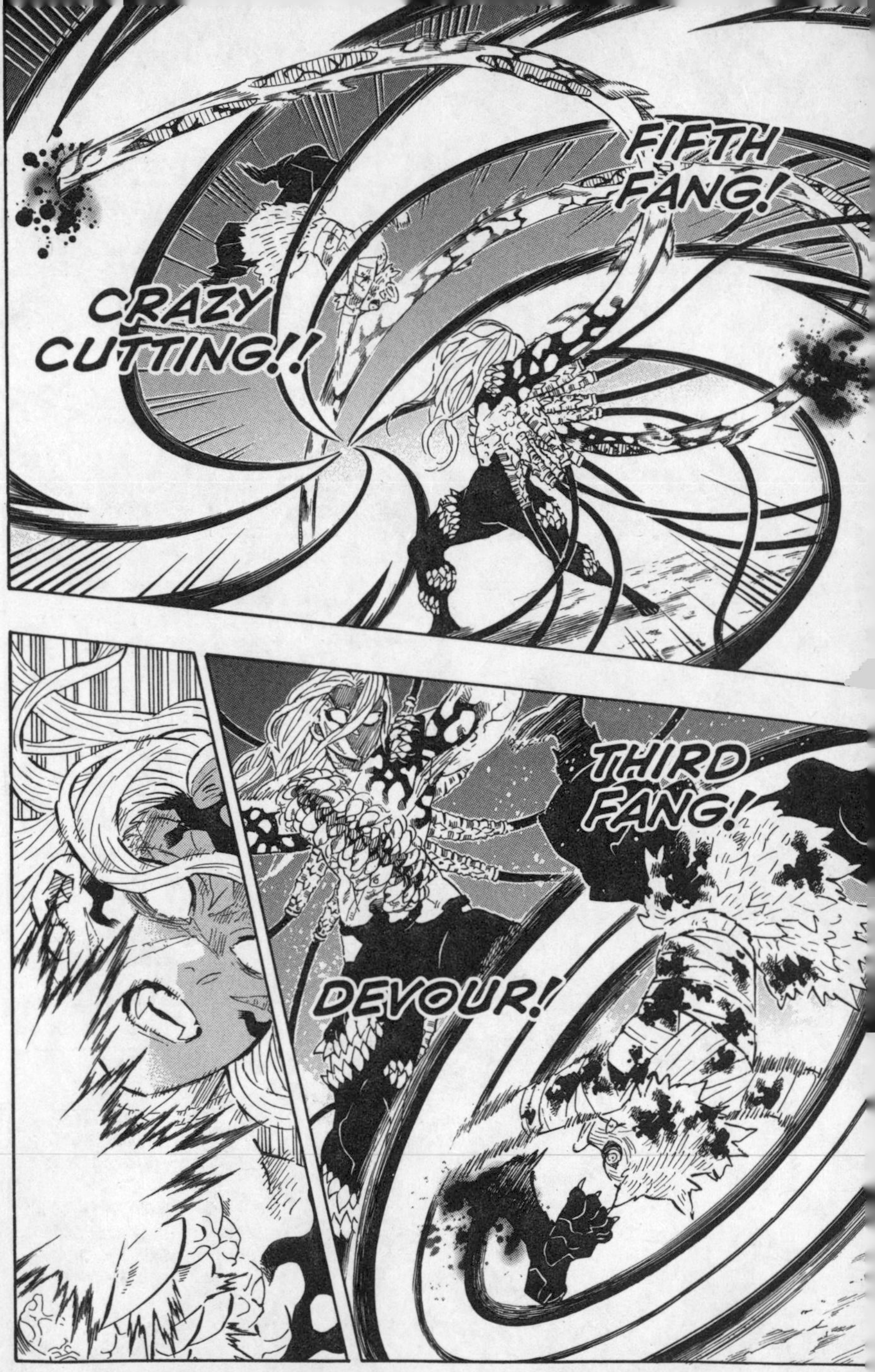
FIFTH FANG!
CRAZY CUTTING!!
THIRD FANG!
DEVOUR!

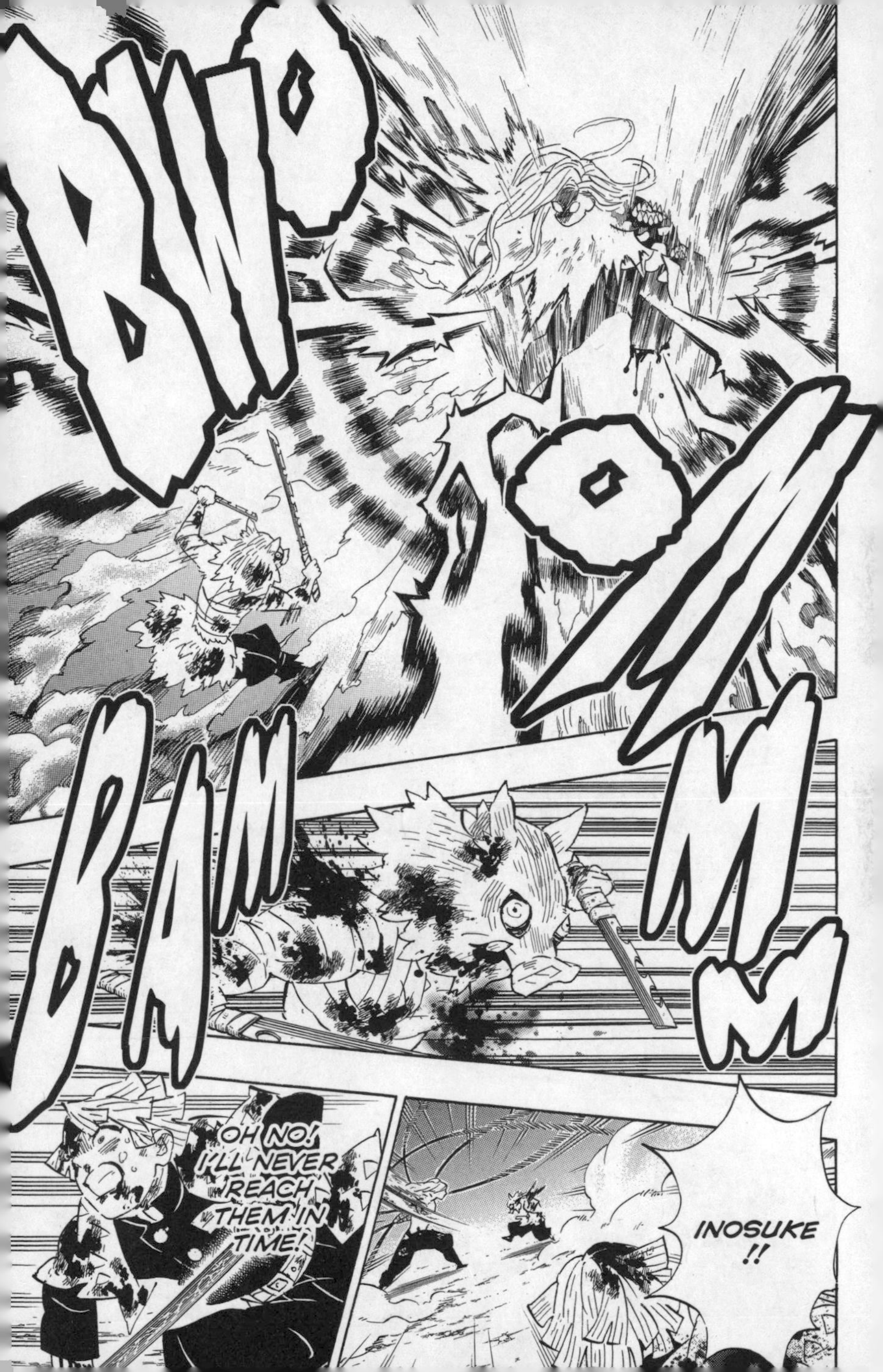
BOOM
BAMM
INOSUKE!!
OH NO! I'LL NEVER REACH THEM IN TIME!

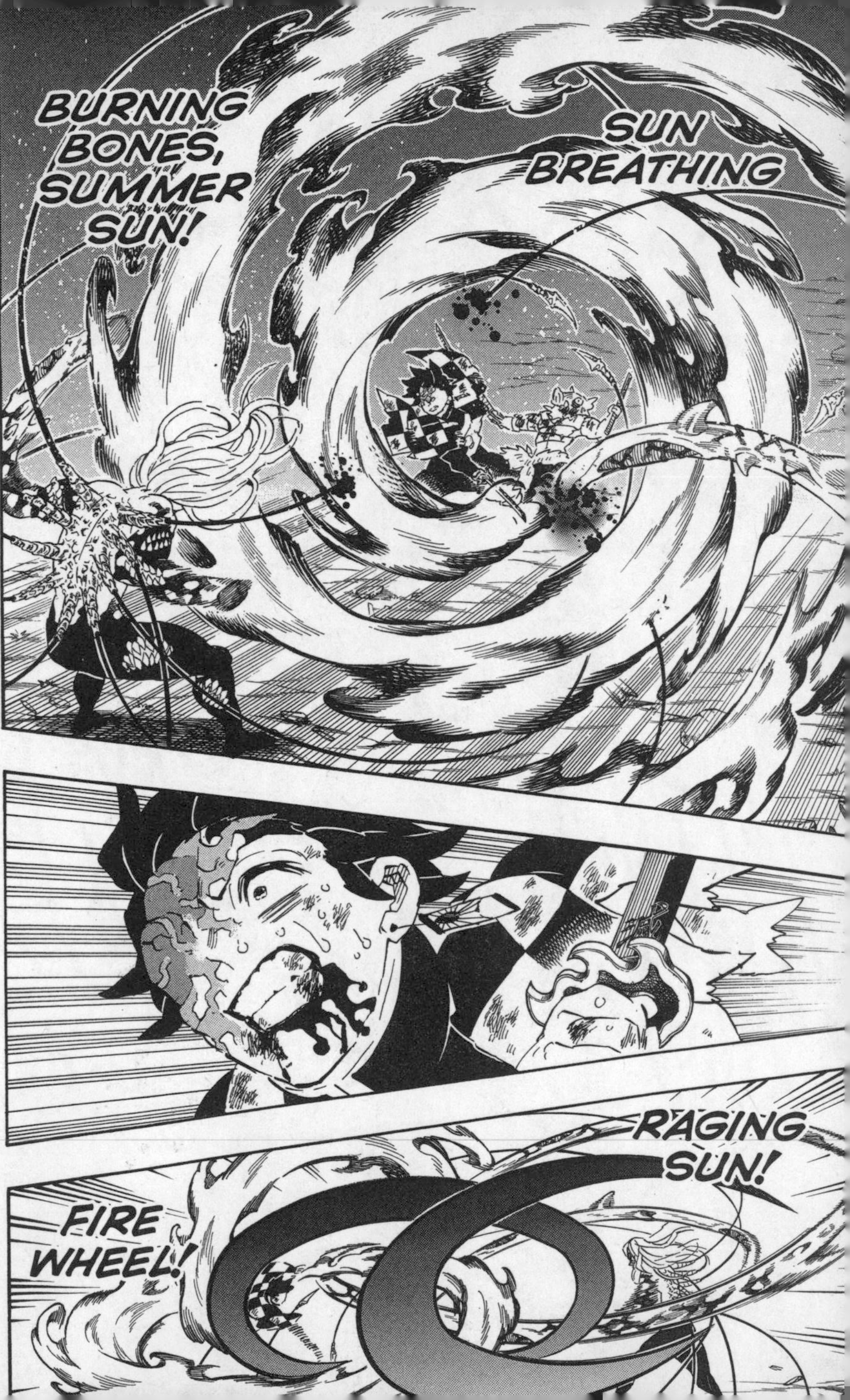
SUN BREATHING
BURNING BONES, SUMMER SUN!
RAGING SUN!
FIRE WHEEL!

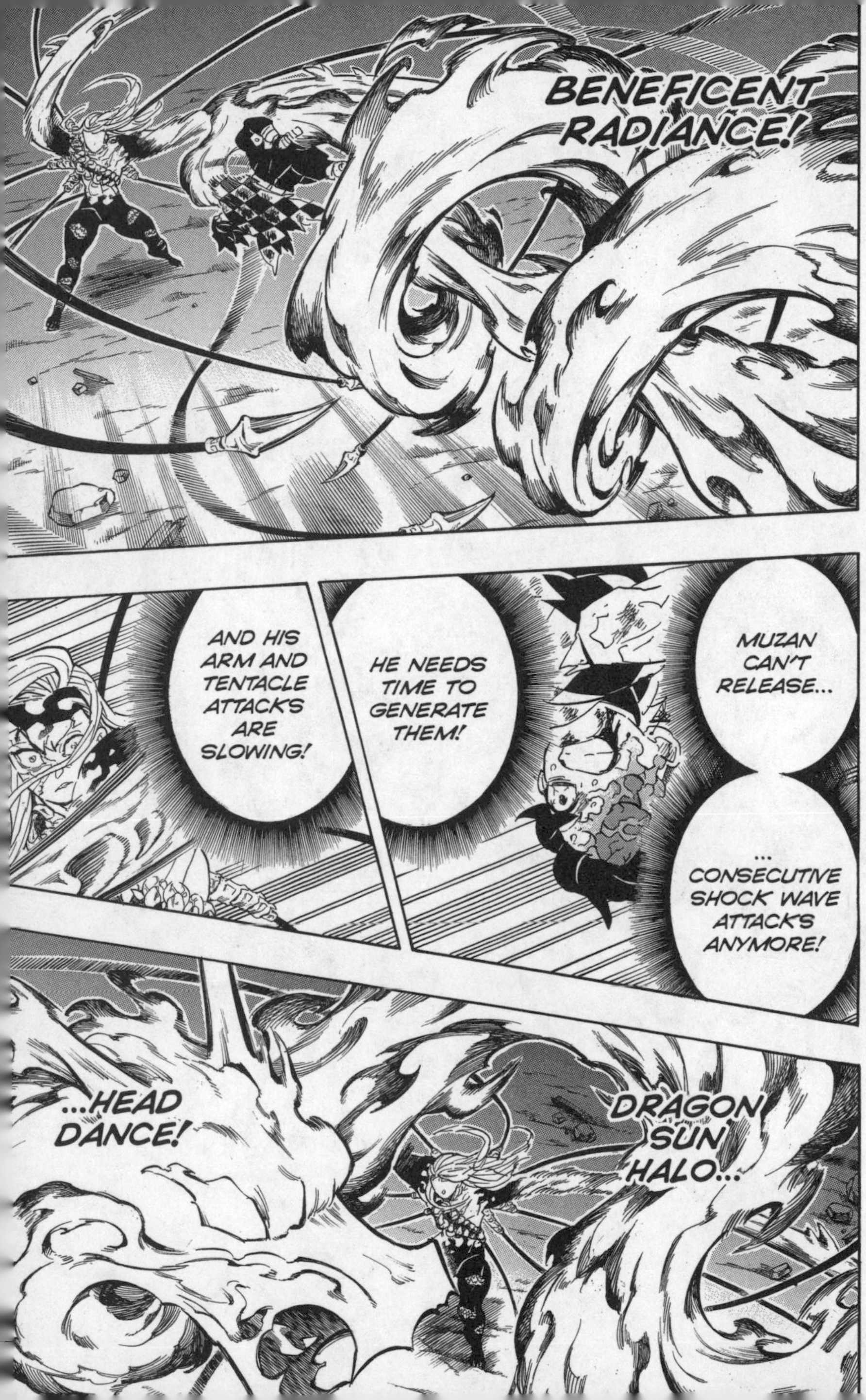
BENEFICENT RADIANCE!
MUZAN CAN'T RELEASE...
...CONSECUTIVE SHOCK WAVE ATTACKS ANYMORE!
HE NEEDS TIME TO GENERATE THEM!
AND HIS ARM AND TENTACLE ATTACKS ARE SLOWING!
DRAGON SUN HALO...
...HEAD DANCE!

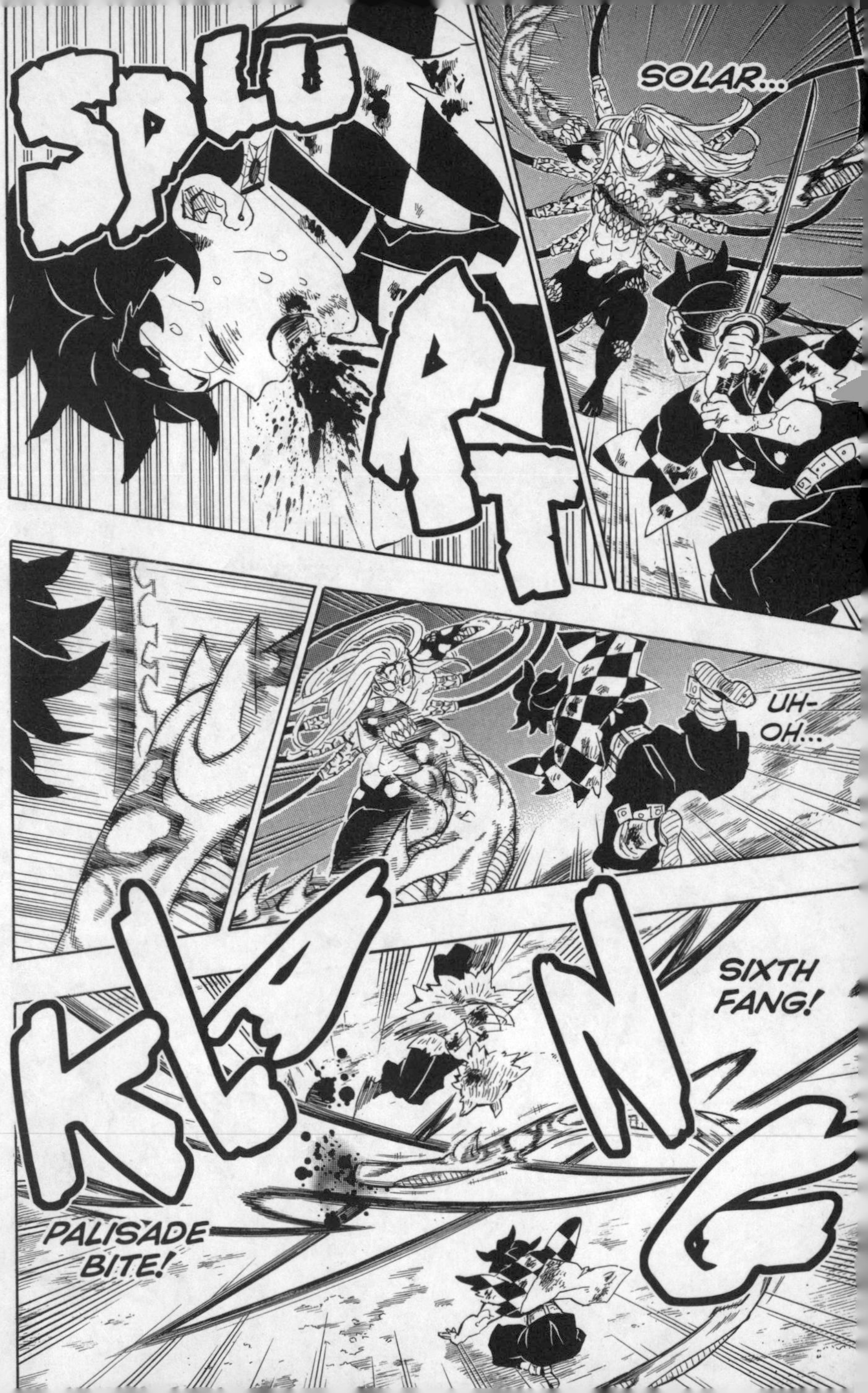
SOLAR...
SPLURT
UH-OH...
SIXTH FANG!
KLANG
PALISADE BITE!

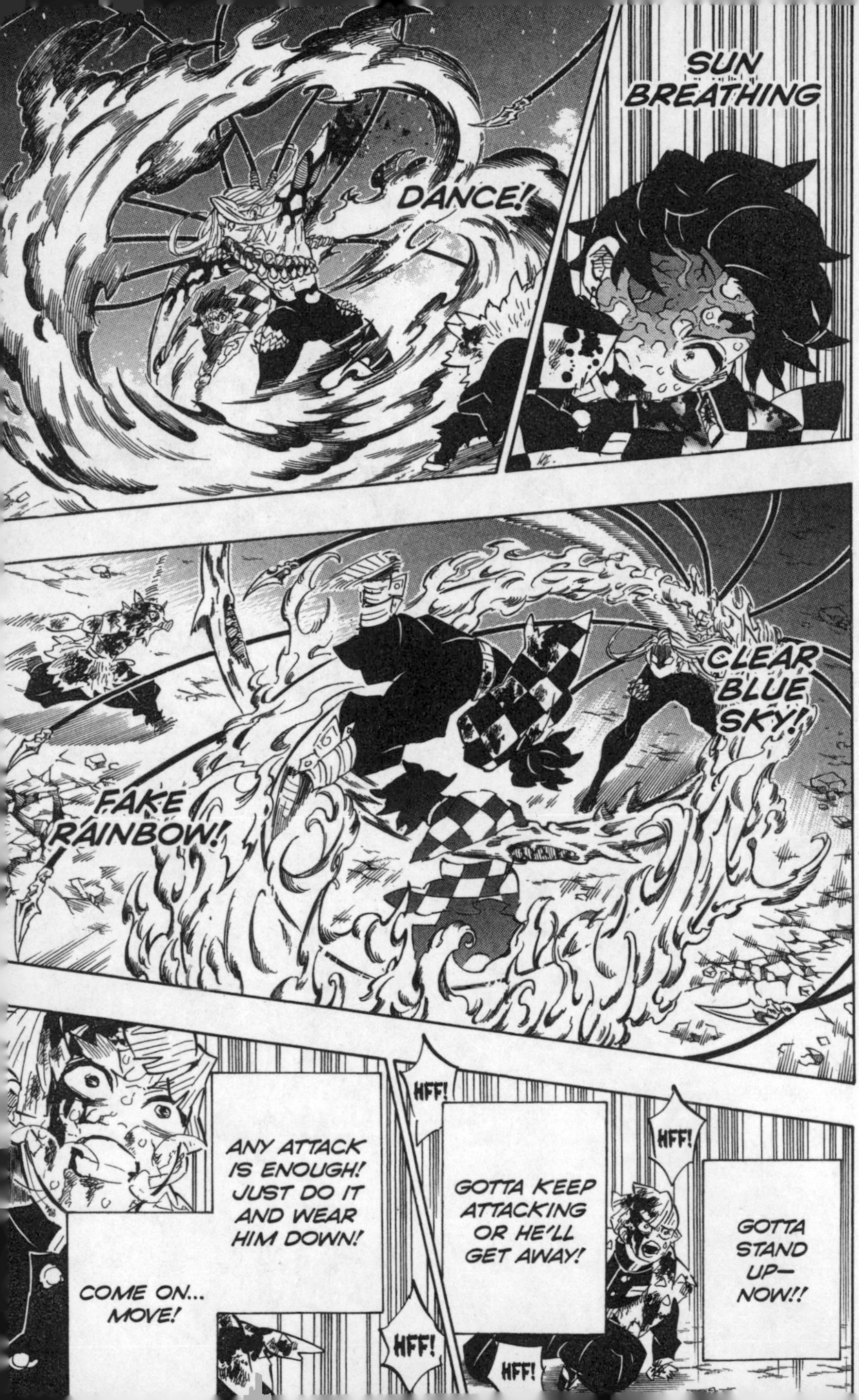
SUN BREATHING
DANCE!
CLEAR BLUE SKY!
FAKE RAINBOW!
HFF!
GOTTA STAND UP— NOW!!
HFF!
GOTTA KEEP ATTACKING OR HE'LL GET AWAY!
HFF!
HFF!
ANY ATTACK IS ENOUGH! JUST DO IT AND WEAR HIM DOWN!
COME ON... MOVE!

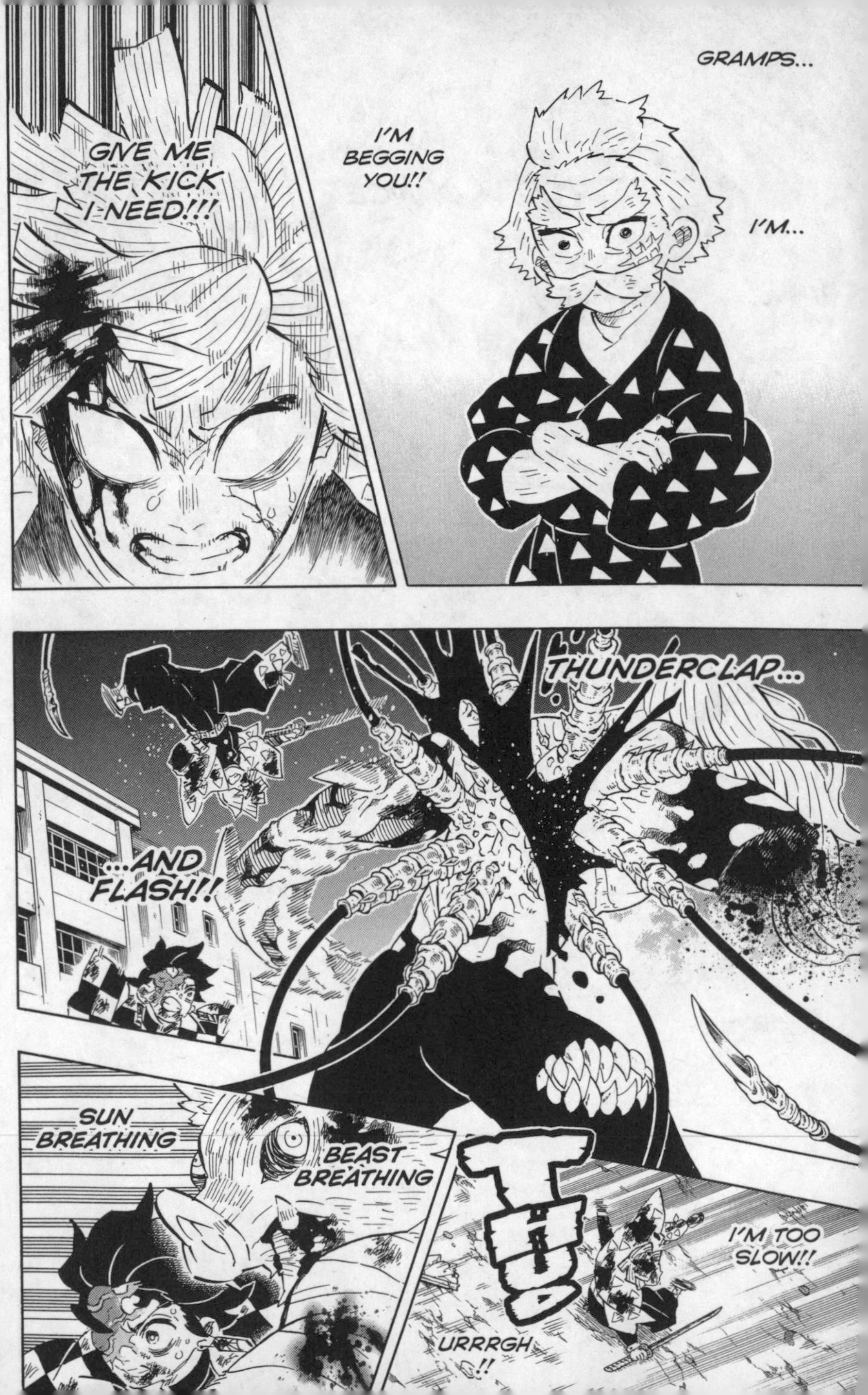

GRAMPS...
I'M...
I'M BEGGING YOU!!
GIVE ME THE KICK I NEED!!!
THUNDERCLAP...
...AND FLASH!!
THUD
I'M TOO SLOW!!
URRRGH!!
BEAST BREATHING
SUN BREATHING

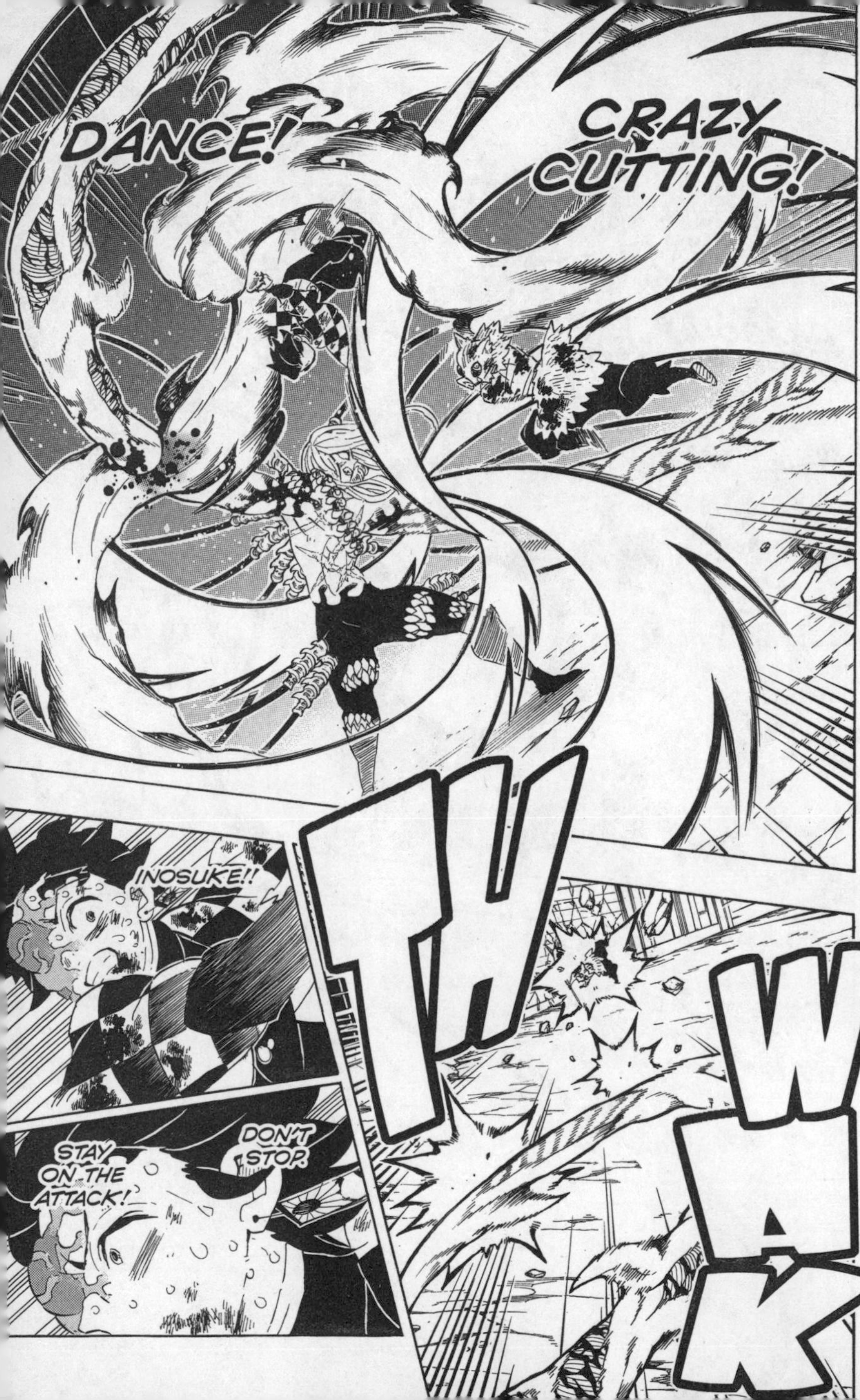
CRAZY CUTTING!
DANCE!
THWAK
INOSUKE!!
DON'T STOP.
STAY ON THE ATTACK!

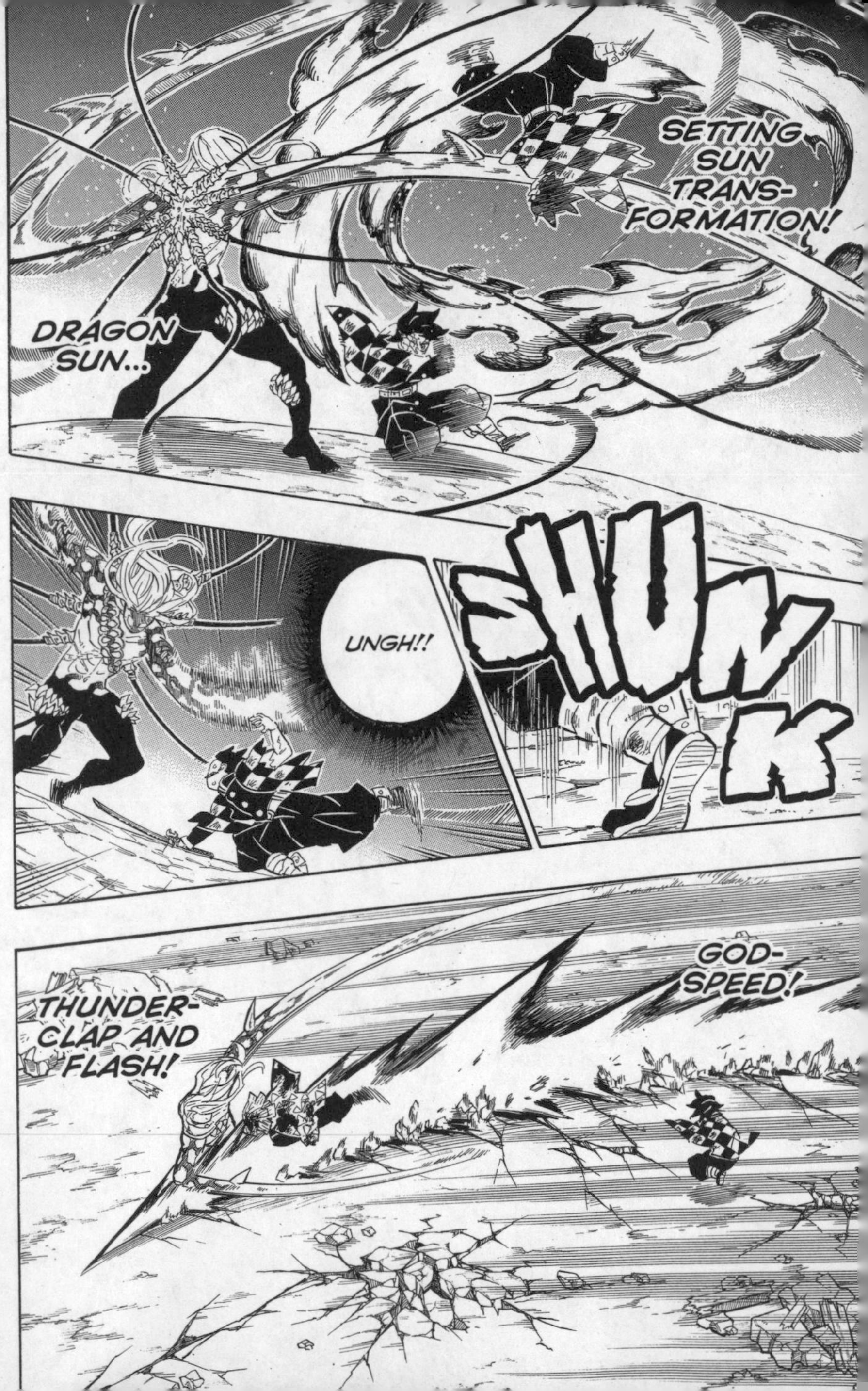
SETTING SUN TRANS-FORMATION!
DRAGON SUN...
SHUNK
UNGH!!
GOD-SPEED!
THUNDER-CLAP AND FLASH!

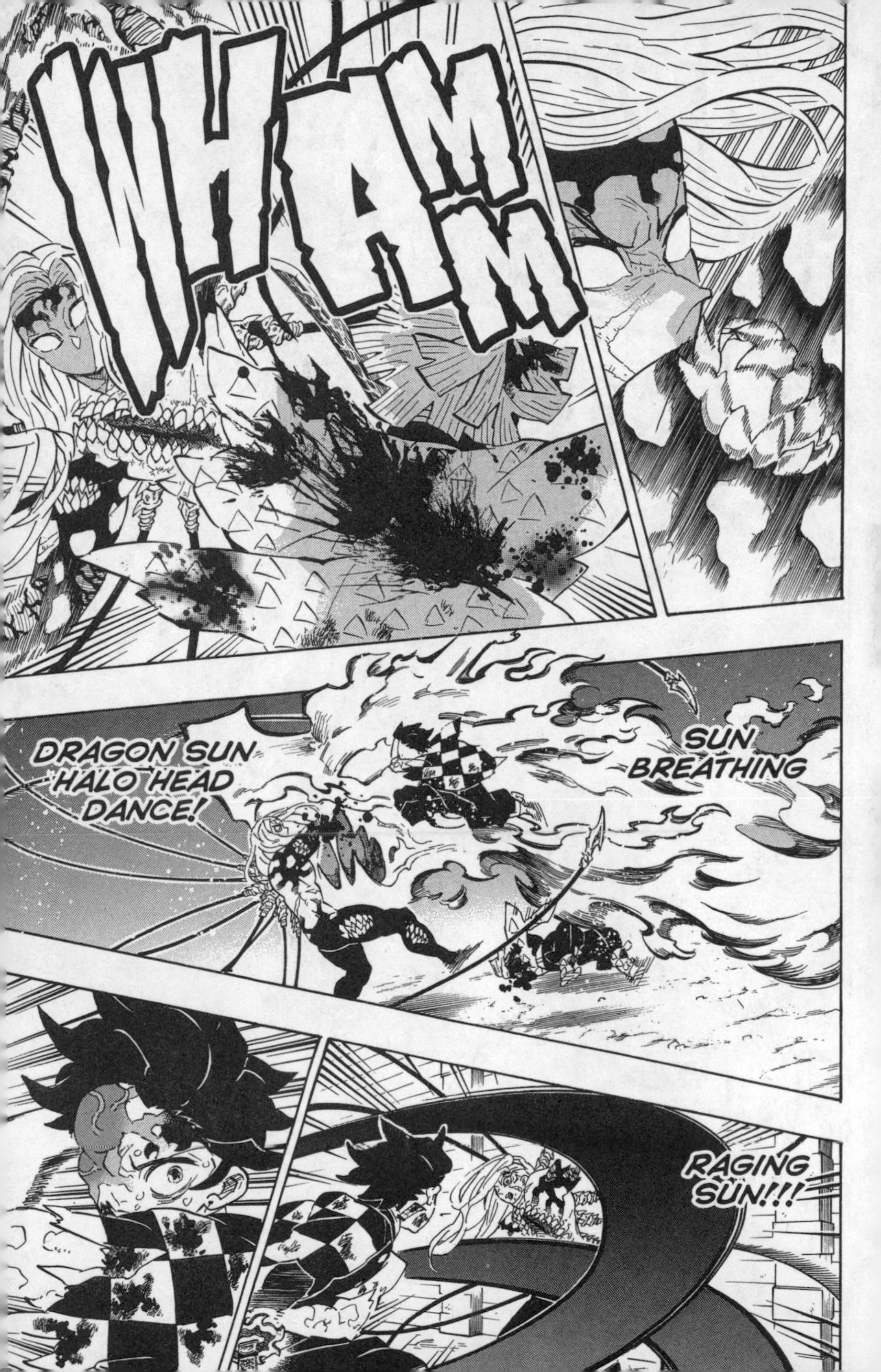
WHAM
SUN BREATHING
DRAGON SUN HALO HEAD DANCE!
RAGING SUN!!!

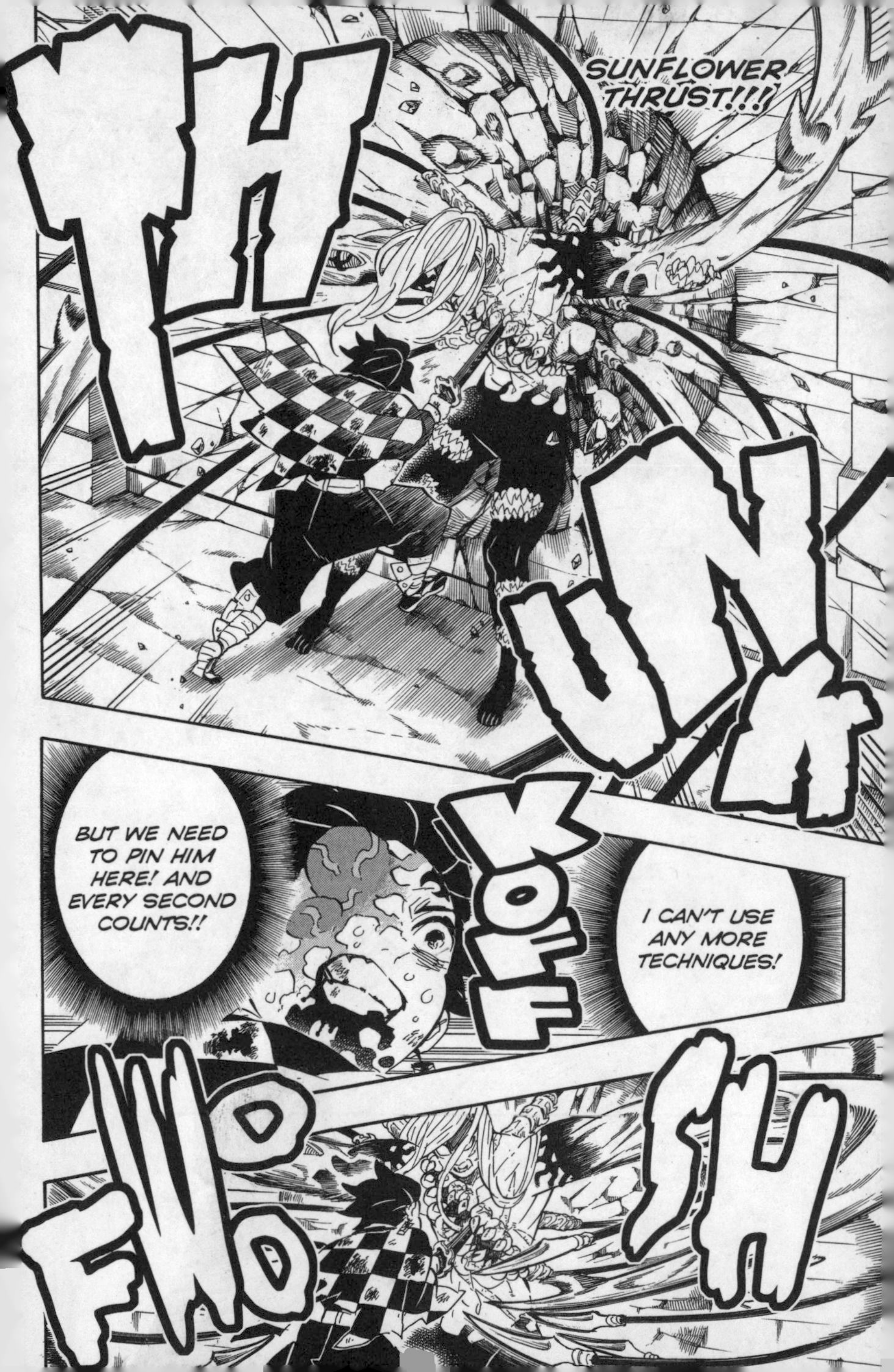
SUNFLOWER THRUST!!!
THUNK
I CAN'T USE ANY MORE TECHNIQUES!
KOFF
BUT WE NEED TO PIN HIM HERE! AND EVERY SECOND COUNTS!!
FWOOSH

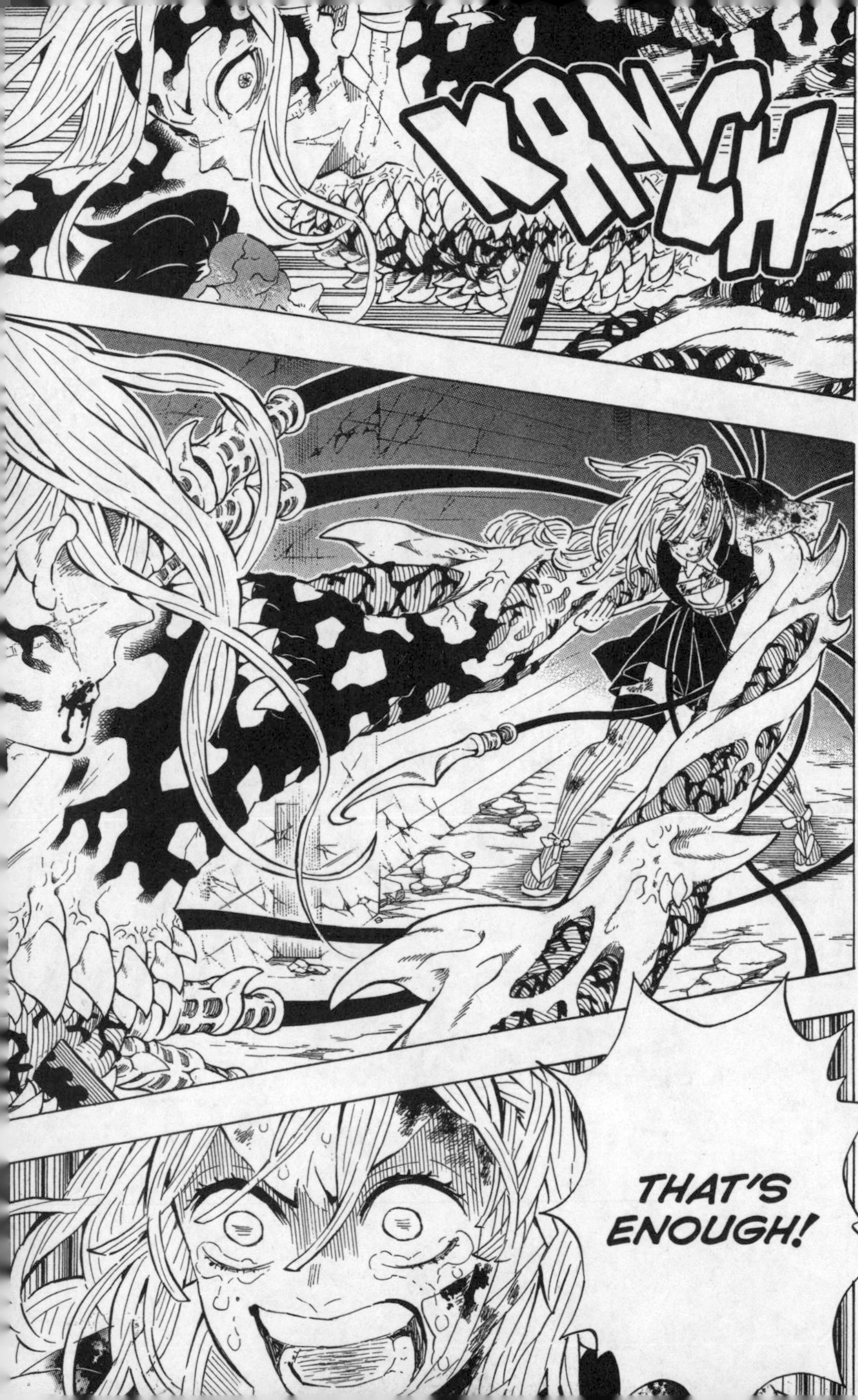
KRNCH
THAT'S ENOUGH!

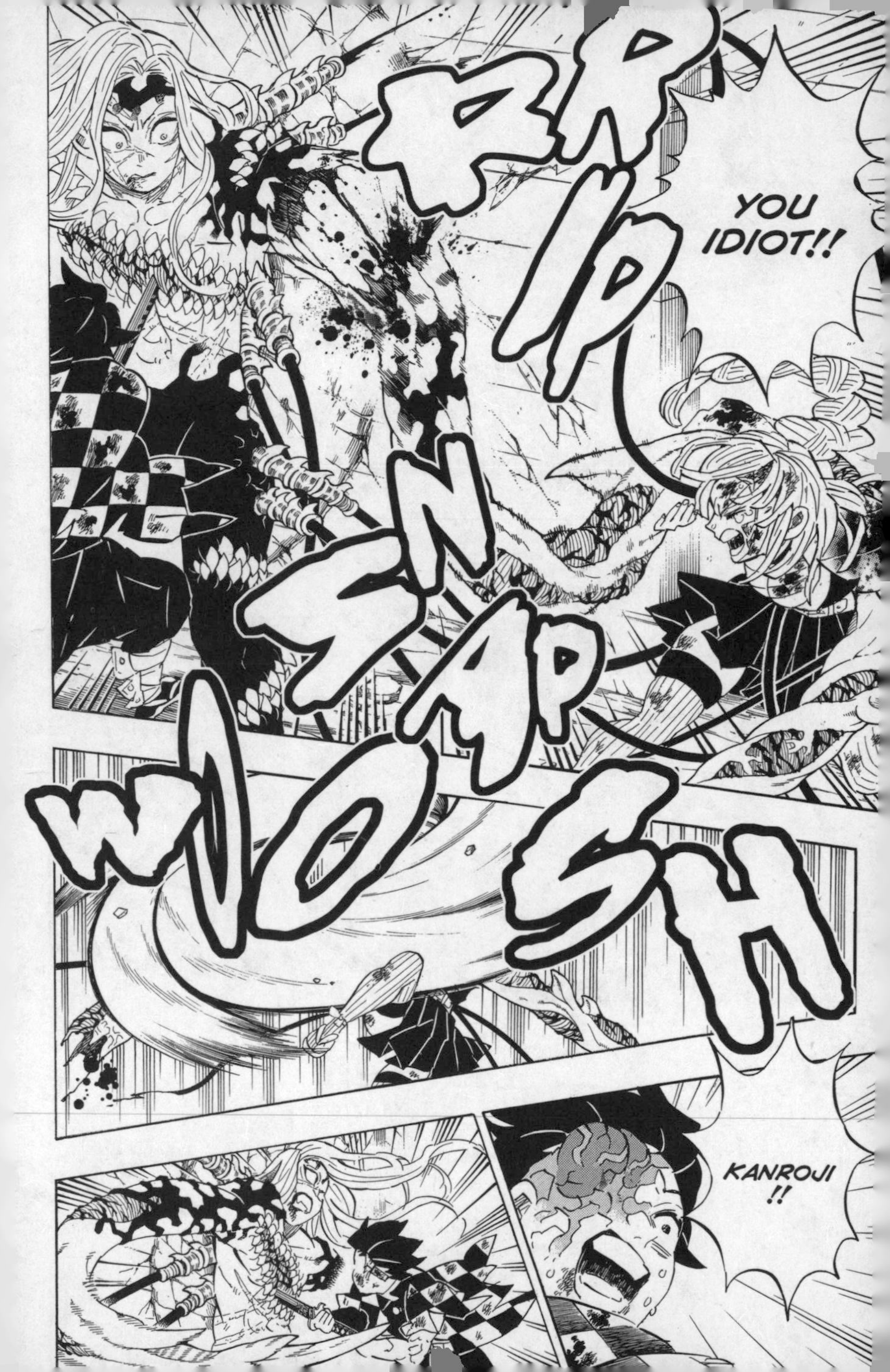
YOU IDIOT!!
RIP
SNAP
WHOOSH
KANROJI !!

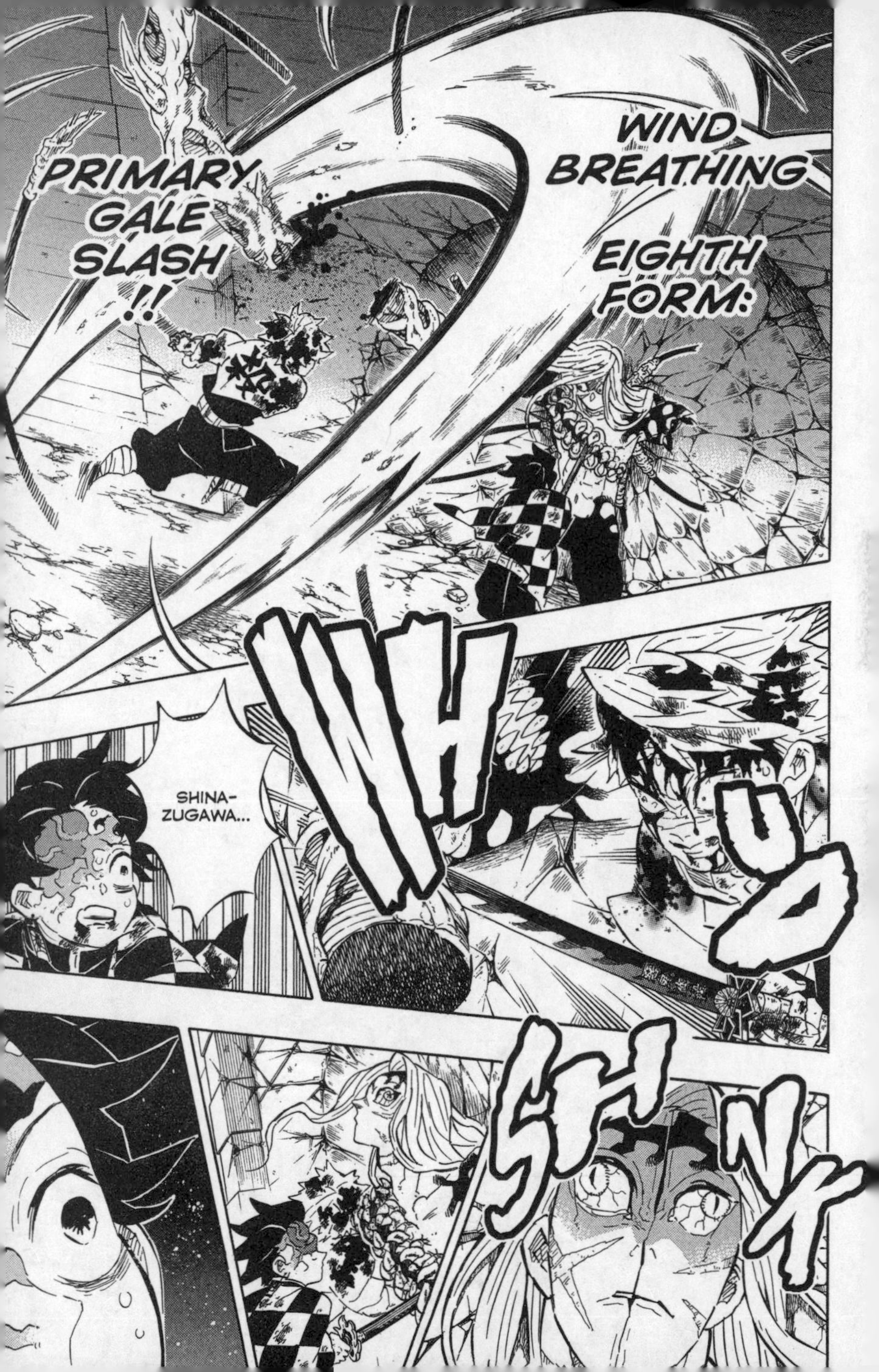
WIND BREATHING
EIGHTH FORM:
PRIMARY GALE SLASH!!
WHUD
SHINA-ZUGAWA...
SHINK

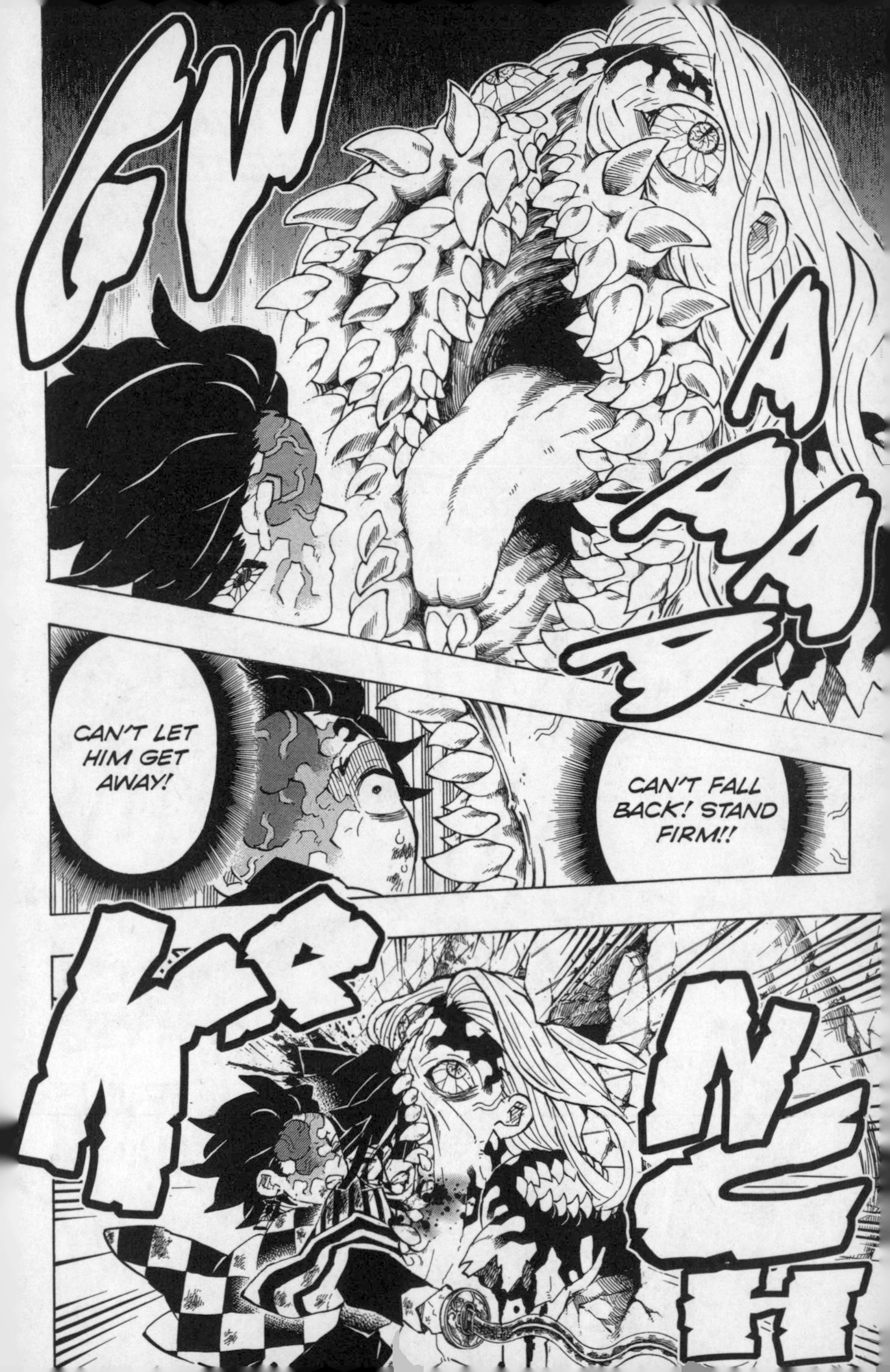
CAN'T FALL BACK! STAND FIRM!!
CAN'T LET HIM GET AWAY!

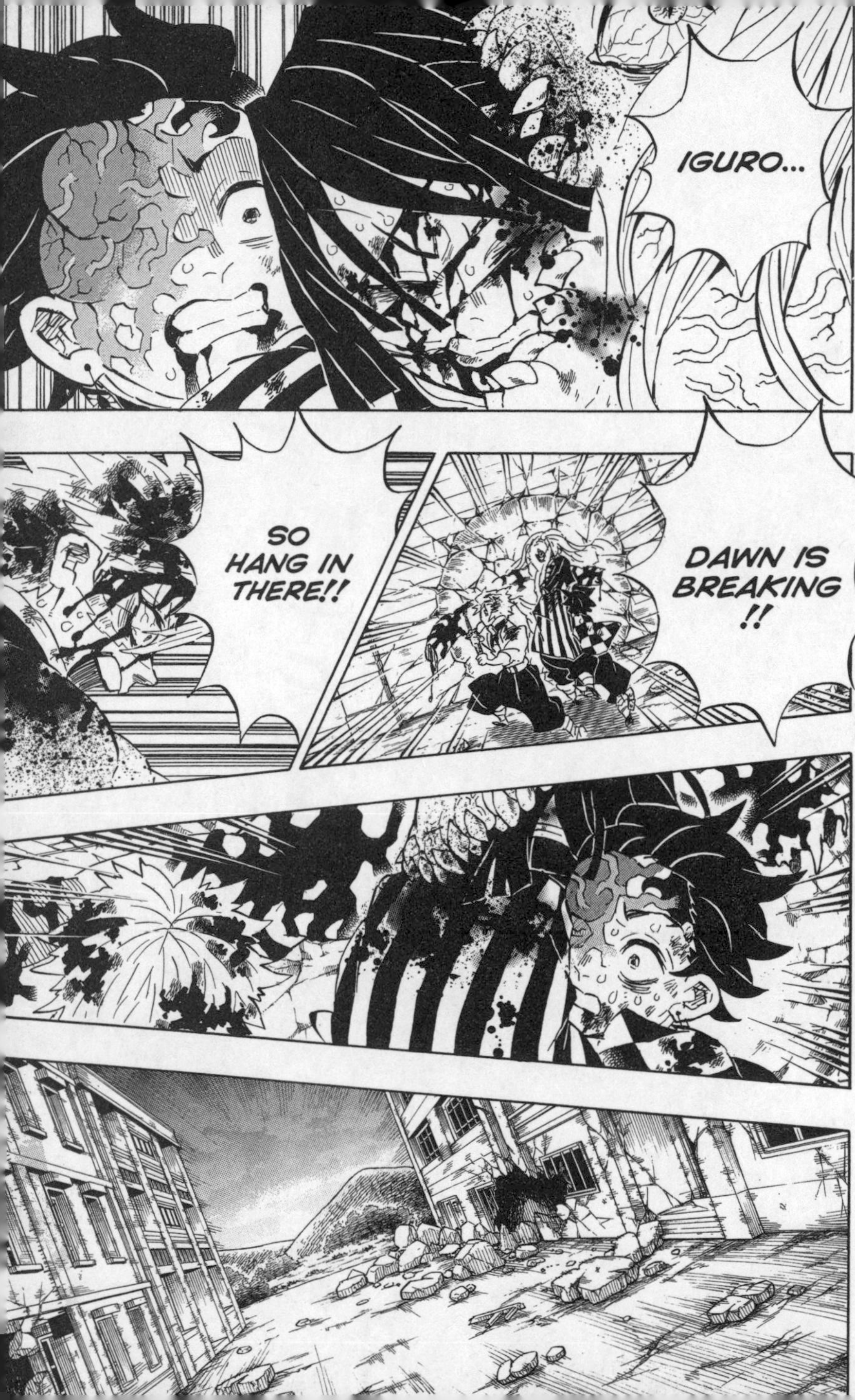
IGURO...
DAWN IS BREAKING!!
SO HANG IN THERE!!

CHAPTER 199: MILLENNIAL DAWN

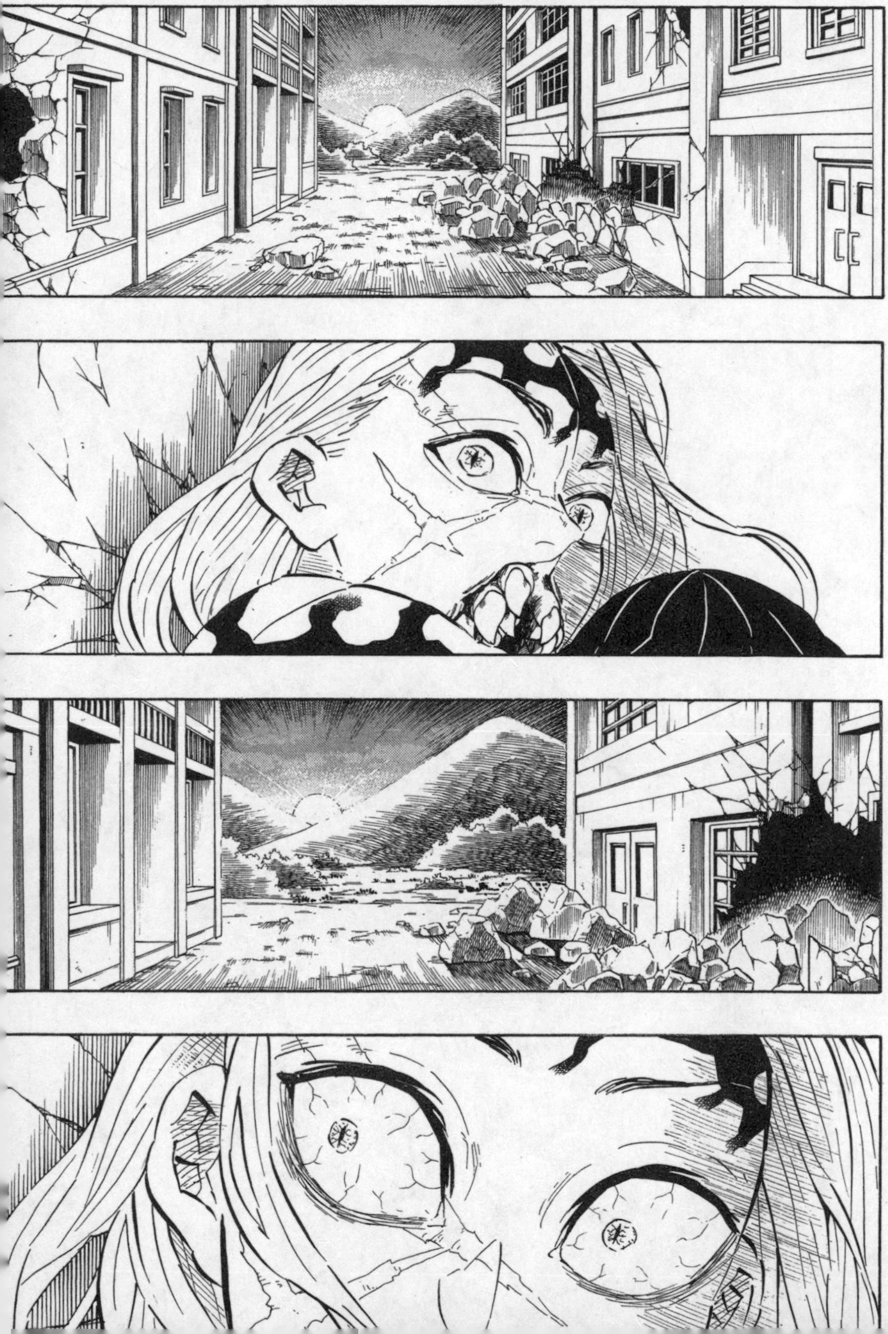

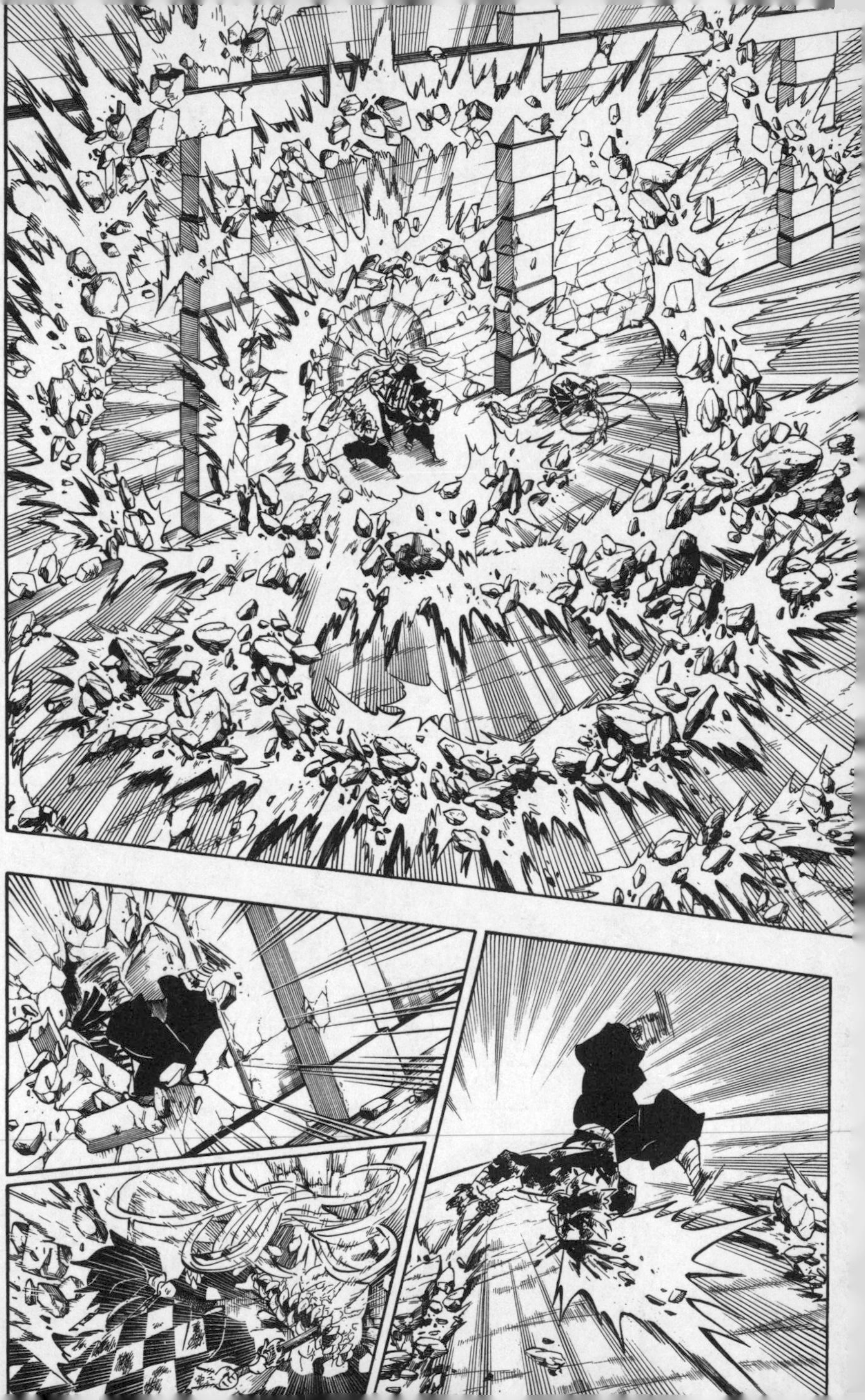

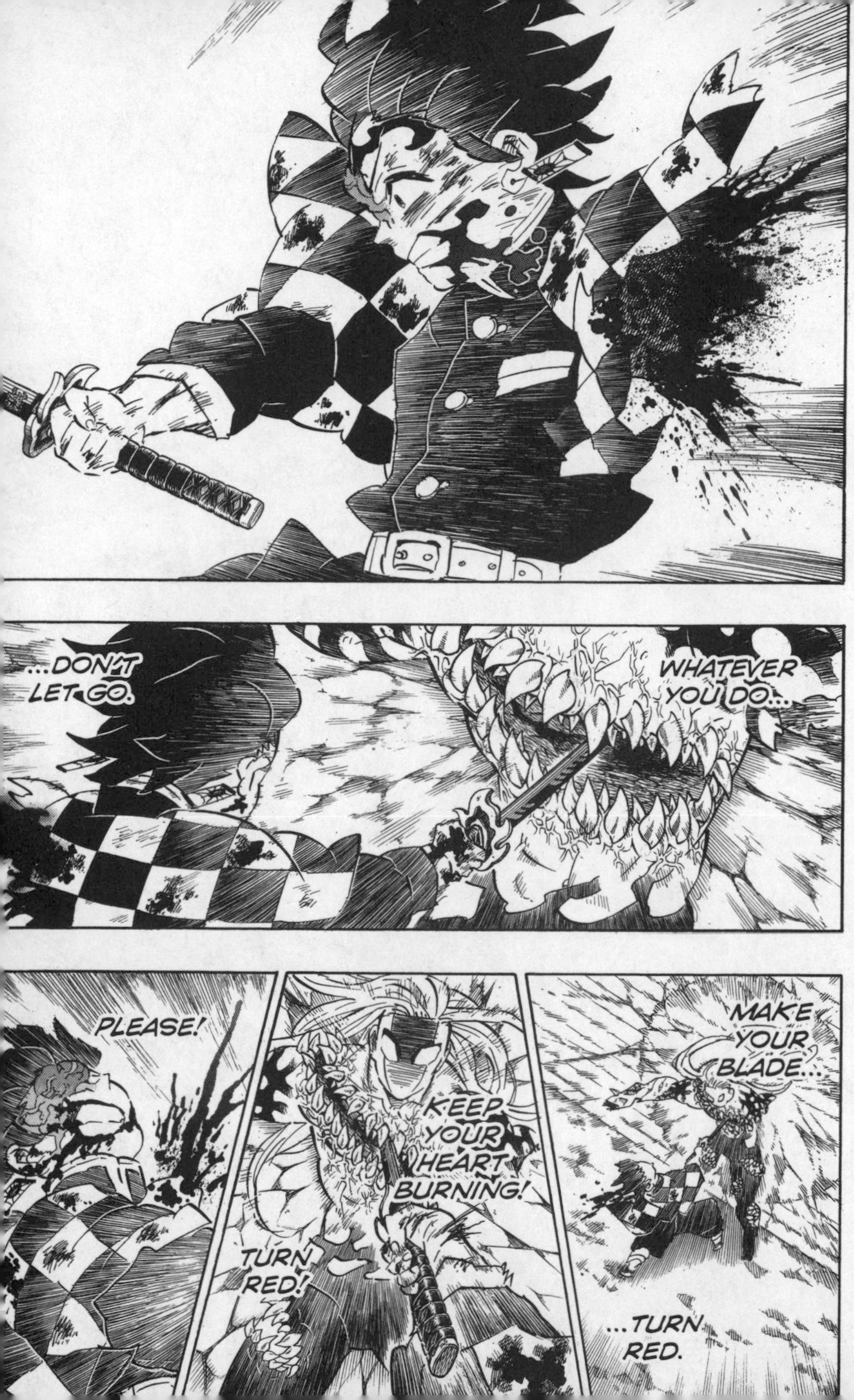
WHATEVER YOU DO...
...DON'T LET GO.
MAKE YOUR BLADE...
...TURN RED.
KEEP YOUR HEART BURNING!
TURN RED!
PLEASE!

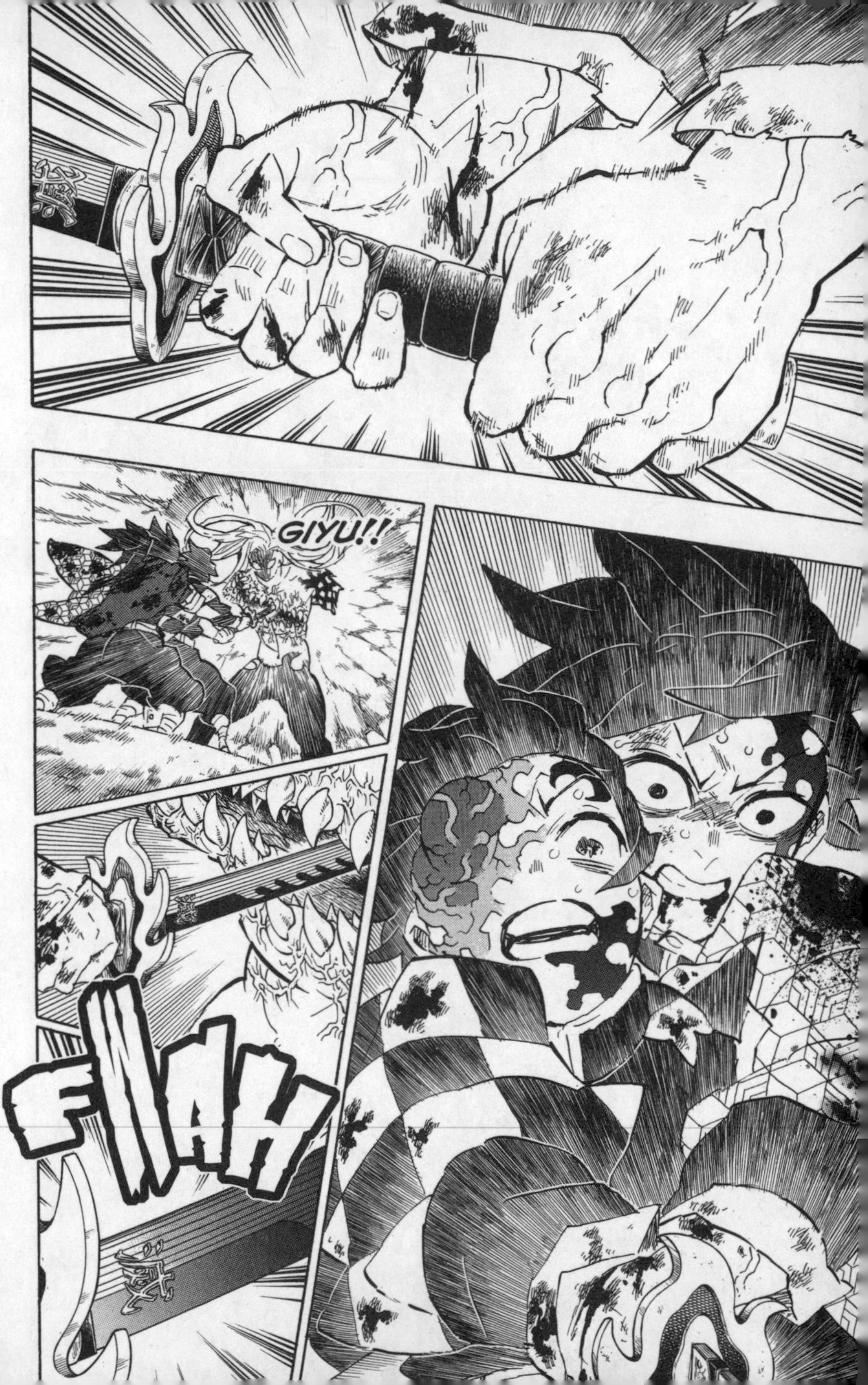
GIYU!!
FWAH

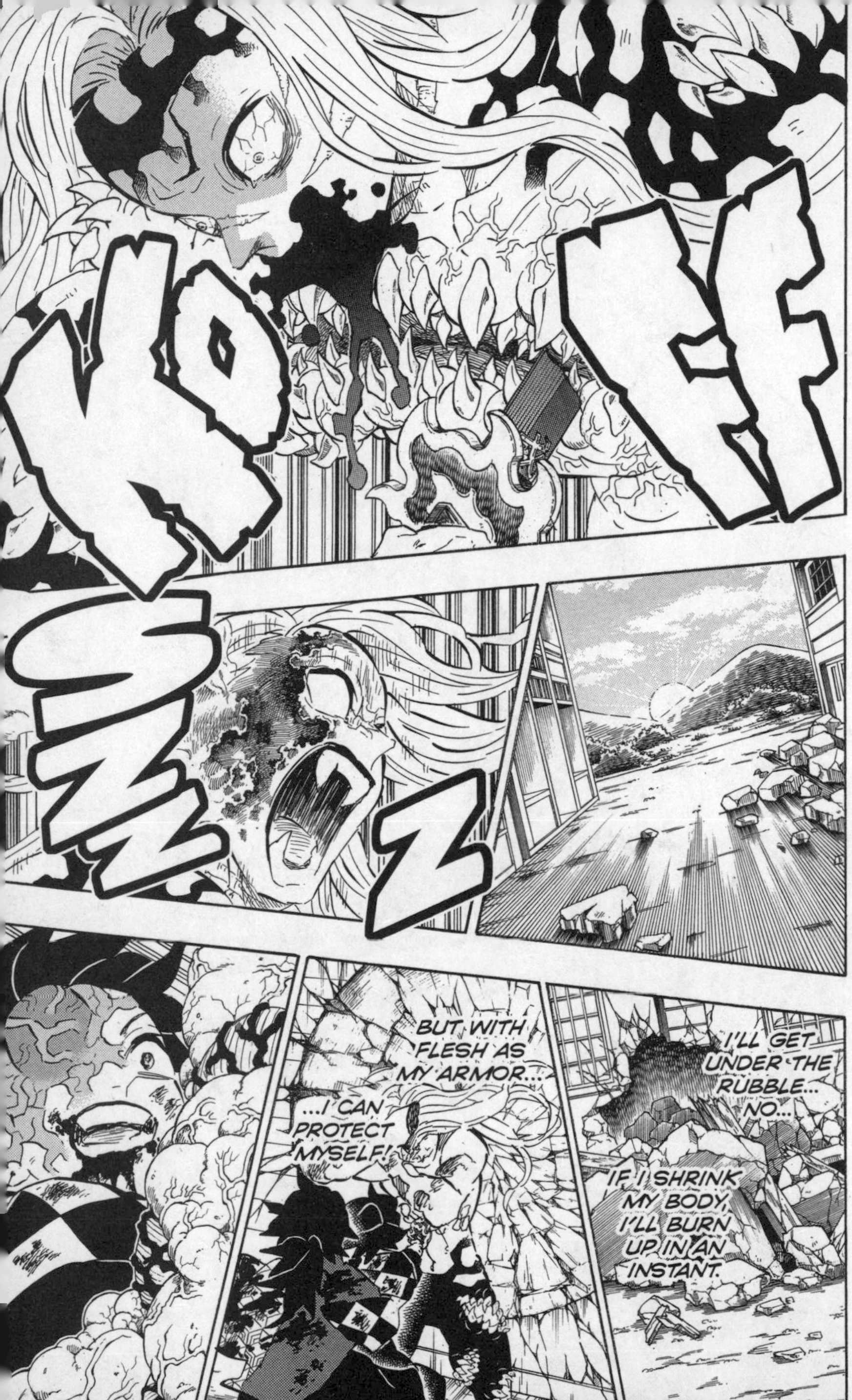
I'LL GET UNDER THE RUBBLE... NO...
IF I SHRINK MY BODY, I'LL BURN UP IN AN INSTANT.
BUT WITH FLESH AS MY ARMOR...
...I CAN PROTECT MYSELF!

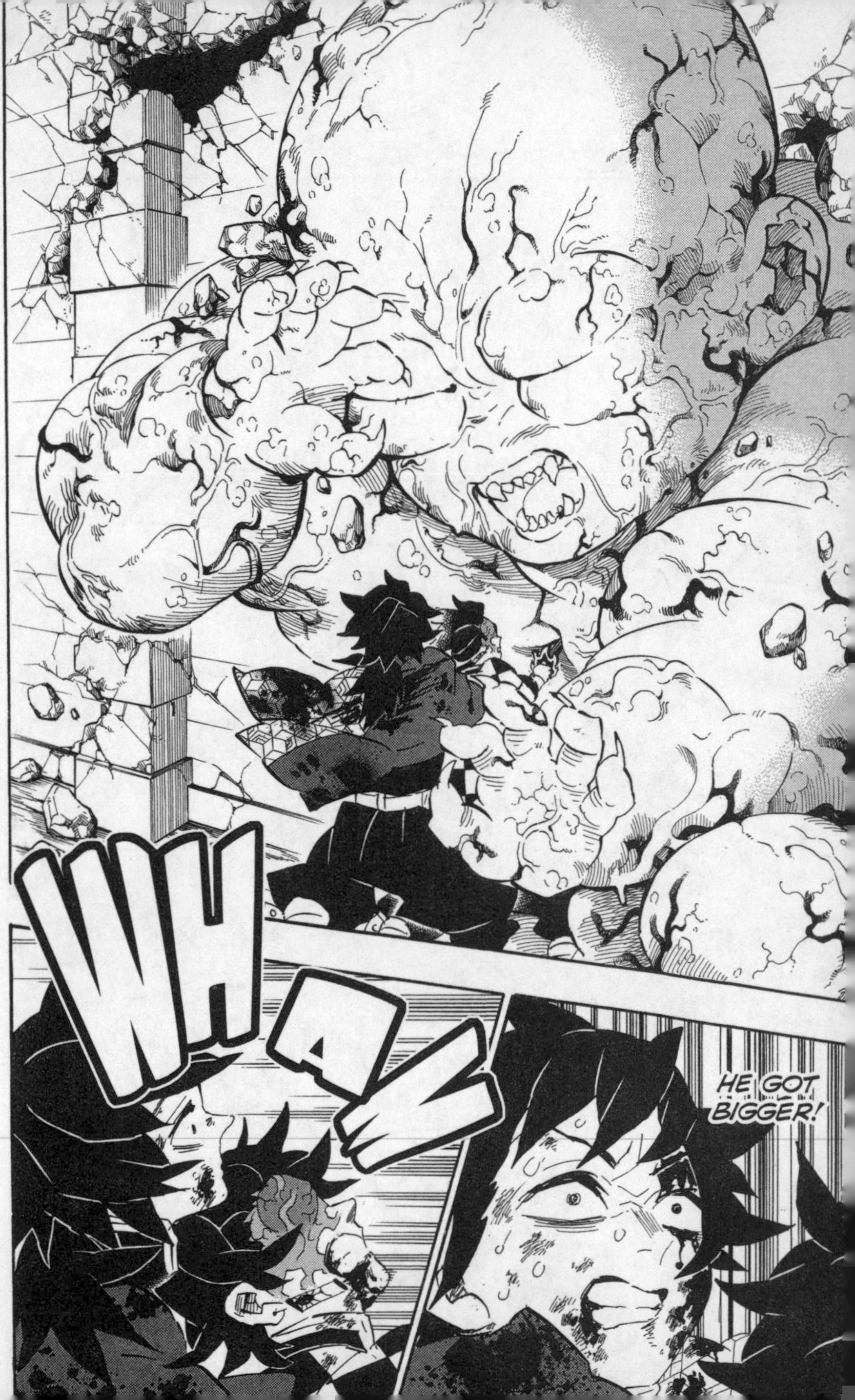
HE GOT BIGGER!
WHA

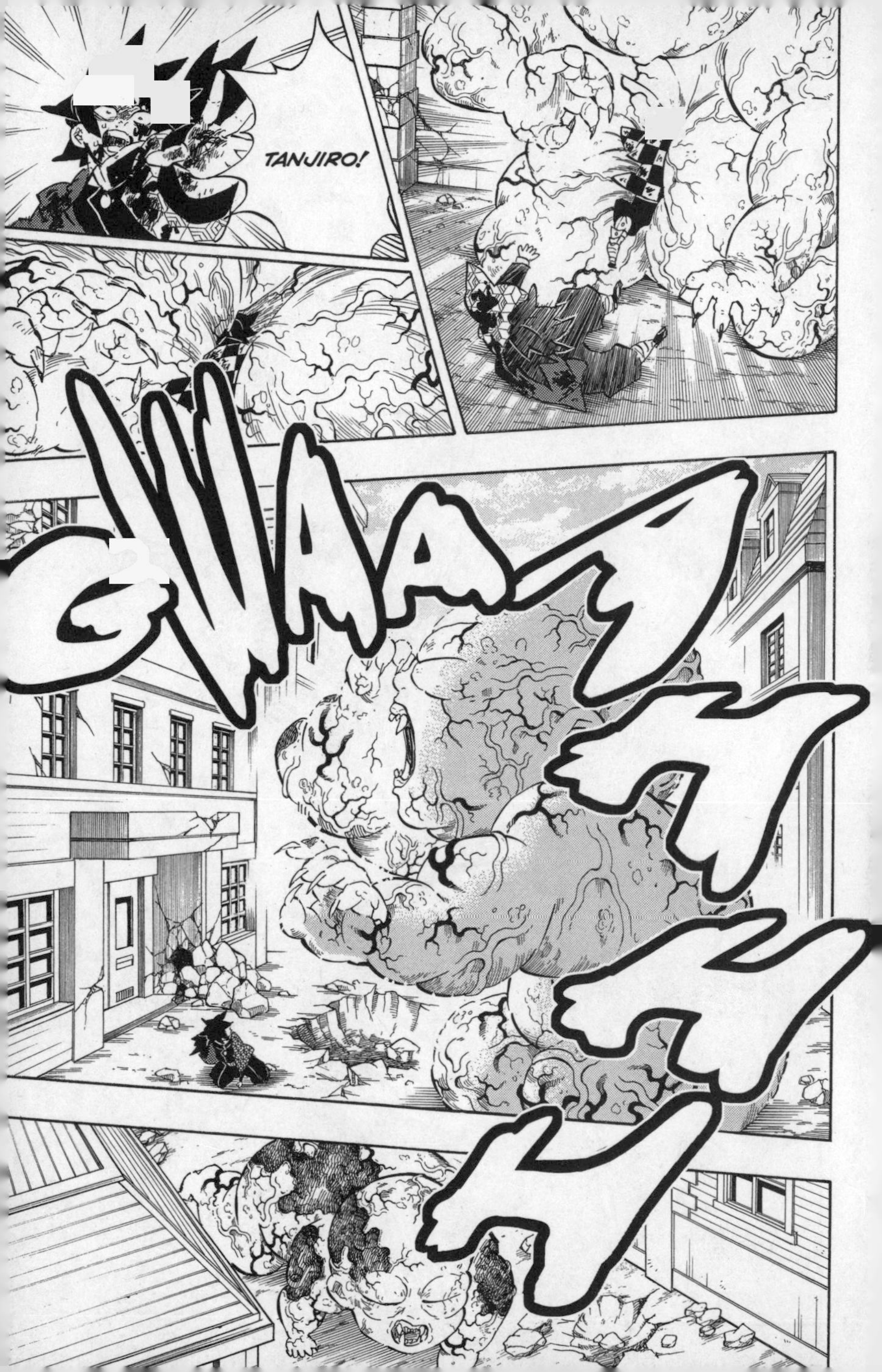
TANJIRO!

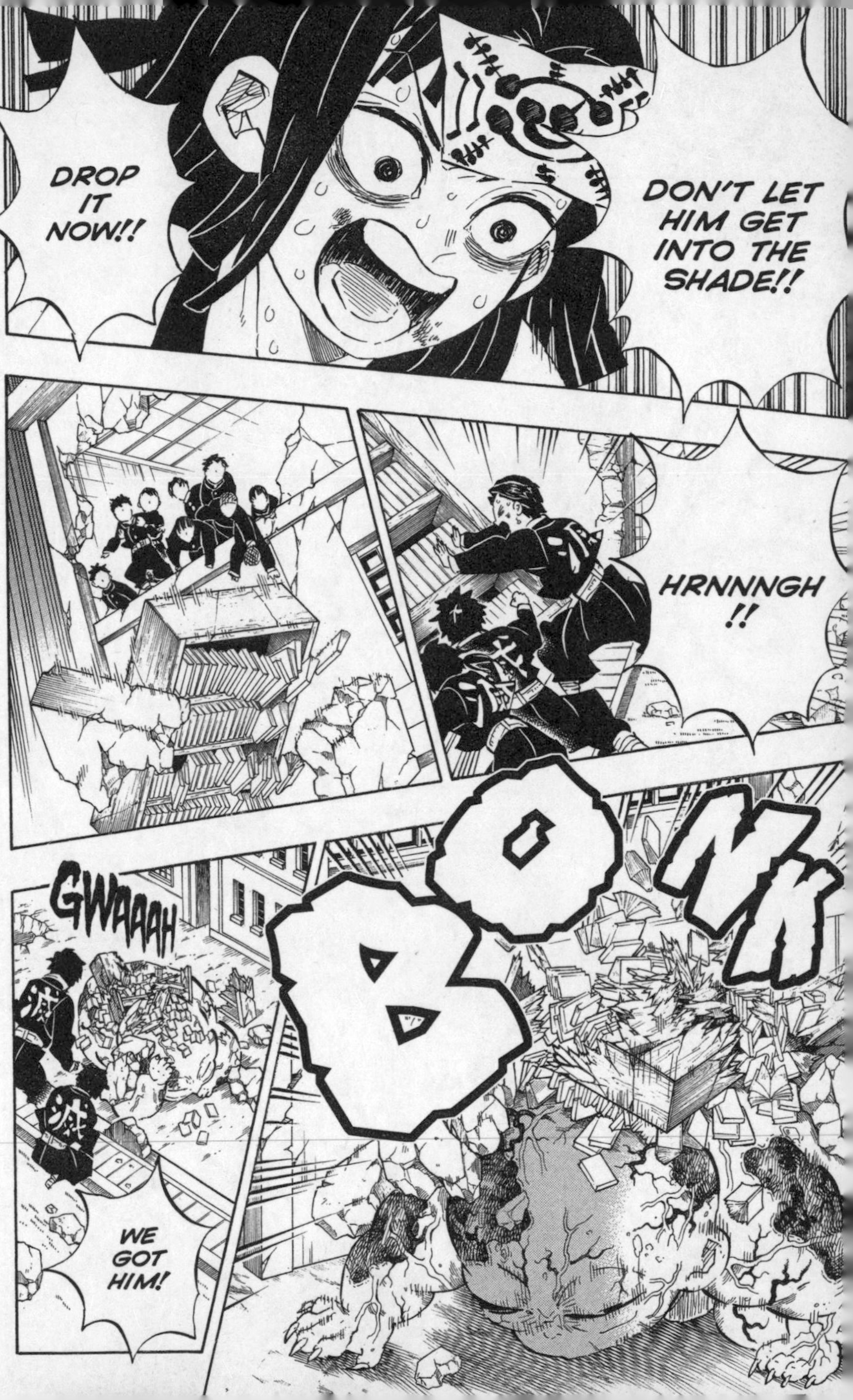
DON'T LET HIM GET INTO THE SHADE!!
DROP IT NOW!!
HRNNNGH !!
BOOM
GWAAAH
WE GOT HIM!

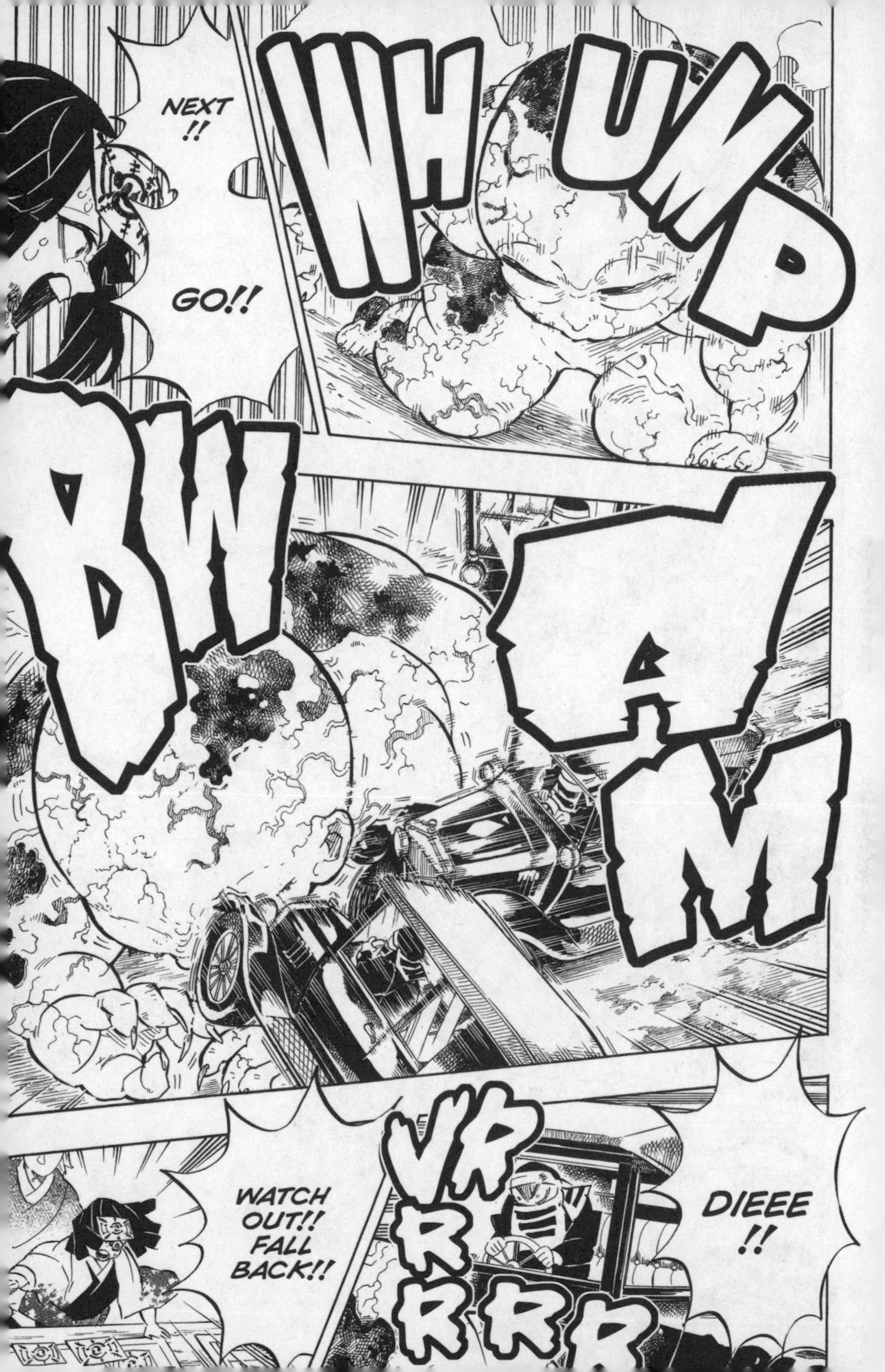
WHUMP
NEXT!!
GO!!
BWAM
DIEEE!!
VRRRRRR
WATCH OUT!! FALL BACK!!

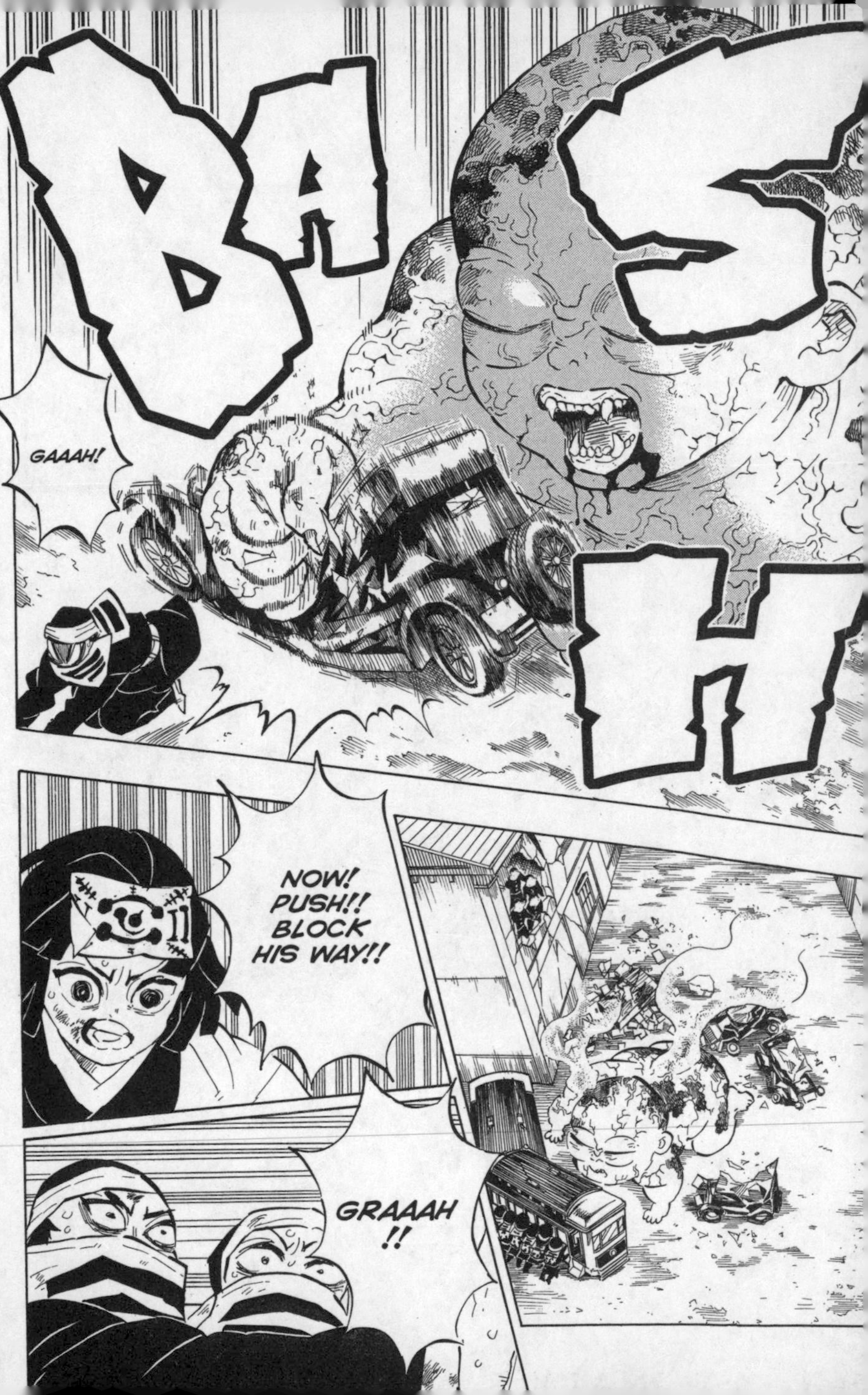
BASH
GAAAH!
NOW! PUSH!! BLOCK HIS WAY!!
GRAAAH !!

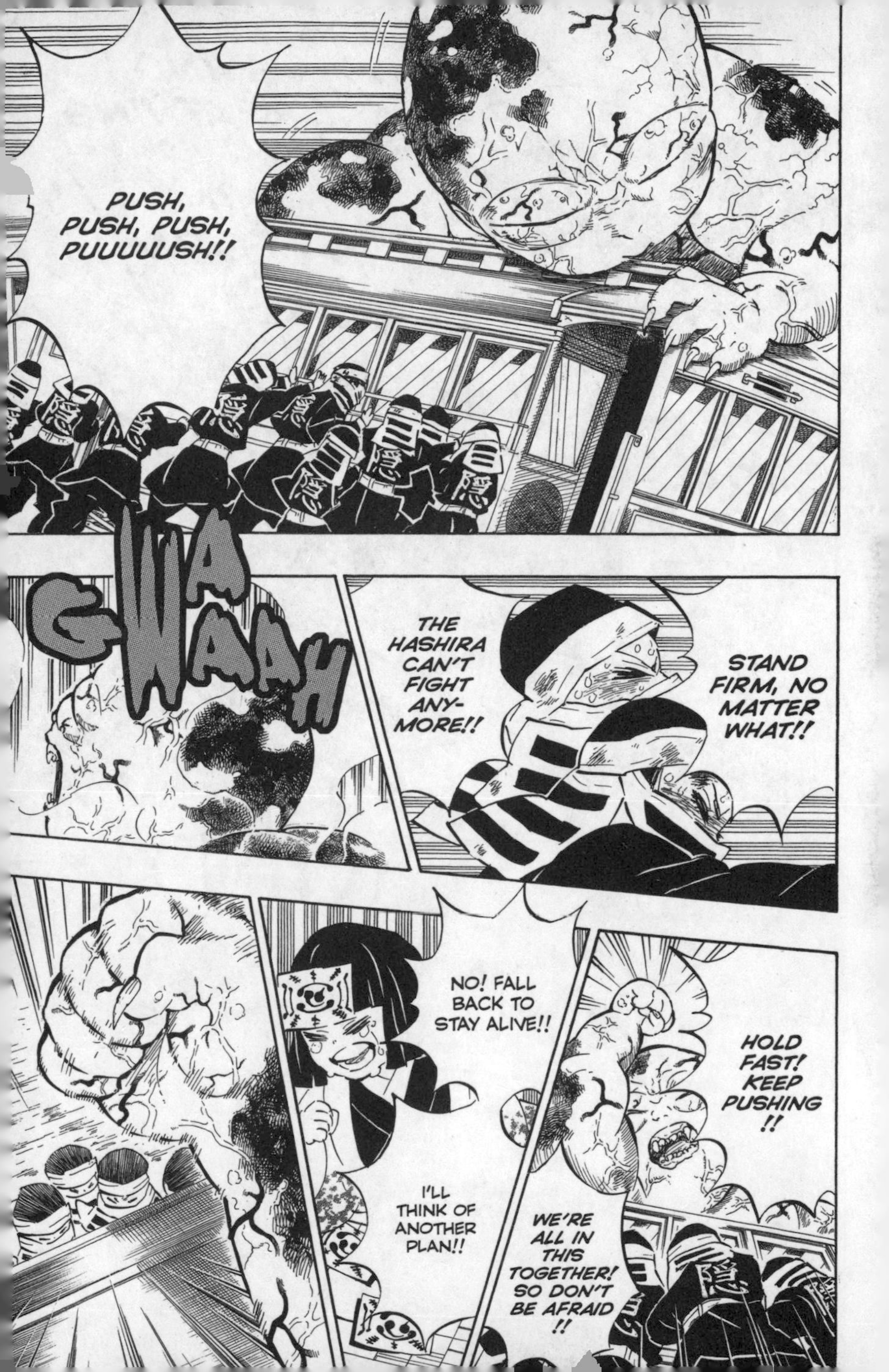
PUSH, PUSH, PUSH, PUUUUUSH!!
THE HASHIRA CAN'T FIGHT ANYMORE!!
STAND FIRM, NO MATTER WHAT!!
GWAAAH
HOLD FAST! KEEP PUSHING!!
WE'RE ALL IN THIS TOGETHER! SO DON'T BE AFRAID!!
NO! FALL BACK TO STAY ALIVE!!
I'LL THINK OF ANOTHER PLAN!!

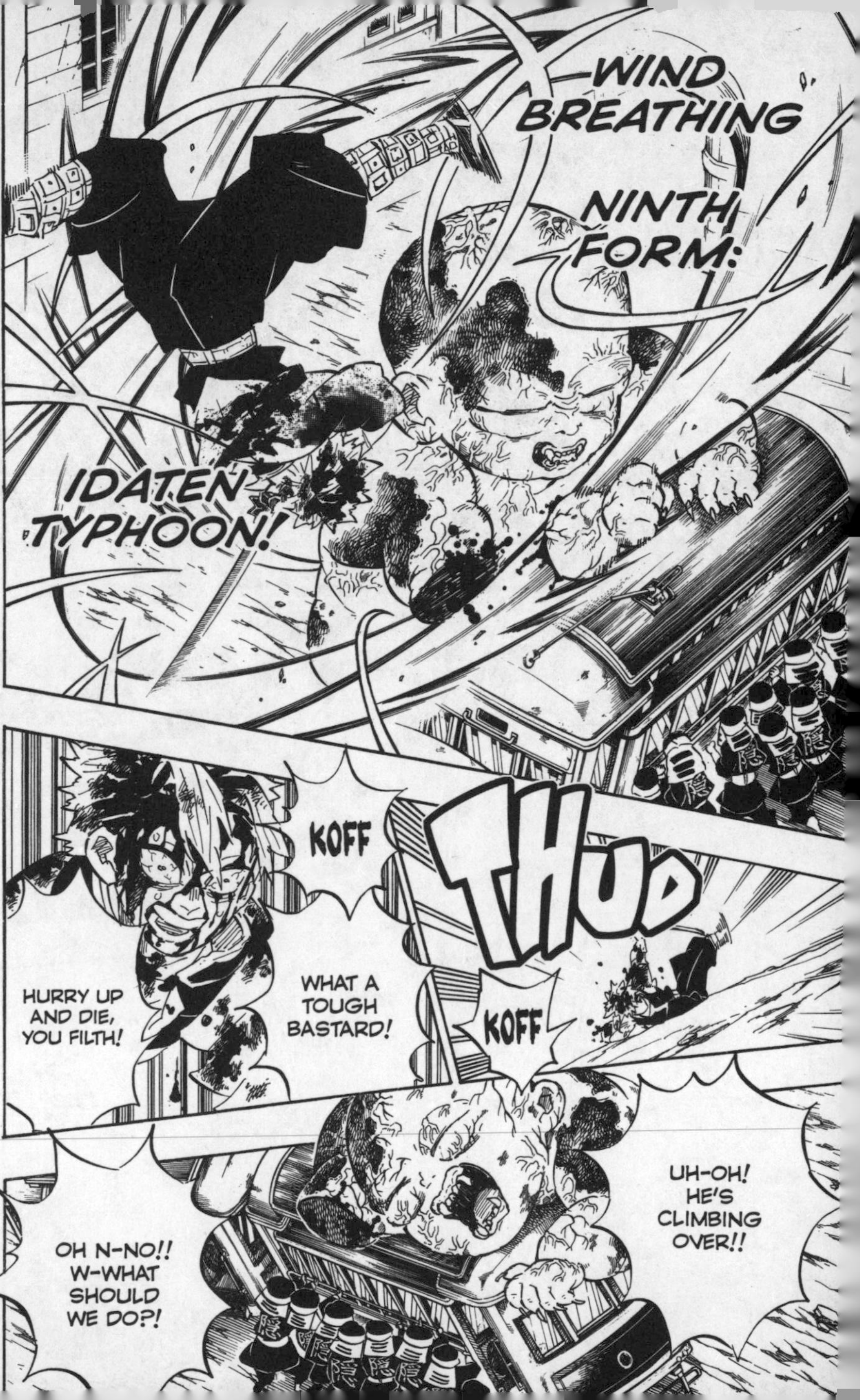
WIND BREATHING
NINTH FORM:
IDATEN TYPHOON!
THUD
KOFF
KOFF
WHAT A TOUGH BASTARD!
HURRY UP AND DIE, YOU FILTH!
UH-OH! HE'S CLIMBING OVER!!
OH N-NO!! W-WHAT SHOULD WE DO?!

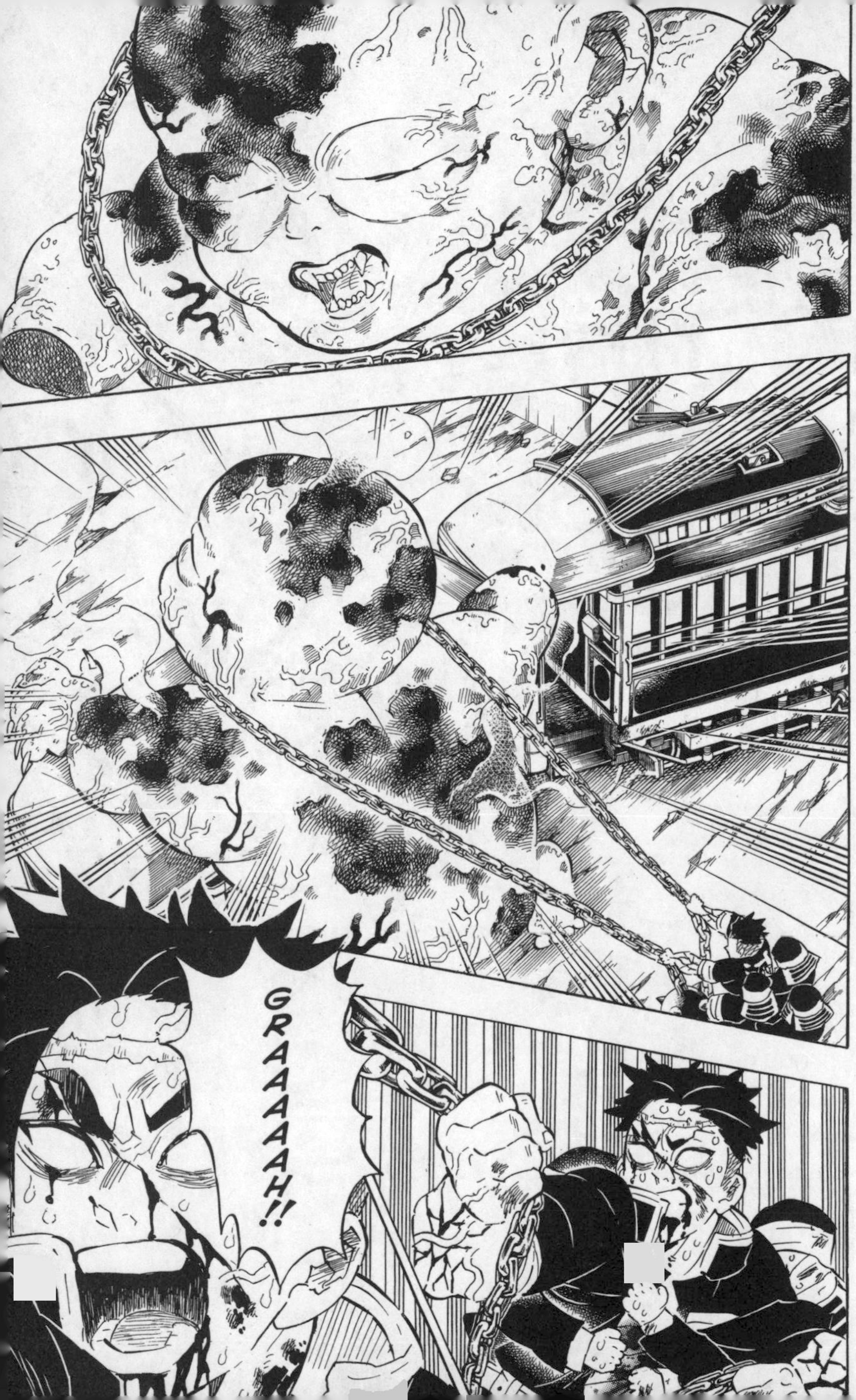
GRAAAAAAH!!

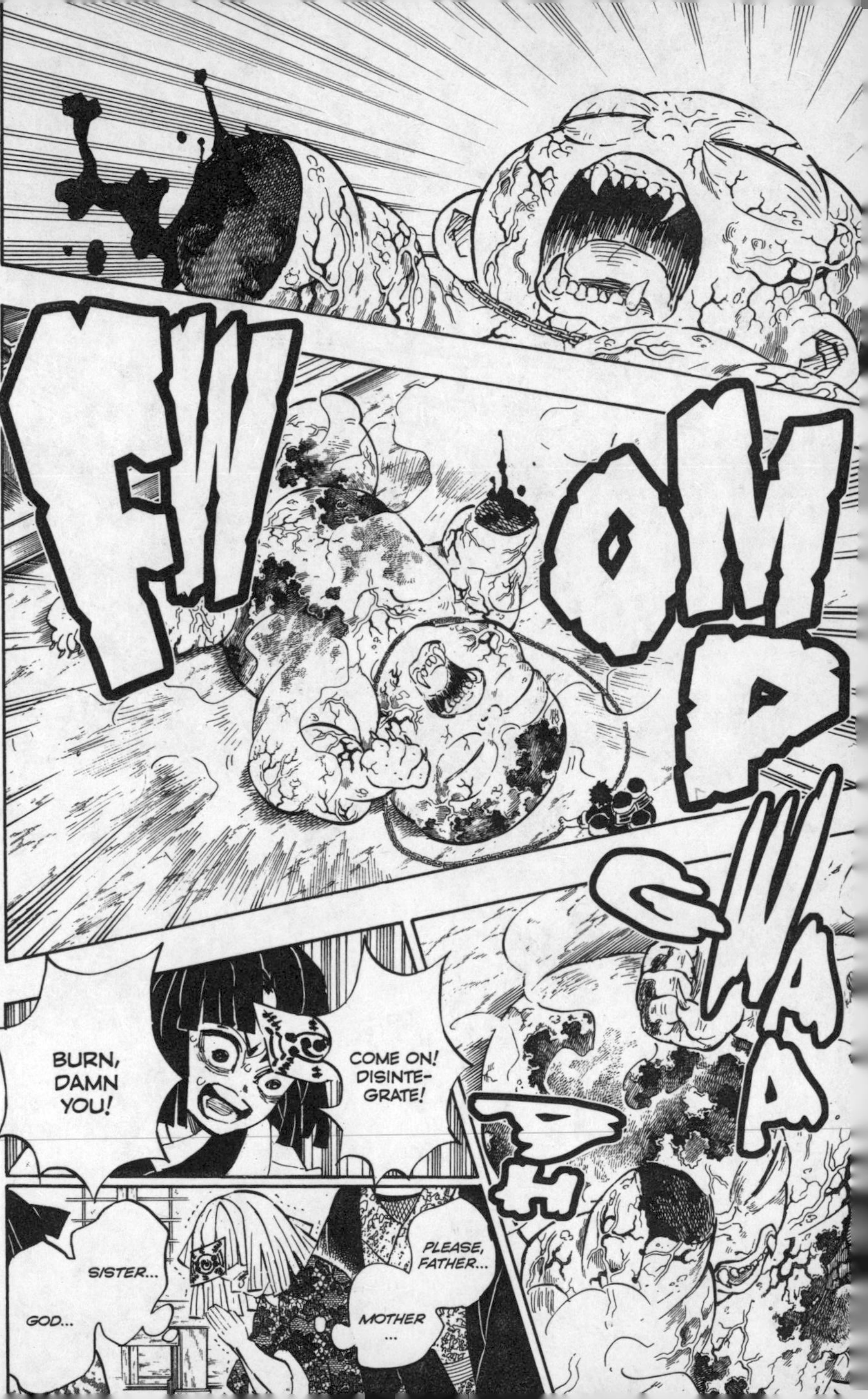

FWOMP
COME ON! DISINTE-GRATE!
BURN, DAMN YOU!
PLEASE, FATHER...
MOTHER...
SISTER...
GOD...

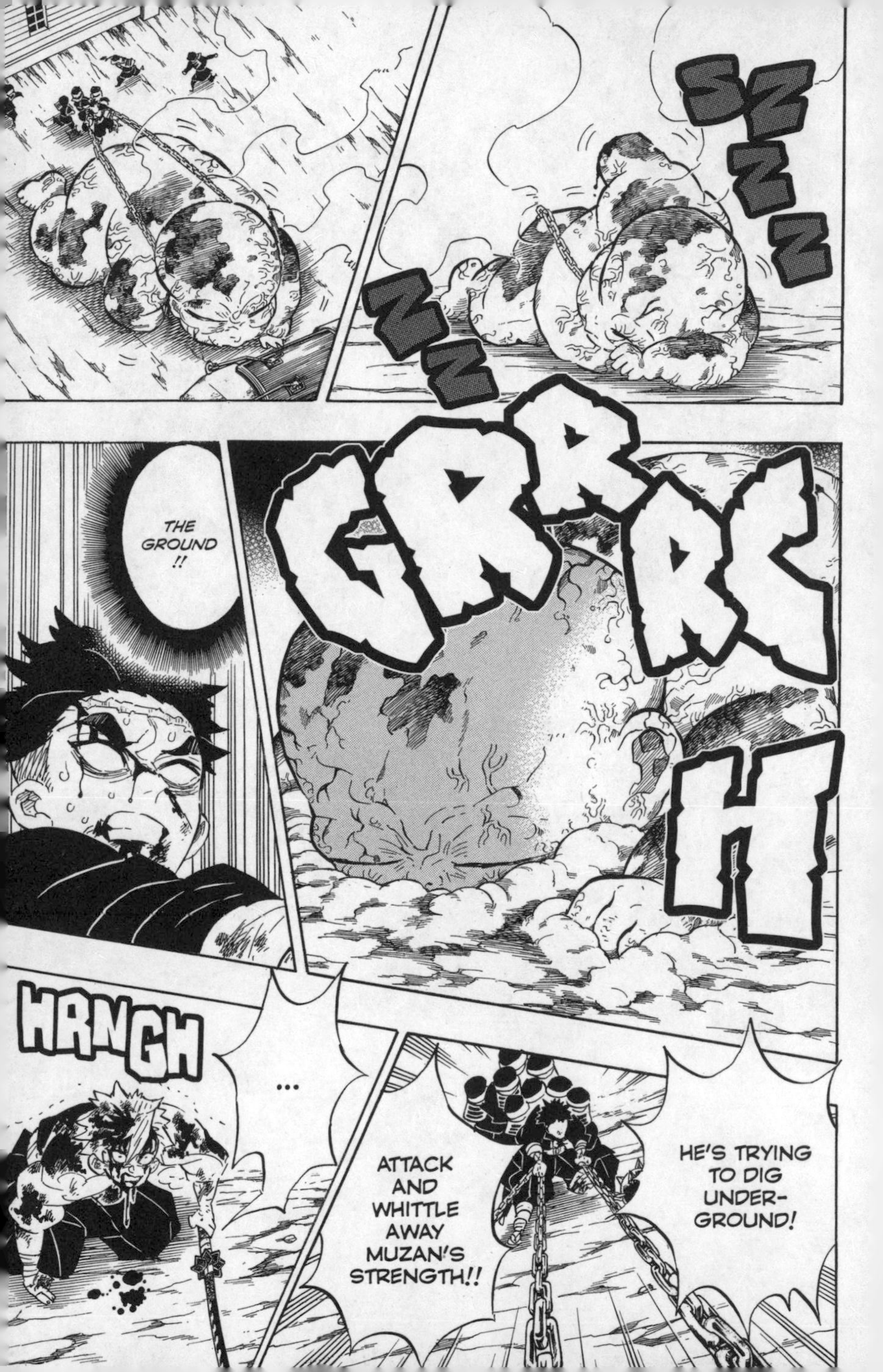
SZZZ
ZZZ
GRRRKH
THE GROUND !!
HE'S TRYING TO DIG UNDER-GROUND!
ATTACK AND WHITTLE AWAY MUZAN'S STRENGTH!!
...
HRNGH

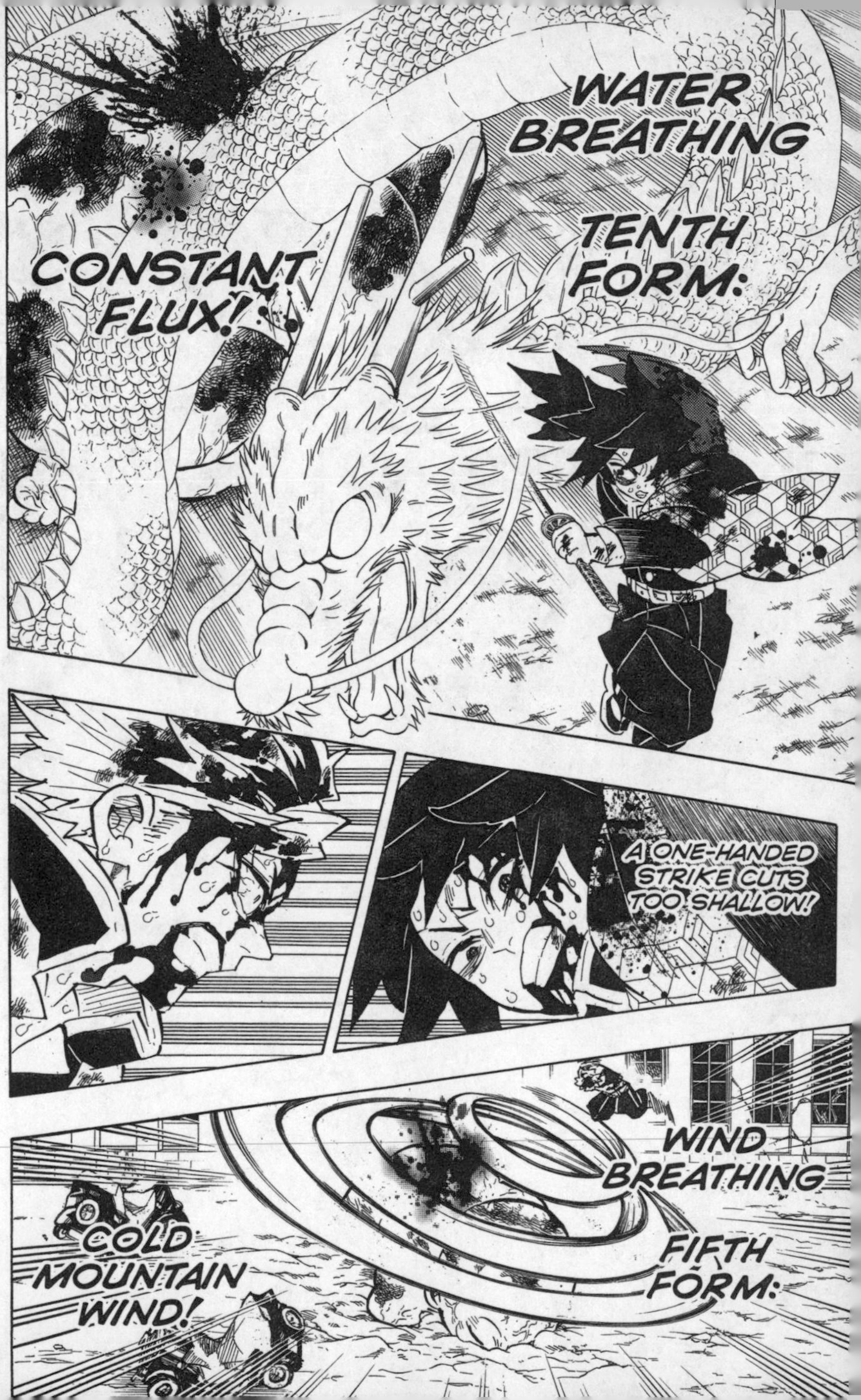
WATER BREATHING
TENTH FORM:
CONSTANT FLUX!
A ONE-HANDED STRIKE CUTS TOO SHALLOW!
WIND BREATHING
FIFTH FORM:
COLD MOUNTAIN WIND!

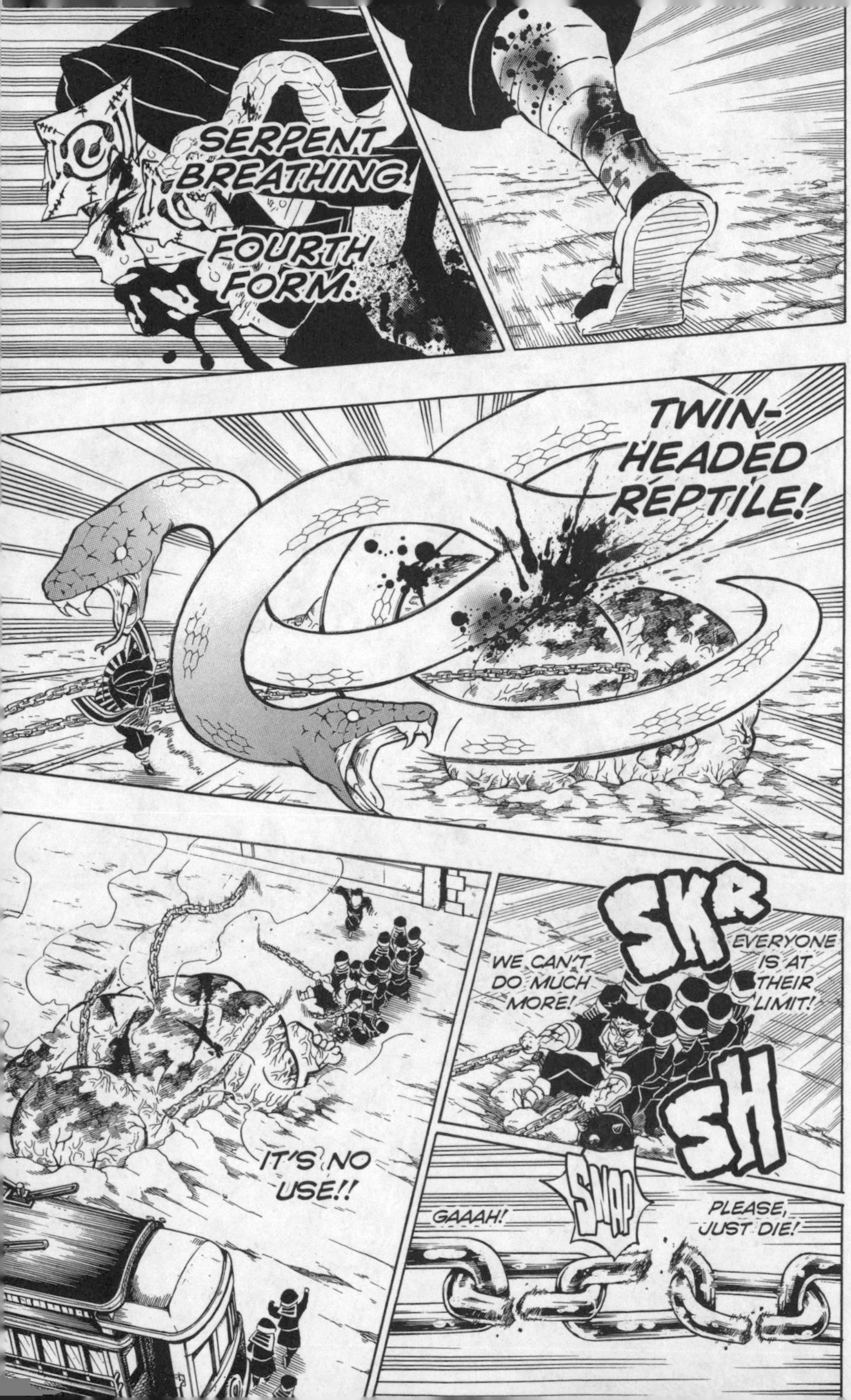
SERPENT BREATHING!
FOURTH FORM:
TWIN-HEADED REPTILE!
SKR
EVERYONE IS AT THEIR LIMIT!
WE CAN'T DO MUCH MORE!
SH
PLEASE, JUST DIE!
SNAP
GAAAH!
IT'S NO USE!!

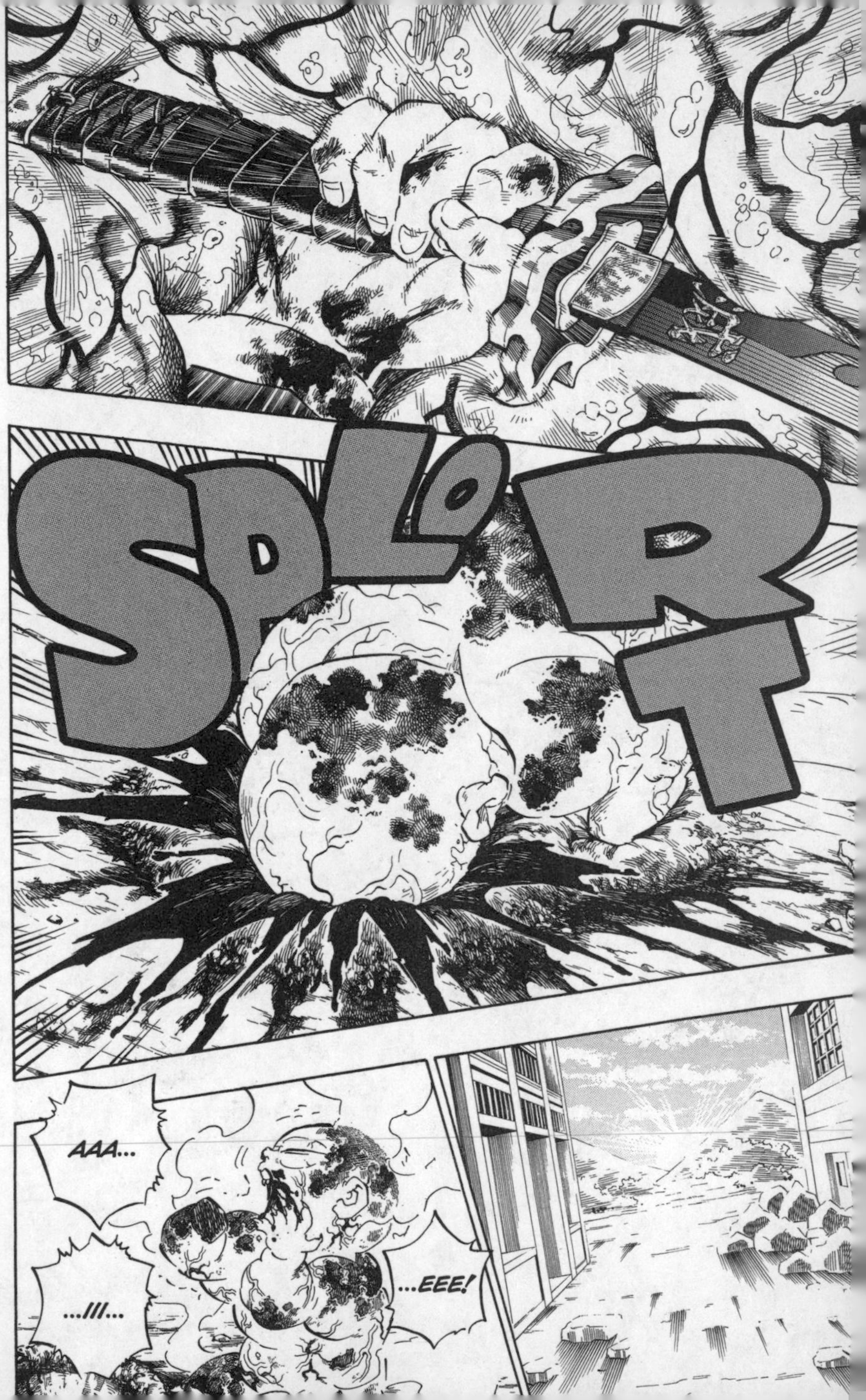
SPLORT
AAA...
...III...
...EEE!

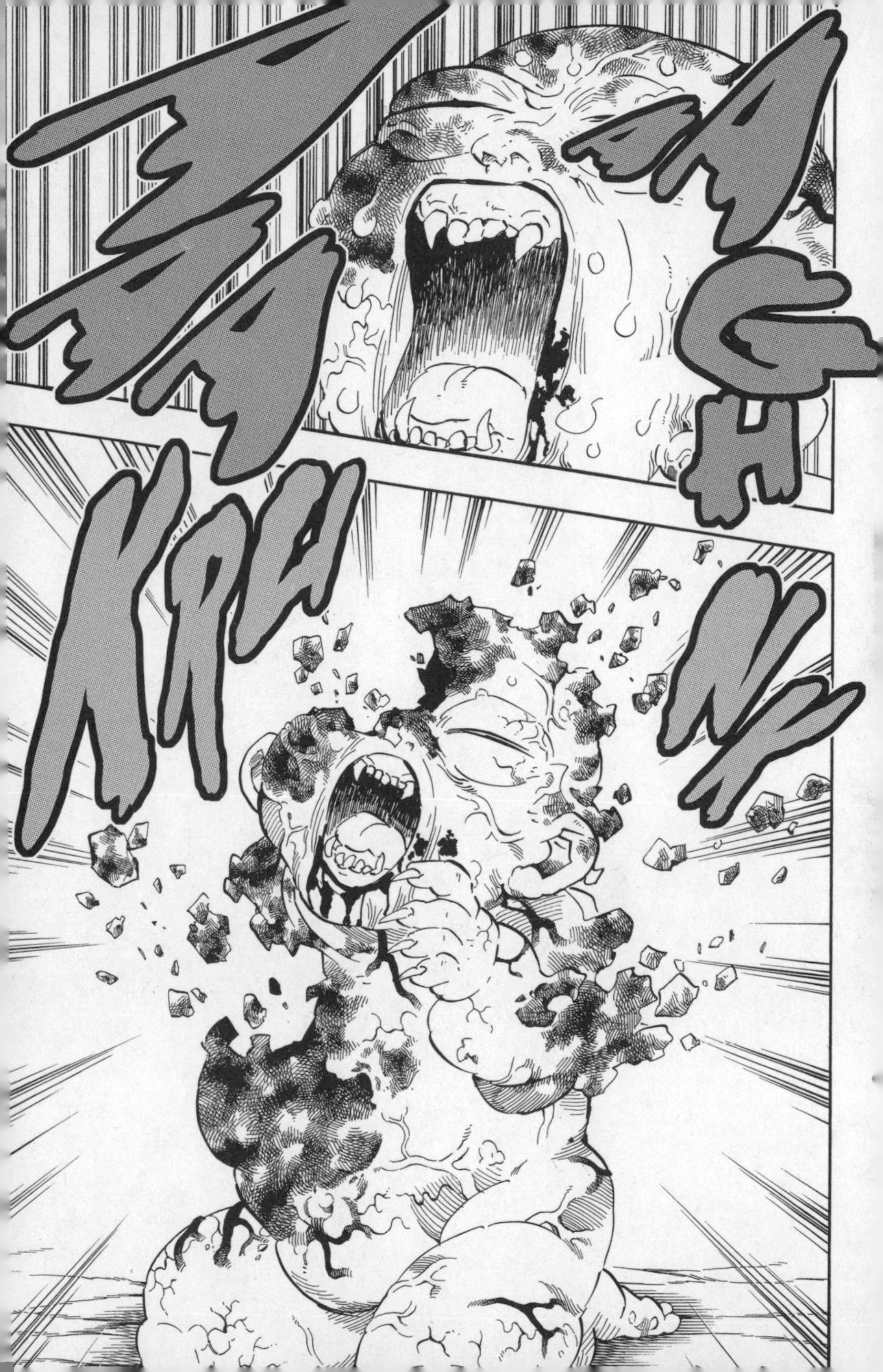
AAAAGH
KRANK

CHAPTER 200: THE PRICE OF VICTORY

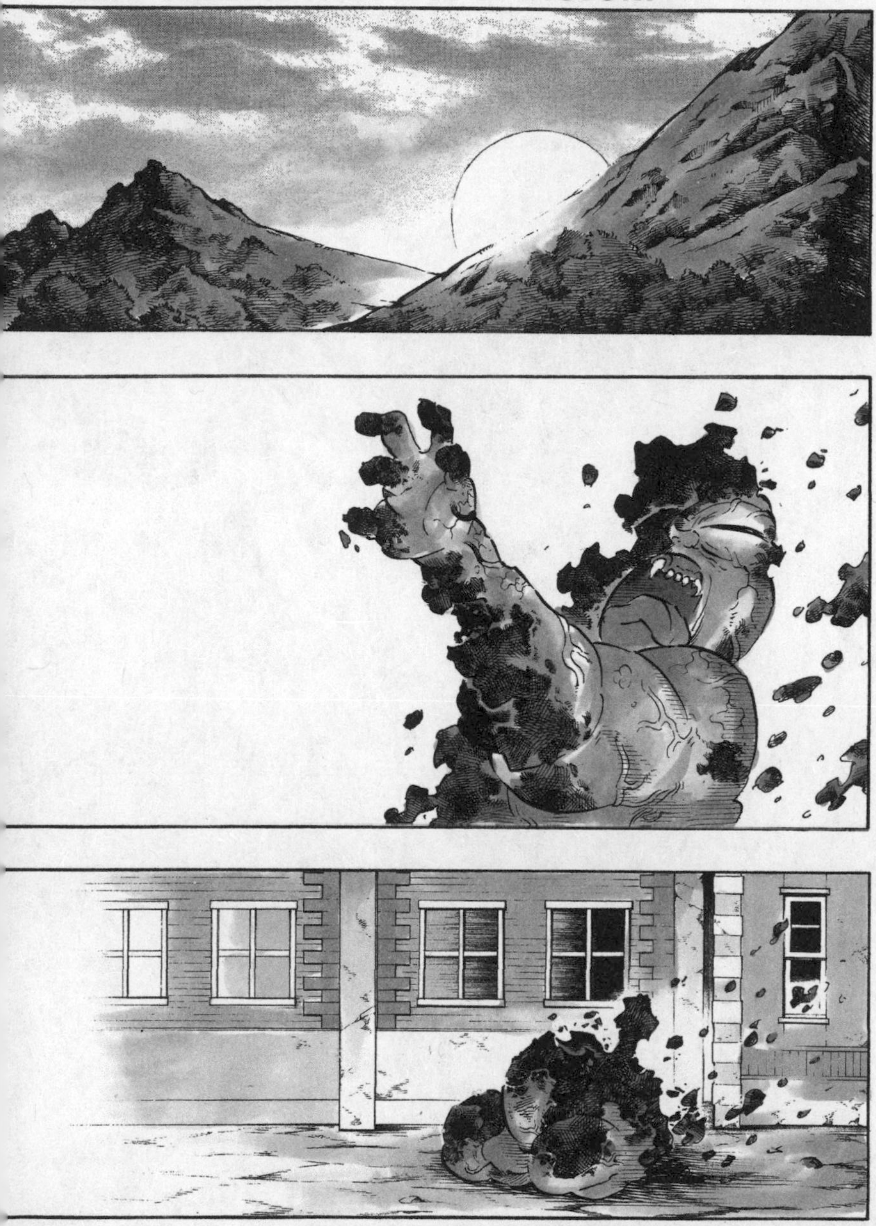

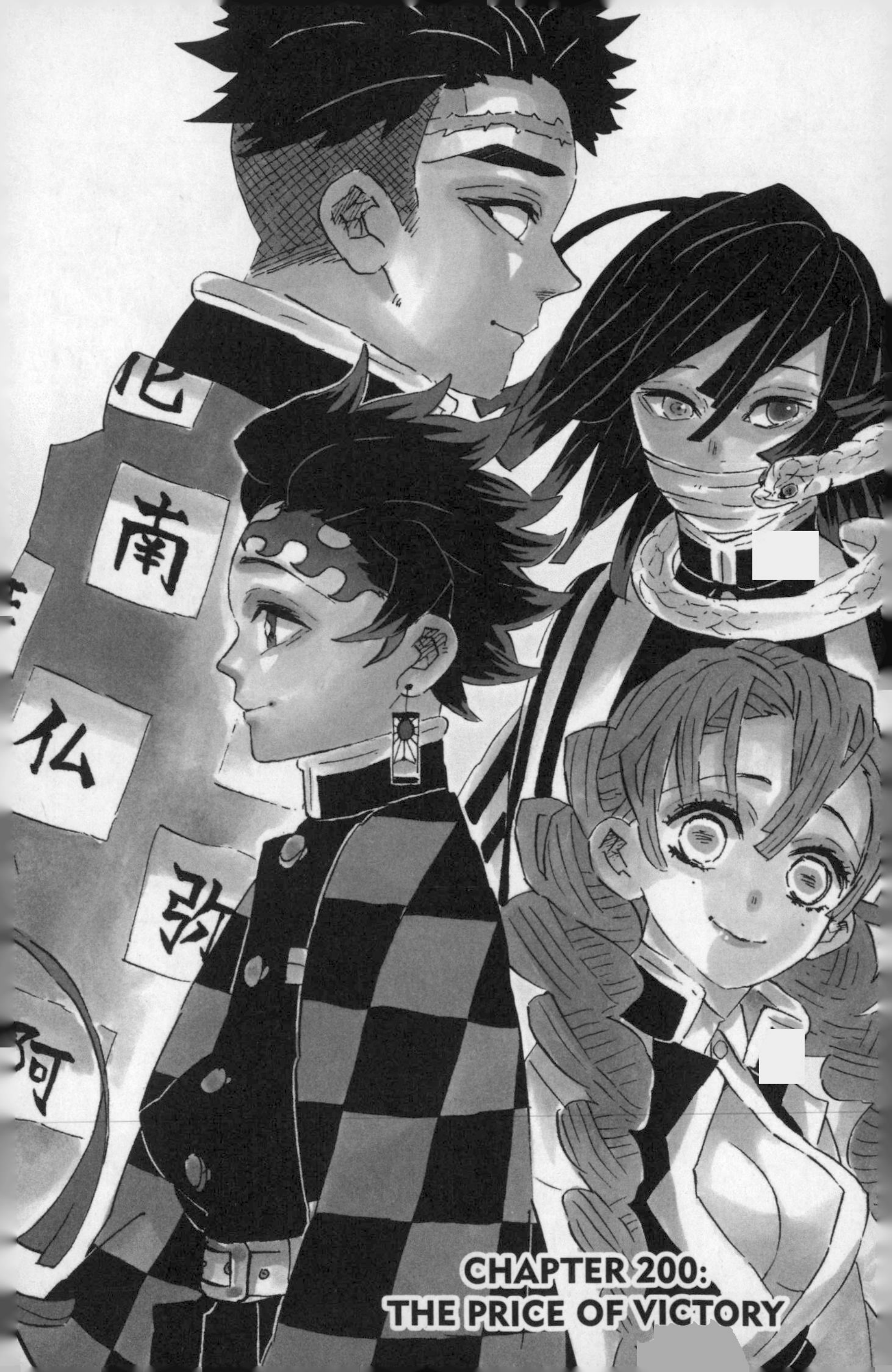
CHAPTER 200:
THE PRICE OF VICTORY

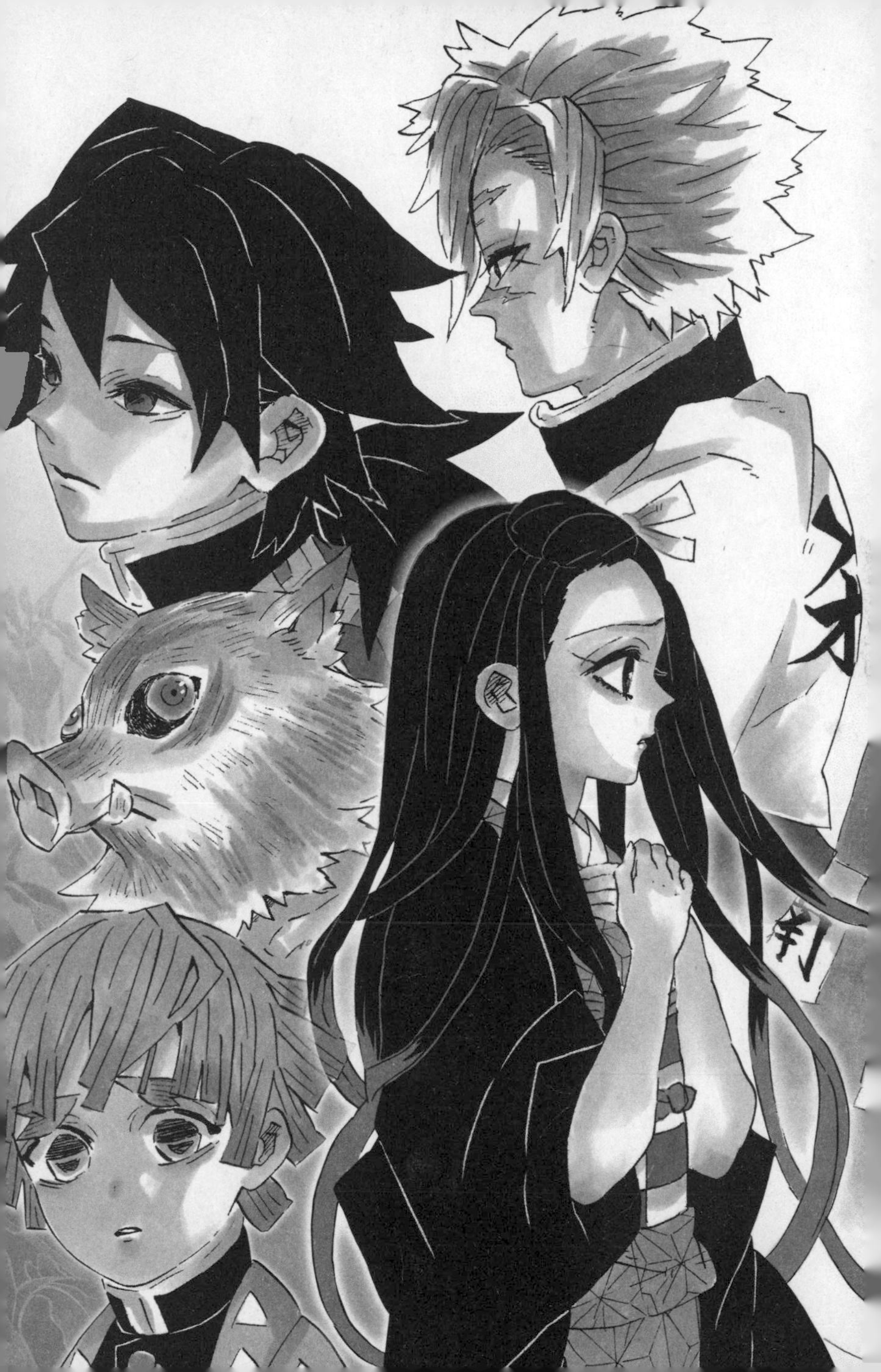

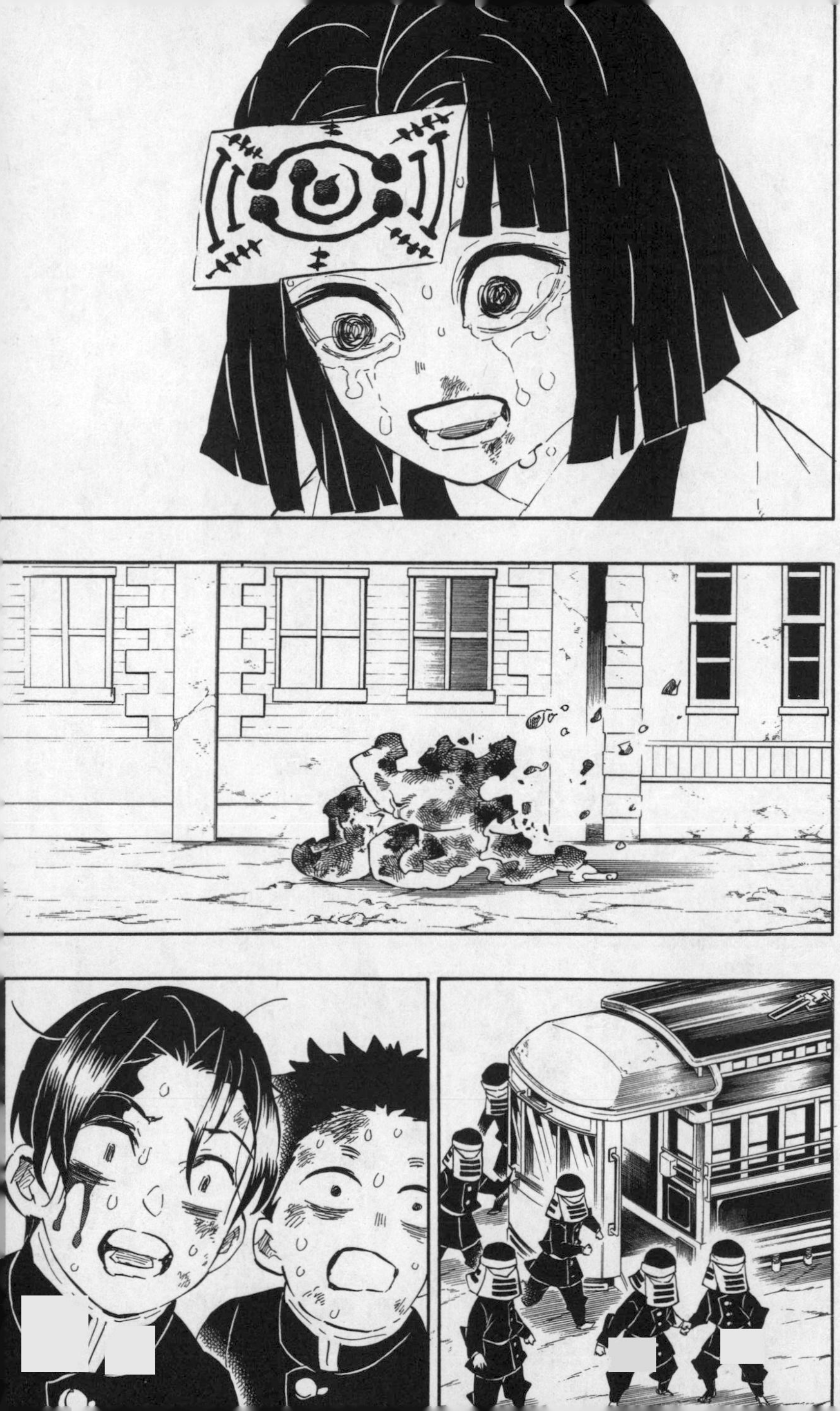

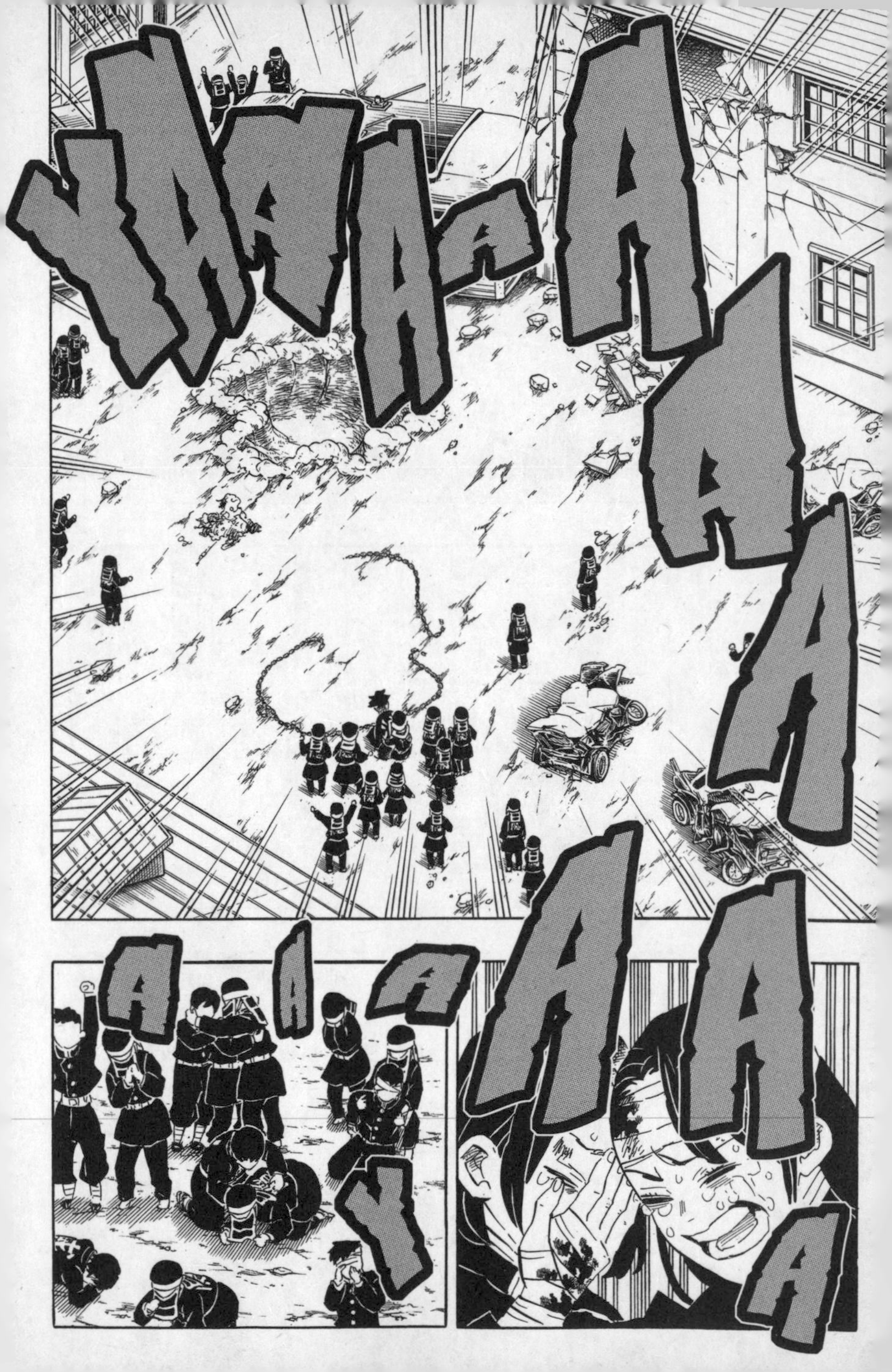

WAA-AAAA
AAA
AAAY

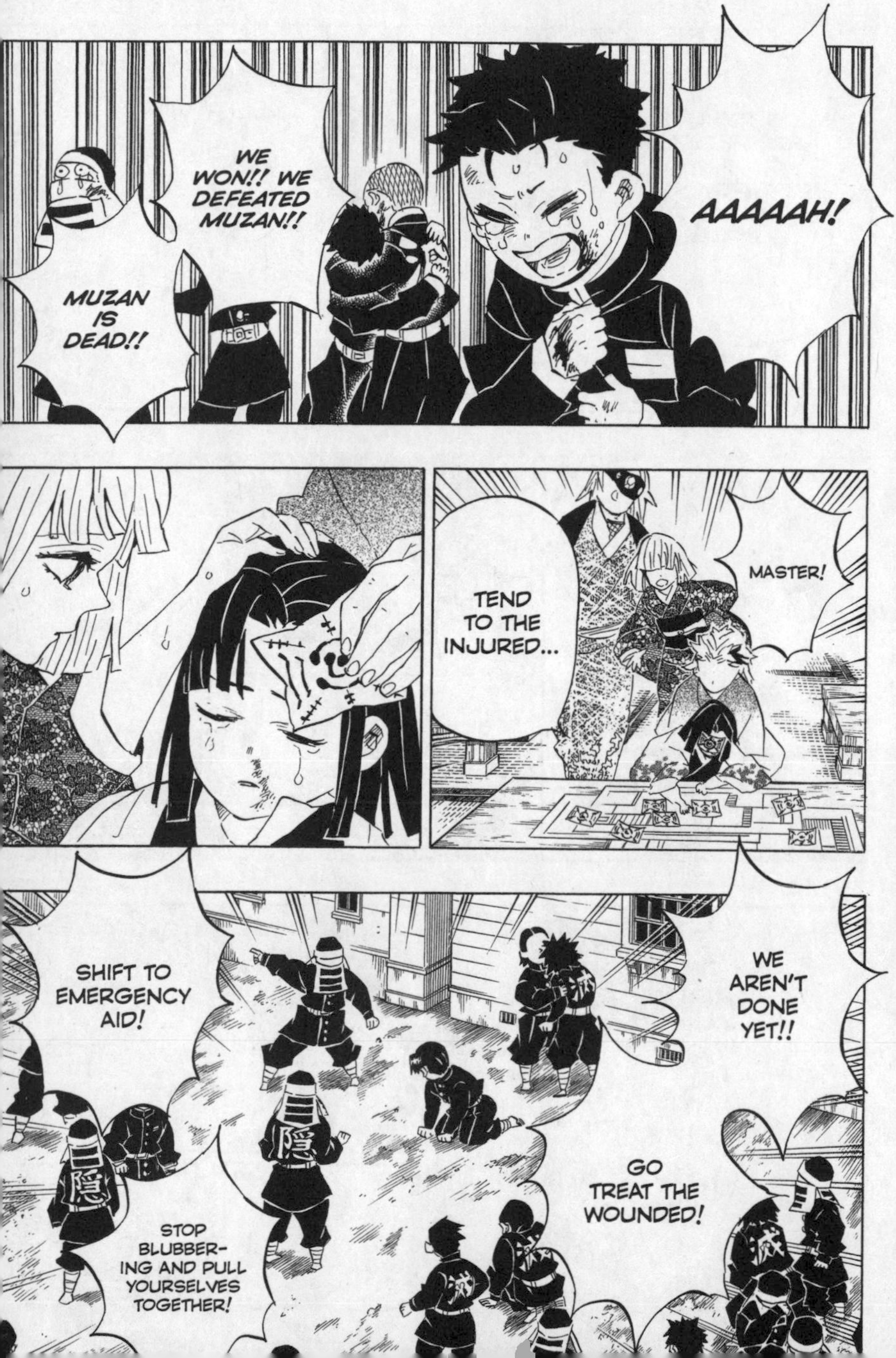
AAAAAH!
WE WON!! WE DEFEATED MUZAN!!
MUZAN IS DEAD!!
MASTER!
TEND TO THE INJURED...
WE AREN'T DONE YET!!
SHIFT TO EMERGENCY AID!
GO TREAT THE WOUNDED!
STOP BLUBBERING AND PULL YOURSELVES TOGETHER!

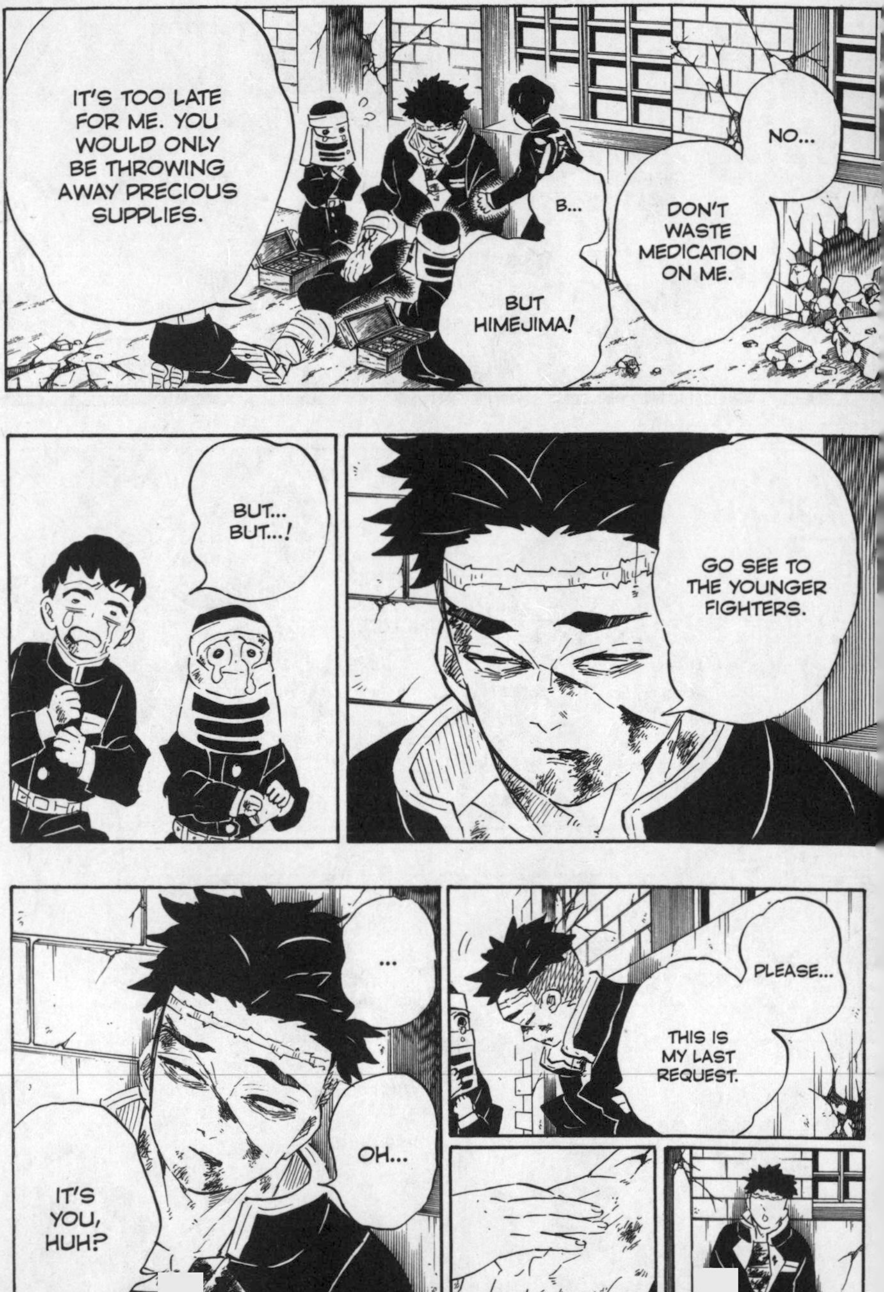
NO...
DON'T WASTE MEDICATION ON ME.
B...
BUT HIMEJIMA!
IT'S TOO LATE FOR ME. YOU WOULD ONLY BE THROWING AWAY PRECIOUS SUPPLIES.
GO SEE TO THE YOUNGER FIGHTERS.
BUT... BUT...!
PLEASE...
THIS IS MY LAST REQUEST.
...
OH...
IT'S YOU, HUH?

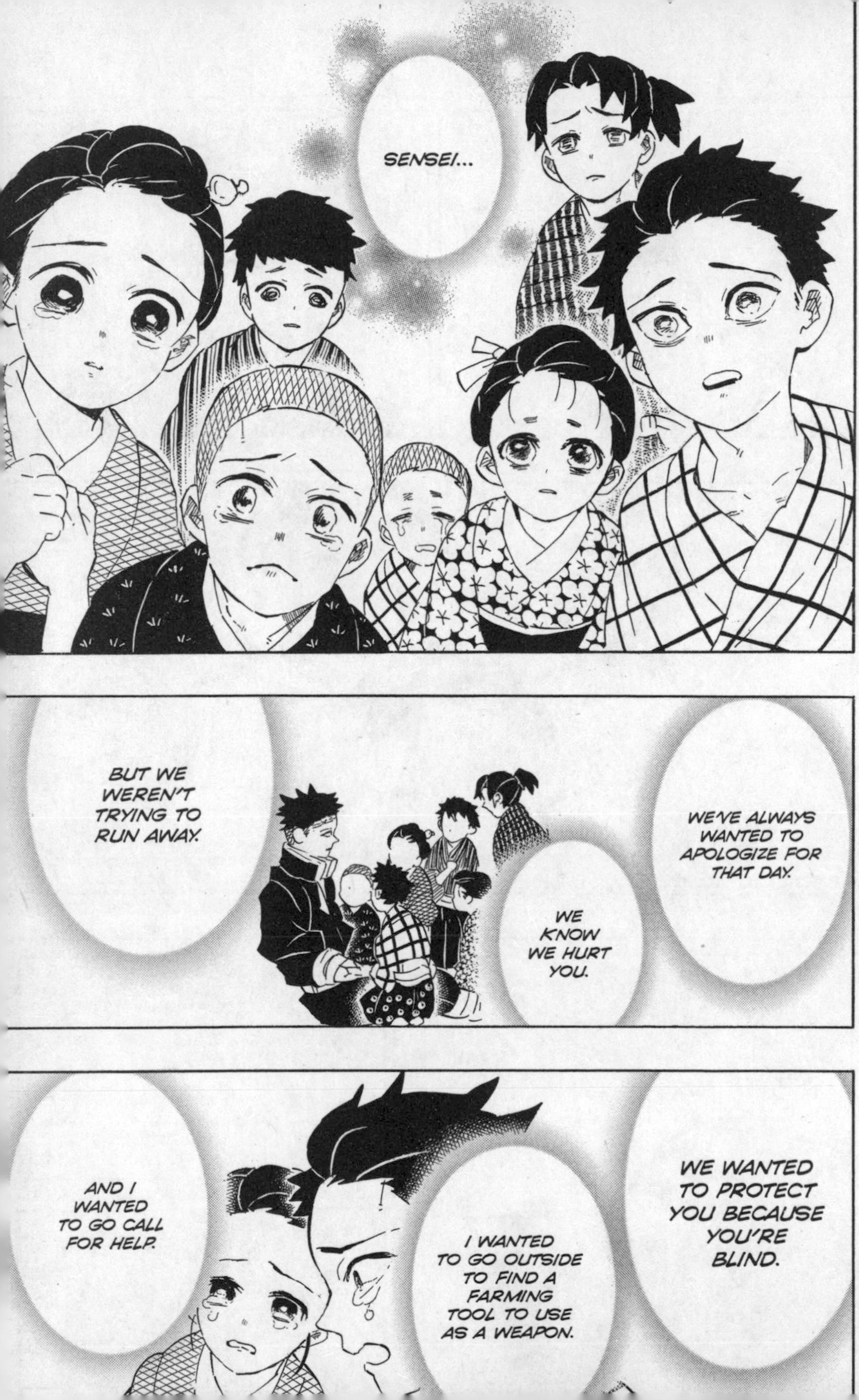
SENSEI...
WE'VE ALWAYS WANTED TO APOLOGIZE FOR THAT DAY.
WE KNOW WE HURT YOU.
BUT WE WEREN'T TRYING TO RUN AWAY.
WE WANTED TO PROTECT YOU BECAUSE YOU'RE BLIND.
I WANTED TO GO OUTSIDE TO FIND A FARMING TOOL TO USE AS A WEAPON.
AND I WANTED TO GO CALL FOR HELP.

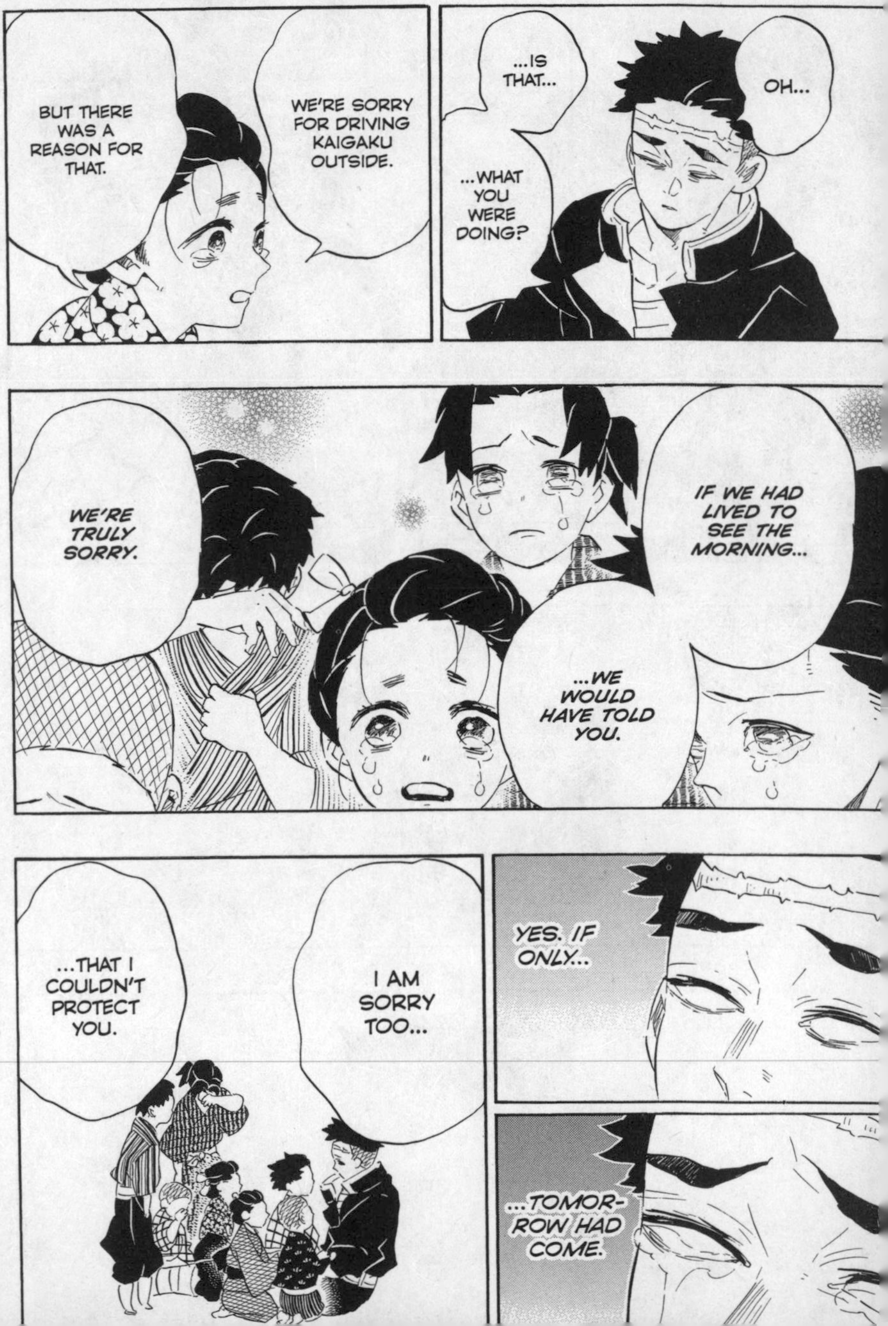
OH...
...IS THAT...
...WHAT YOU WERE DOING?
WE'RE SORRY FOR DRIVING KAIGAKU OUTSIDE.
BUT THERE WAS A REASON FOR THAT.
IF WE HAD LIVED TO SEE THE MORNING...
...WE WOULD HAVE TOLD YOU.
WE'RE TRULY SORRY.
YES. IF ONLY...
...TOMOR-ROW HAD COME.
I AM SORRY TOO...
...THAT I COULDN'T PROTECT YOU.

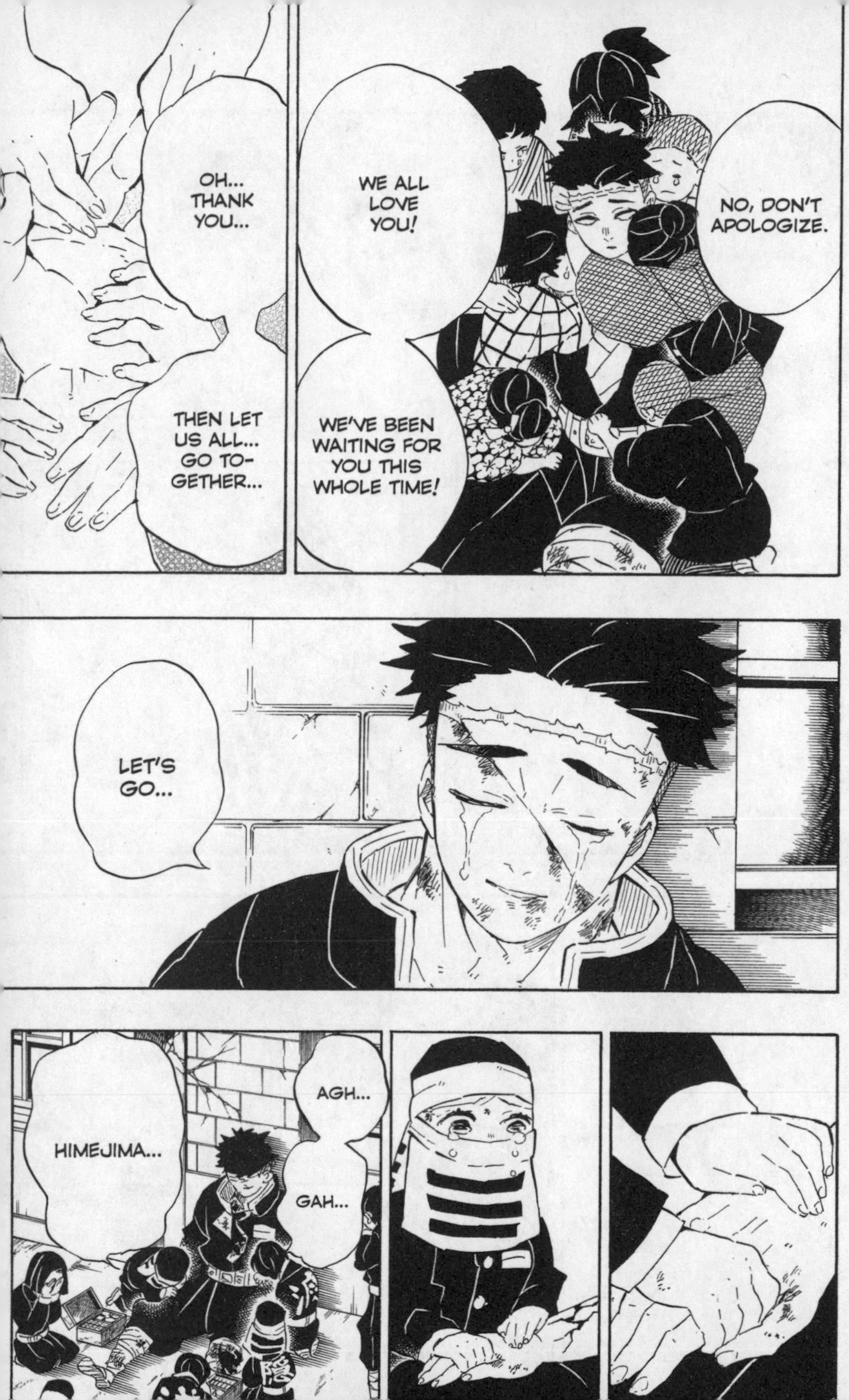
NO, DON'T APOLOGIZE.
WE ALL LOVE YOU!
WE'VE BEEN WAITING FOR YOU THIS WHOLE TIME!
OH... THANK YOU...
THEN LET US ALL... GO TO-GETHER...
LET'S GO...
AGH...
GAH...
HIMEJIMA...

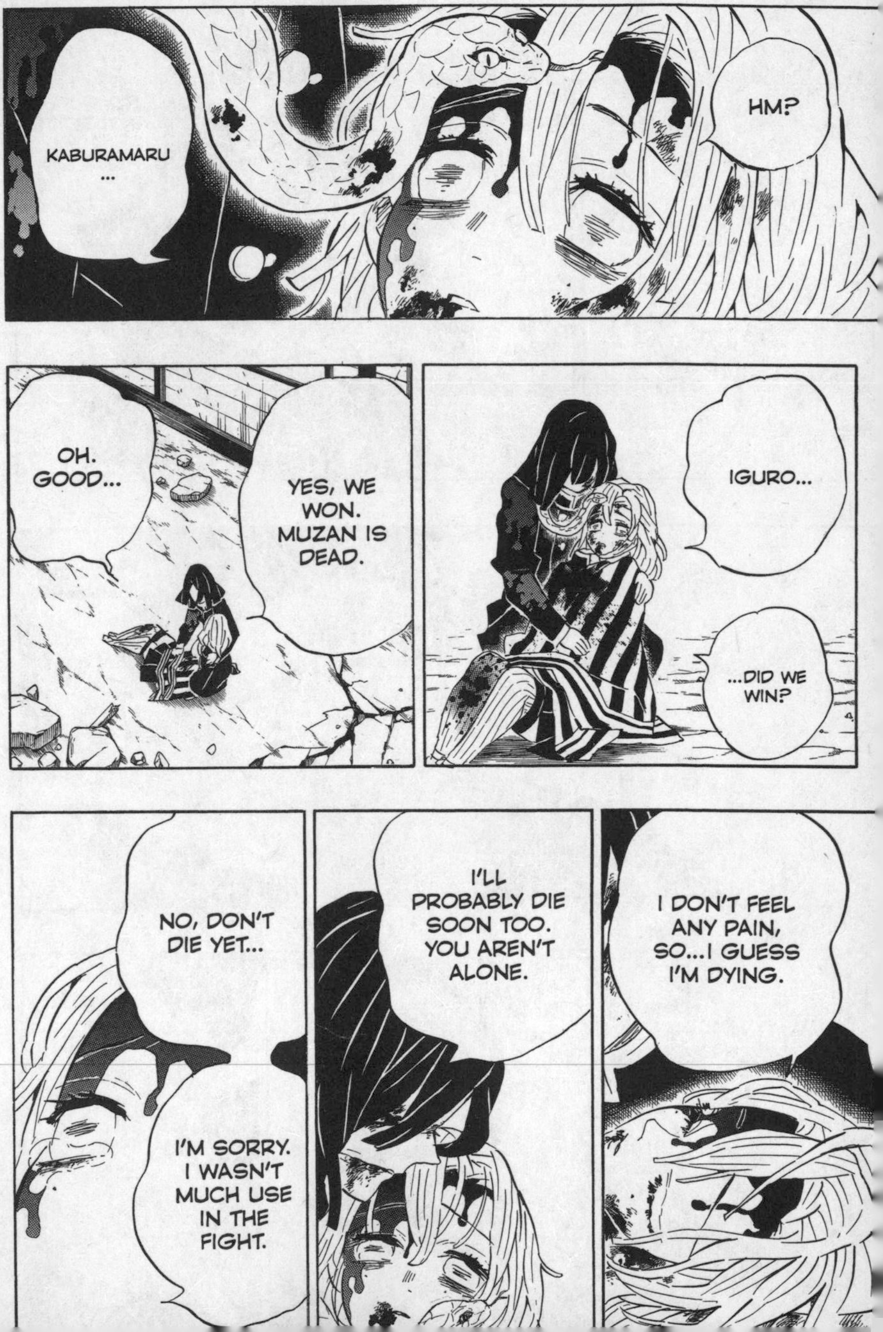
HM?
KABURAMARU ...
IGURO...
...DID WE WIN?
YES, WE WON. MUZAN IS DEAD.
OH. GOOD...
I DON'T FEEL ANY PAIN, SO...I GUESS I'M DYING.
I'LL PROBABLY DIE SOON TOO. YOU AREN'T ALONE.
NO, DON'T DIE YET...
I'M SORRY. I WASN'T MUCH USE IN THE FIGHT.

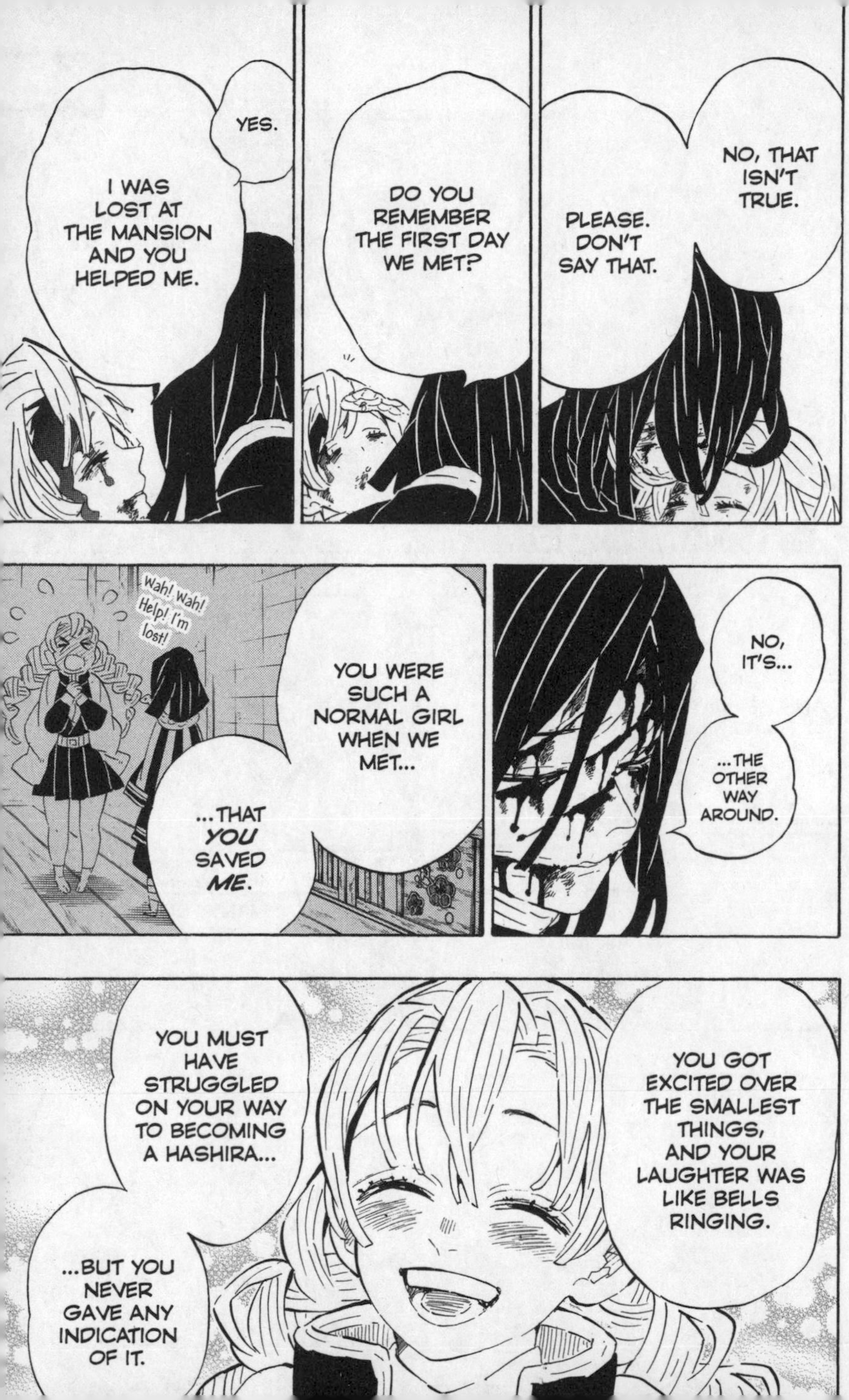
NO, THAT ISN'T TRUE.
PLEASE. DON'T SAY THAT.
DO YOU REMEMBER THE FIRST DAY WE MET?
YES.
I WAS LOST AT THE MANSION AND YOU HELPED ME.
NO, IT'S...
...THE OTHER WAY AROUND.
YOU WERE SUCH A NORMAL GIRL WHEN WE MET...
Wah! Wah! Help! I'm lost!
...THAT *YOU* SAVED *ME*.
YOU GOT EXCITED OVER THE SMALLEST THINGS, AND YOUR LAUGHTER WAS LIKE BELLS RINGING.
YOU MUST HAVE STRUGGLED ON YOUR WAY TO BECOMING A HASHIRA...
...BUT YOU NEVER GAVE ANY INDICATION OF IT.

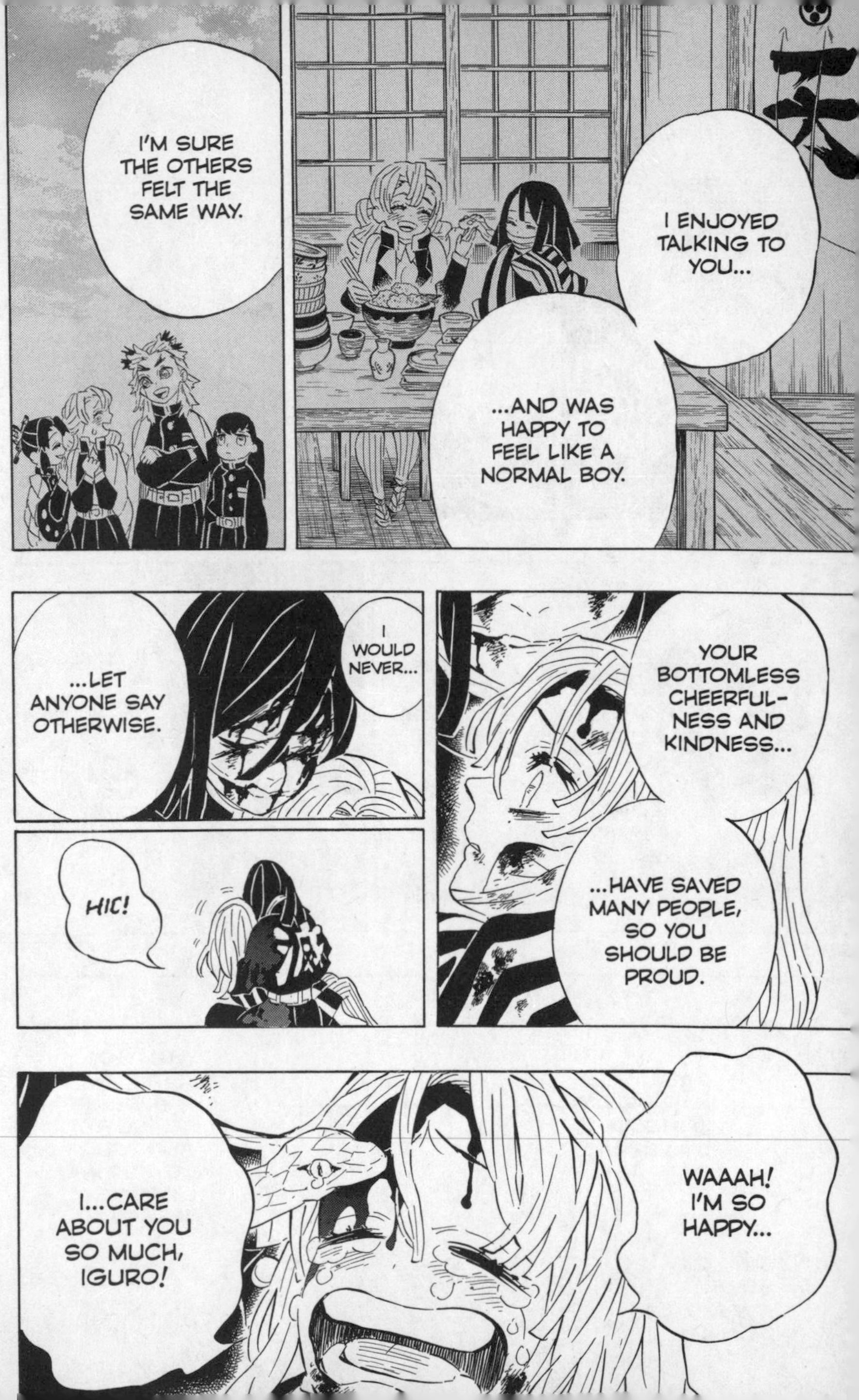
I ENJOYED TALKING TO YOU...
...AND WAS HAPPY TO FEEL LIKE A NORMAL BOY.
I'M SURE THE OTHERS FELT THE SAME WAY.
YOUR BOTTOMLESS CHEERFUL-NESS AND KINDNESS...
...HAVE SAVED MANY PEOPLE, SO YOU SHOULD BE PROUD.
I WOULD NEVER...
...LET ANYONE SAY OTHERWISE.
HIC!
WAAAH! I'M SO HAPPY...
I...CARE ABOUT YOU SO MUCH, IGURO!

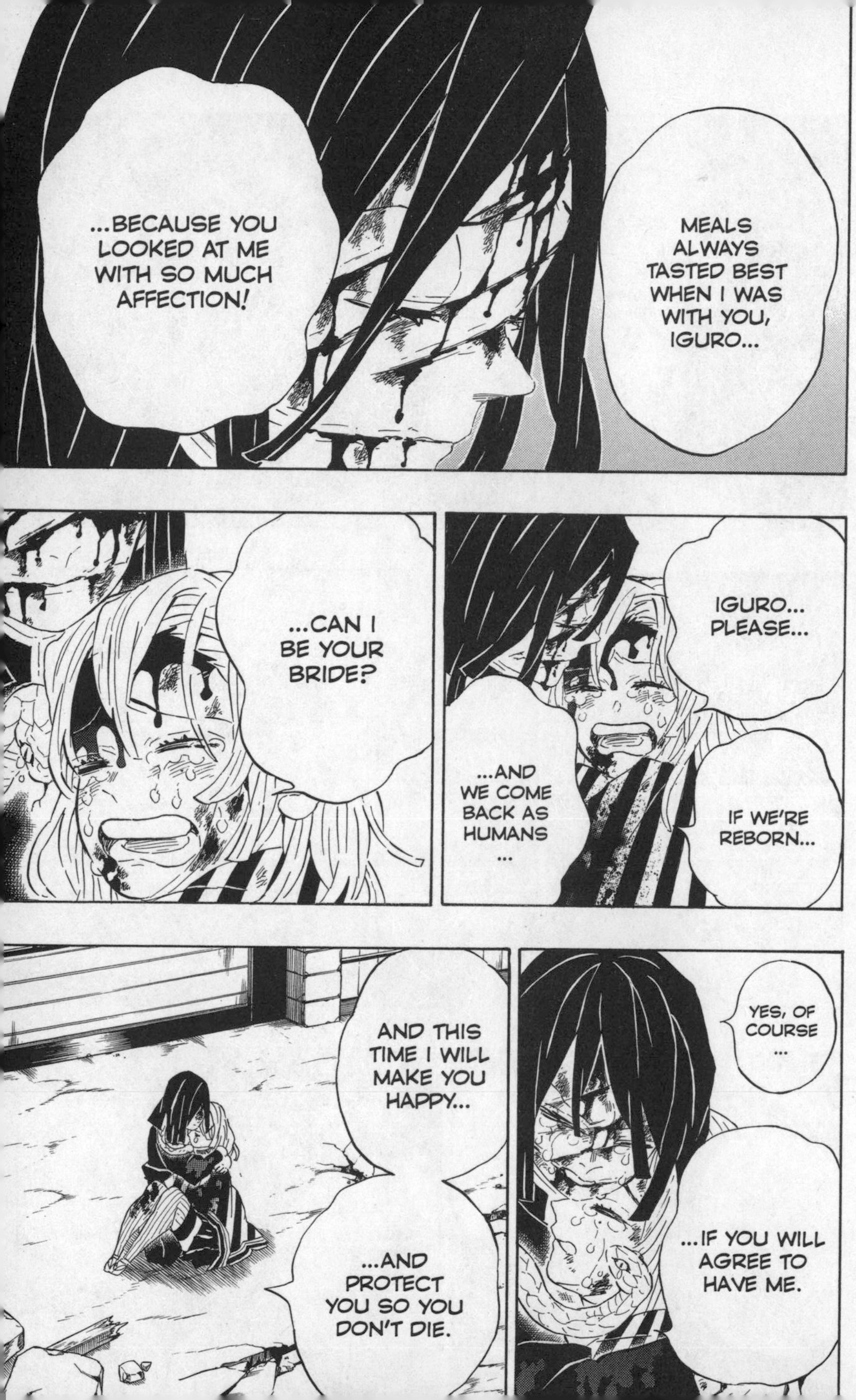
MEALS ALWAYS TASTED BEST WHEN I WAS WITH YOU, IGURO...
...BECAUSE YOU LOOKED AT ME WITH SO MUCH AFFECTION!
IGURO... PLEASE...
IF WE'RE REBORN...
...AND WE COME BACK AS HUMANS ...
...CAN I BE YOUR BRIDE?
YES, OF COURSE ...
...IF YOU WILL AGREE TO HAVE ME.
AND THIS TIME I WILL MAKE YOU HAPPY...
...AND PROTECT YOU SO YOU DON'T DIE.

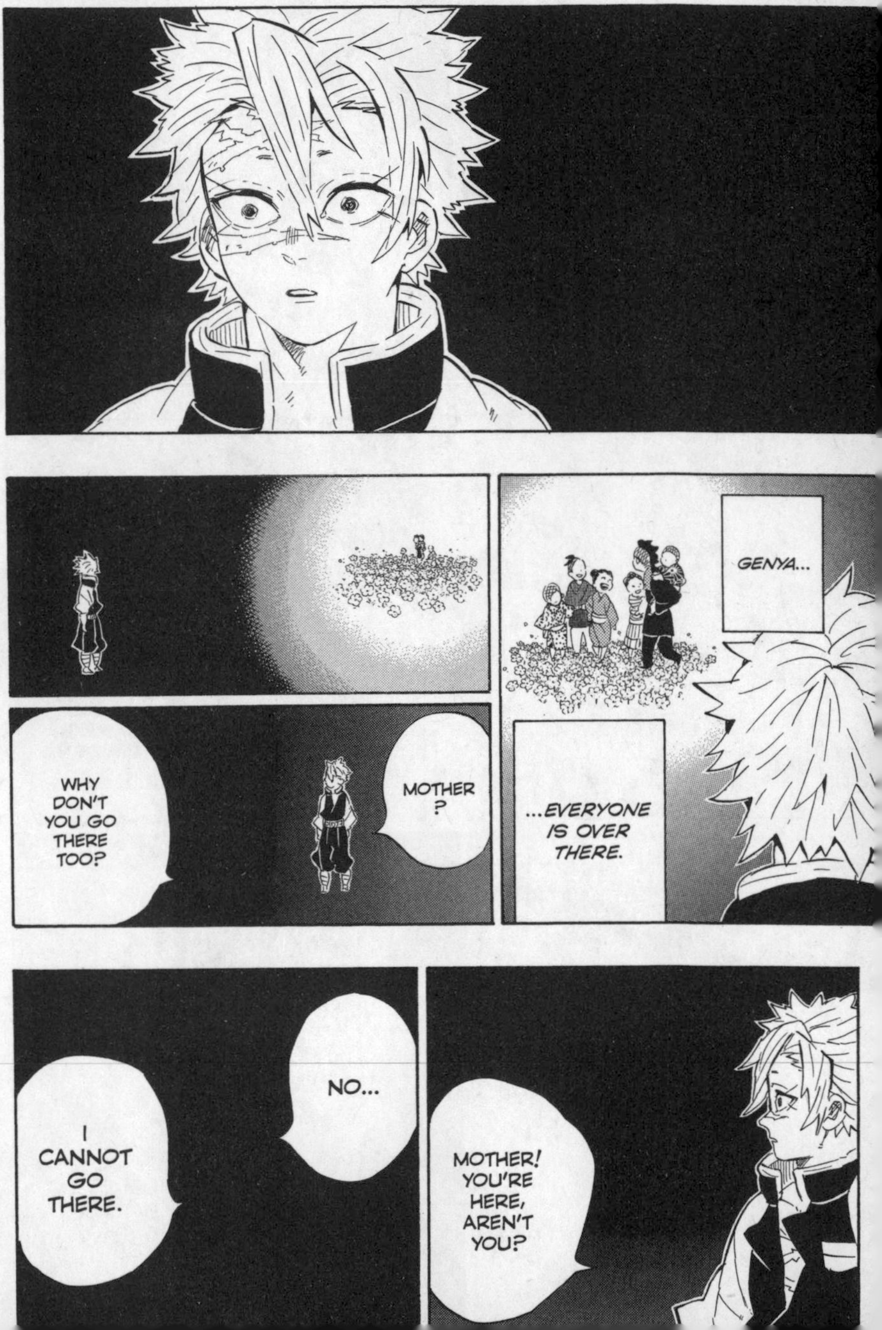
GENYA...
...EVERYONE IS OVER THERE.
MOTHER?
WHY DON'T YOU GO THERE TOO?
MOTHER! YOU'RE HERE, AREN'T YOU?
NO...
I CANNOT GO THERE.

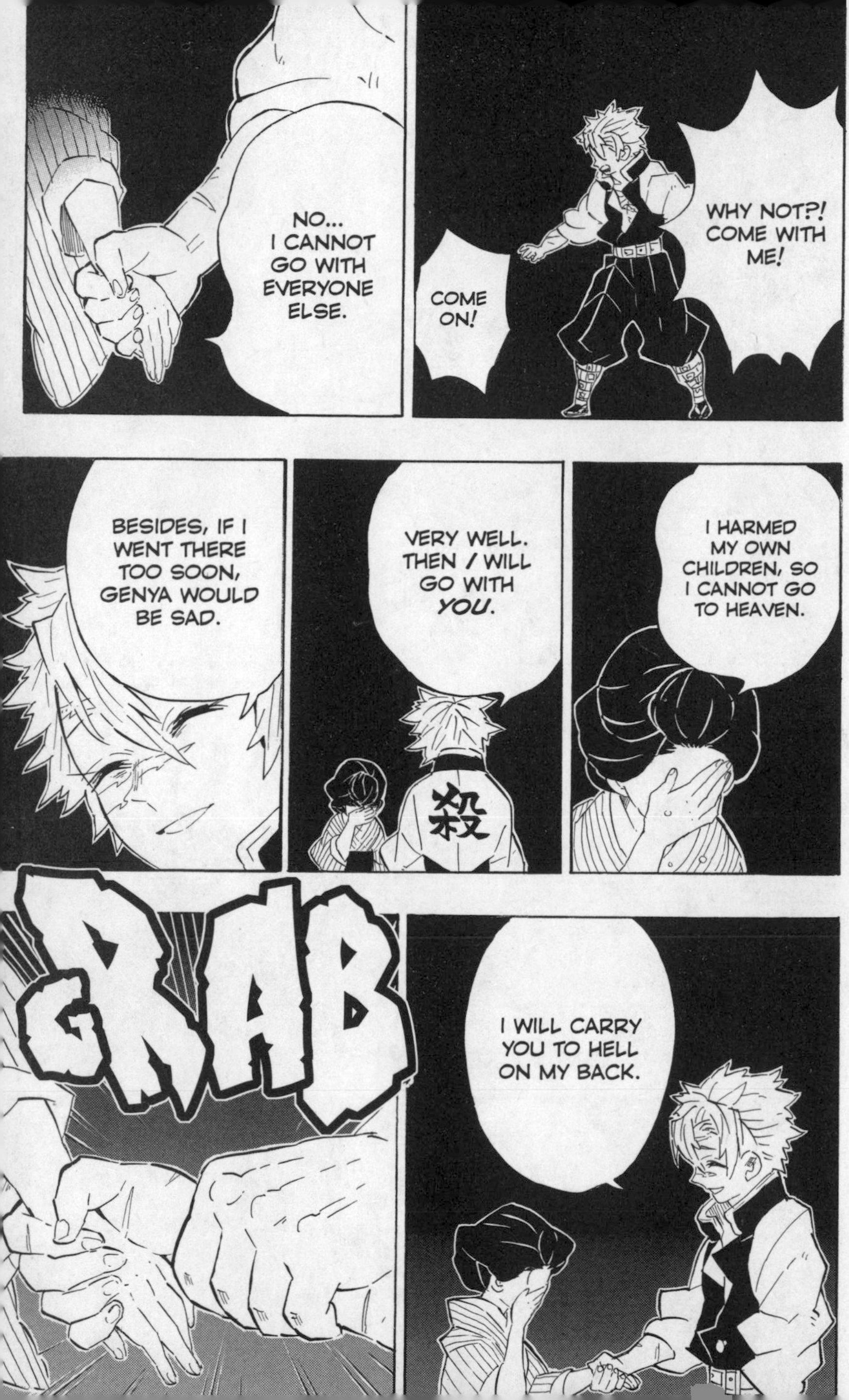
WHY NOT?! COME WITH ME!
COME ON!
NO... I CANNOT GO WITH EVERYONE ELSE.
I HARMED MY OWN CHILDREN, SO I CANNOT GO TO HEAVEN.
VERY WELL. THEN I WILL GO WITH YOU.
BESIDES, IF I WENT THERE TOO SOON, GENYA WOULD BE SAD.
I WILL CARRY YOU TO HELL ON MY BACK.
GRAB

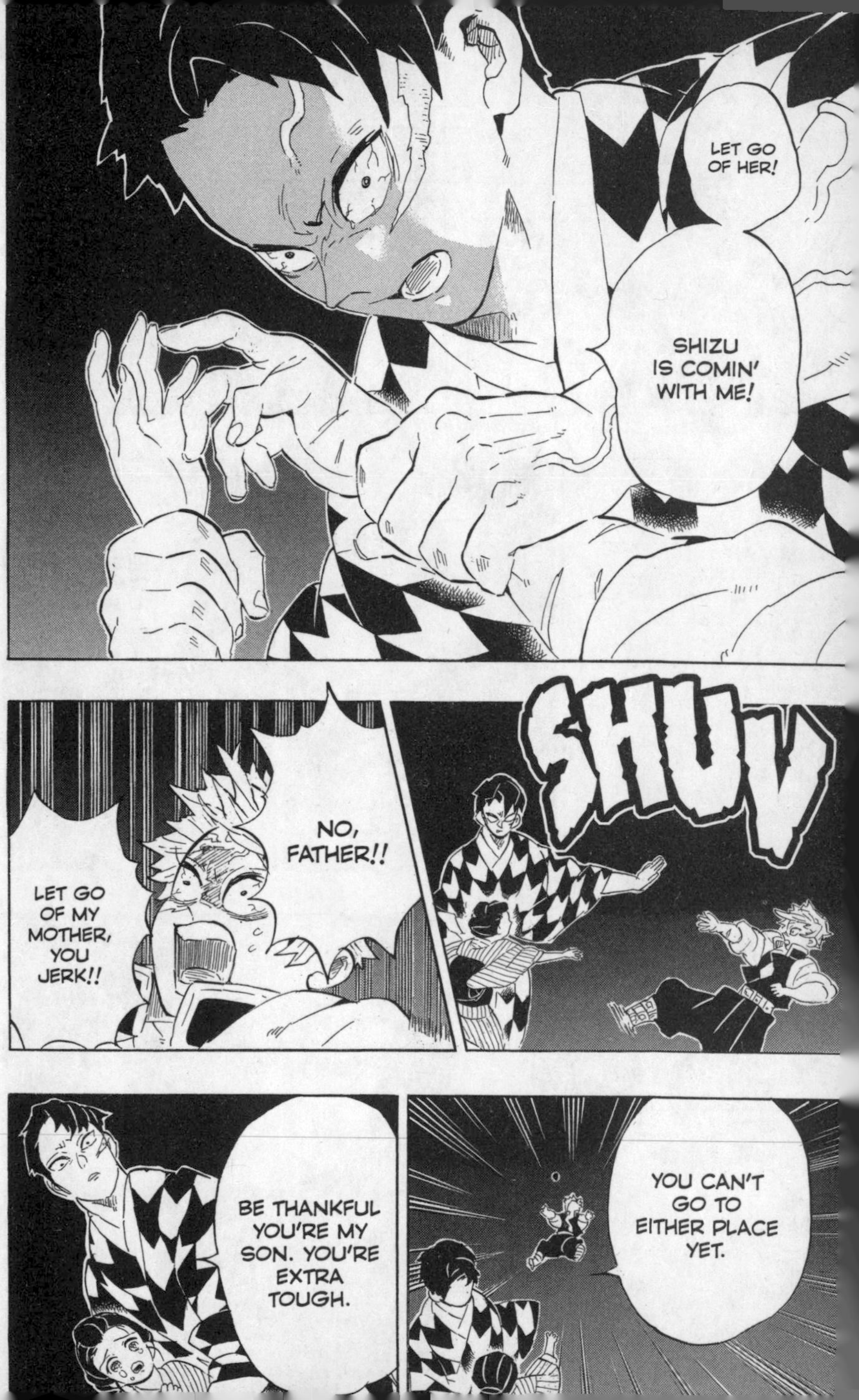
LET GO OF HER!
SHIZU IS COMIN' WITH ME!
SHUV
NO, FATHER!!
LET GO OF MY MOTHER, YOU JERK!!
YOU CAN'T GO TO EITHER PLACE YET.
BE THANKFUL YOU'RE MY SON. YOU'RE EXTRA TOUGH.

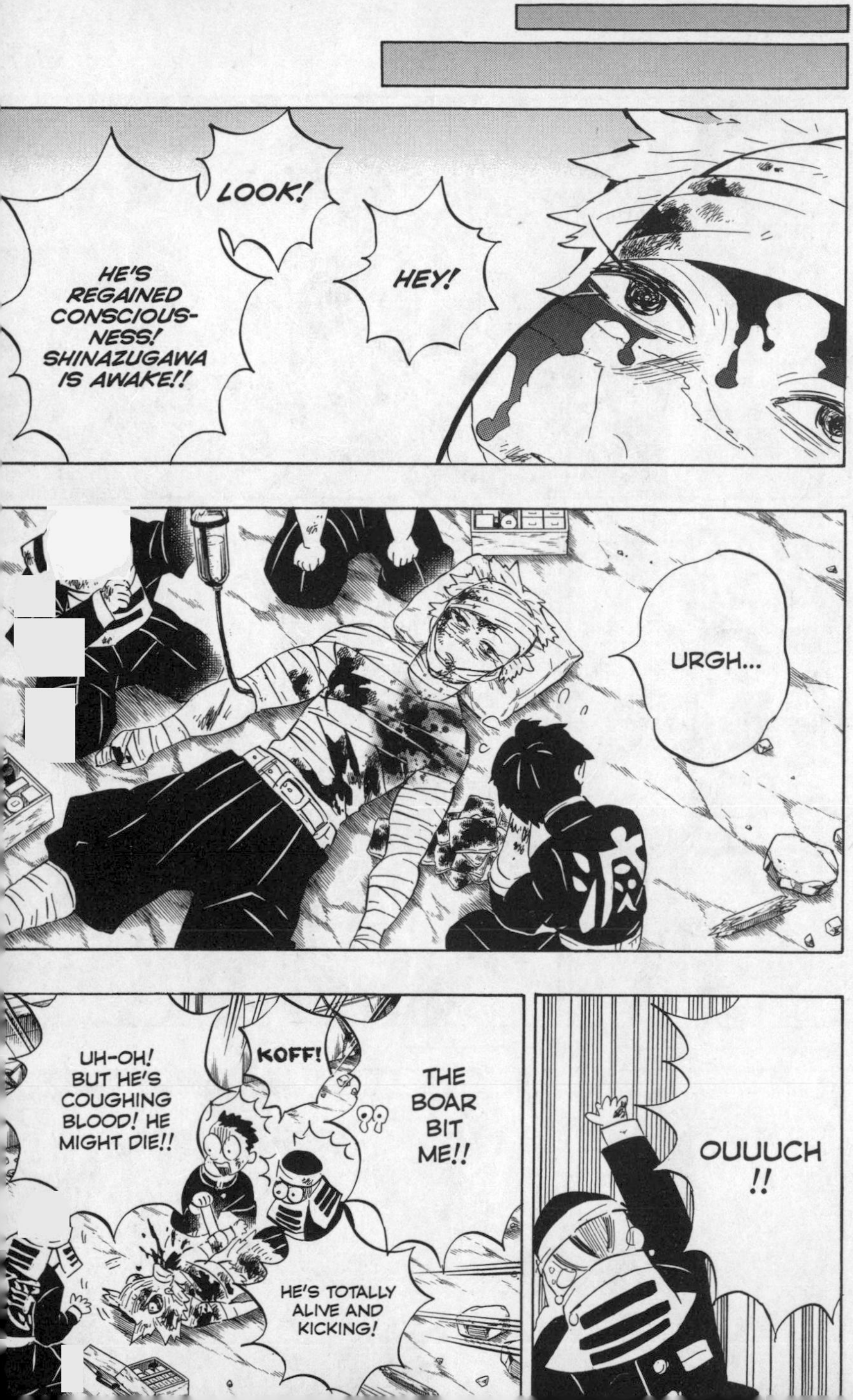
HEY!
LOOK!
HE'S REGAINED CONSCIOUS-NESS! SHINAZUGAWA IS AWAKE!!
URGH...
OUUUCH!!
THE BOAR BIT ME!!
KOFF!
UH-OH! BUT HE'S COUGHING BLOOD! HE MIGHT DIE!!
HE'S TOTALLY ALIVE AND KICKING!

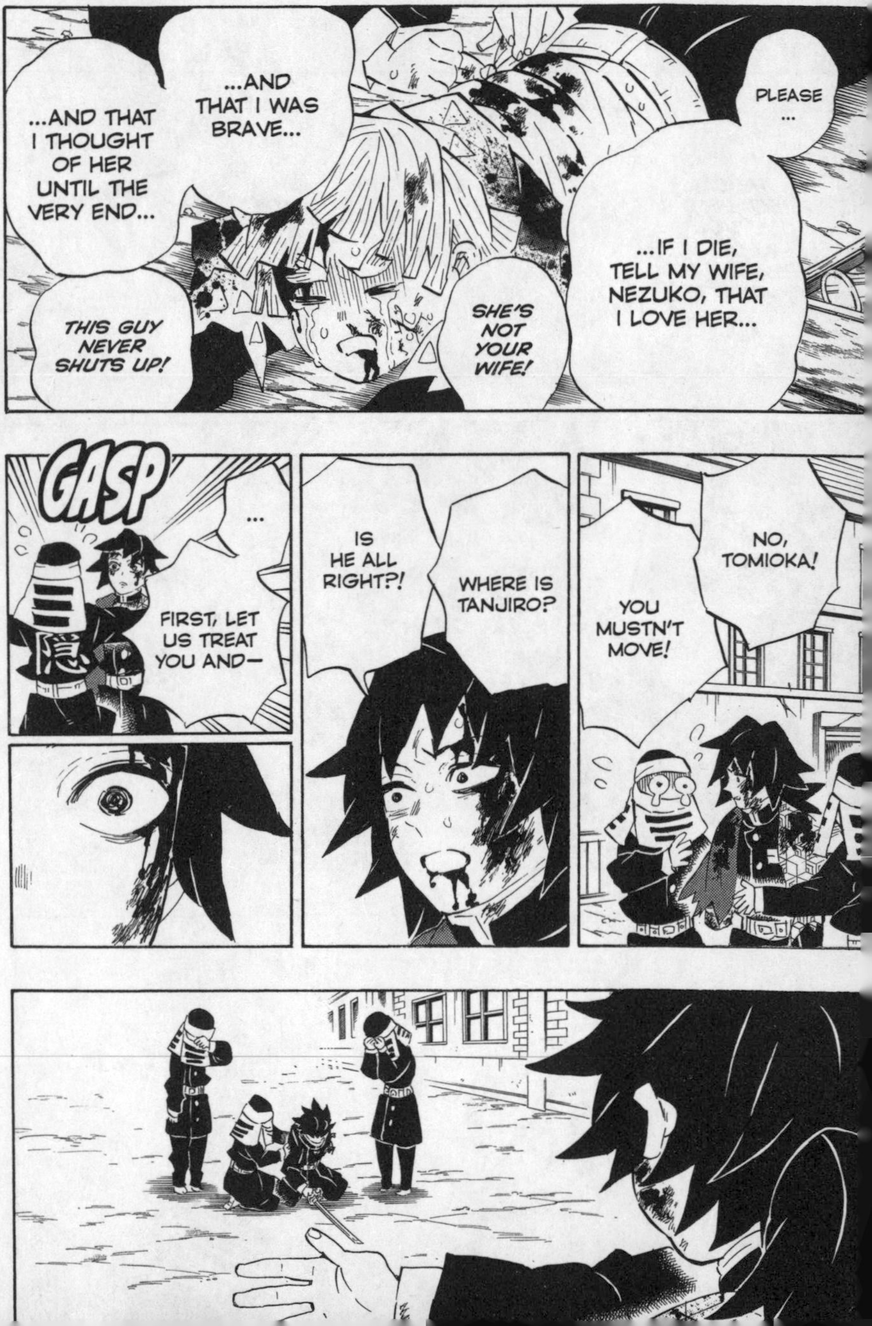
PLEASE ...
...IF I DIE, TELL MY WIFE, NEZUKO, THAT I LOVE HER...
SHE'S NOT YOUR WIFE!
...AND THAT I WAS BRAVE...
...AND THAT I THOUGHT OF HER UNTIL THE VERY END...
THIS GUY NEVER SHUTS UP!
NO, TOMIOKA!
YOU MUSTN'T MOVE!
WHERE IS TANJIRO?
IS HE ALL RIGHT?!
...
GASP
FIRST, LET US TREAT YOU AND—

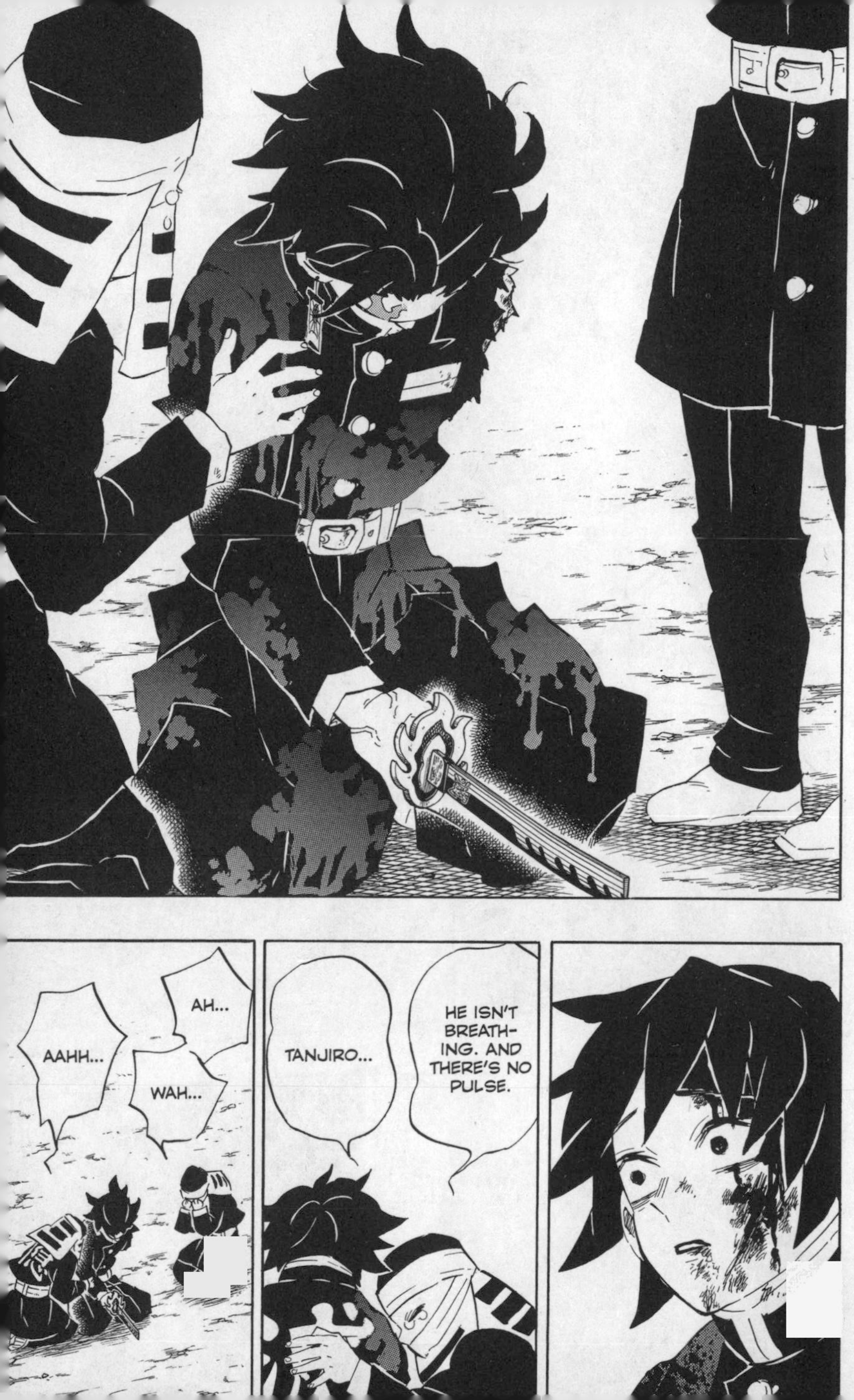
HE ISN'T BREATHING. AND THERE'S NO PULSE.
TANJIRO...
AH...
WAH...
AAHH...

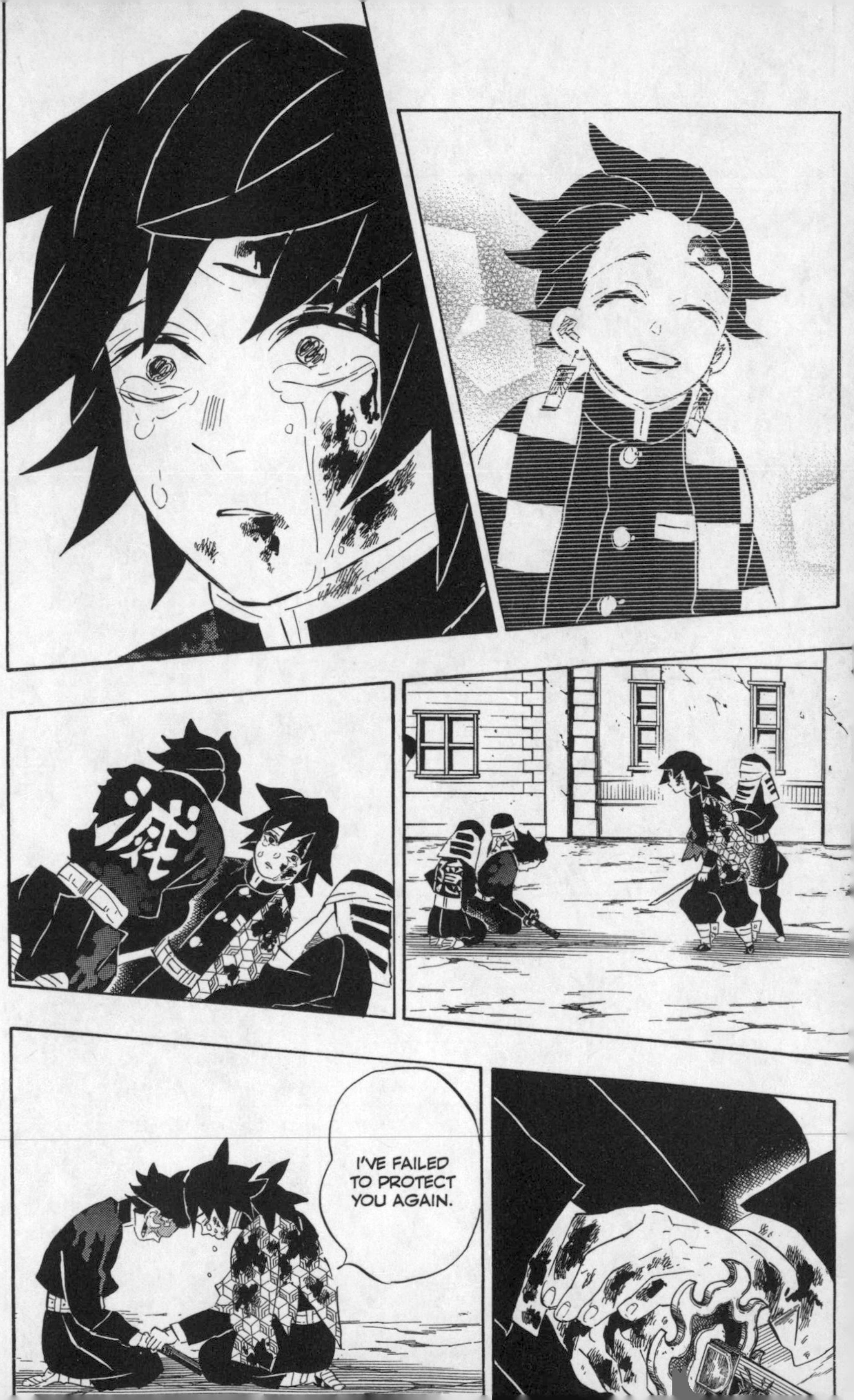
I'VE FAILED TO PROTECT YOU AGAIN.

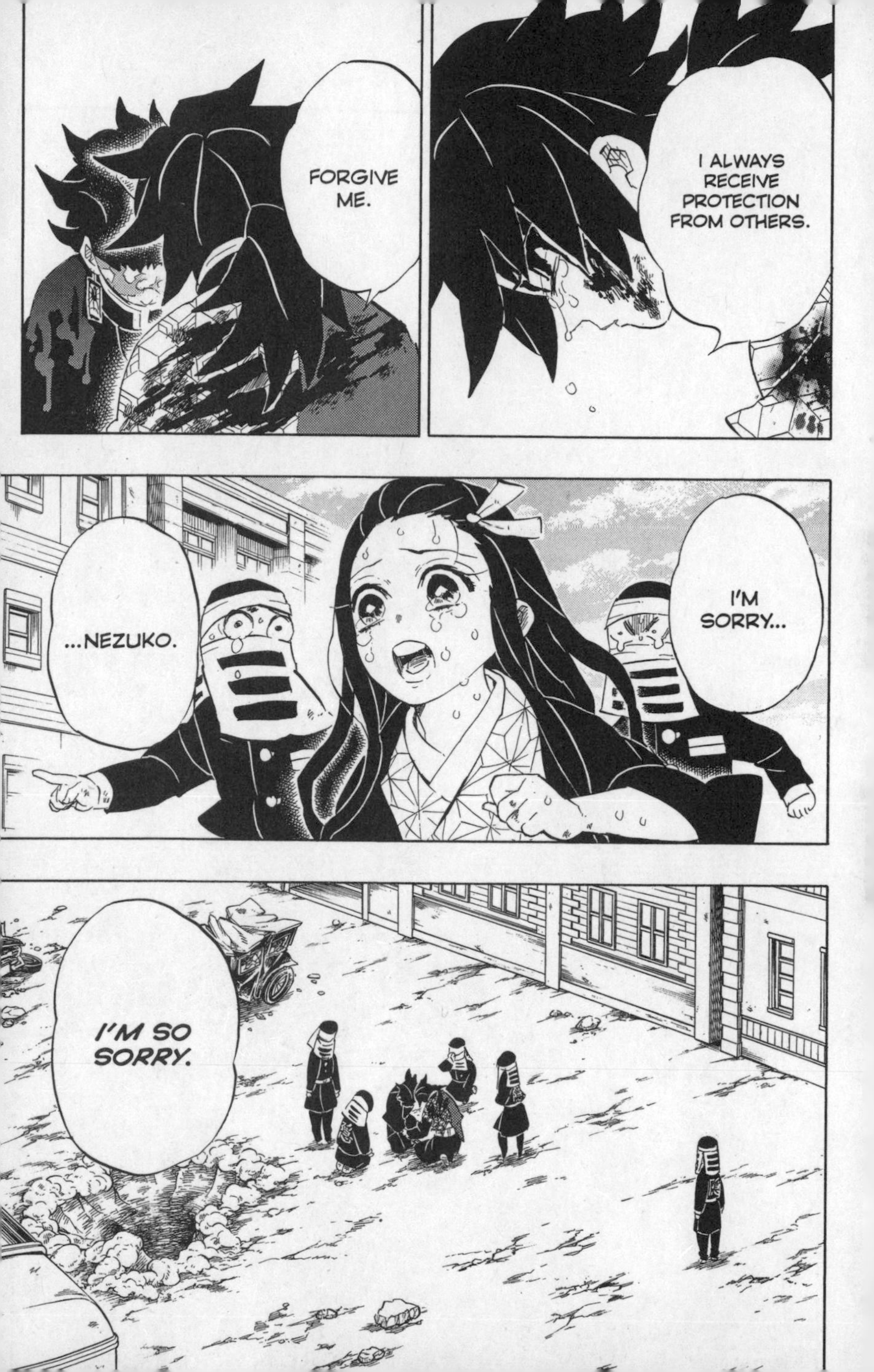
I ALWAYS RECEIVE PROTECTION FROM OTHERS.
FORGIVE ME.
I'M SORRY...
...NEZUKO.
I'M SO SORRY.

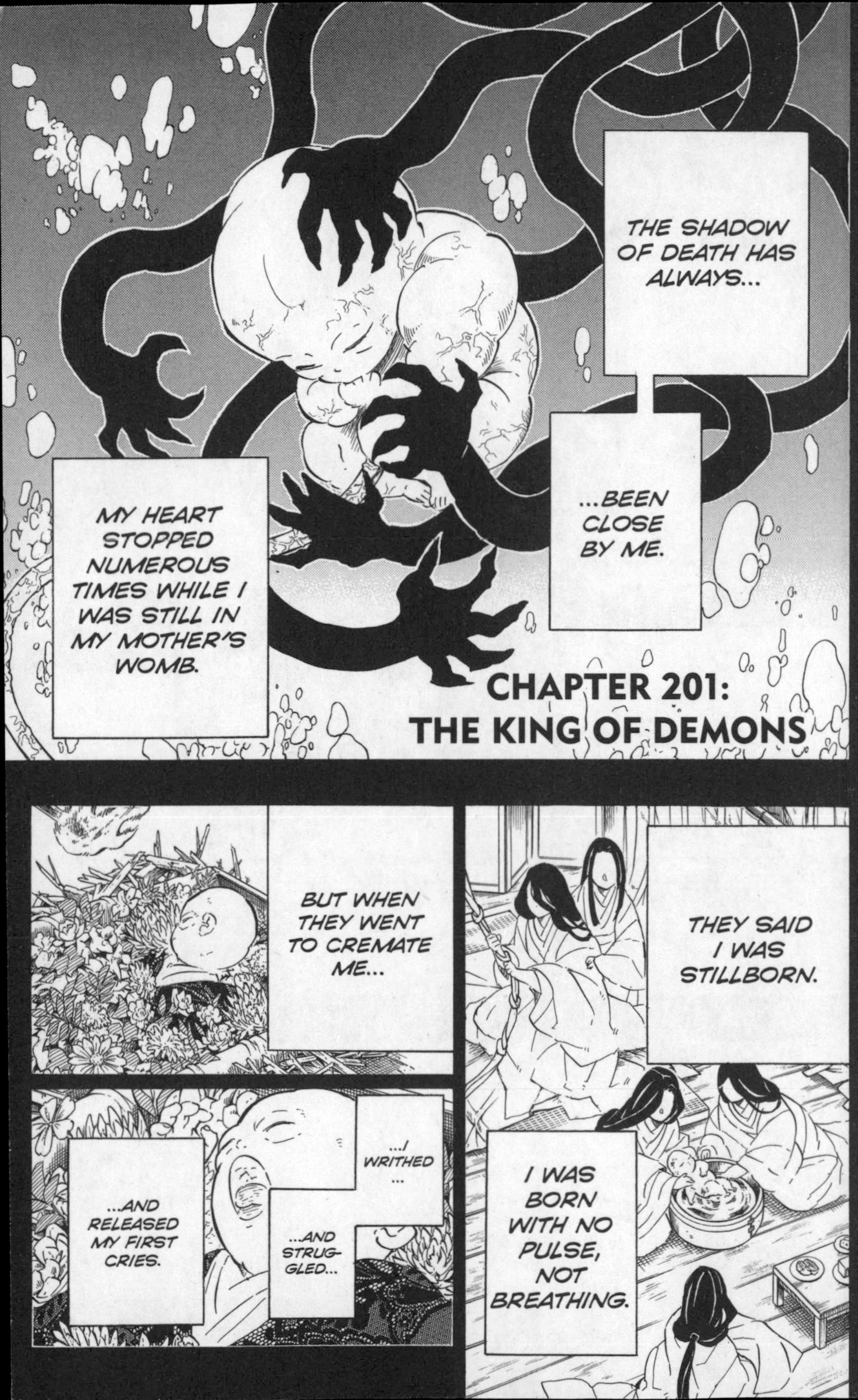
THE SHADOW OF DEATH HAS ALWAYS...
...BEEN CLOSE BY ME.
MY HEART STOPPED NUMEROUS TIMES WHILE I WAS STILL IN MY MOTHER'S WOMB.
CHAPTER 201: THE KING OF DEMONS
THEY SAID I WAS STILLBORN.
I WAS BORN WITH NO PULSE, NOT BREATHING.
BUT WHEN THEY WENT TO CREMATE ME...
...I WRITHED...
...AND STRUG-GLED...
...AND RELEASED MY FIRST CRIES.

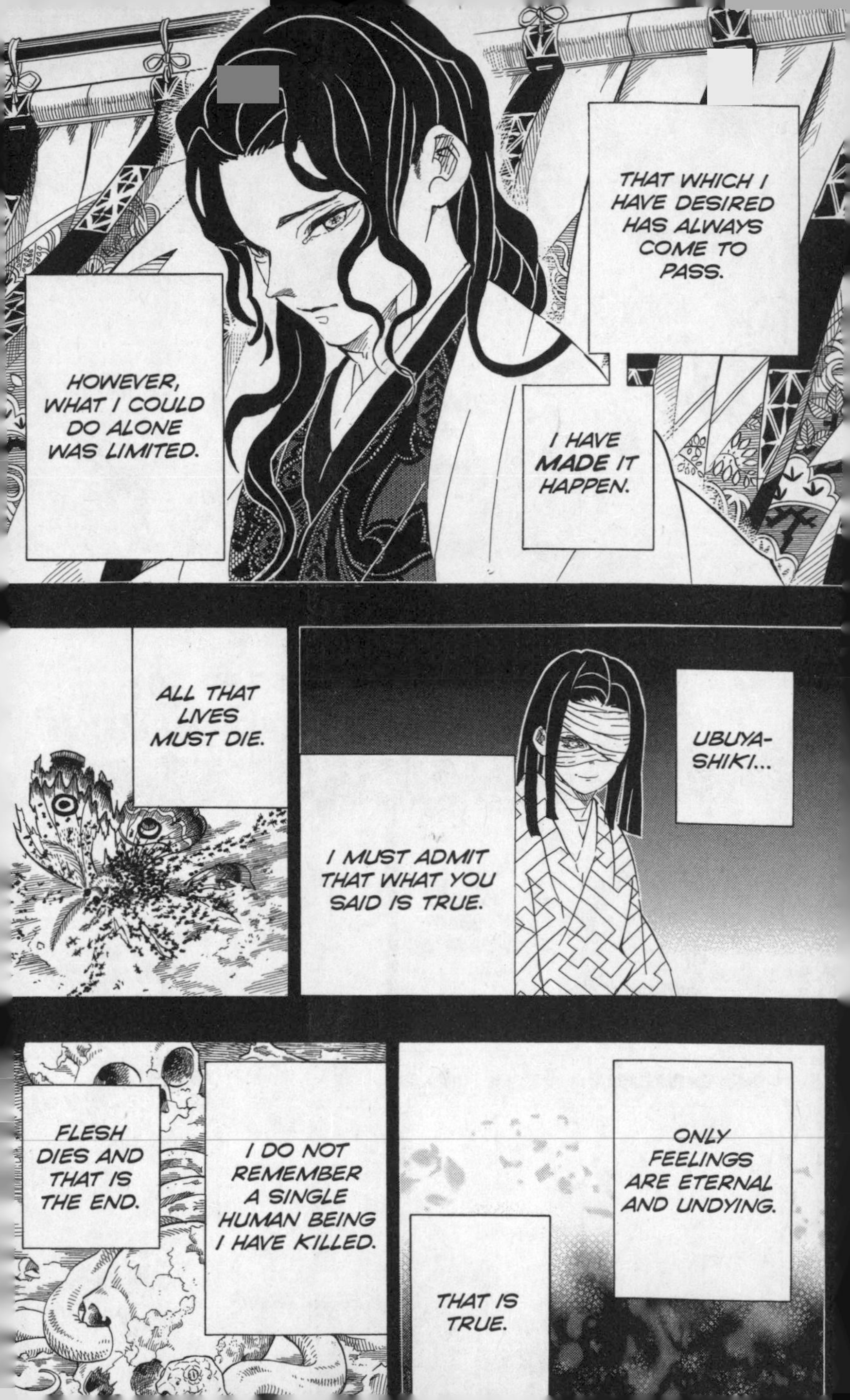
THAT WHICH I HAVE DESIRED HAS ALWAYS COME TO PASS.
I HAVE MADE IT HAPPEN.
HOWEVER, WHAT I COULD DO ALONE WAS LIMITED.
UBUYA-SHIKI...
I MUST ADMIT THAT WHAT YOU SAID IS TRUE.
ALL THAT LIVES MUST DIE.
ONLY FEELINGS ARE ETERNAL AND UNDYING.
THAT IS TRUE.
I DO NOT REMEMBER A SINGLE HUMAN BEING I HAVE KILLED.
FLESH DIES AND THAT IS THE END.

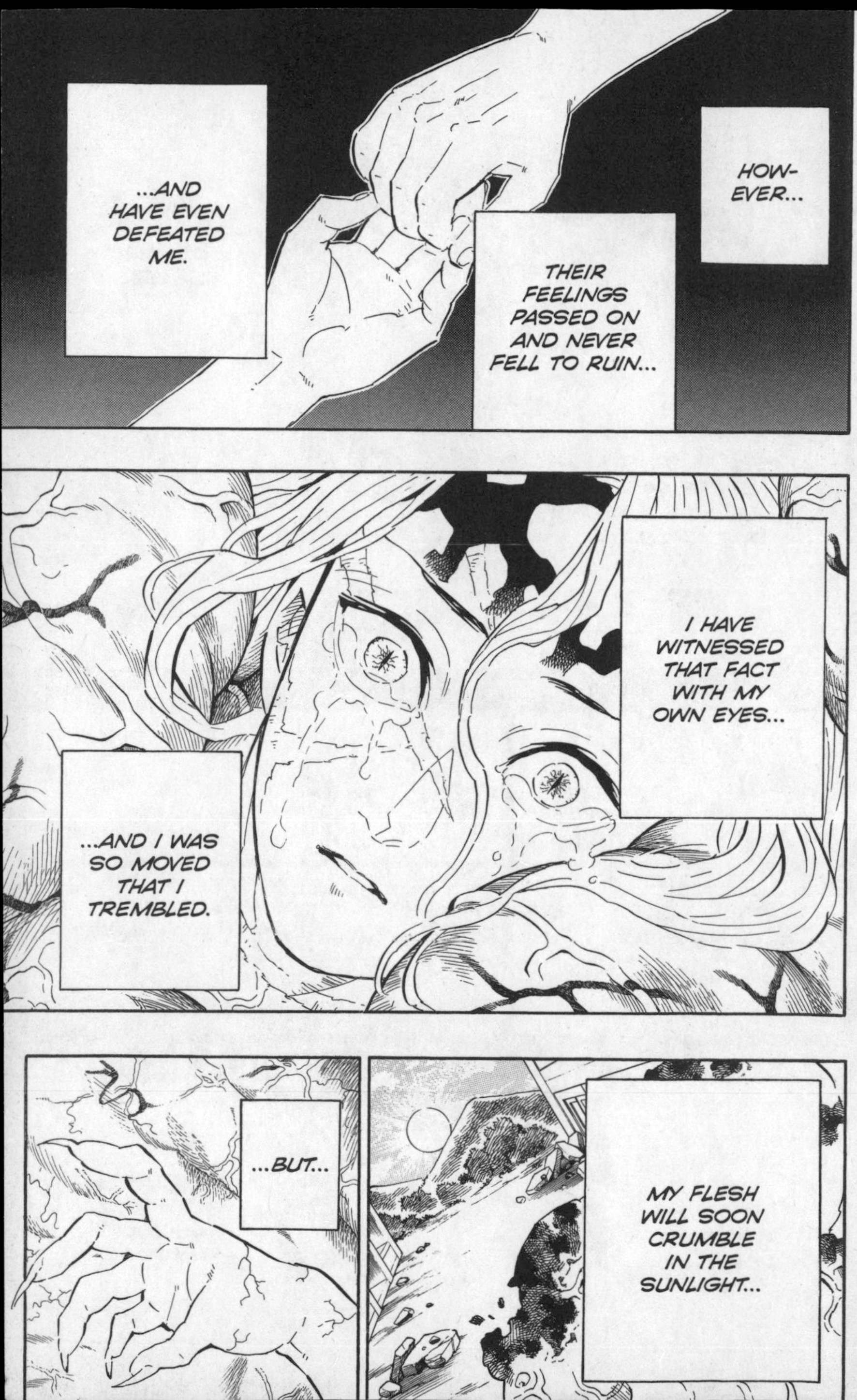
HOW-EVER...
THEIR FEELINGS PASSED ON AND NEVER FELL TO RUIN...
...AND HAVE EVEN DEFEATED ME.
I HAVE WITNESSED THAT FACT WITH MY OWN EYES...
...AND I WAS SO MOVED THAT I TREMBLED.
MY FLESH WILL SOON CRUMBLE IN THE SUNLIGHT...
...BUT...

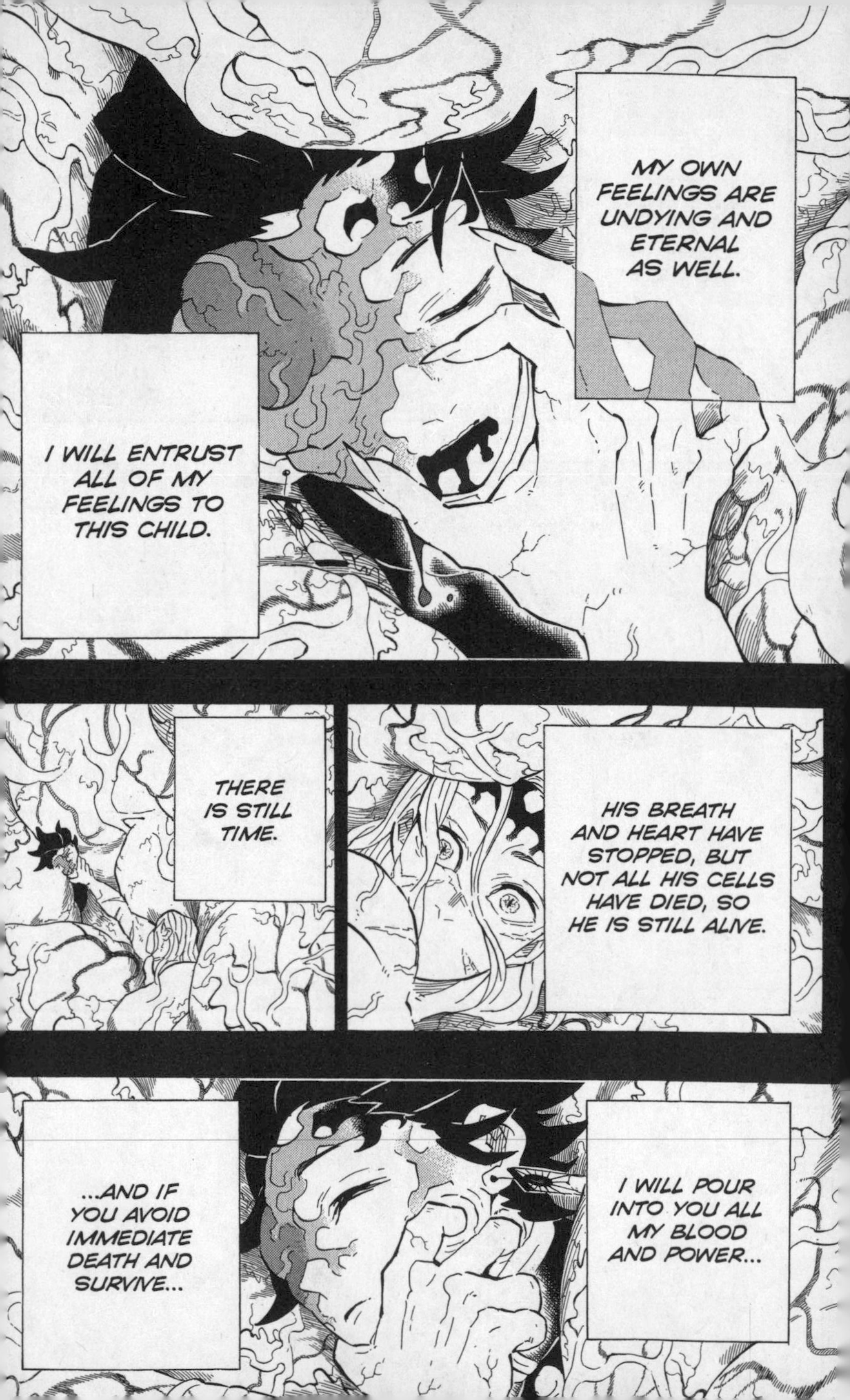
MY OWN FEELINGS ARE UNDYING AND ETERNAL AS WELL.
I WILL ENTRUST ALL OF MY FEELINGS TO THIS CHILD.
HIS BREATH AND HEART HAVE STOPPED, BUT NOT ALL HIS CELLS HAVE DIED, SO HE IS STILL ALIVE.
THERE IS STILL TIME.
I WILL POUR INTO YOU ALL MY BLOOD AND POWER...
...AND IF YOU AVOID IMMEDIATE DEATH AND SURVIVE...

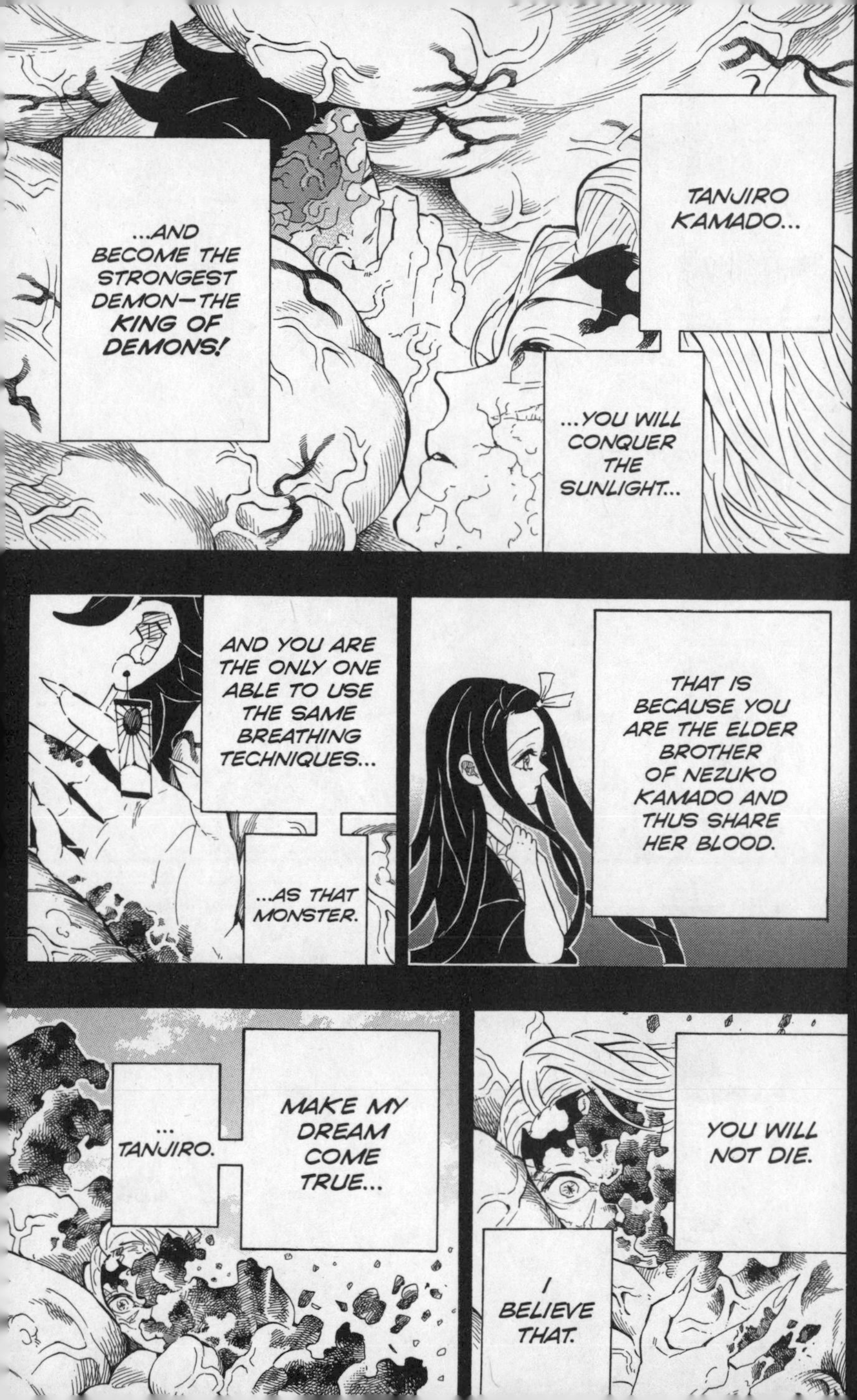
TANJIRO KAMADO...
...YOU WILL CONQUER THE SUNLIGHT...
...AND BECOME THE STRONGEST DEMON—THE KING OF DEMONS!
THAT IS BECAUSE YOU ARE THE ELDER BROTHER OF NEZUKO KAMADO AND THUS SHARE HER BLOOD.
AND YOU ARE THE ONLY ONE ABLE TO USE THE SAME BREATHING TECHNIQUES...
...AS THAT MONSTER.
YOU WILL NOT DIE.
I BELIEVE THAT.
MAKE MY DREAM COME TRUE...
...TANJIRO.

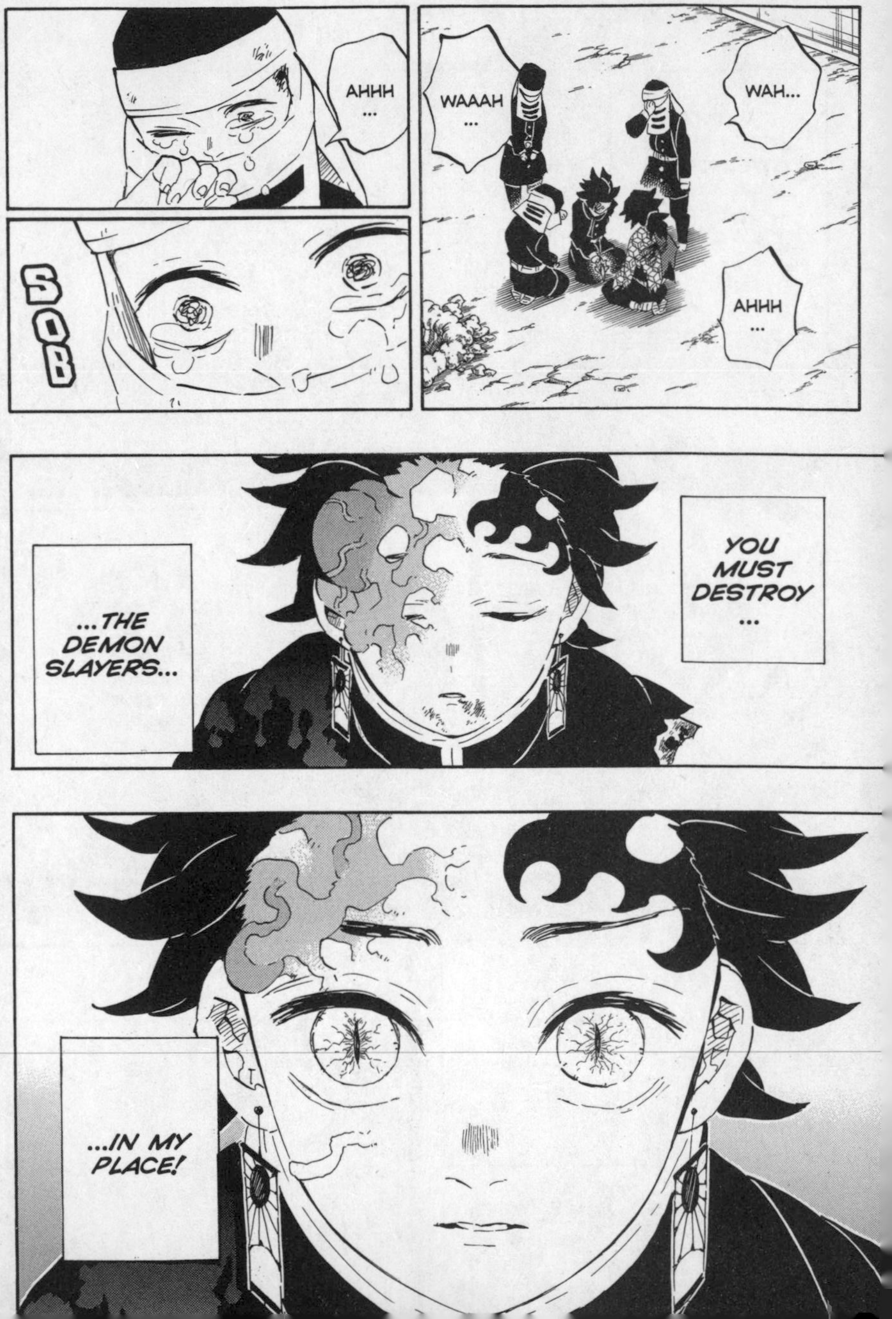
WAH...
WAAAH ...
AHHH ...
AHHH ...
SOB
YOU MUST DESTROY ...
...THE DEMON SLAYERS...
...IN MY PLACE!

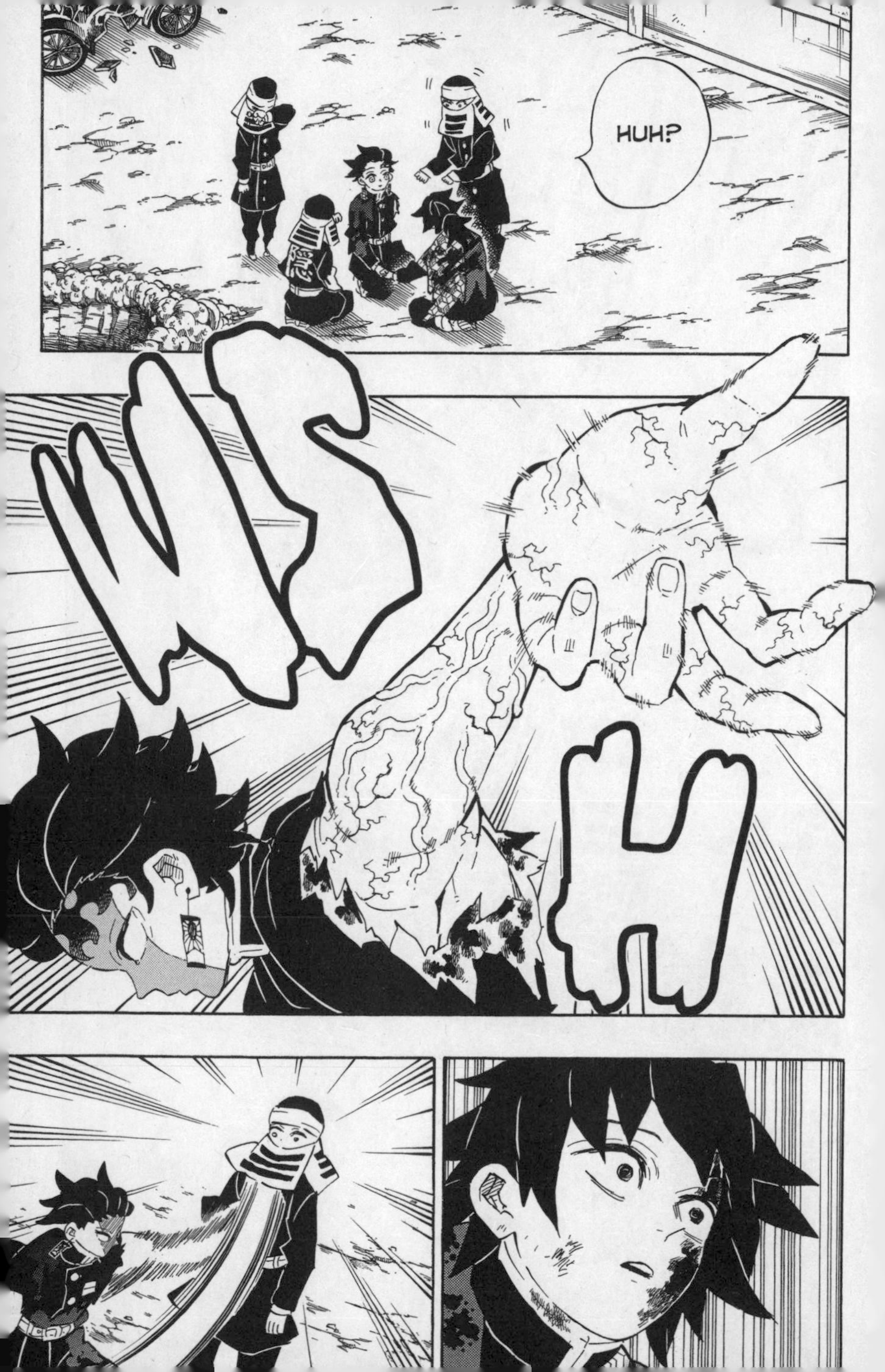
HUH?

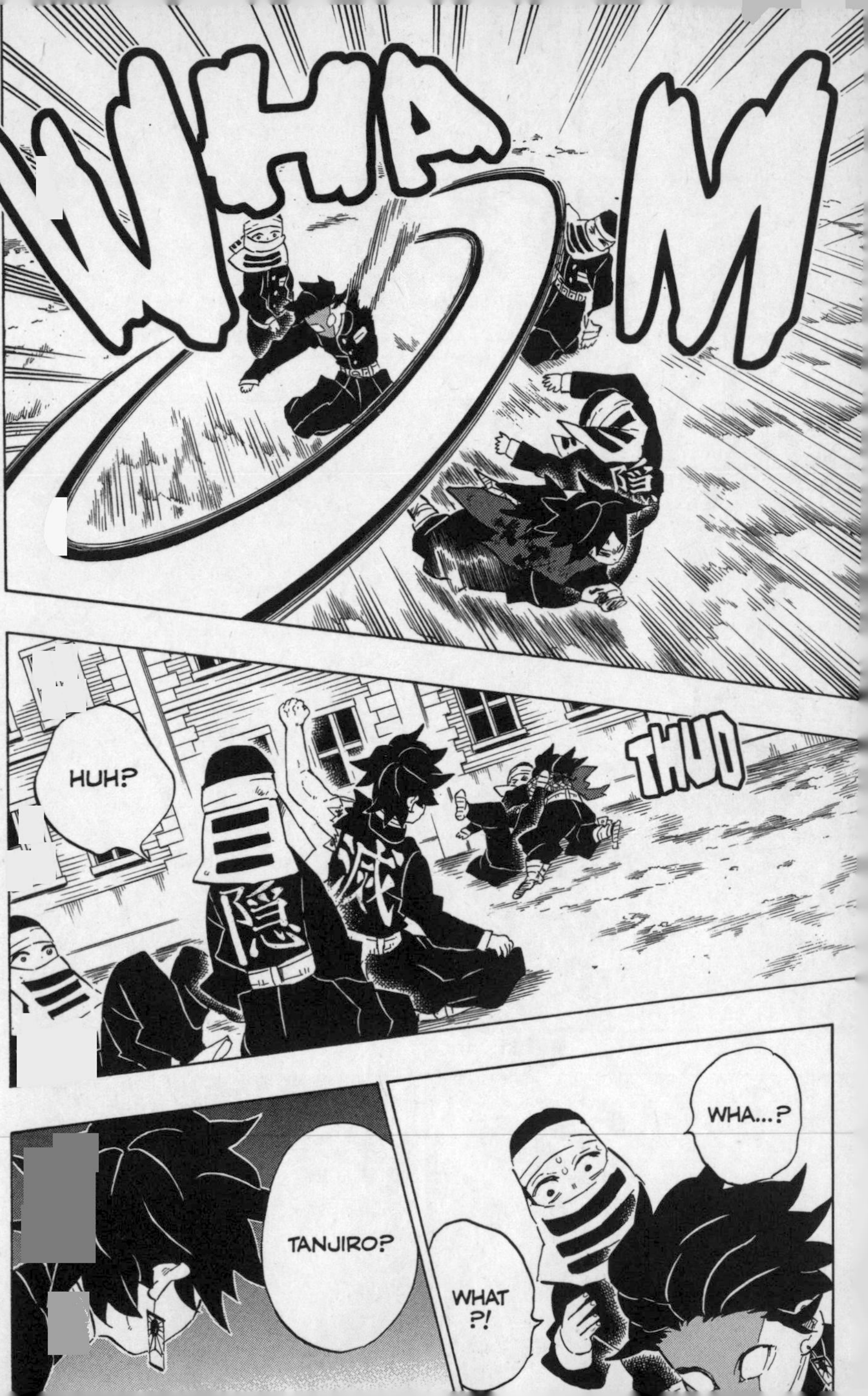
WHAM
THUD
HUH?
WHA...?
WHAT?!
TANJIRO?

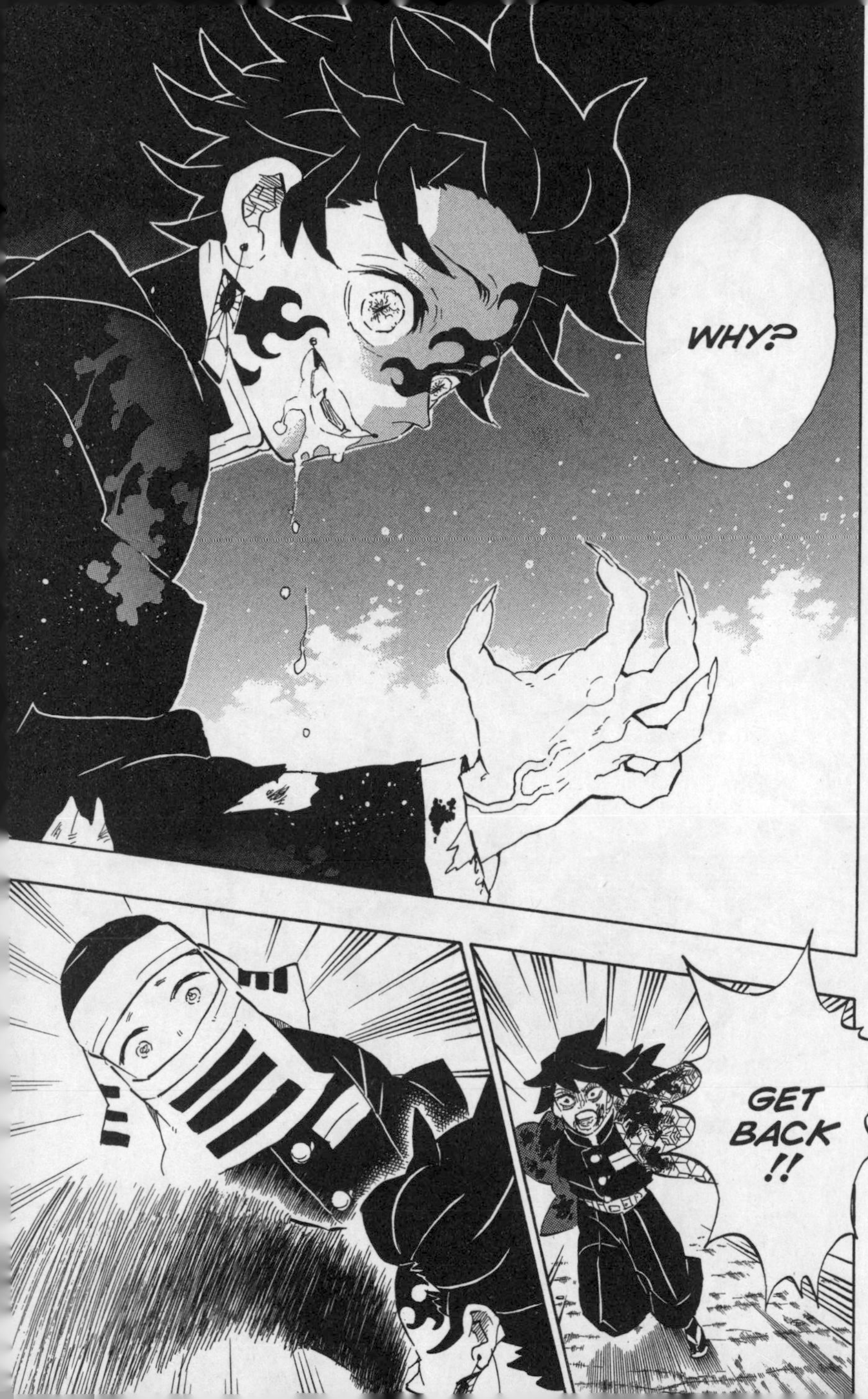
WHY?
GET BACK !!

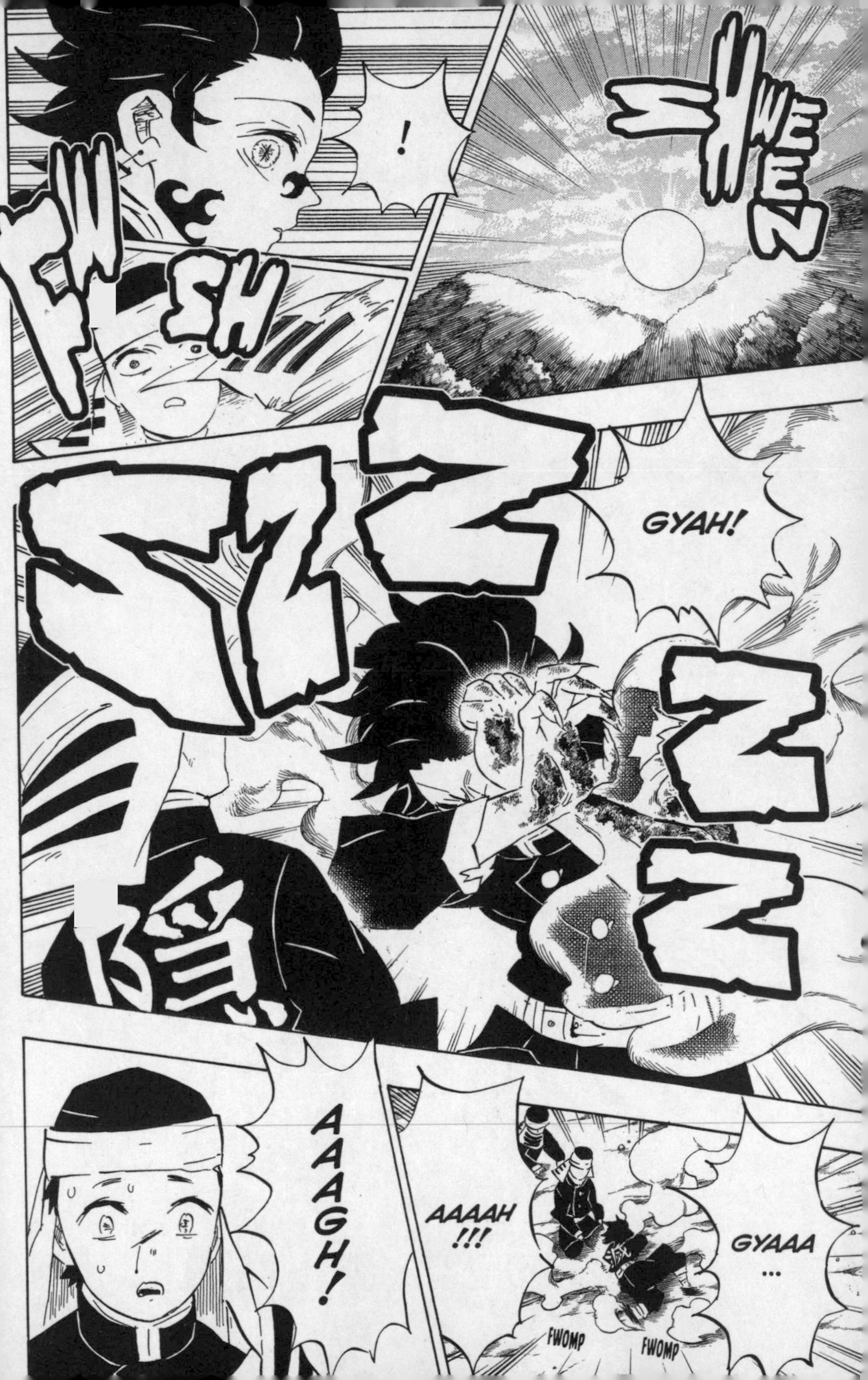
SHWEEN
!
FWISH
GYAH!
SIZZZZ
GYAAA...
AAAAH!!!
FWOMP
FWOMP
AAAAGH!

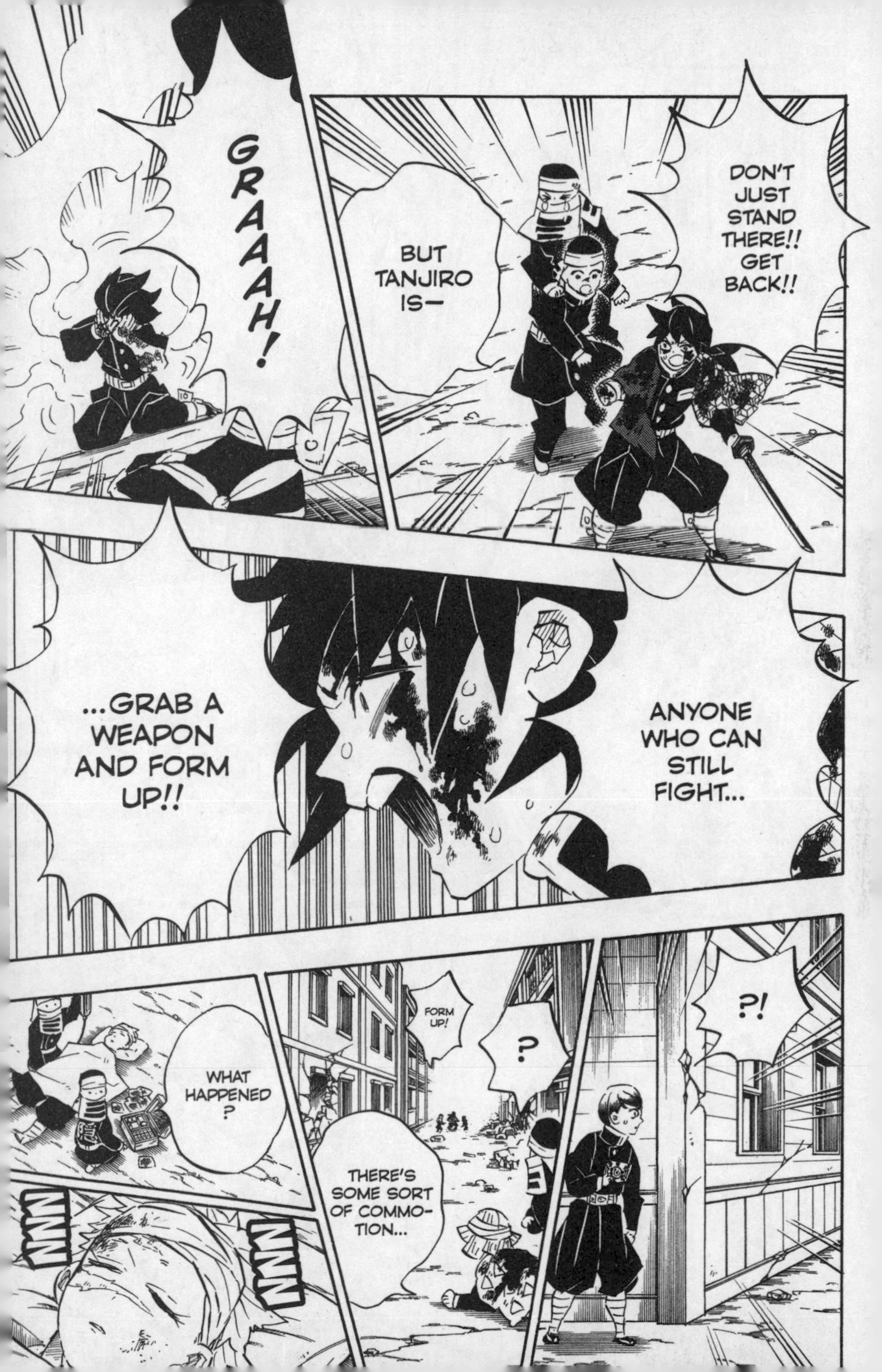
DON'T JUST STAND THERE!! GET BACK!!
BUT TANJIRO IS—
GRAAAAH!
ANYONE WHO CAN STILL FIGHT...
...GRAB A WEAPON AND FORM UP!!
?!
?
FORM UP!
THERE'S SOME SORT OF COMMOTION...
WHAT HAPPENED?
NNN
NNN

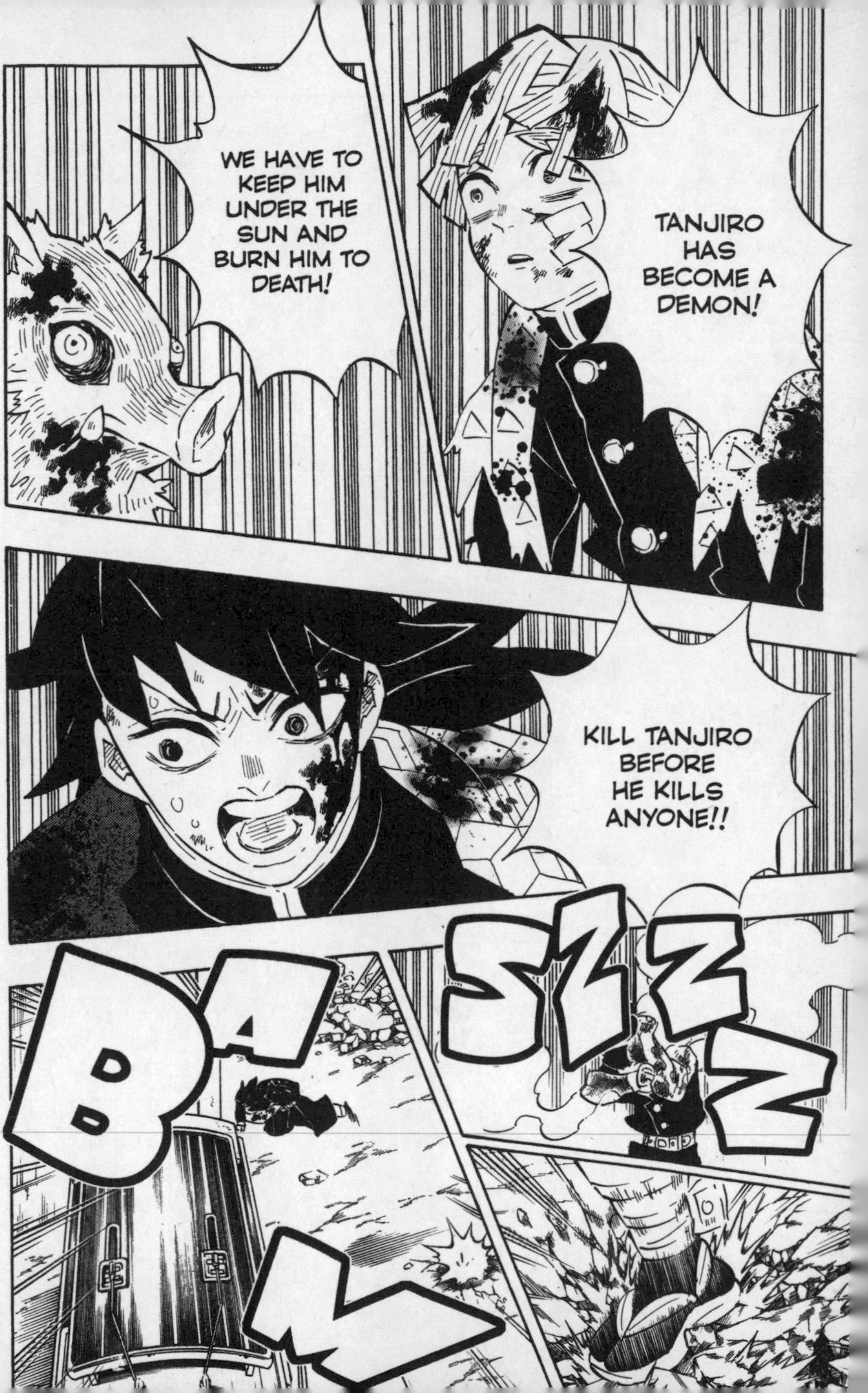
TANJIRO HAS BECOME A DEMON!
WE HAVE TO KEEP HIM UNDER THE SUN AND BURN HIM TO DEATH!
KILL TANJIRO BEFORE HE KILLS ANYONE!!
SZZZ
BAM

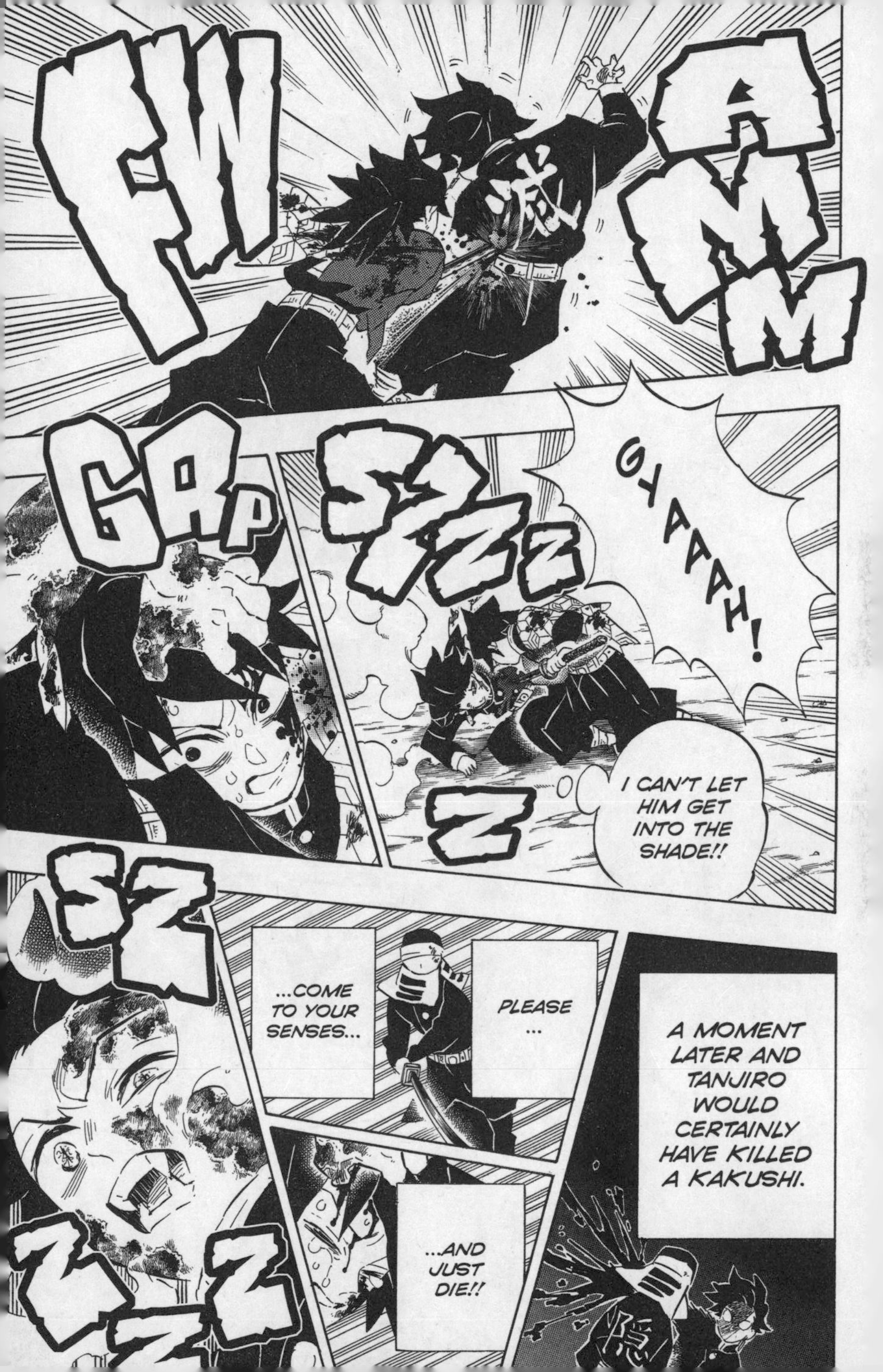
GYAAAAH!
SZZZ
I CAN'T LET HIM GET INTO THE SHADE!!
A MOMENT LATER AND TANJIRO WOULD CERTAINLY HAVE KILLED A KAKUSHI.
PLEASE ...
...COME TO YOUR SENSES...
...AND JUST DIE!!
SZZZ

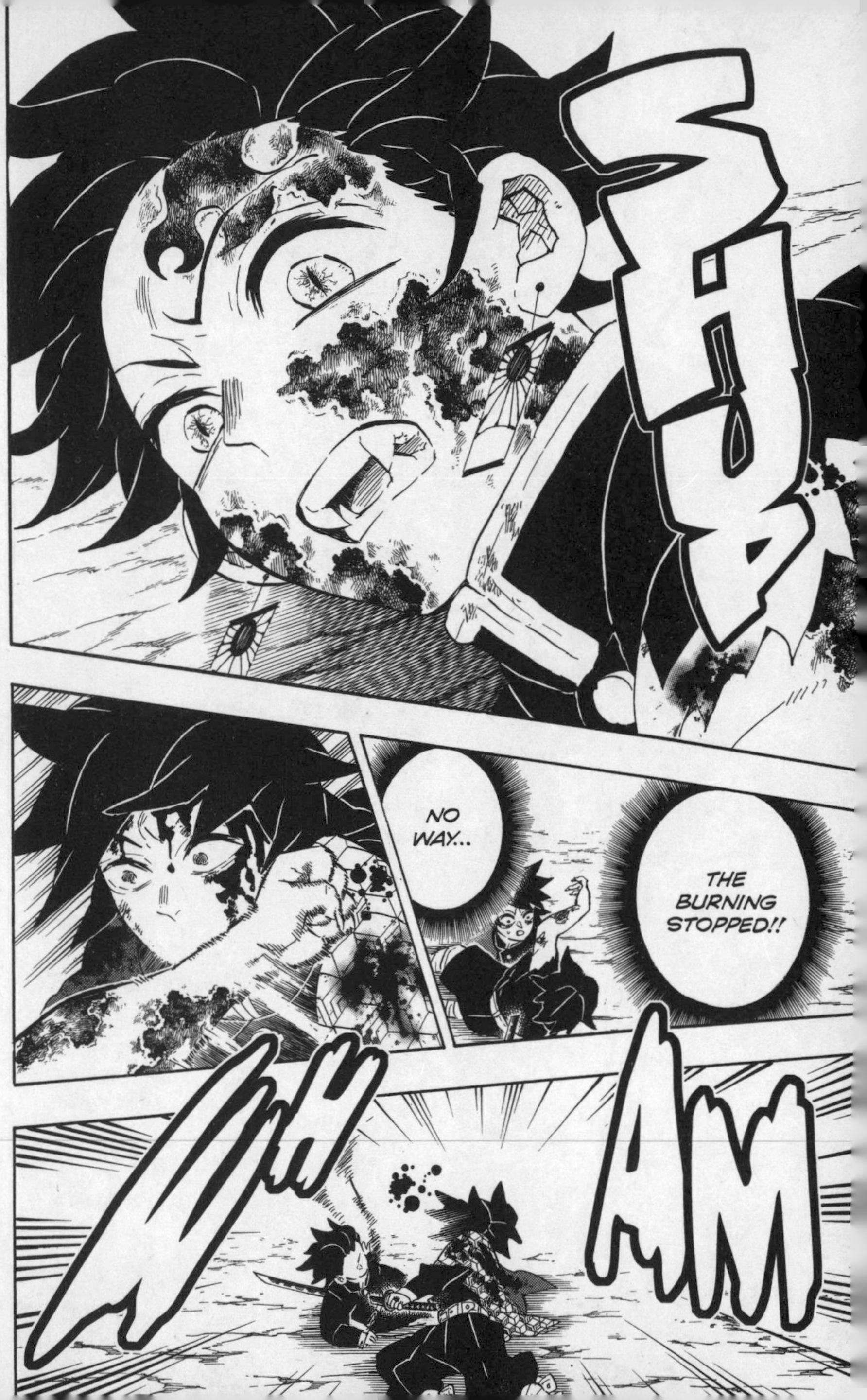
NO WAY...
THE BURNING STOPPED!!

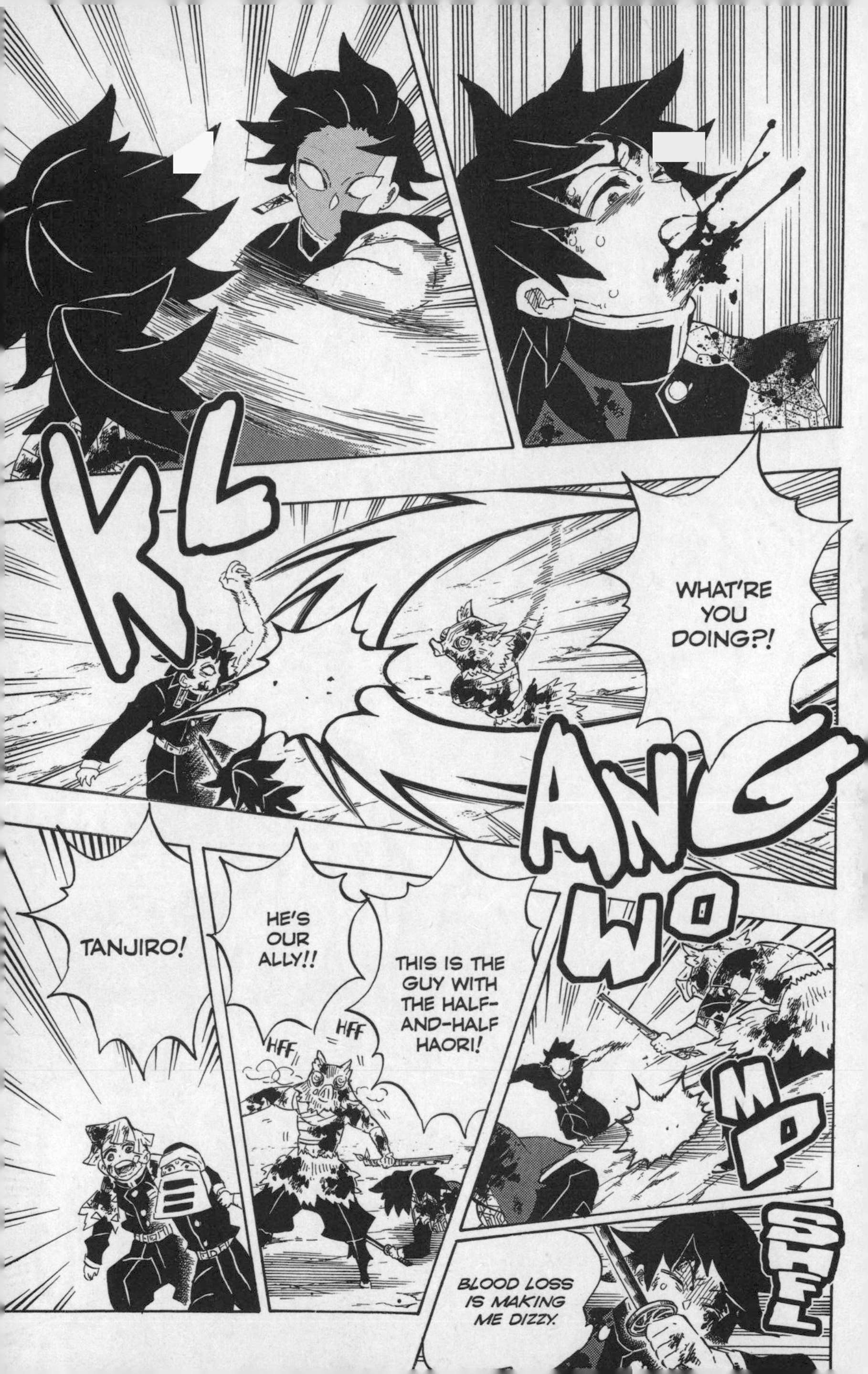
KLANG
WHAT'RE YOU DOING?!
WOMP
SHFL
BLOOD LOSS IS MAKING ME DIZZY.
THIS IS THE GUY WITH THE HALF-AND-HALF HAORI!
HE'S OUR ALLY!!
HFF
HFF
TANJIRO!

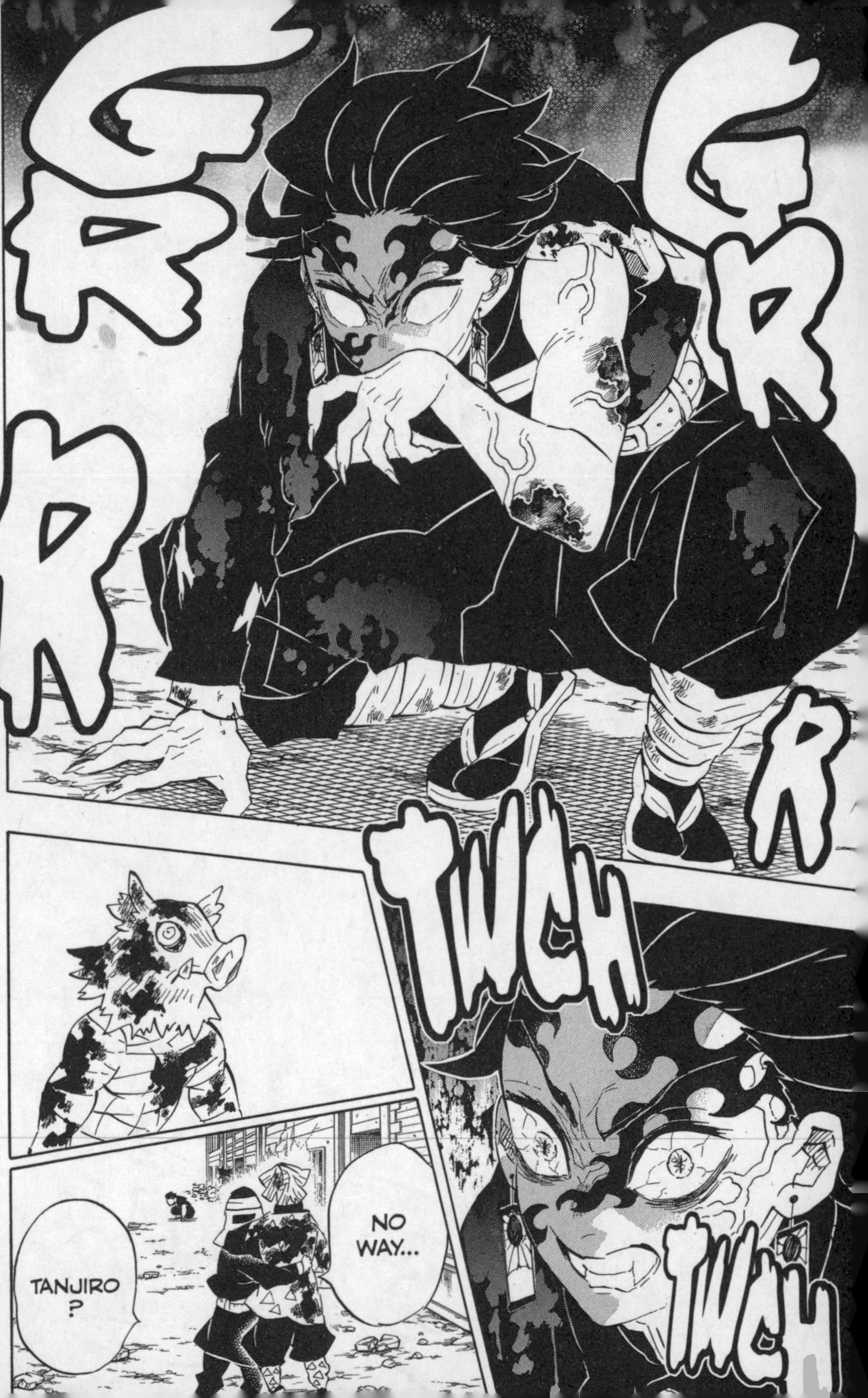
GRR
GRR
TWCH
TWCH
NO WAY...
TANJIRO ?

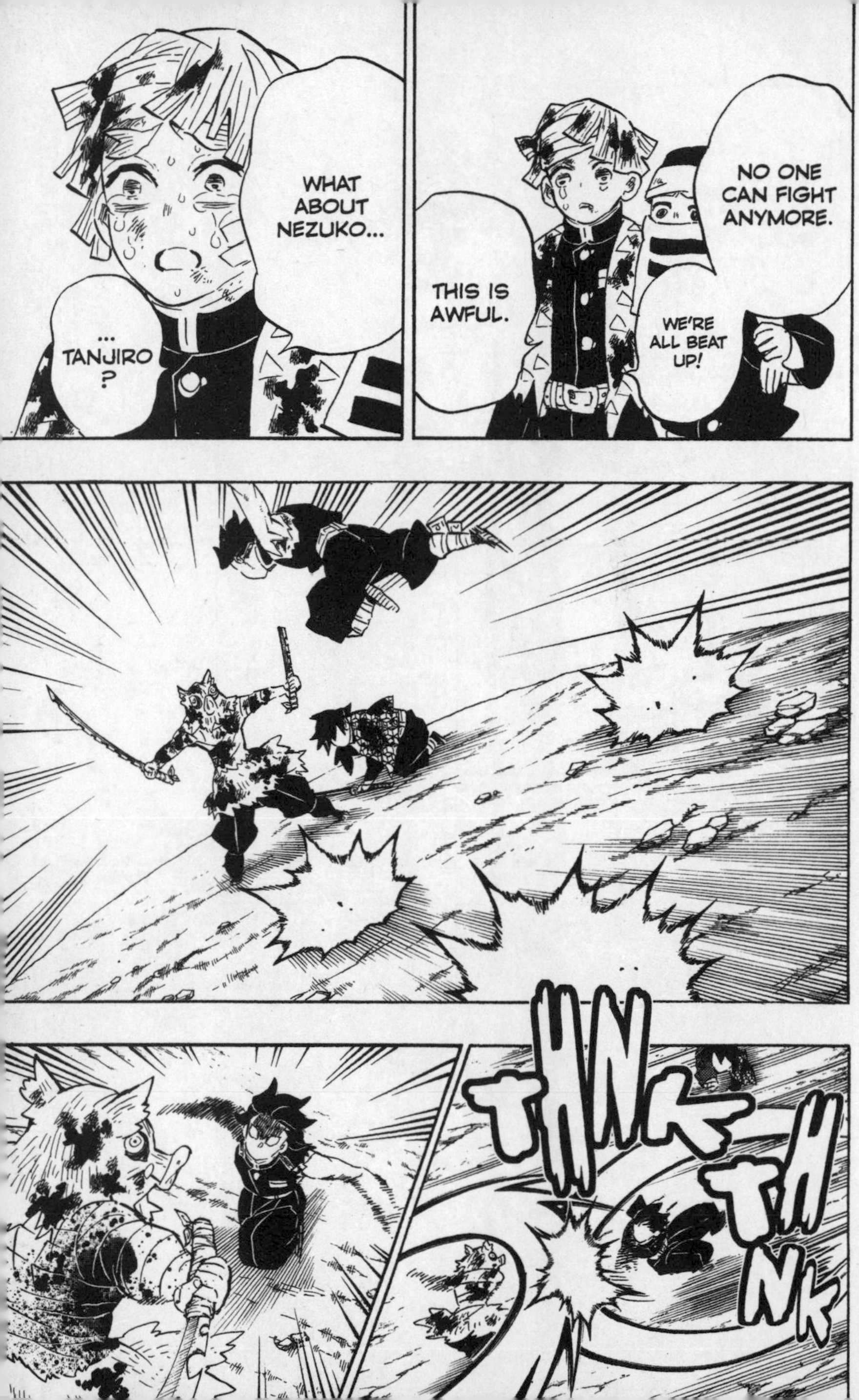
NO ONE CAN FIGHT ANYMORE.
WE'RE ALL BEAT UP!
THIS IS AWFUL.
WHAT ABOUT NEZUKO...
... TANJIRO ?
THNK
THTHNK

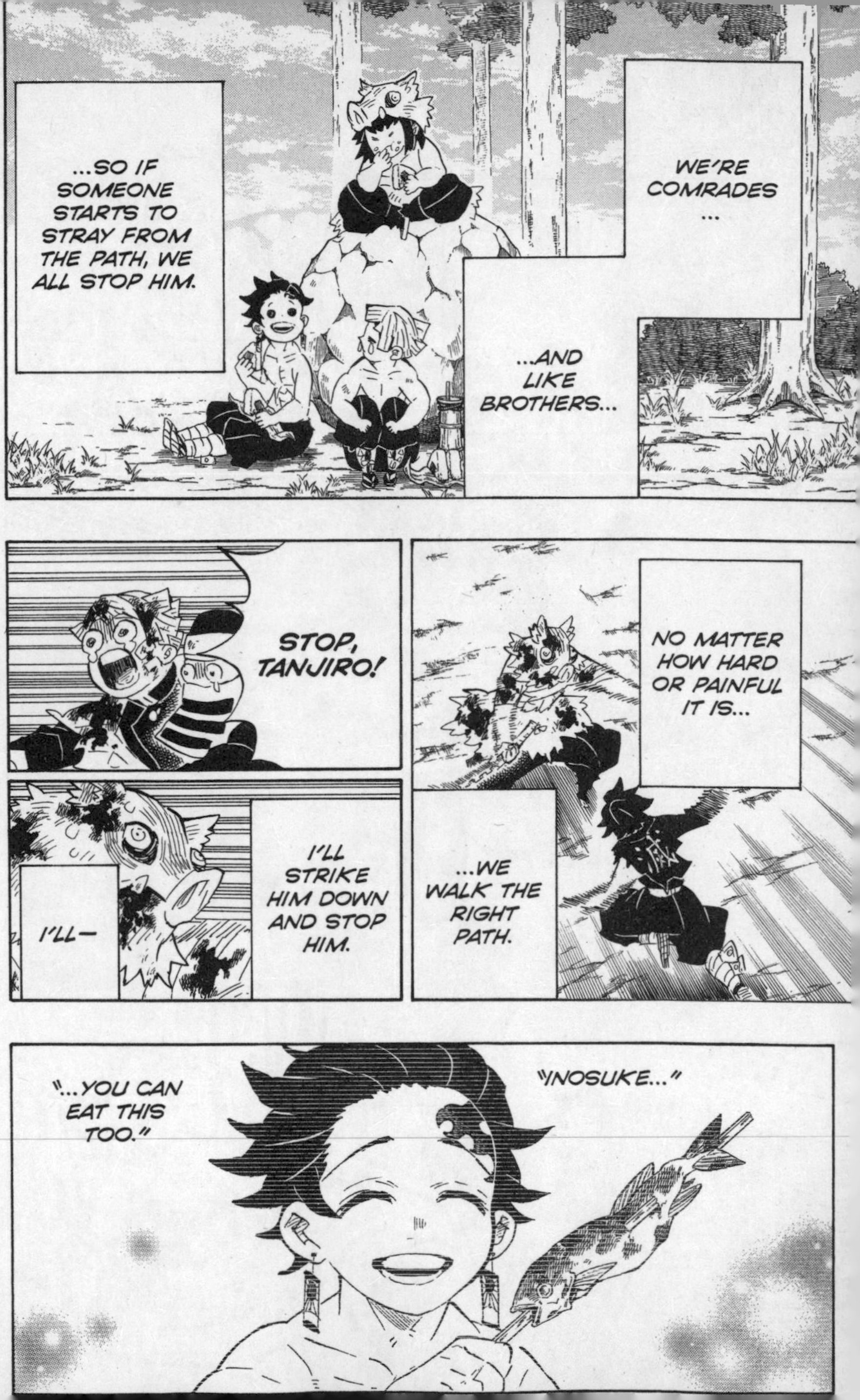
WE'RE COMRADES ...
...AND LIKE BROTHERS...
...SO IF SOMEONE STARTS TO STRAY FROM THE PATH, WE ALL STOP HIM.
NO MATTER HOW HARD OR PAINFUL IT IS...
...WE WALK THE RIGHT PATH.
STOP, TANJIRO!
I'LL STRIKE HIM DOWN AND STOP HIM.
I'LL—
"INOSUKE..."
"...YOU CAN EAT THIS TOO."

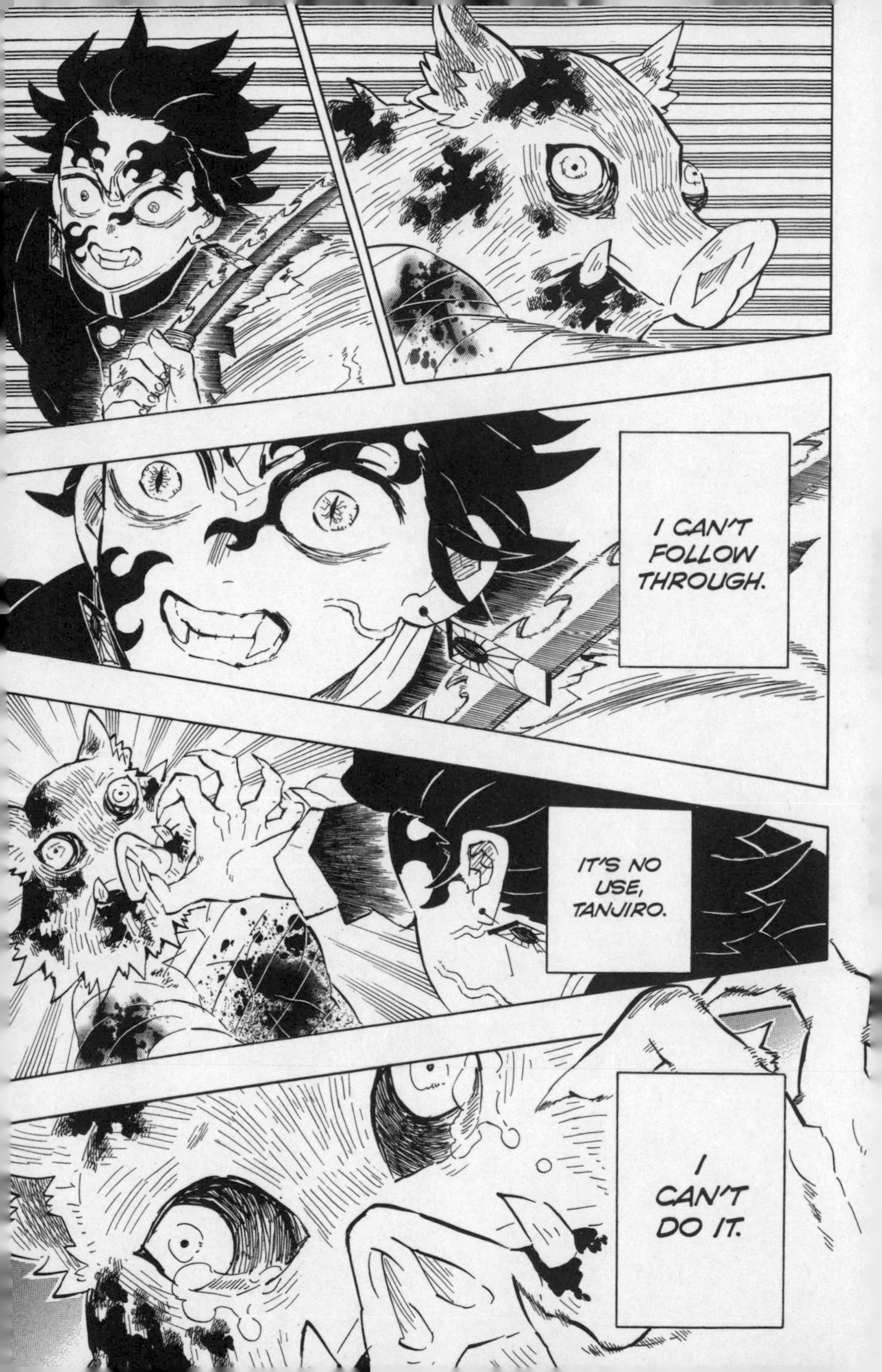
I CAN'T FOLLOW THROUGH.
IT'S NO USE, TANJIRO.
I CAN'T DO IT.

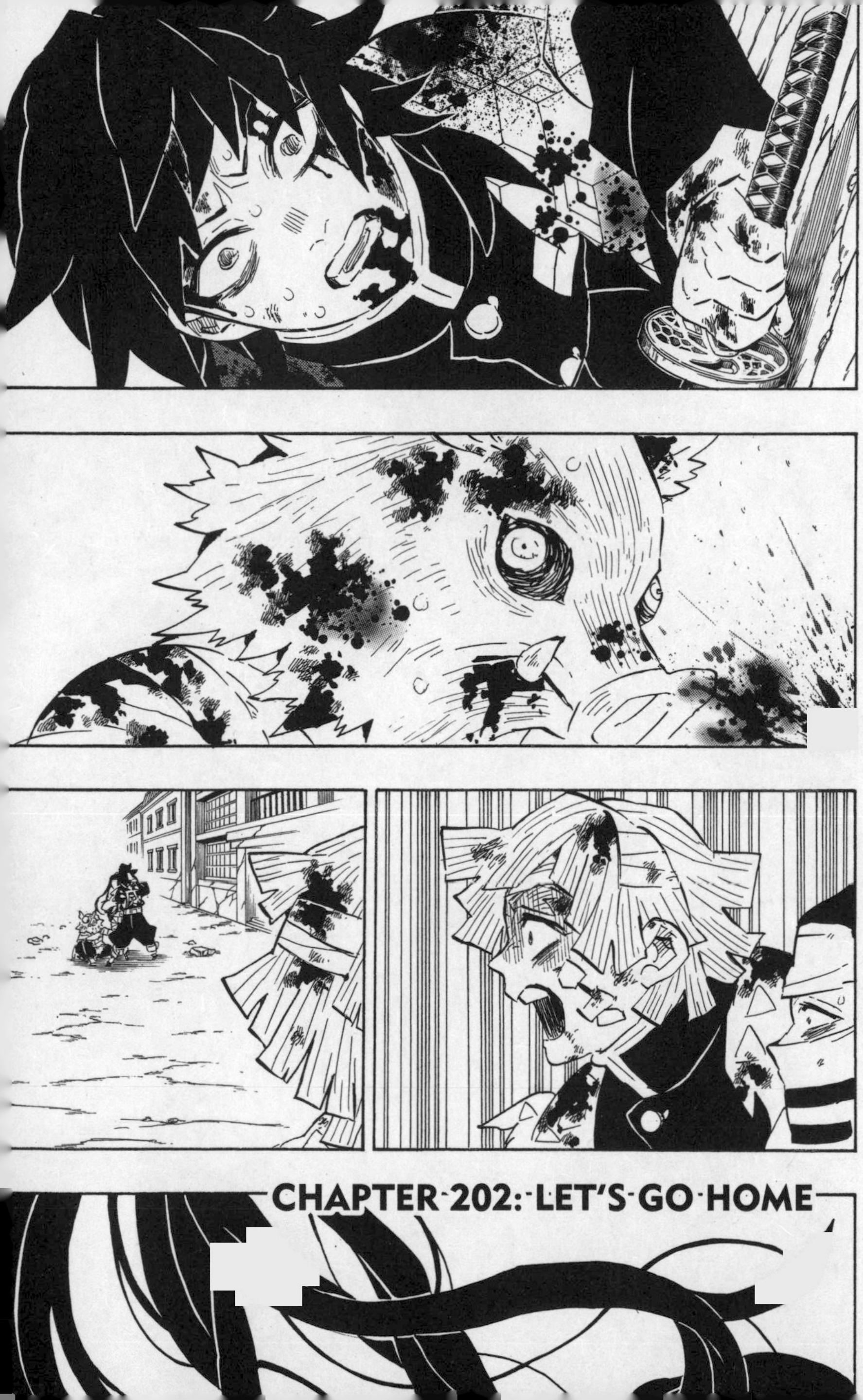
CHAPTER 202: LET'S GO HOME

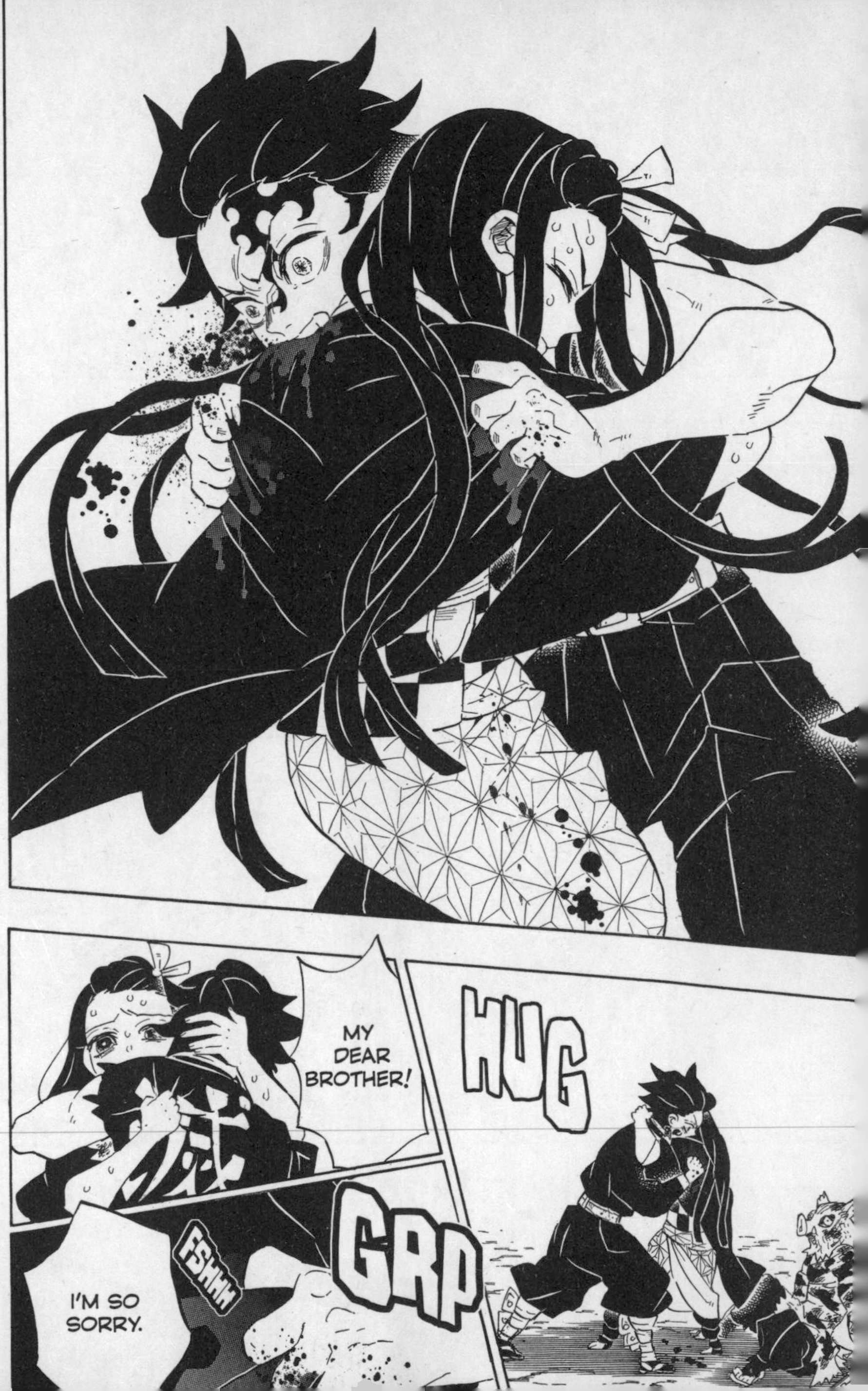
HUG
MY DEAR BROTHER!
GRP
FSHHH
I'M SO SORRY.

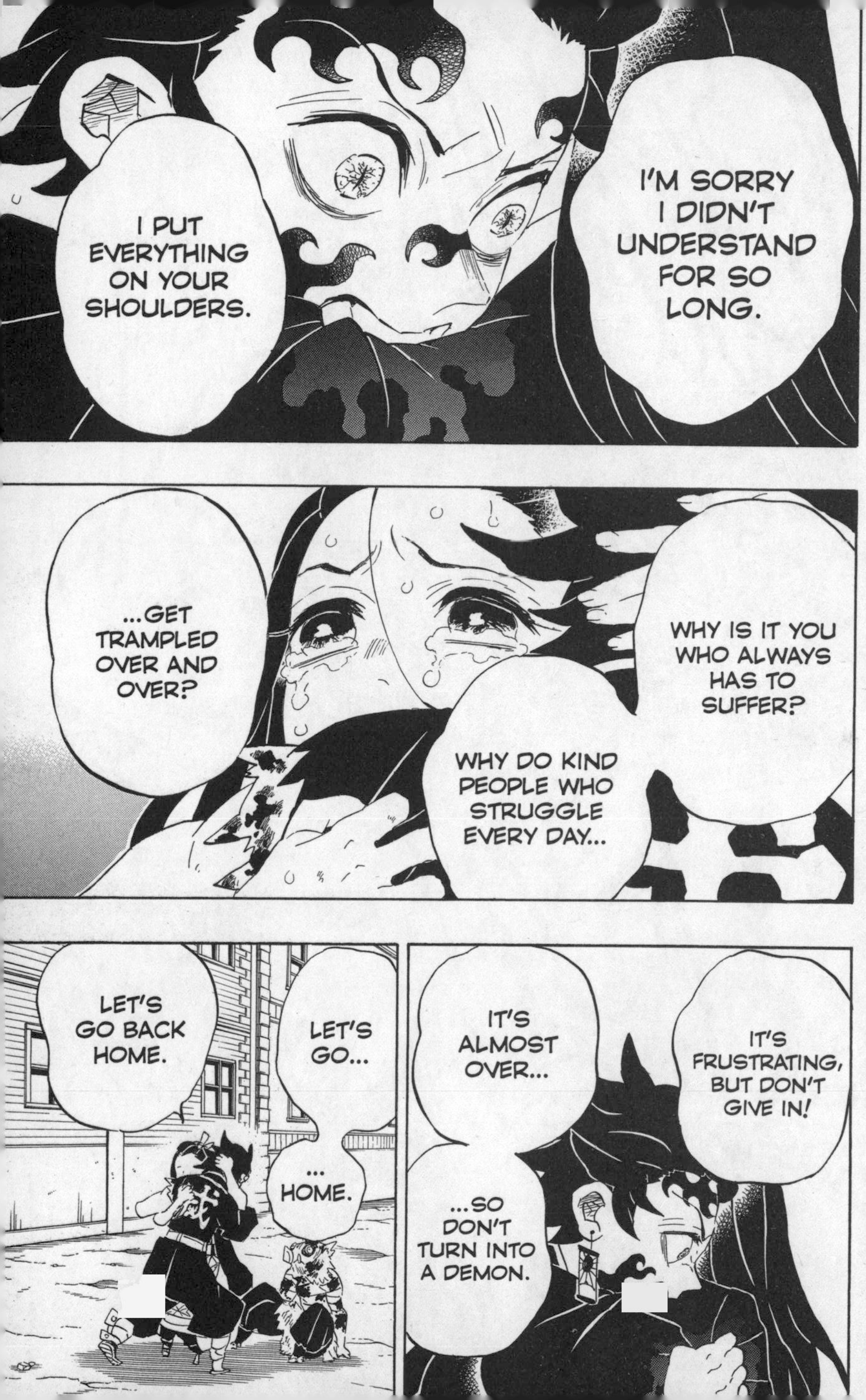
I'M SORRY I DIDN'T UNDERSTAND FOR SO LONG.
I PUT EVERYTHING ON YOUR SHOULDERS.
WHY IS IT YOU WHO ALWAYS HAS TO SUFFER?
WHY DO KIND PEOPLE WHO STRUGGLE EVERY DAY...
...GET TRAMPLED OVER AND OVER?
IT'S FRUSTRATING, BUT DON'T GIVE IN!
IT'S ALMOST OVER...
...SO DON'T TURN INTO A DEMON.
LET'S GO...
... HOME.
LET'S GO BACK HOME.

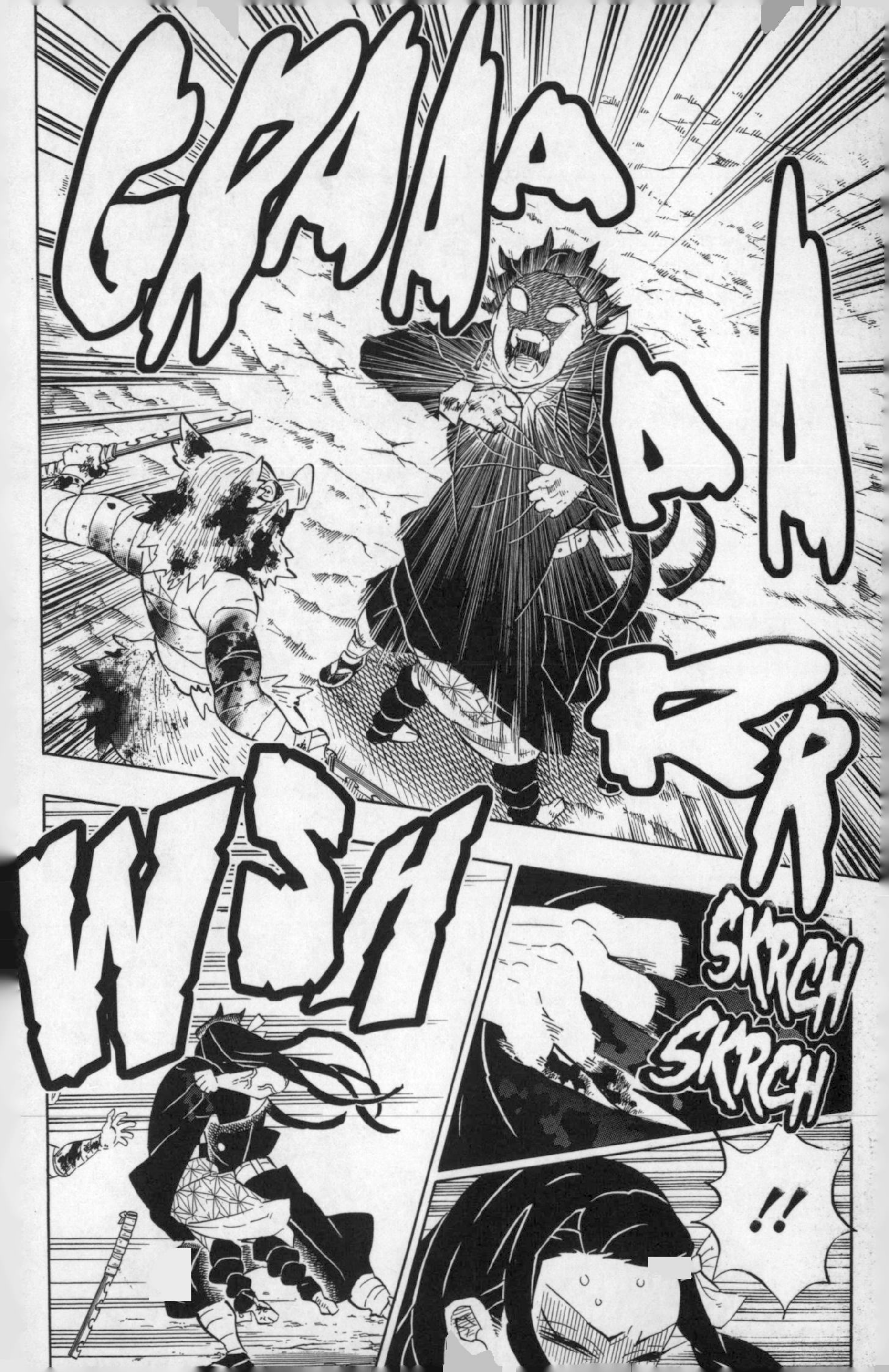
SKRCH
SKRCH
!!
WSH

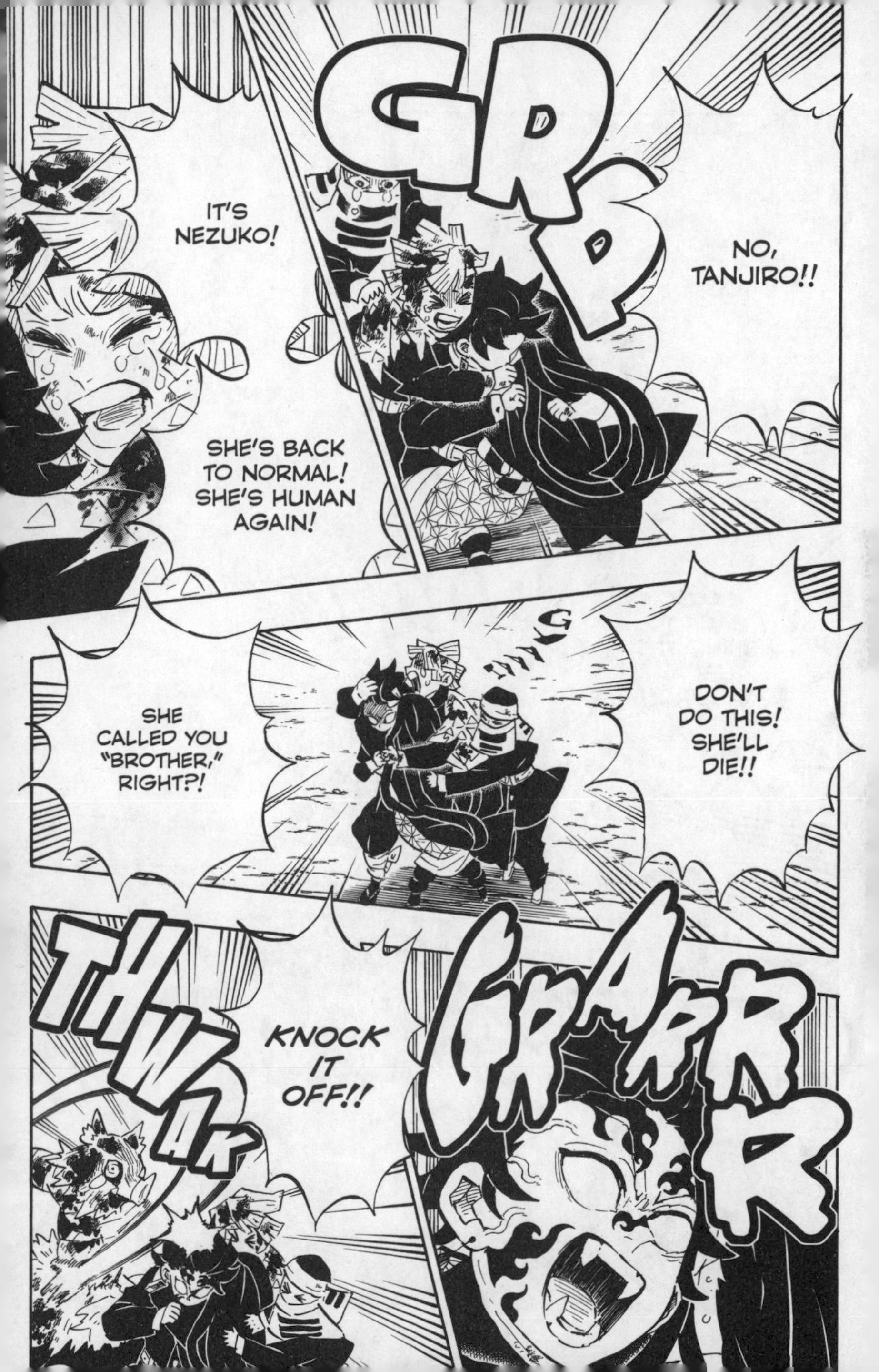
NO, TANJIRO!!
IT'S NEZUKO!
SHE'S BACK TO NORMAL! SHE'S HUMAN AGAIN!
DON'T DO THIS! SHE'LL DIE!!
SHE CALLED YOU "BROTHER," RIGHT?!
KNOCK IT OFF!!
THWAK

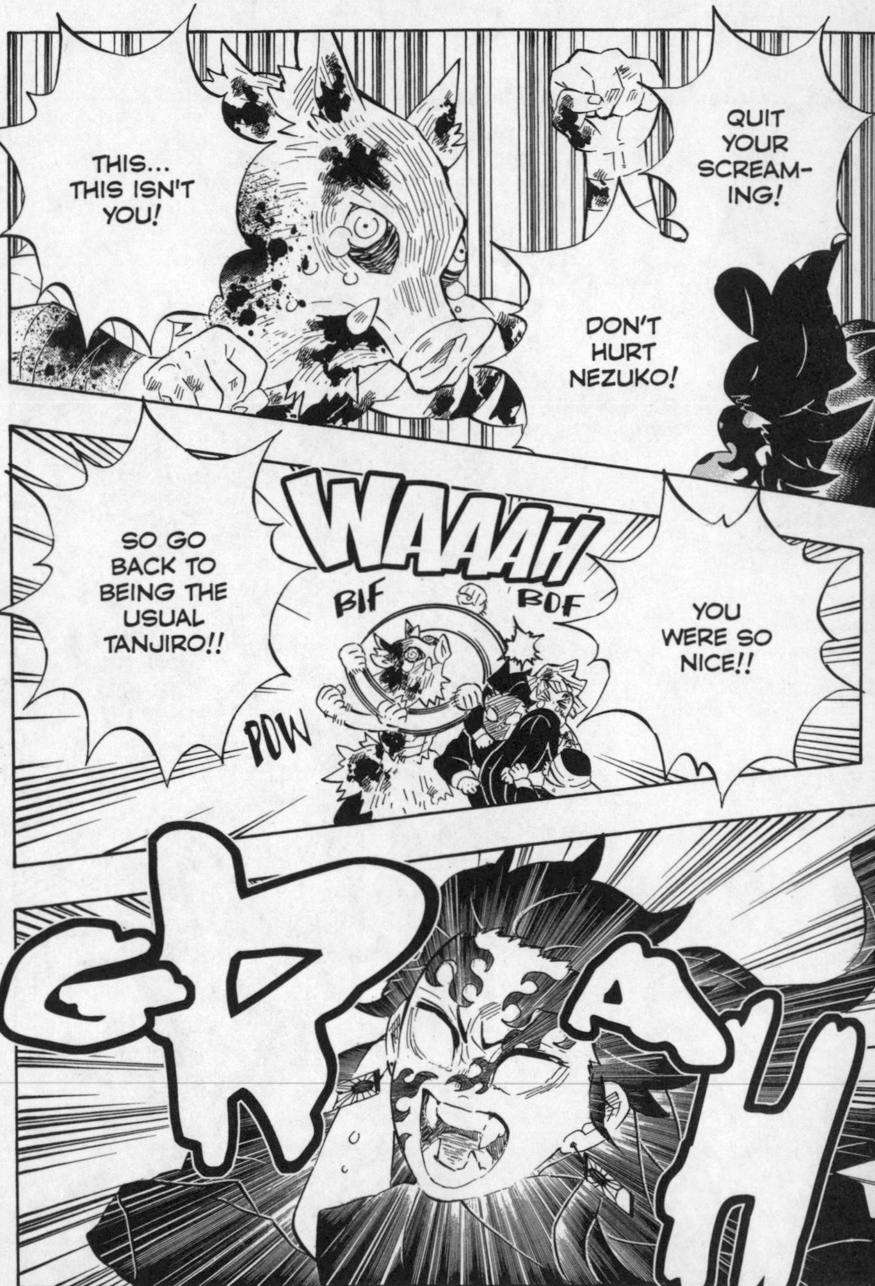
QUIT YOUR SCREAMING!
DON'T HURT NEZUKO!
THIS... THIS ISN'T YOU!
YOU WERE SO NICE!!
WAAAH
BOF
BIF
SO GO BACK TO BEING THE USUAL TANJIRO!!
POW
GRAH

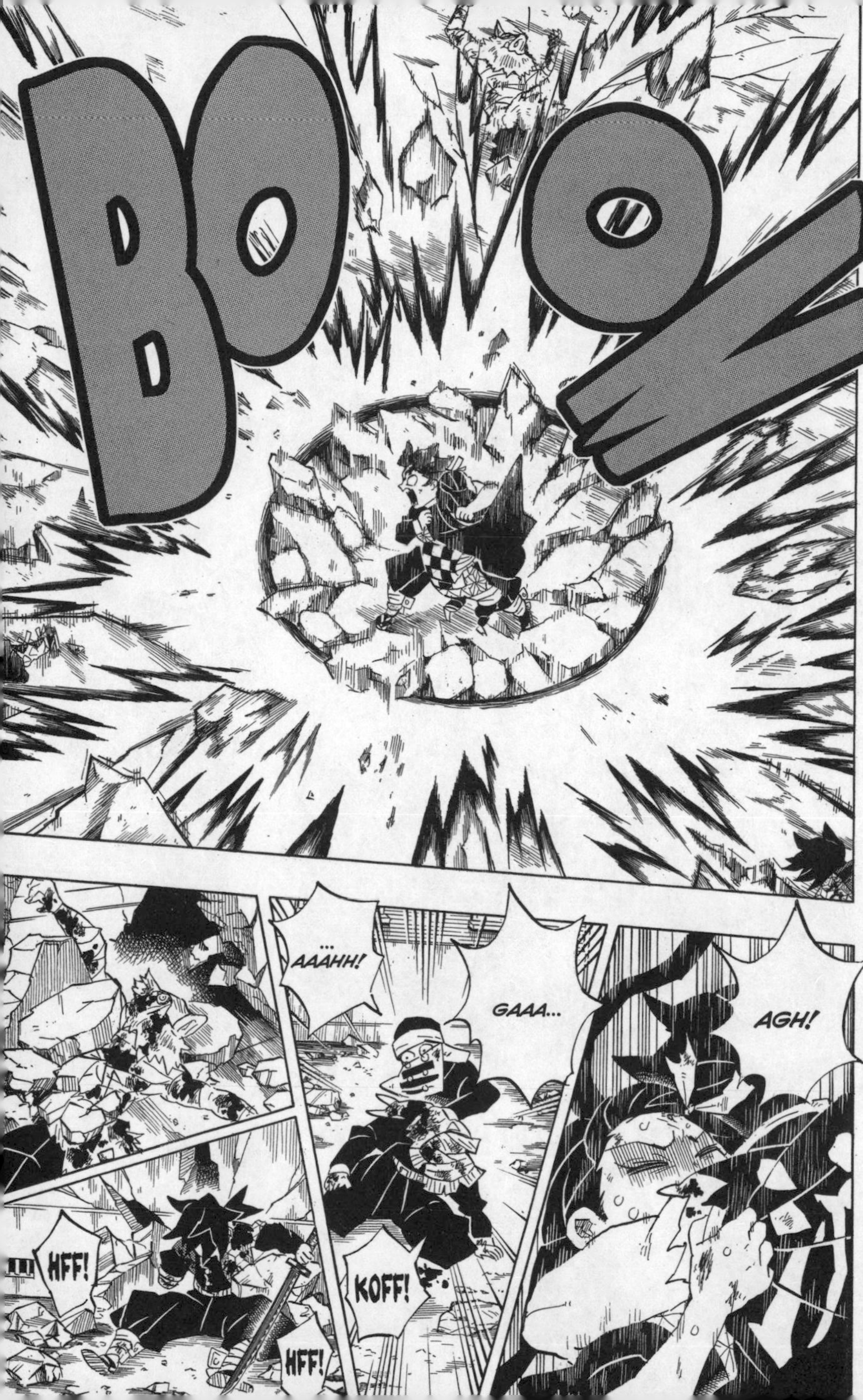
BOOM
AGH!
... AAAHH!
GAAA...
KOFF!
HFF!
HFF!

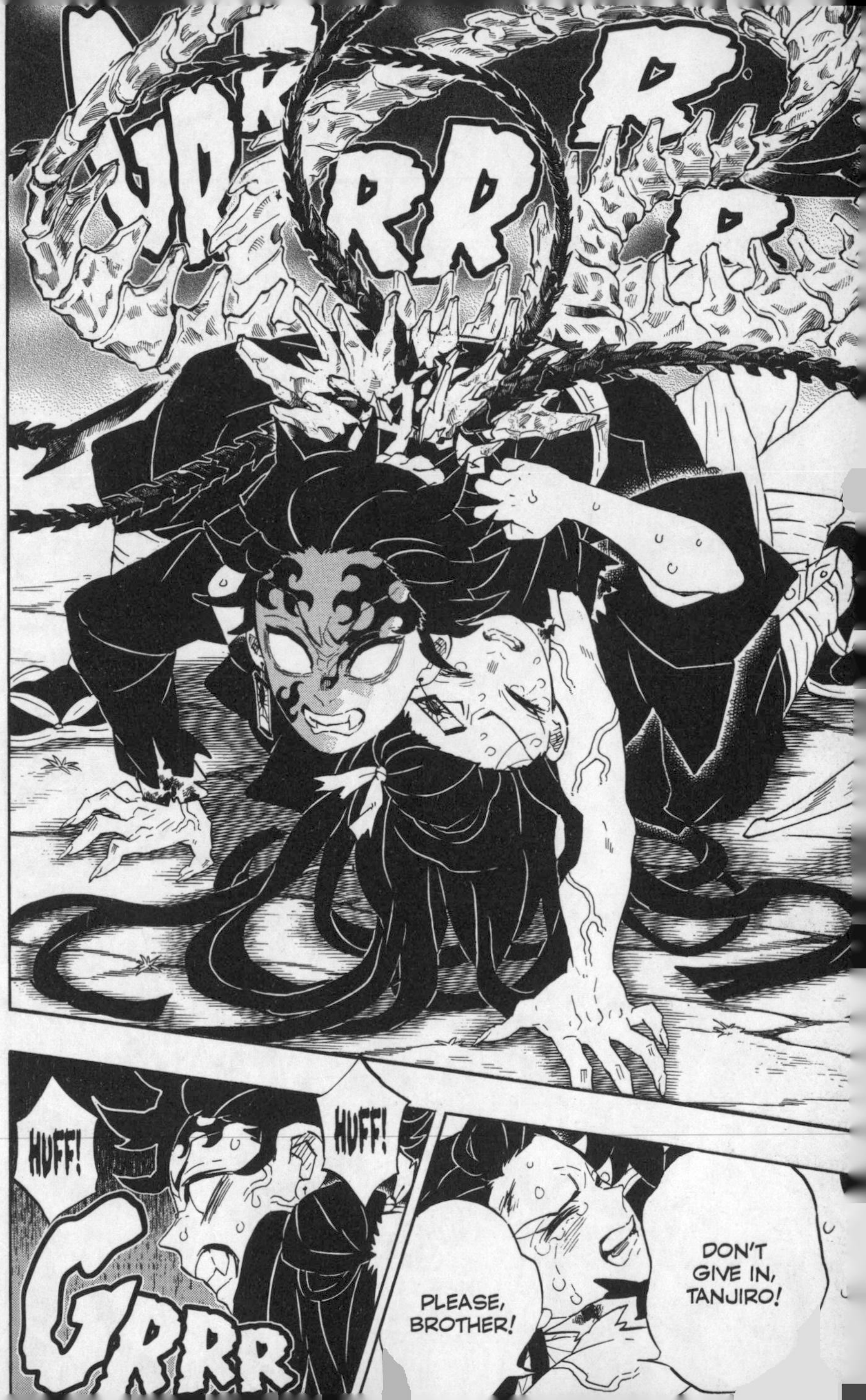
DON'T GIVE IN, TANJIRO!
PLEASE, BROTHER!
HUFF!
HUFF!
GRRR

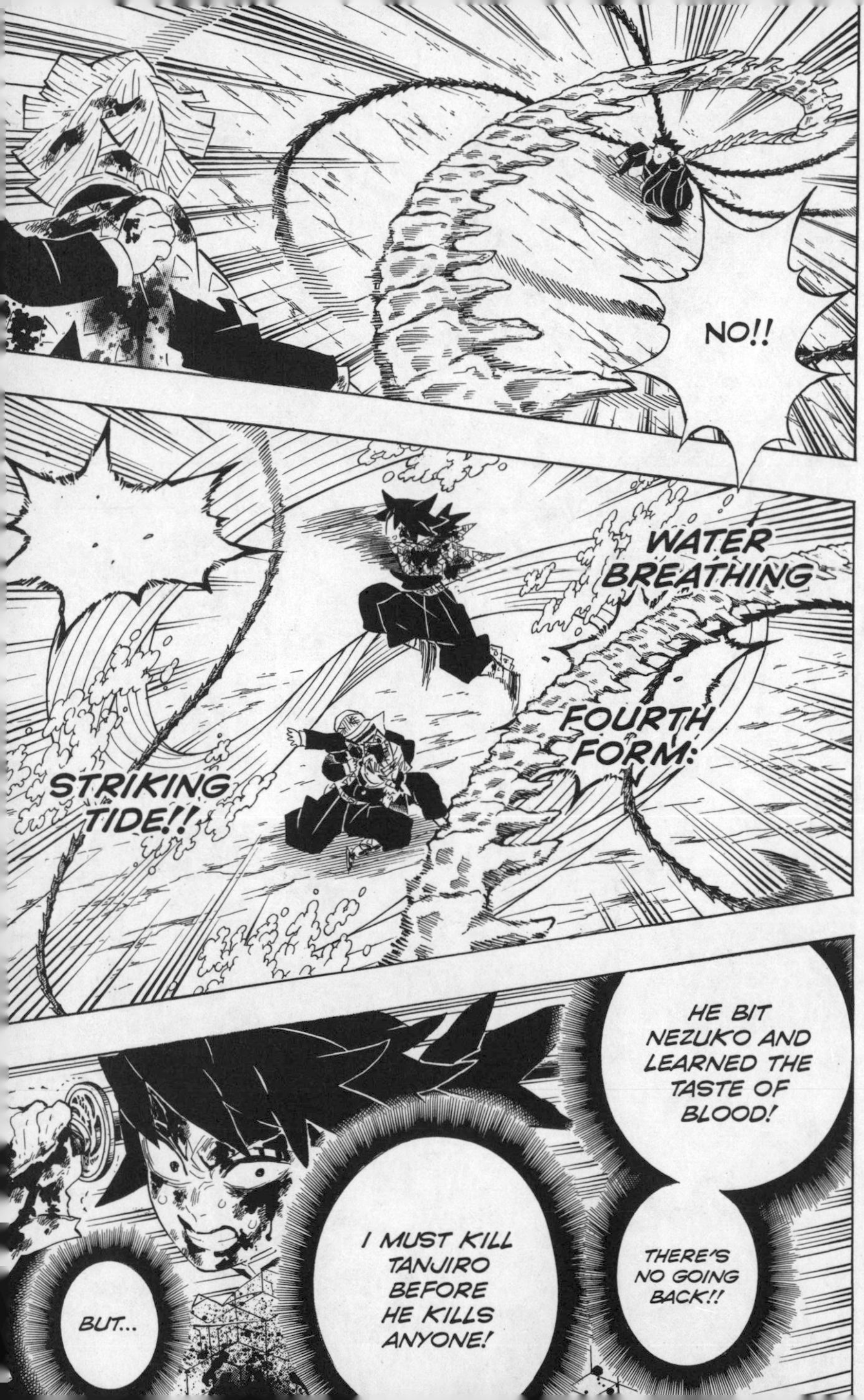
NO!!
WATER BREATHING
FOURTH FORM:
STRIKING TIDE!!
HE BIT NEZUKO AND LEARNED THE TASTE OF BLOOD!
THERE'S NO GOING BACK!!
I MUST KILL TANJIRO BEFORE HE KILLS ANYONE!
BUT...

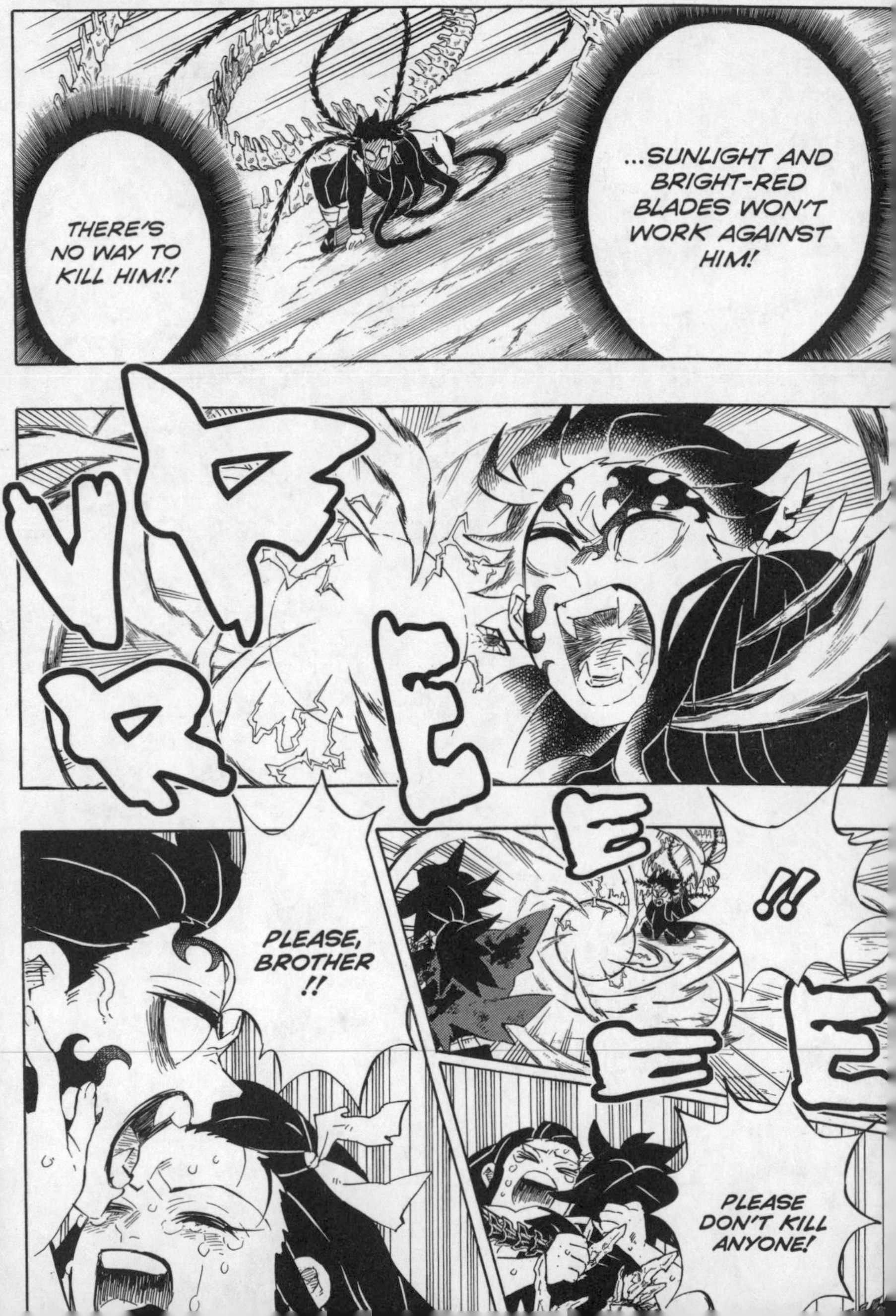
...SUNLIGHT AND BRIGHT-RED BLADES WON'T WORK AGAINST HIM!
THERE'S NO WAY TO KILL HIM!!
PLEASE DON'T KILL ANYONE!
PLEASE, BROTHER!!

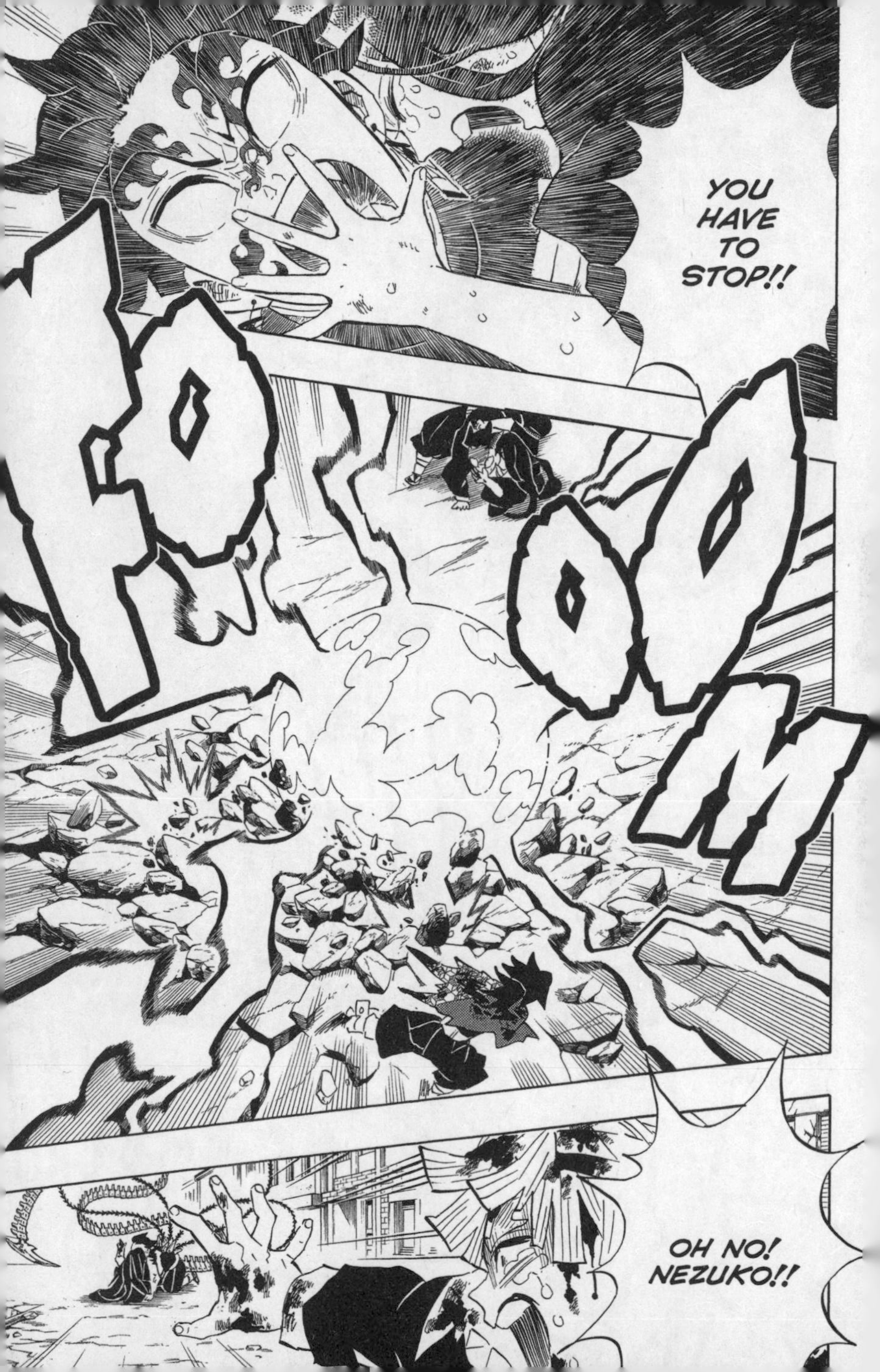
YOU HAVE TO STOP!!
FOOM
OH NO! NEZUKO!!

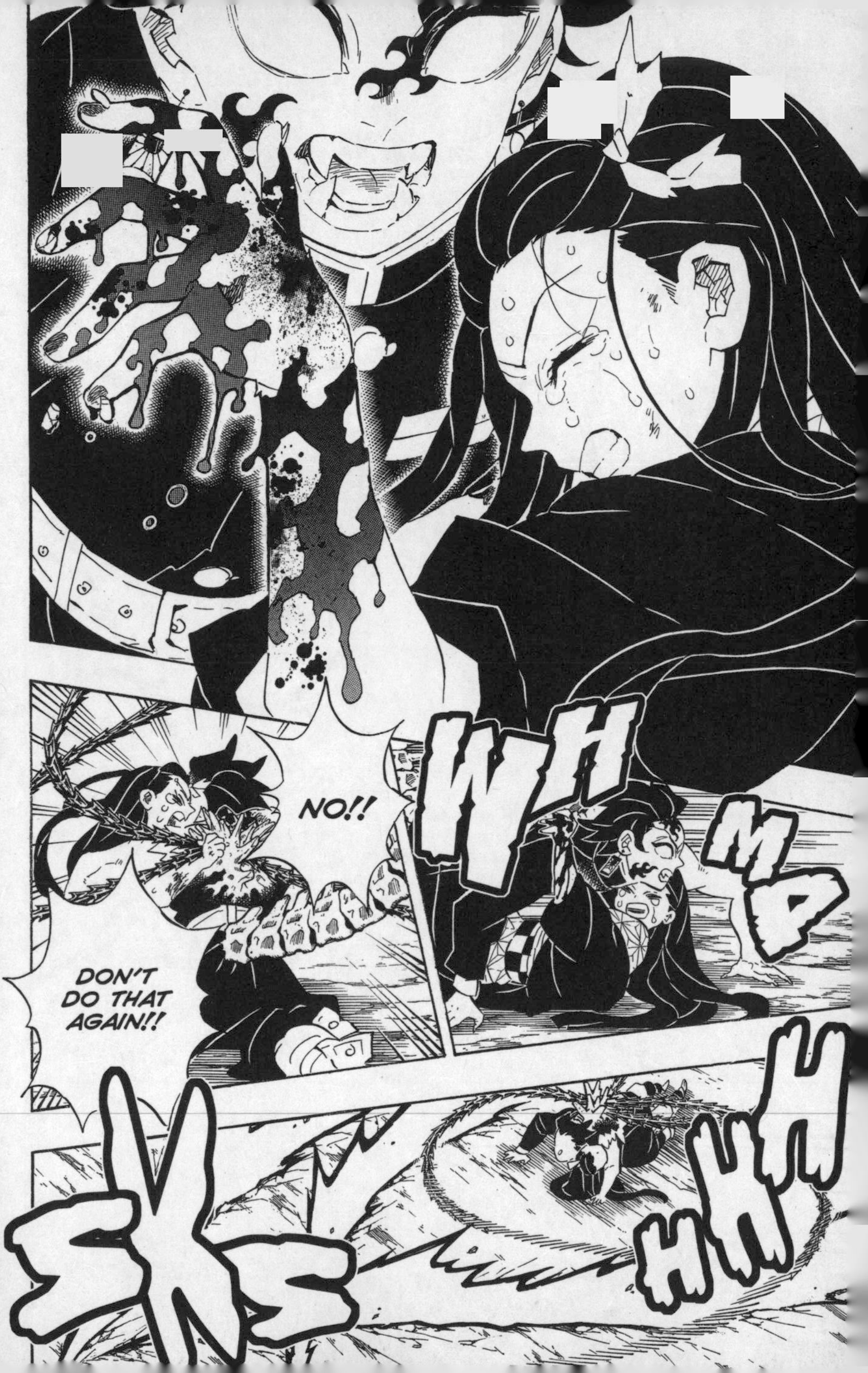
WHMP
NO!!
DON'T DO THAT AGAIN!!
SKSHHHH

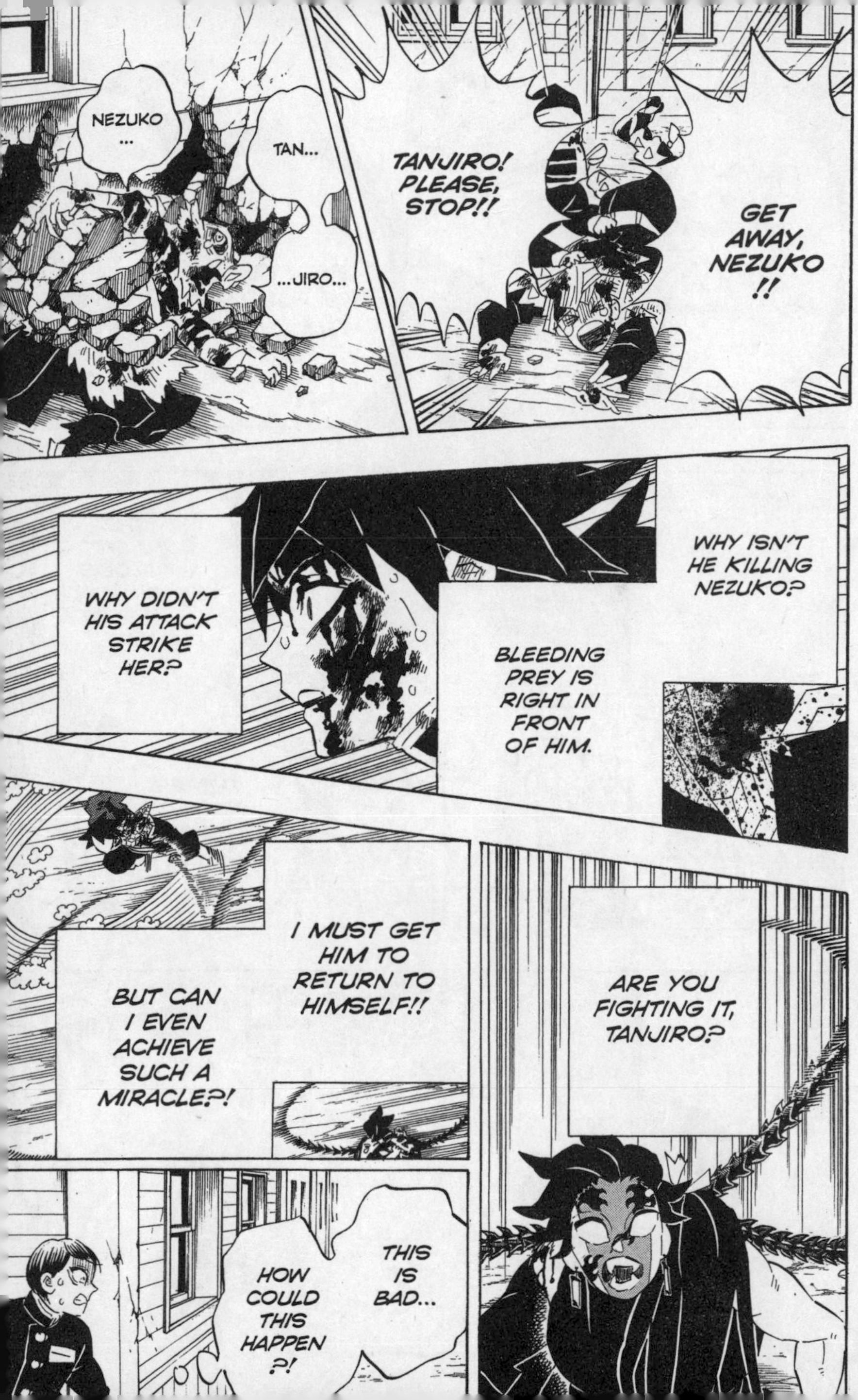
GET AWAY, NEZUKO!!
TANJIRO! PLEASE, STOP!!
TAN...
...JIRO...
NEZUKO...
WHY ISN'T HE KILLING NEZUKO?
BLEEDING PREY IS RIGHT IN FRONT OF HIM.
WHY DIDN'T HIS ATTACK STRIKE HER?
ARE YOU FIGHTING IT, TANJIRO?
I MUST GET HIM TO RETURN TO HIMSELF!!
BUT CAN I EVEN ACHIEVE SUCH A MIRACLE?!
THIS IS BAD...
HOW COULD THIS HAPPEN?!

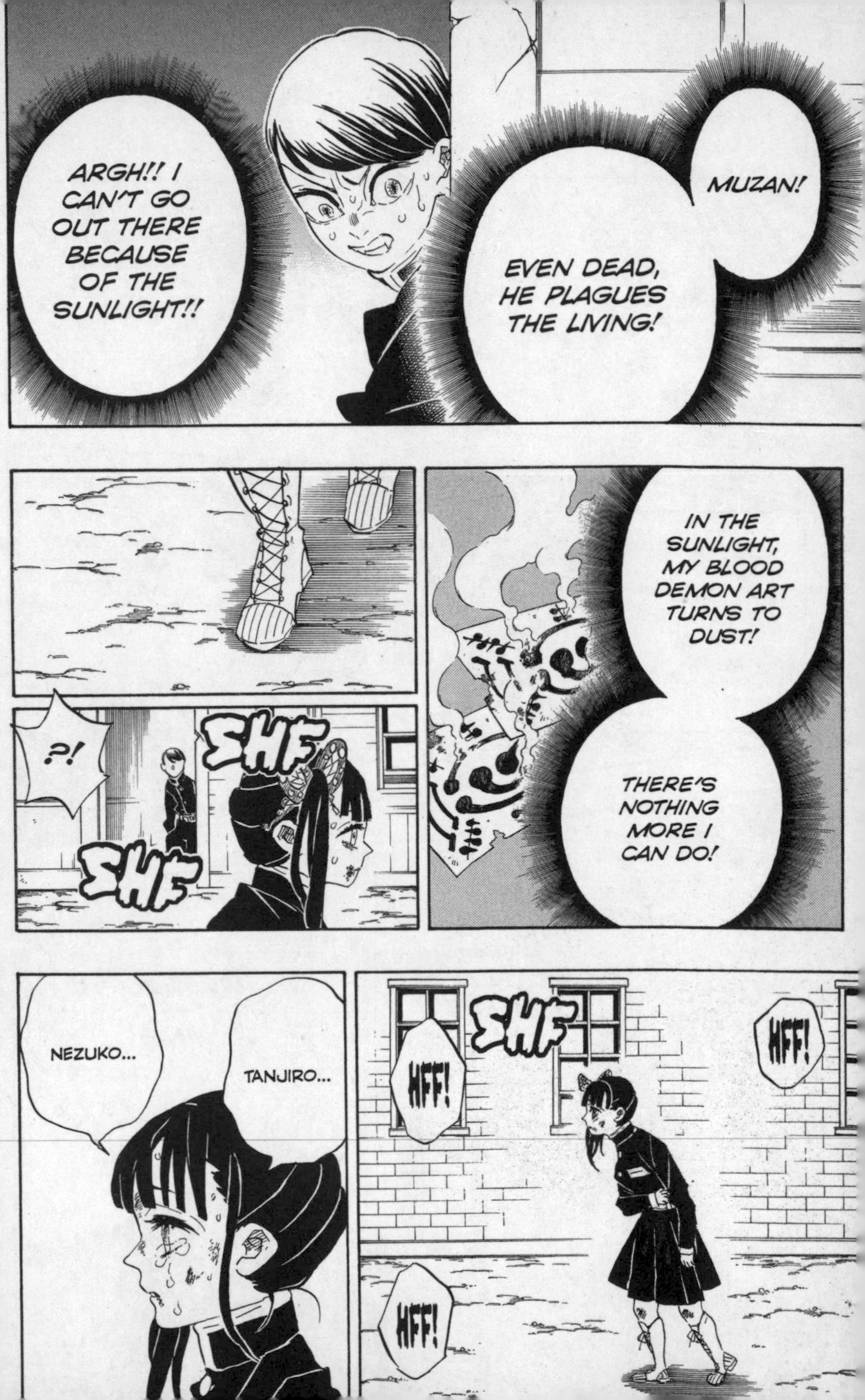
MUZAN!
EVEN DEAD, HE PLAGUES THE LIVING!
ARGH!! I CAN'T GO OUT THERE BECAUSE OF THE SUNLIGHT!!
IN THE SUNLIGHT, MY BLOOD DEMON ART TURNS TO DUST!
THERE'S NOTHING MORE I CAN DO!
SHF
?!
SHF
HFF!
SHF
HFF!
HFF!
TANJIRO...
NEZUKO...

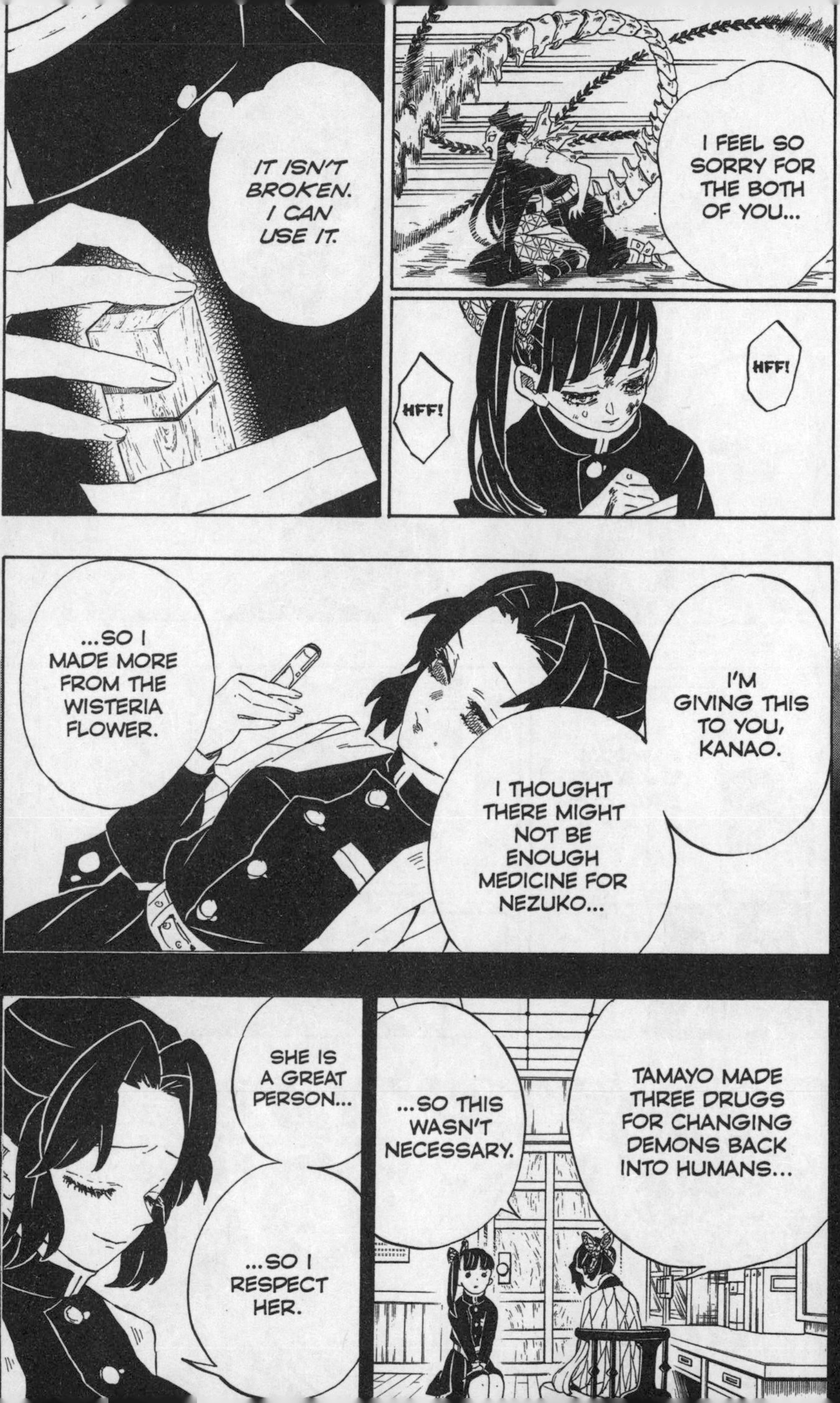
I FEEL SO SORRY FOR THE BOTH OF YOU...
HFF!
HFF!
IT ISN'T BROKEN. I CAN USE IT.
I'M GIVING THIS TO YOU, KANAO.
I THOUGHT THERE MIGHT NOT BE ENOUGH MEDICINE FOR NEZUKO...
...SO I MADE MORE FROM THE WISTERIA FLOWER.
TAMAYO MADE THREE DRUGS FOR CHANGING DEMONS BACK INTO HUMANS...
...SO THIS WASN'T NECESSARY.
SHE IS A GREAT PERSON...
...SO I RESPECT HER.

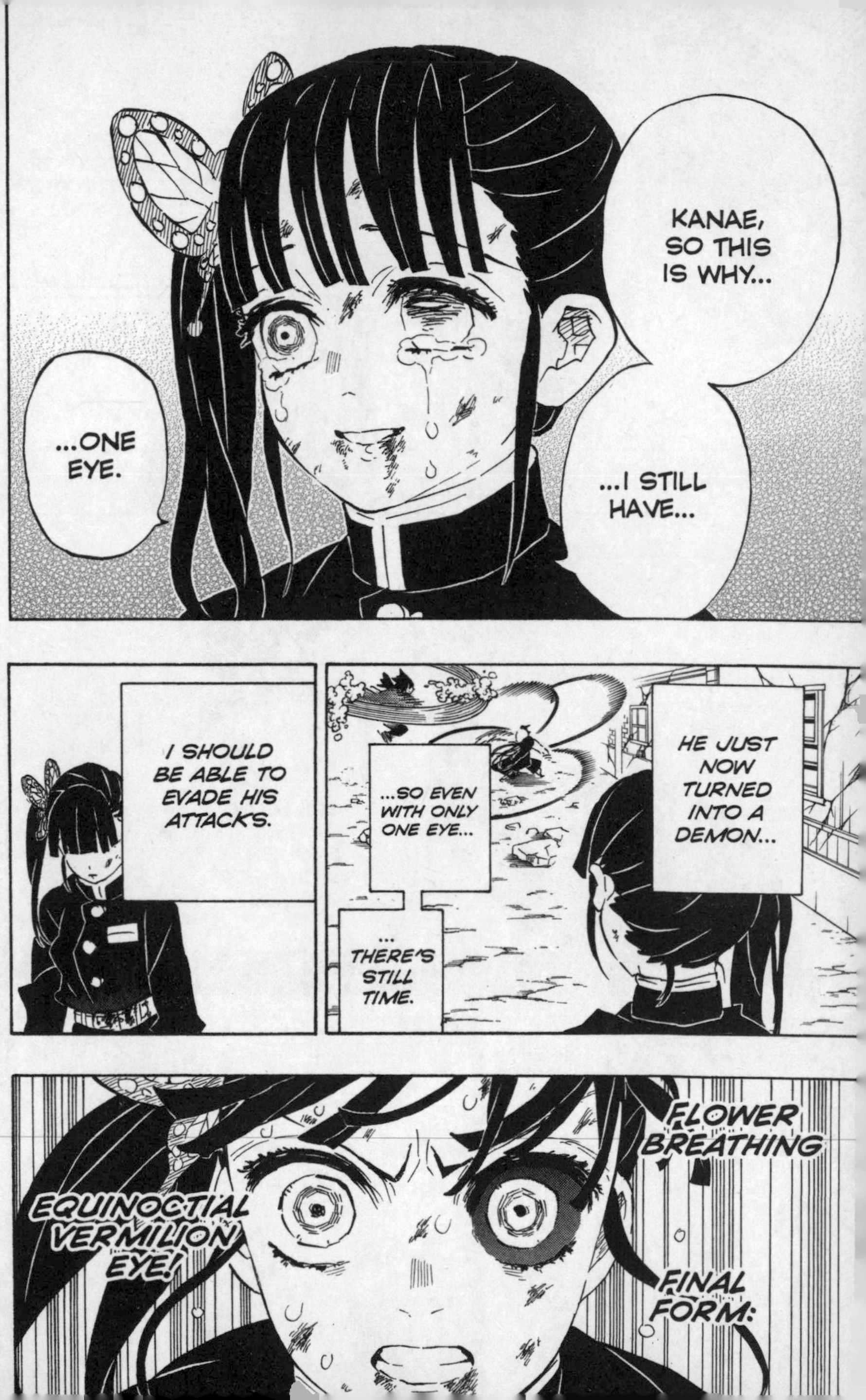
KANAE, SO THIS IS WHY...
...I STILL HAVE...
...ONE EYE.
HE JUST NOW TURNED INTO A DEMON...
...SO EVEN WITH ONLY ONE EYE...
... THERE'S STILL TIME.
I SHOULD BE ABLE TO EVADE HIS ATTACKS.
FLOWER BREATHING
FINAL FORM:
EQUINOCTIAL VERMILION EYE!

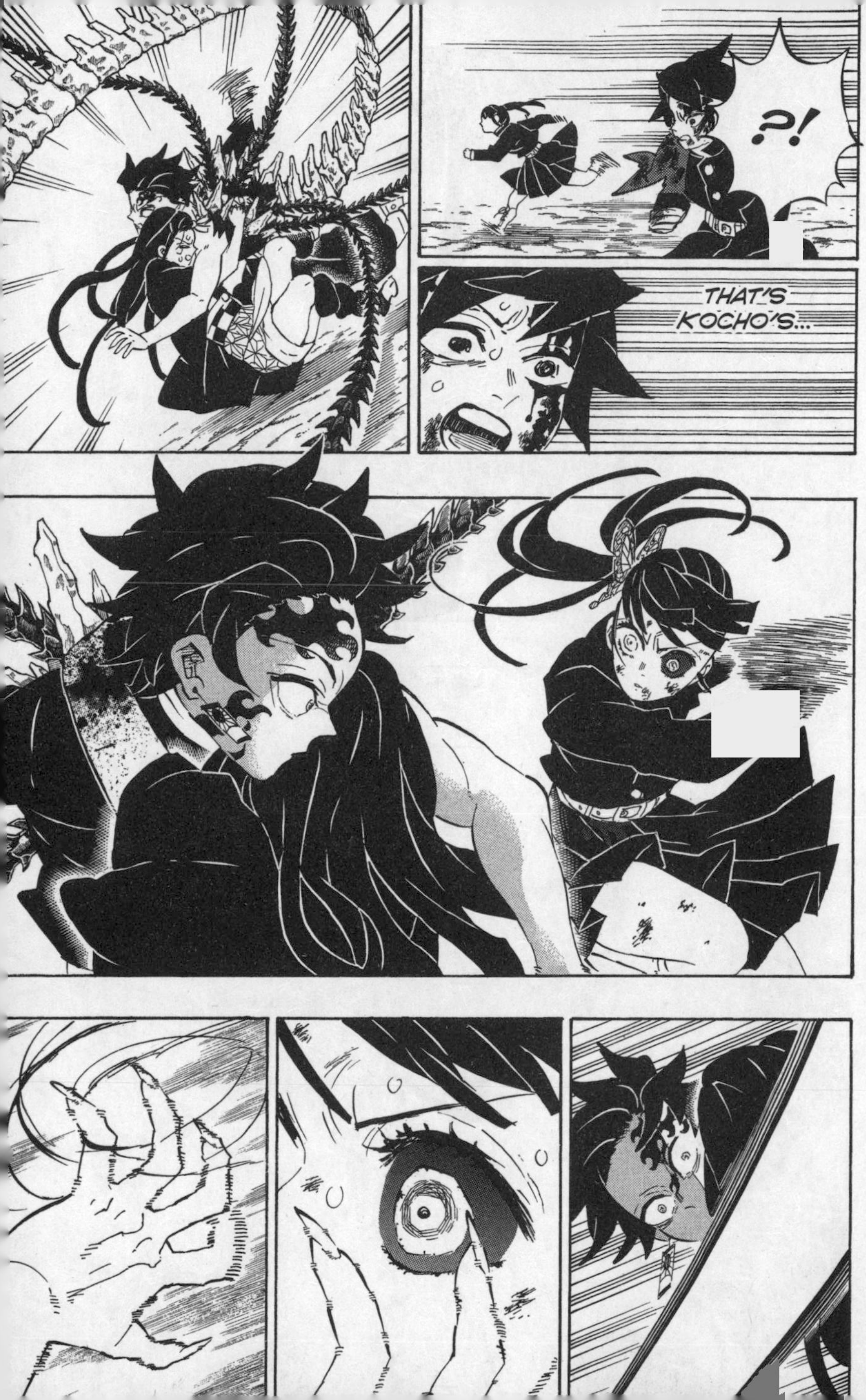
?!
THAT'S KOCHO'S...

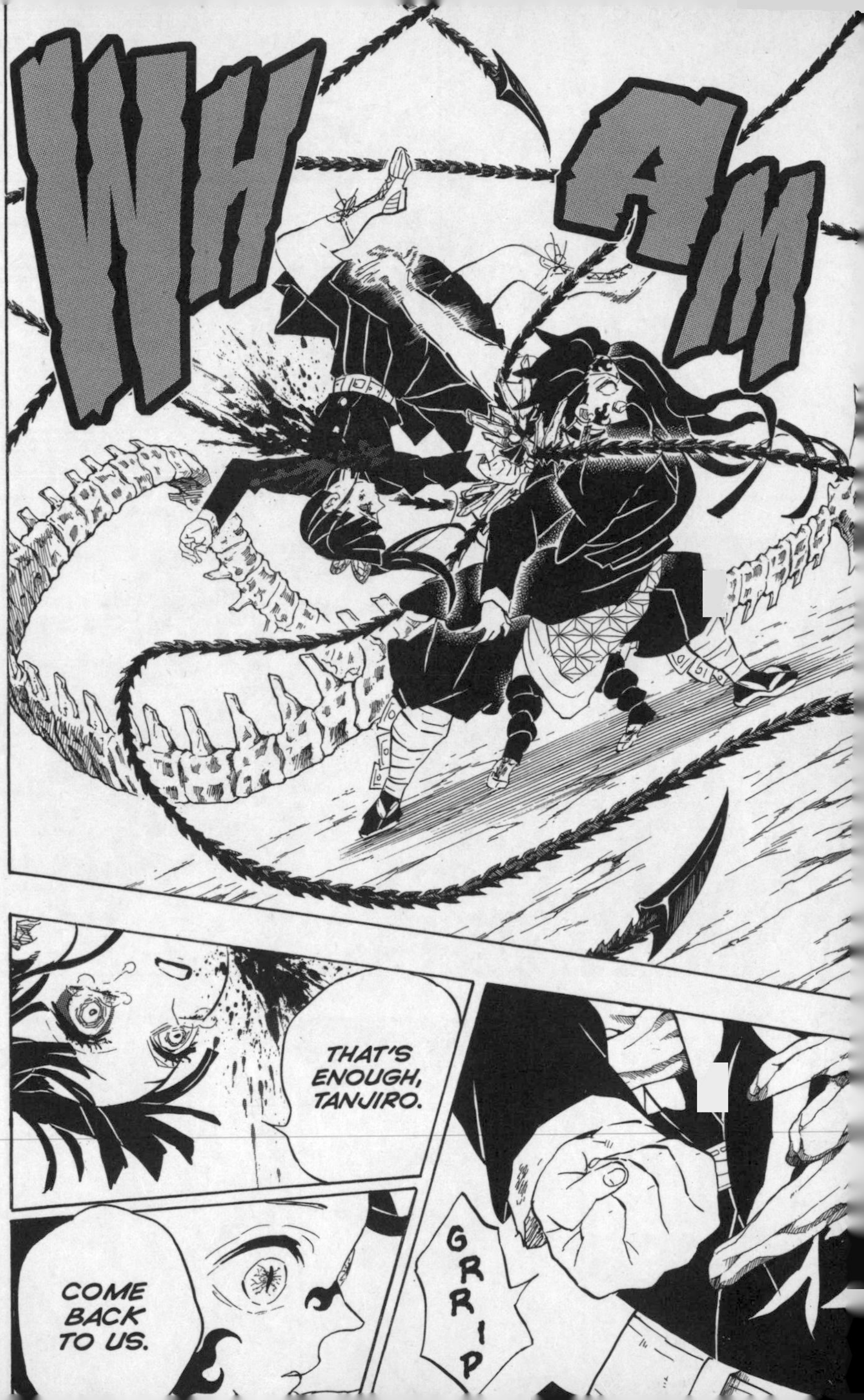
WHAM
GRRIP
THAT'S ENOUGH, TANJIRO.
COME BACK TO US.

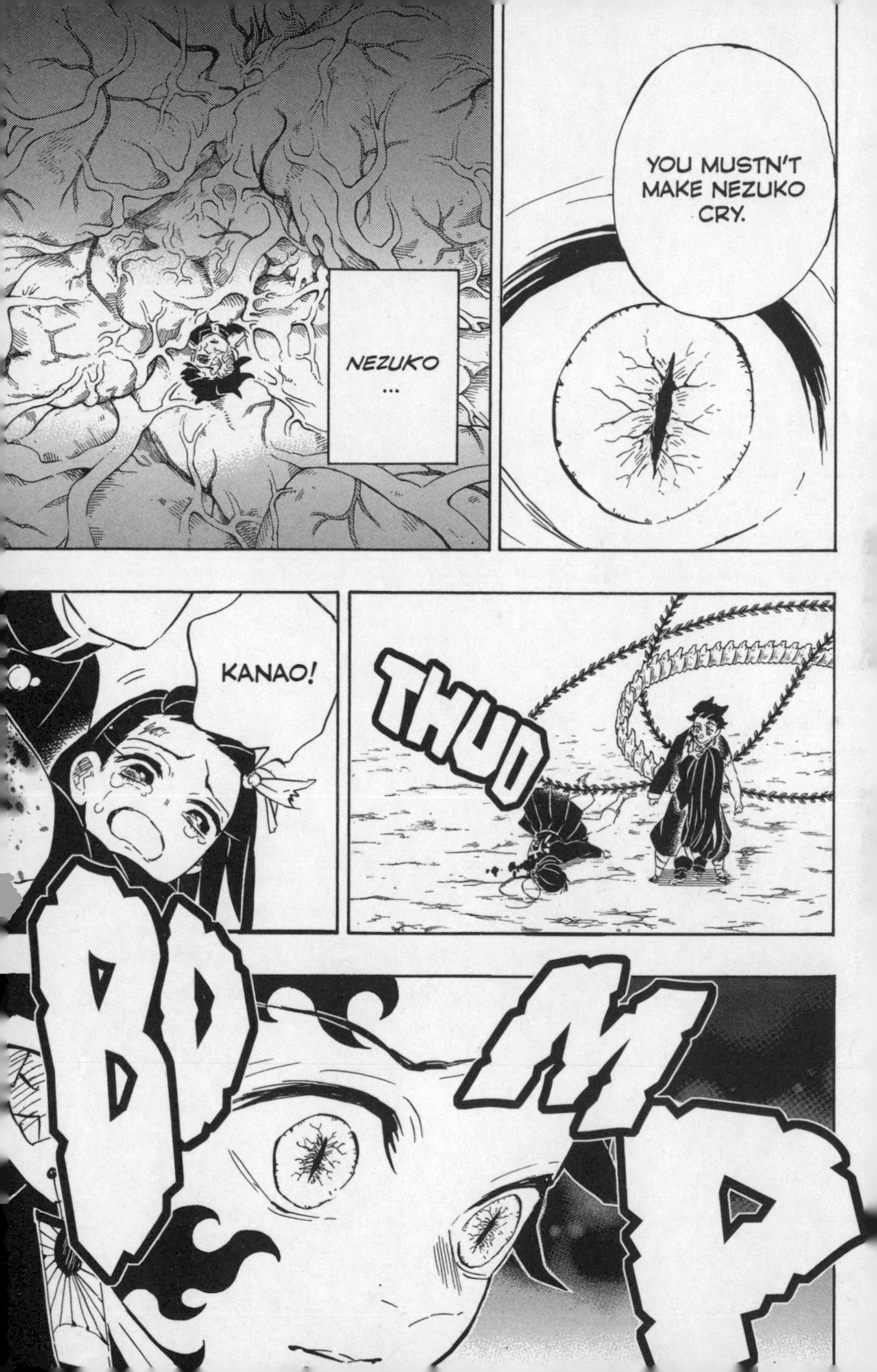
YOU MUSTN'T MAKE NEZUKO CRY.
NEZUKO ...
THUD
KANAO!
BDMP

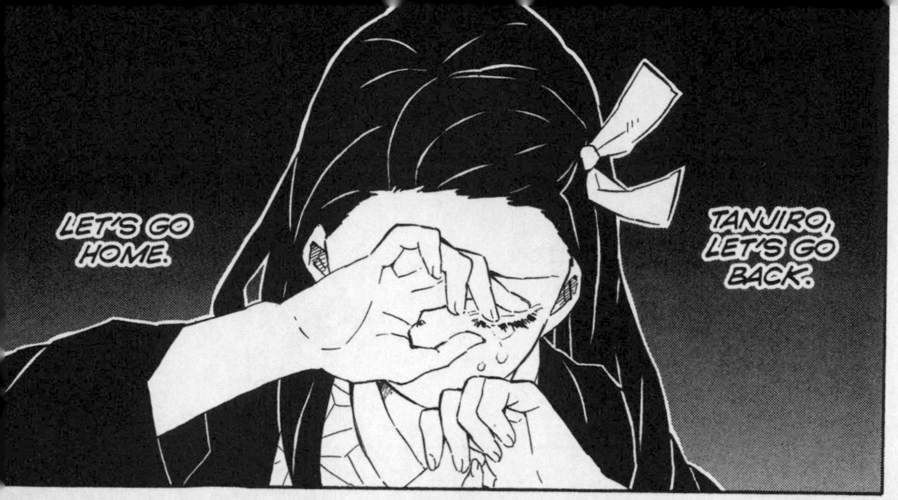
TANJIRO, LET'S GO BACK.
LET'S GO HOME.

CHAPTER 203: VOICES OF ENCOURAGEMENT

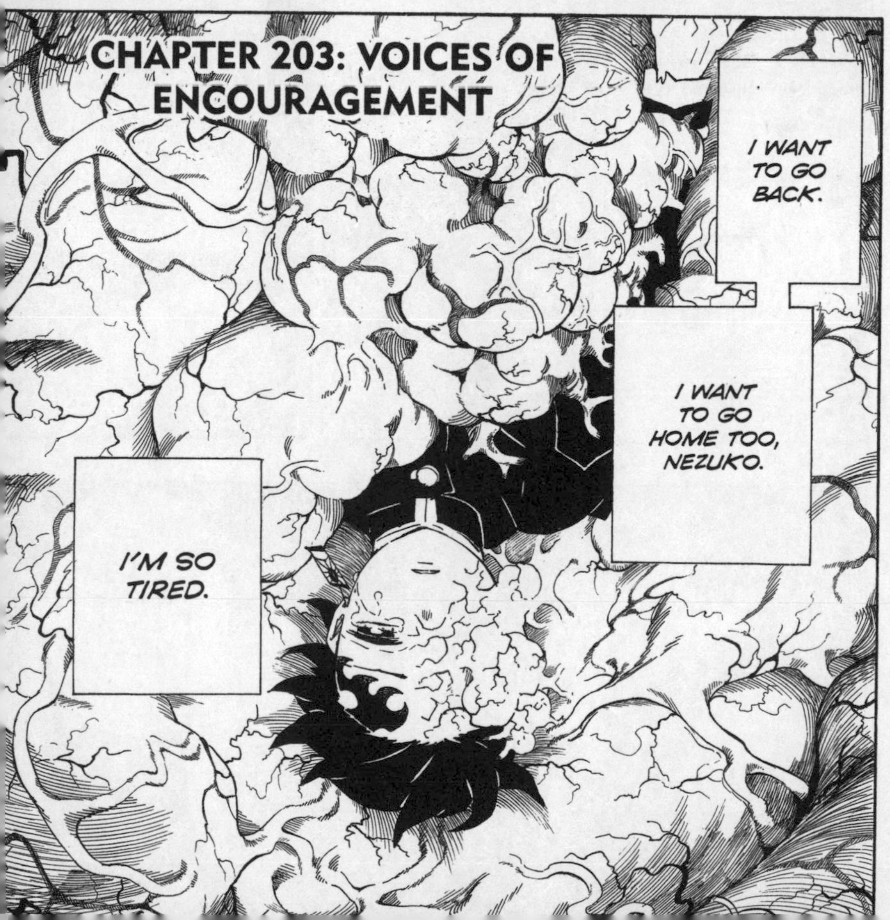
I WANT TO GO BACK.
I WANT TO GO HOME TOO, NEZUKO.
I'M SO TIRED.

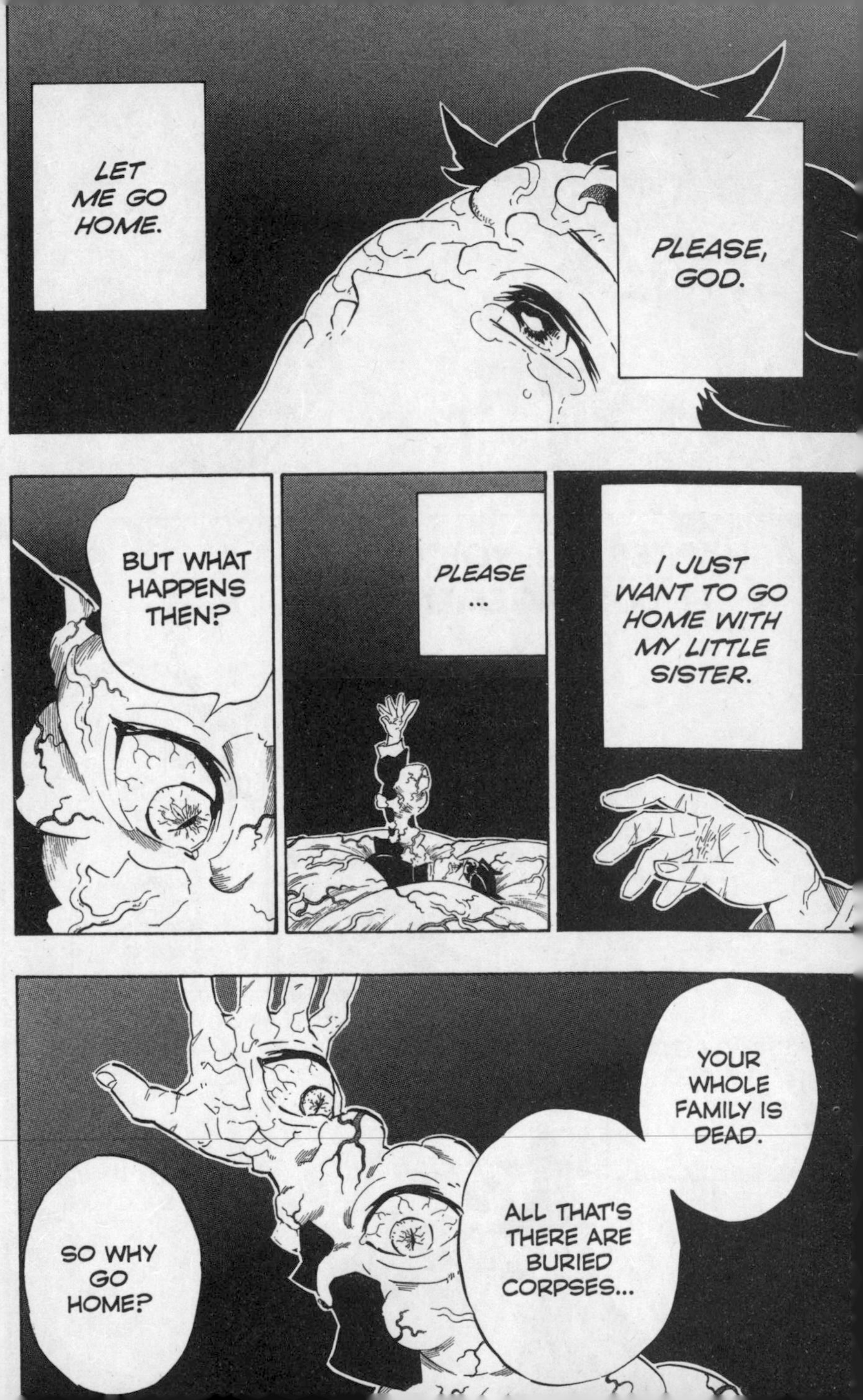
PLEASE, GOD.
LET ME GO HOME.
I JUST WANT TO GO HOME WITH MY LITTLE SISTER.
PLEASE ...
BUT WHAT HAPPENS THEN?
YOUR WHOLE FAMILY IS DEAD.
ALL THAT'S THERE ARE BURIED CORPSES...
SO WHY GO HOME?

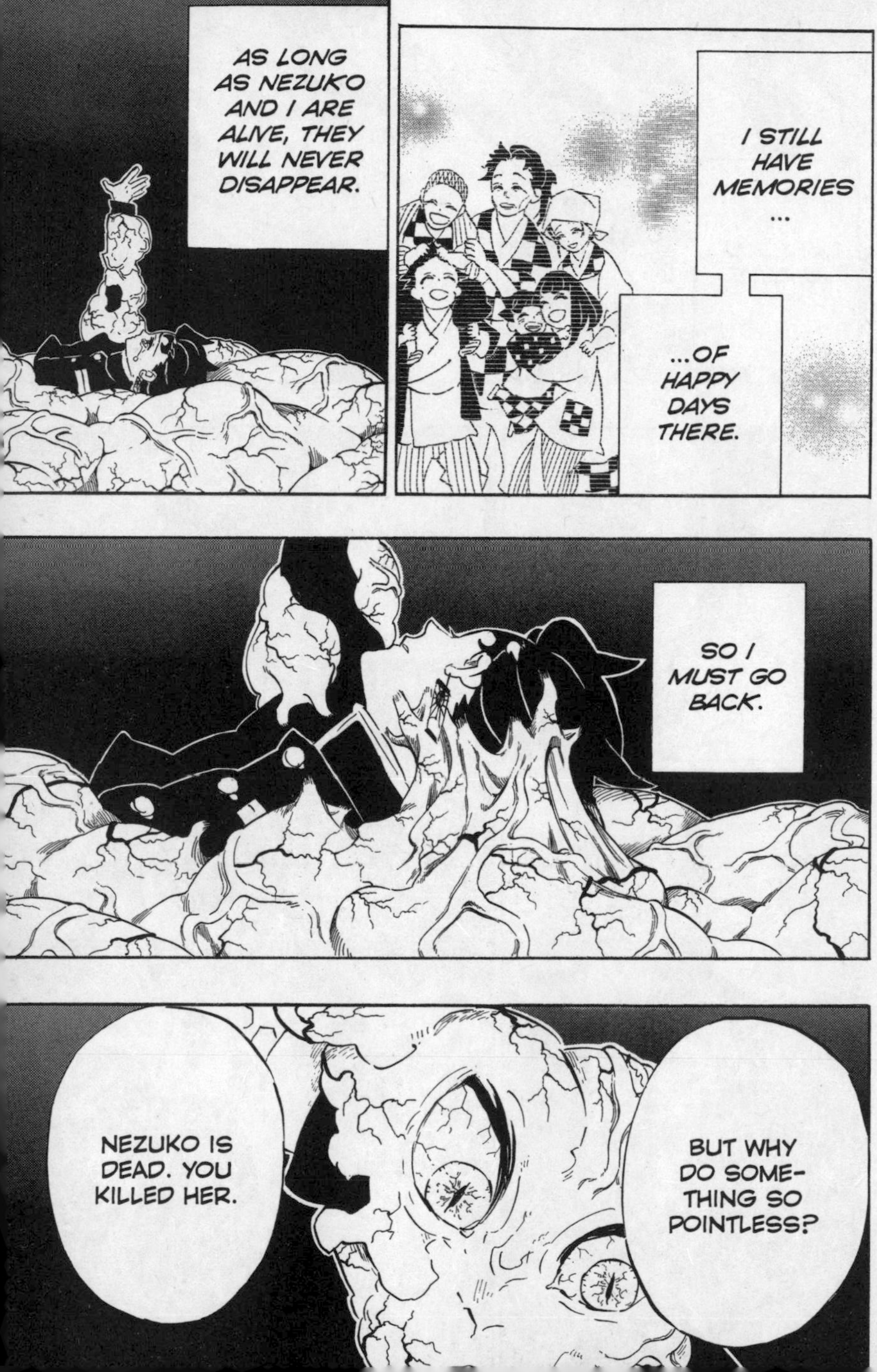
I STILL HAVE MEMORIES ...
...OF HAPPY DAYS THERE.
AS LONG AS NEZUKO AND I ARE ALIVE, THEY WILL NEVER DISAPPEAR.
SO I MUST GO BACK.
BUT WHY DO SOME-THING SO POINTLESS?
NEZUKO IS DEAD. YOU KILLED HER.

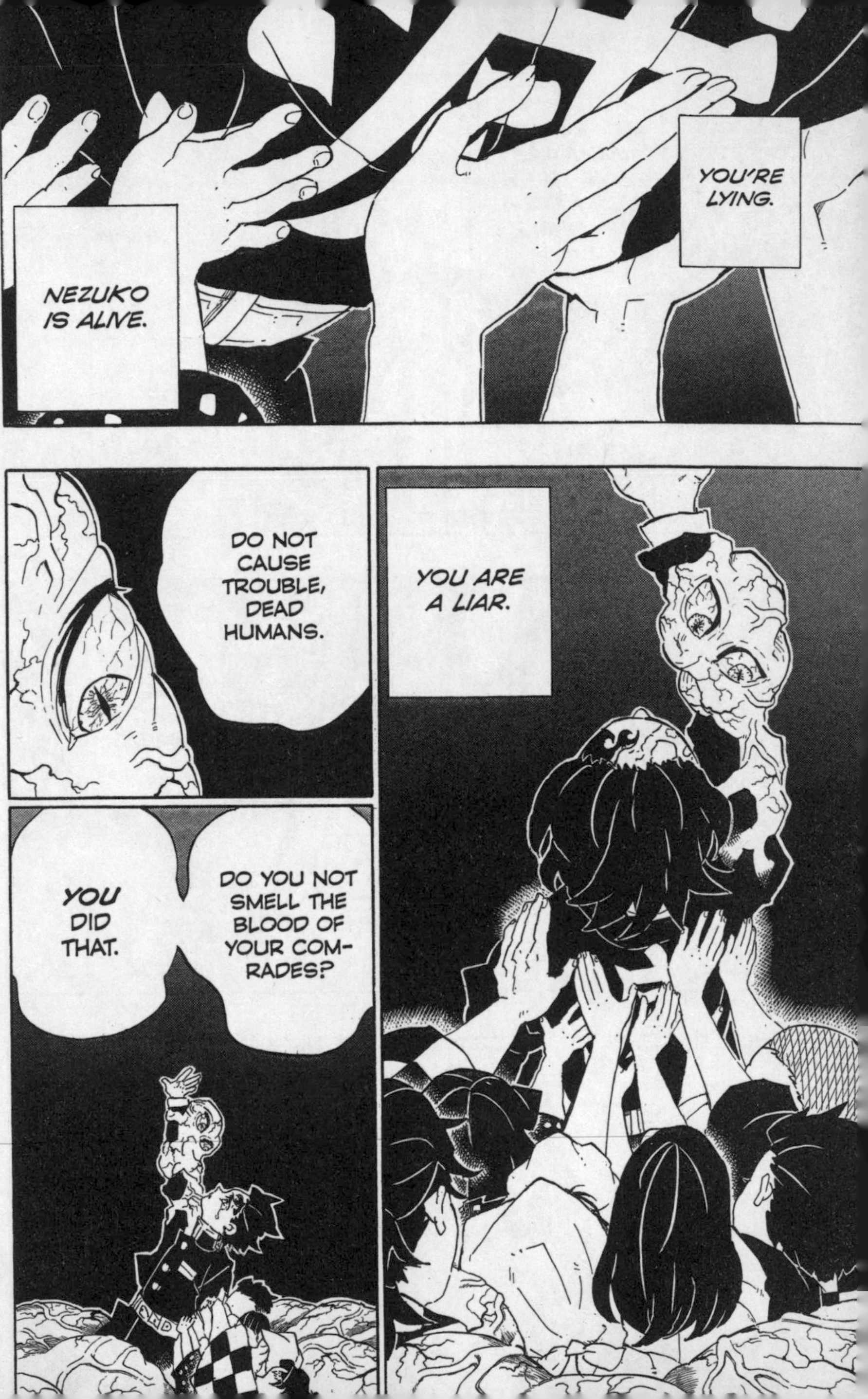
YOU'RE LYING.
NEZUKO IS ALIVE.
YOU ARE A LIAR.
DO NOT CAUSE TROUBLE, DEAD HUMANS.
DO YOU NOT SMELL THE BLOOD OF YOUR COM-RADES?
YOU DID THAT.

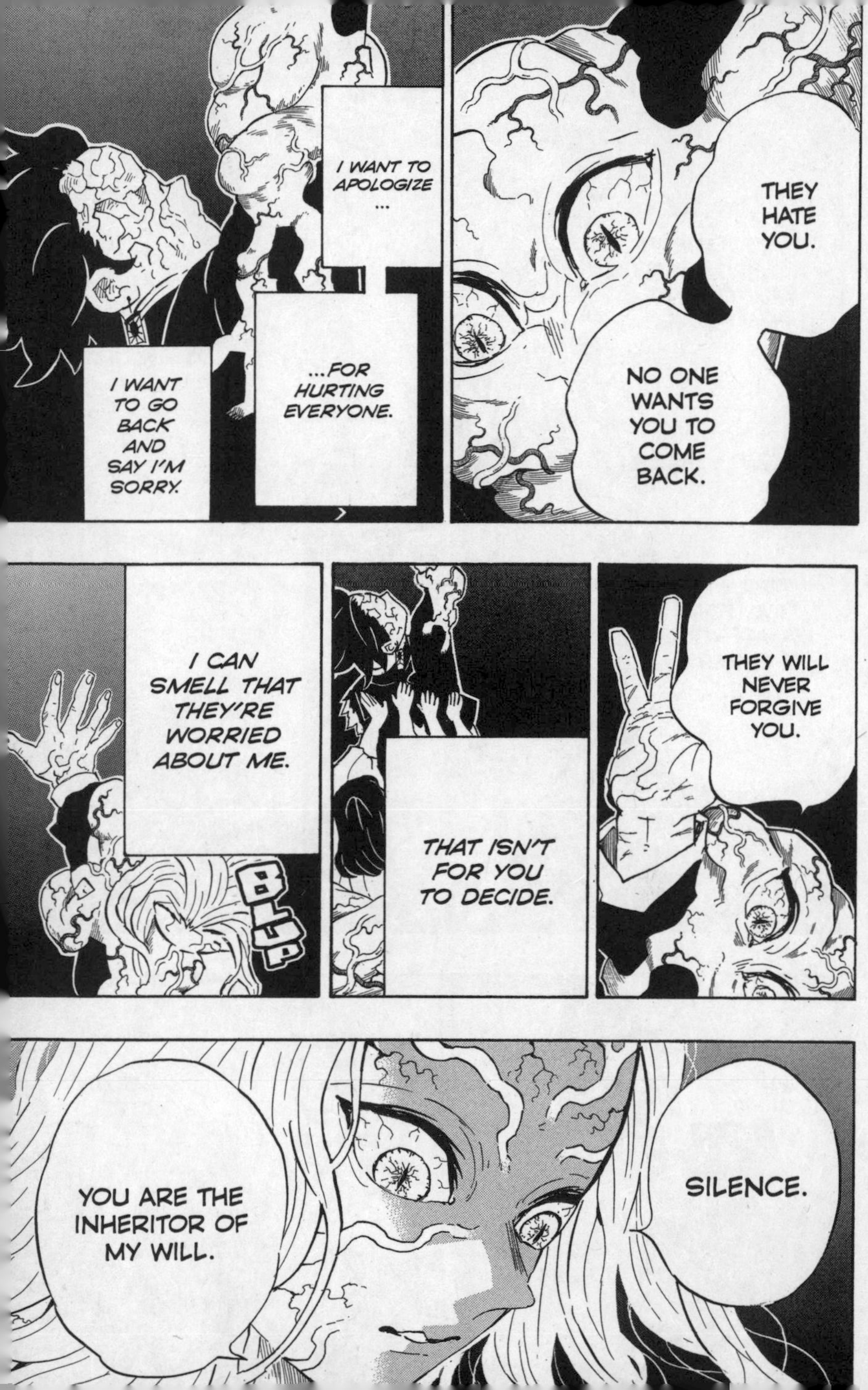
THEY HATE YOU.
NO ONE WANTS YOU TO COME BACK.
I WANT TO APOLOGIZE ...
...FOR HURTING EVERYONE.
I WANT TO GO BACK AND SAY I'M SORRY.
THEY WILL NEVER FORGIVE YOU.
THAT ISN'T FOR YOU TO DECIDE.
I CAN SMELL THAT THEY'RE WORRIED ABOUT ME.
BLUP
SILENCE.
YOU ARE THE INHERITOR OF MY WILL.

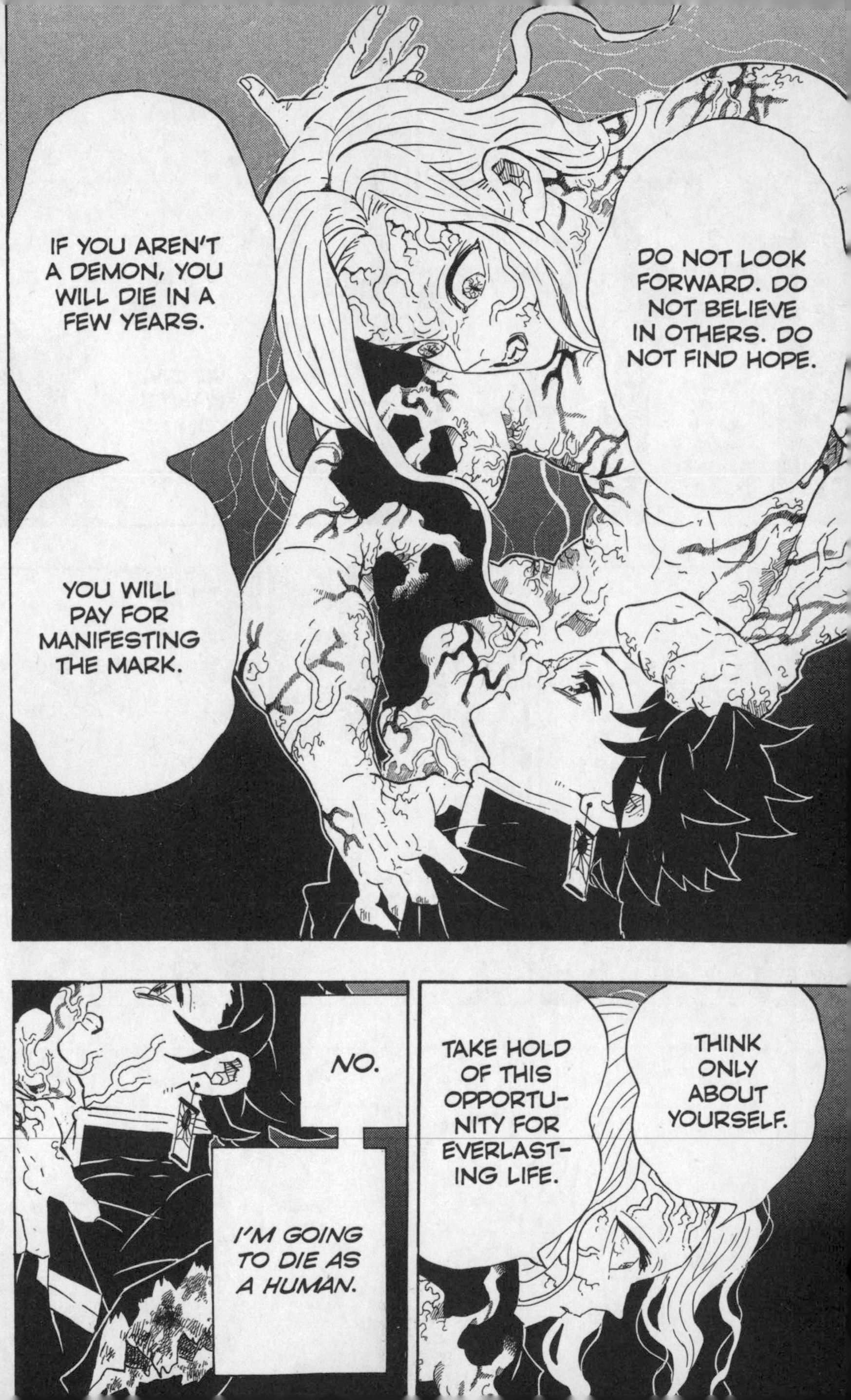
DO NOT LOOK FORWARD. DO NOT BELIEVE IN OTHERS. DO NOT FIND HOPE.
IF YOU AREN'T A DEMON, YOU WILL DIE IN A FEW YEARS.
YOU WILL PAY FOR MANIFESTING THE MARK.
THINK ONLY ABOUT YOURSELF.
TAKE HOLD OF THIS OPPORTUNITY FOR EVERLASTING LIFE.
NO.
I'M GOING TO DIE AS A HUMAN.

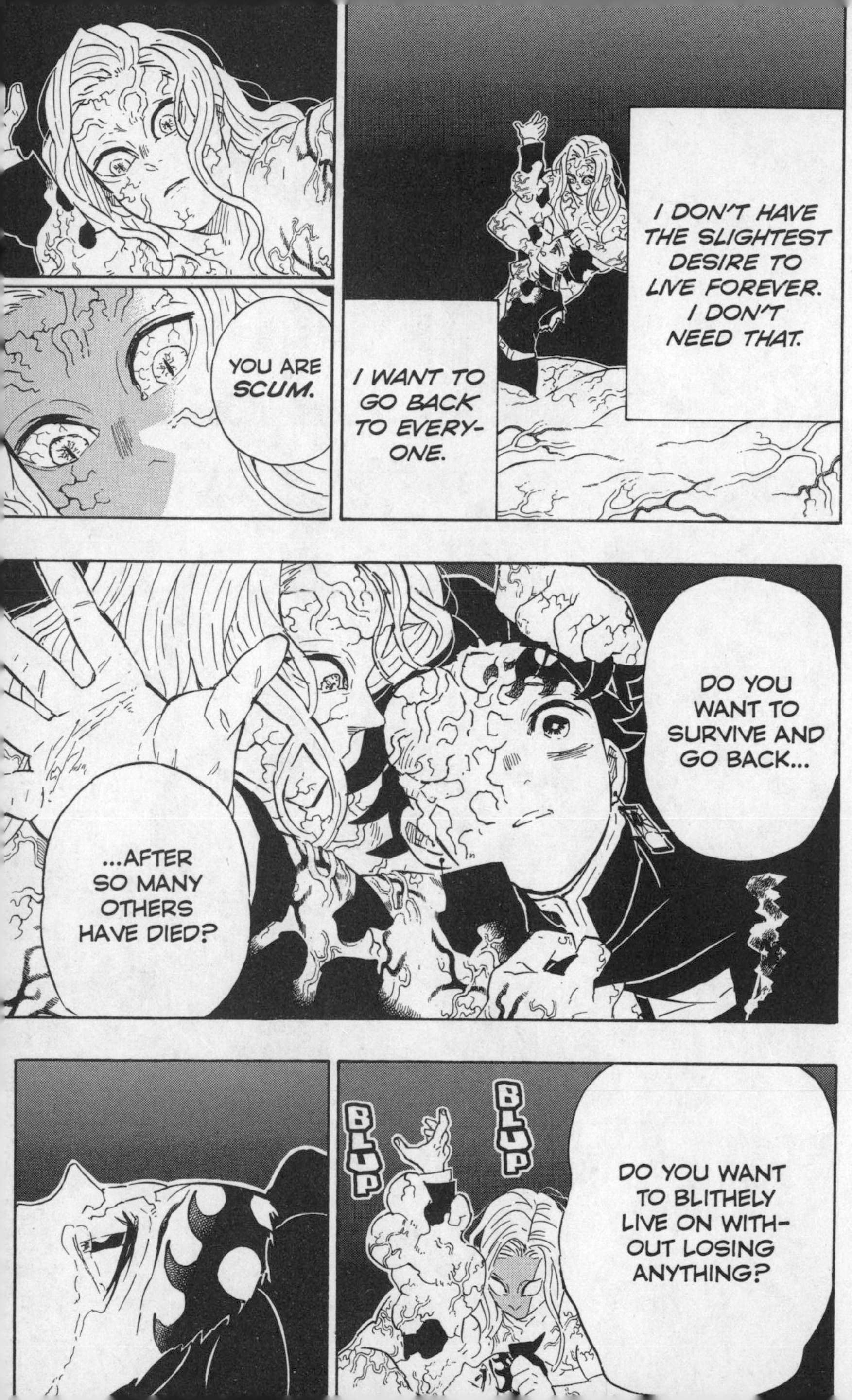
I DON'T HAVE THE SLIGHTEST DESIRE TO LIVE FOREVER. I DON'T NEED THAT.
I WANT TO GO BACK TO EVERY-ONE.
YOU ARE SCUM.
DO YOU WANT TO SURVIVE AND GO BACK...
...AFTER SO MANY OTHERS HAVE DIED?
BLUP
BLUP
DO YOU WANT TO BLITHELY LIVE ON WITH-OUT LOSING ANYTHING?

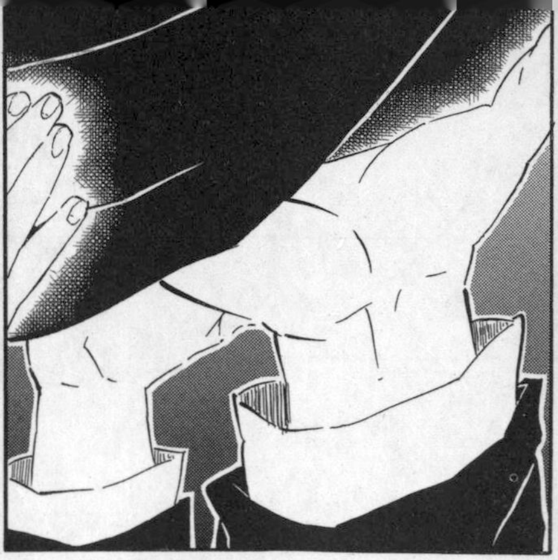
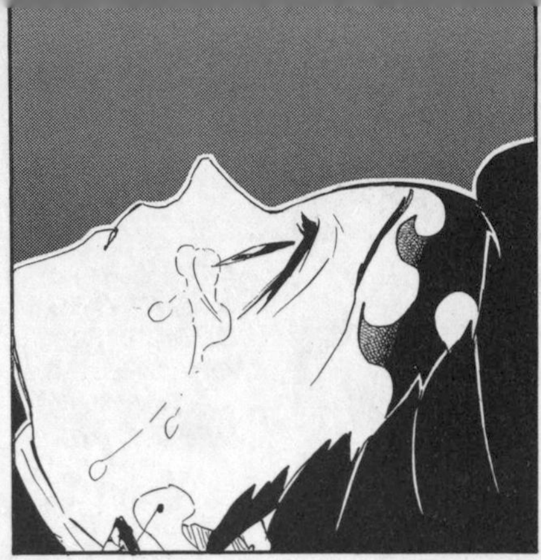
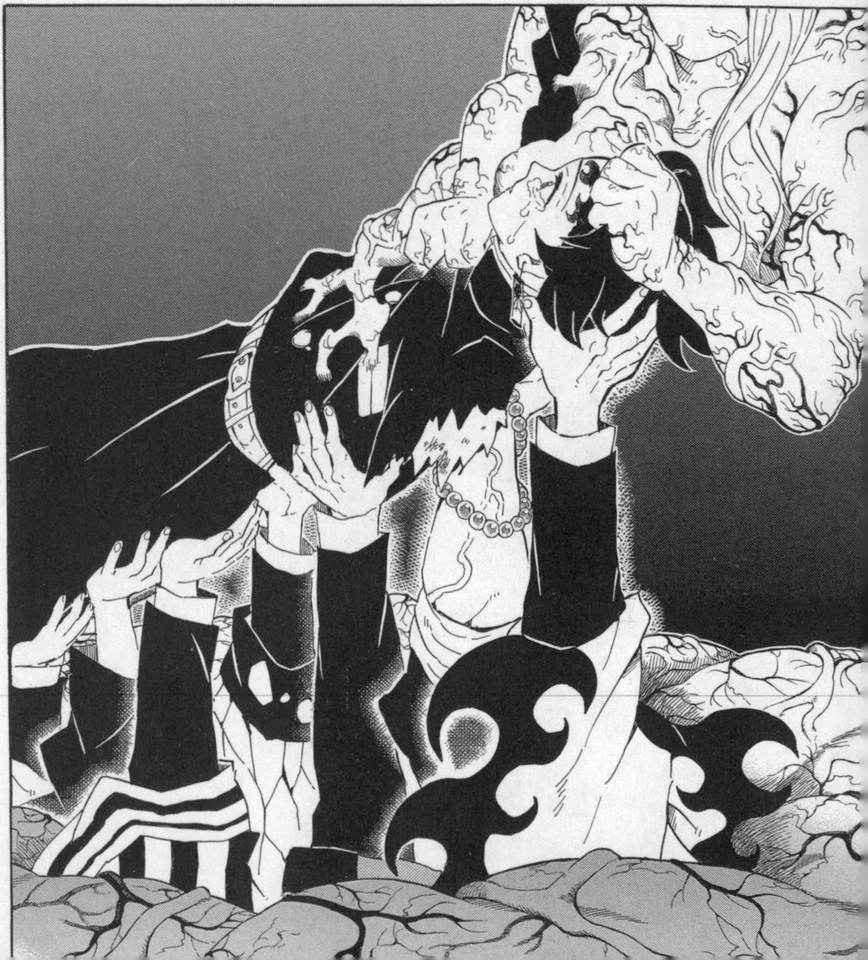

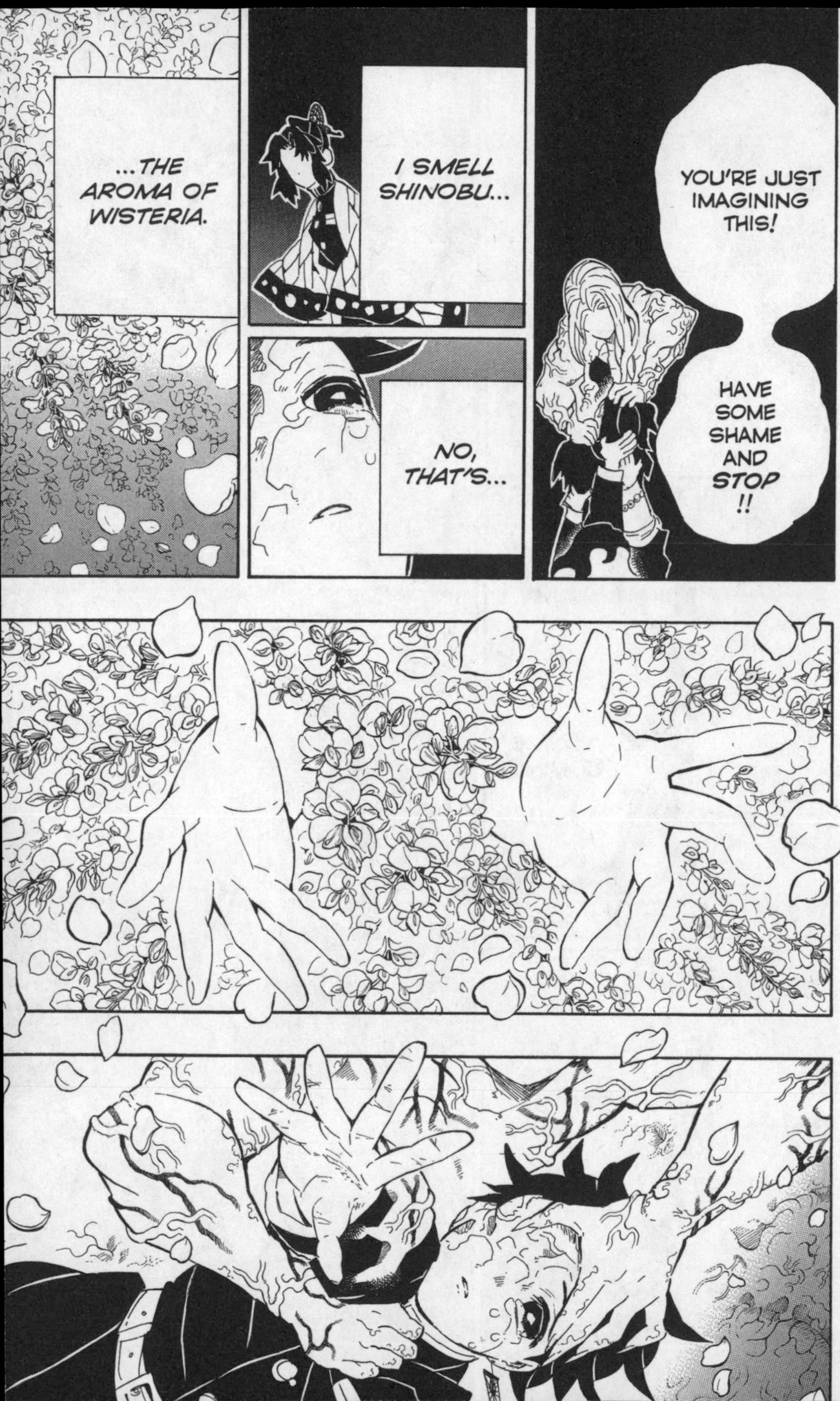
YOU'RE JUST IMAGINING THIS!
HAVE SOME SHAME AND STOP!!
I SMELL SHINOBU...
NO, THAT'S...
...THE AROMA OF WISTERIA.

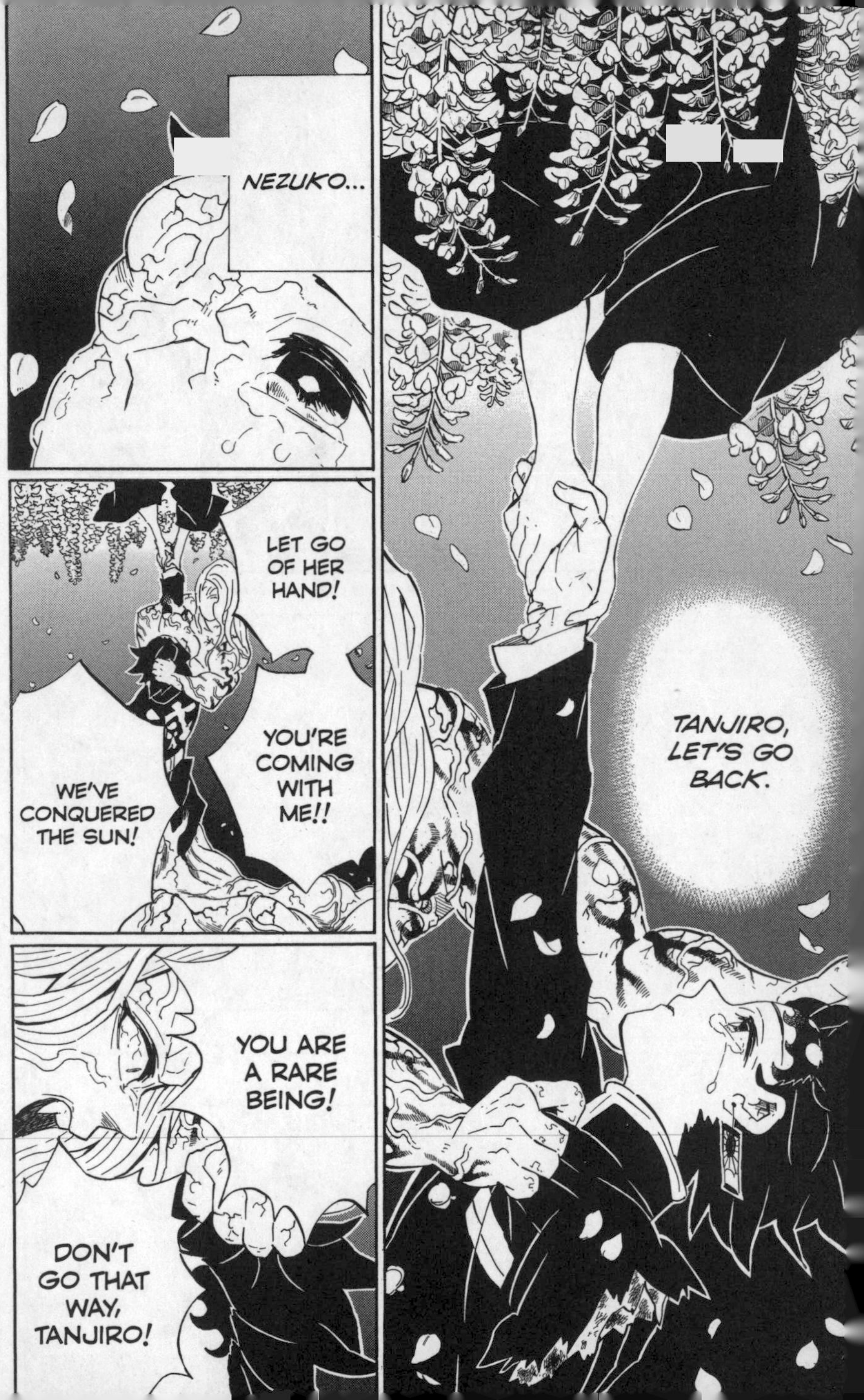
TANJIRO, LET'S GO BACK.
NEZUKO...
LET GO OF HER HAND!
YOU'RE COMING WITH ME!!
WE'VE CONQUERED THE SUN!
YOU ARE A RARE BEING!
DON'T GO THAT WAY, TANJIRO!

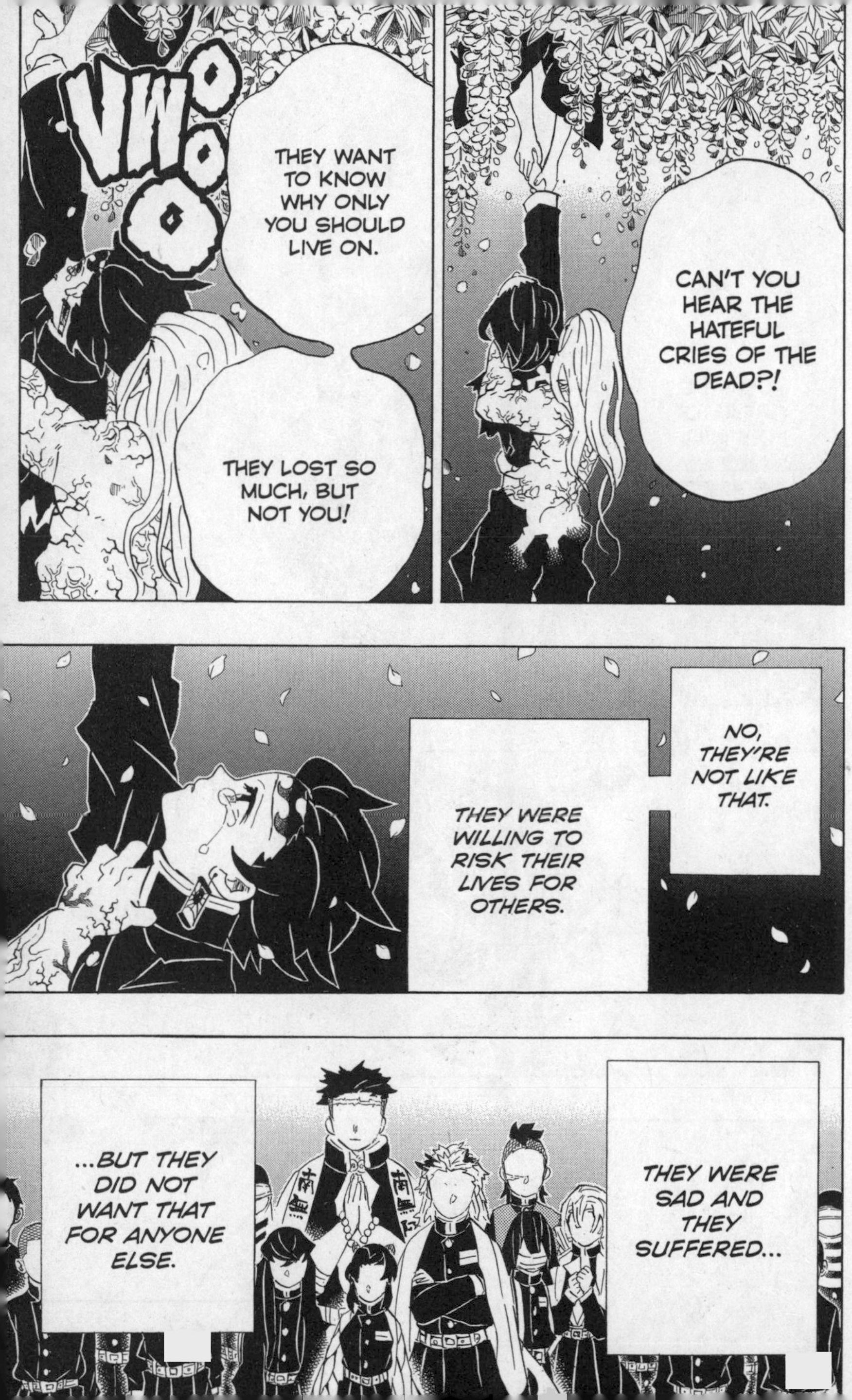
CAN'T YOU HEAR THE HATEFUL CRIES OF THE DEAD?!
THEY WANT TO KNOW WHY ONLY YOU SHOULD LIVE ON.
VWOOO
THEY LOST SO MUCH, BUT NOT YOU!
NO, THEY'RE NOT LIKE THAT.
THEY WERE WILLING TO RISK THEIR LIVES FOR OTHERS.
THEY WERE SAD AND THEY SUFFERED...
...BUT THEY DID NOT WANT THAT FOR ANYONE ELSE.

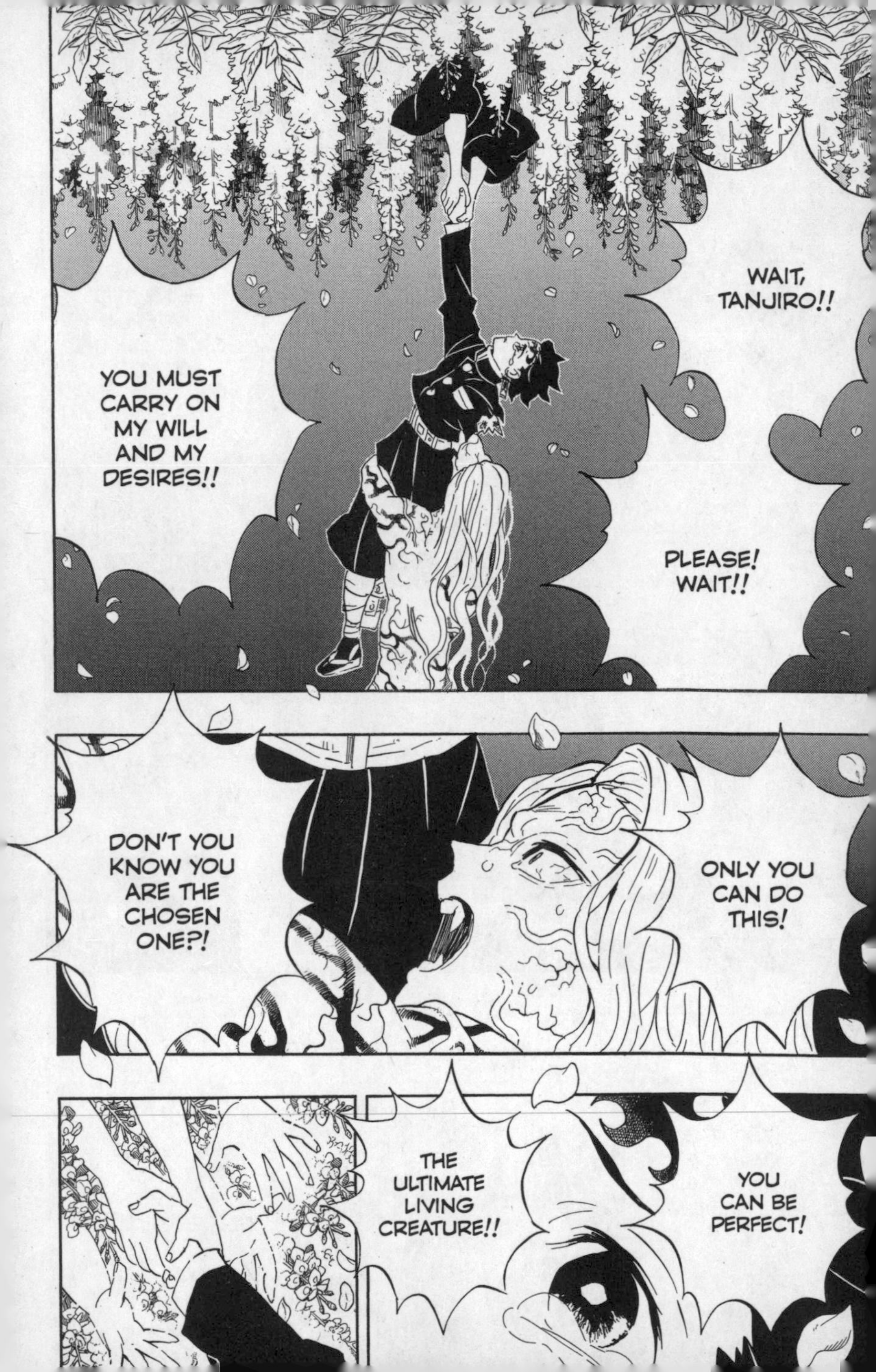
WAIT, TANJIRO!!
PLEASE! WAIT!!
YOU MUST CARRY ON MY WILL AND MY DESIRES!!
ONLY YOU CAN DO THIS!
DON'T YOU KNOW YOU ARE THE CHOSEN ONE?!
YOU CAN BE PERFECT!
THE ULTIMATE LIVING CREATURE!!

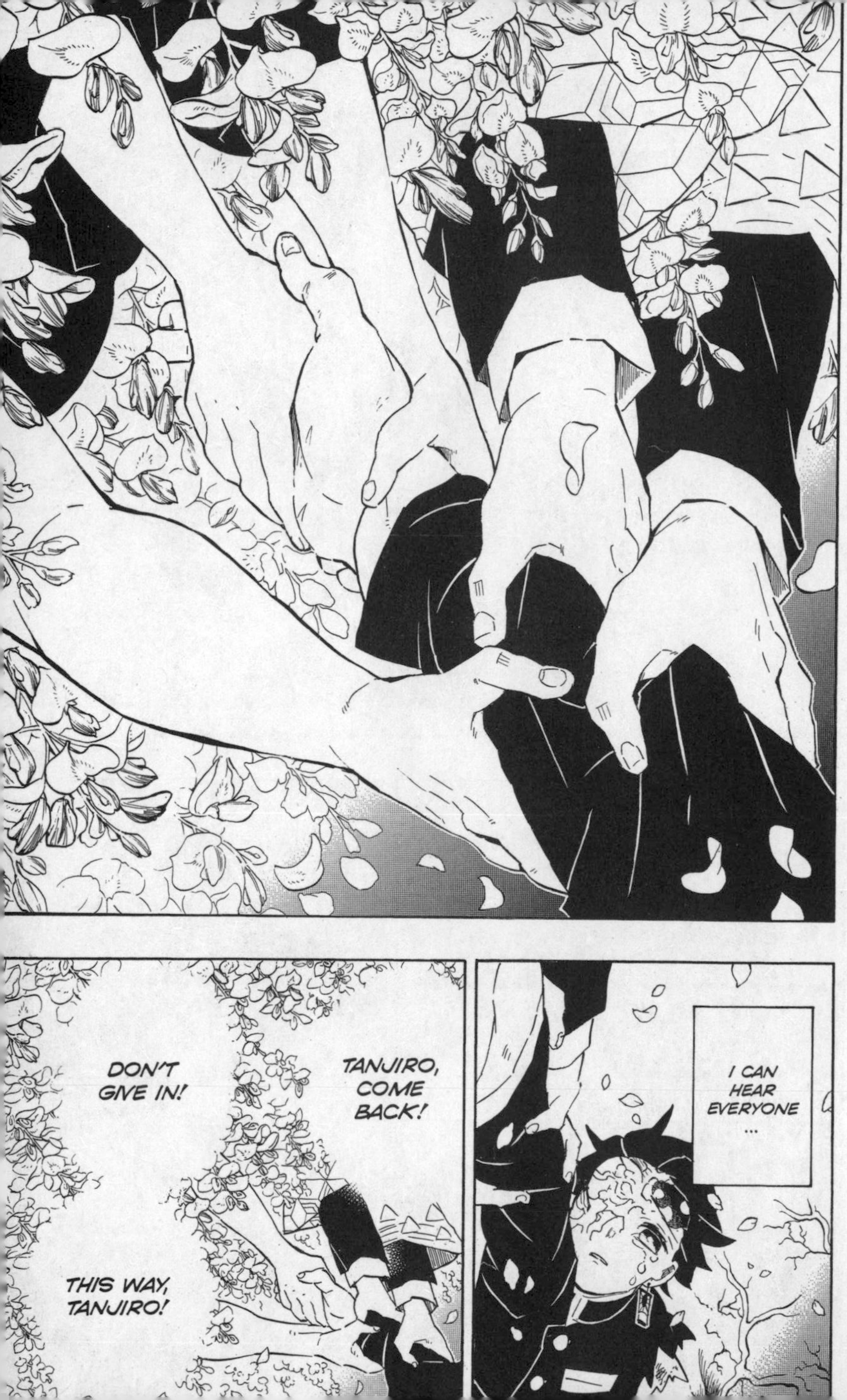
I CAN HEAR EVERYONE ...
TANJIRO, COME BACK!
DON'T GIVE IN!
THIS WAY, TANJIRO!

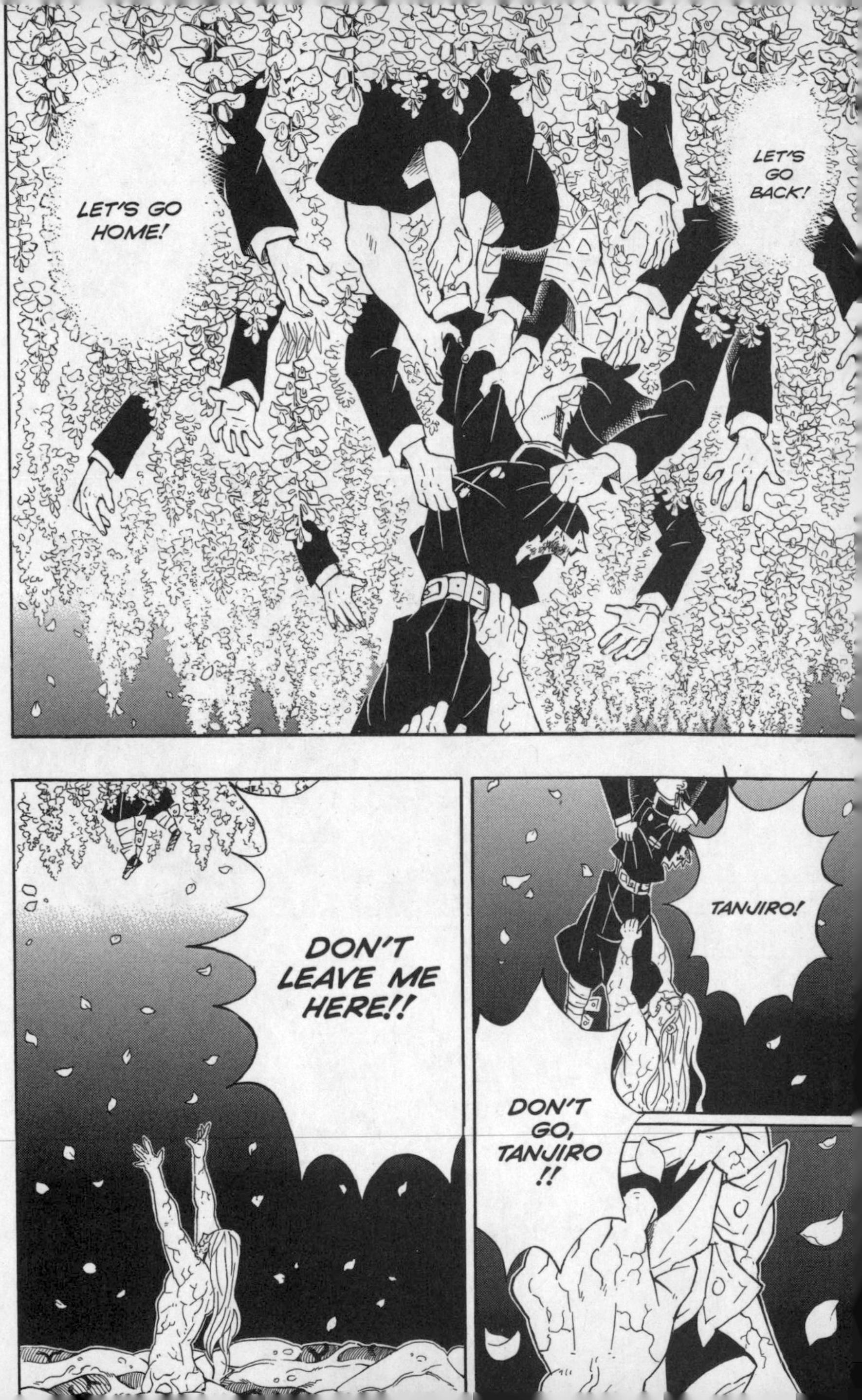
LET'S GO BACK!
LET'S GO HOME!
TANJIRO!
DON'T GO, TANJIRO!!
DON'T LEAVE ME HERE!!

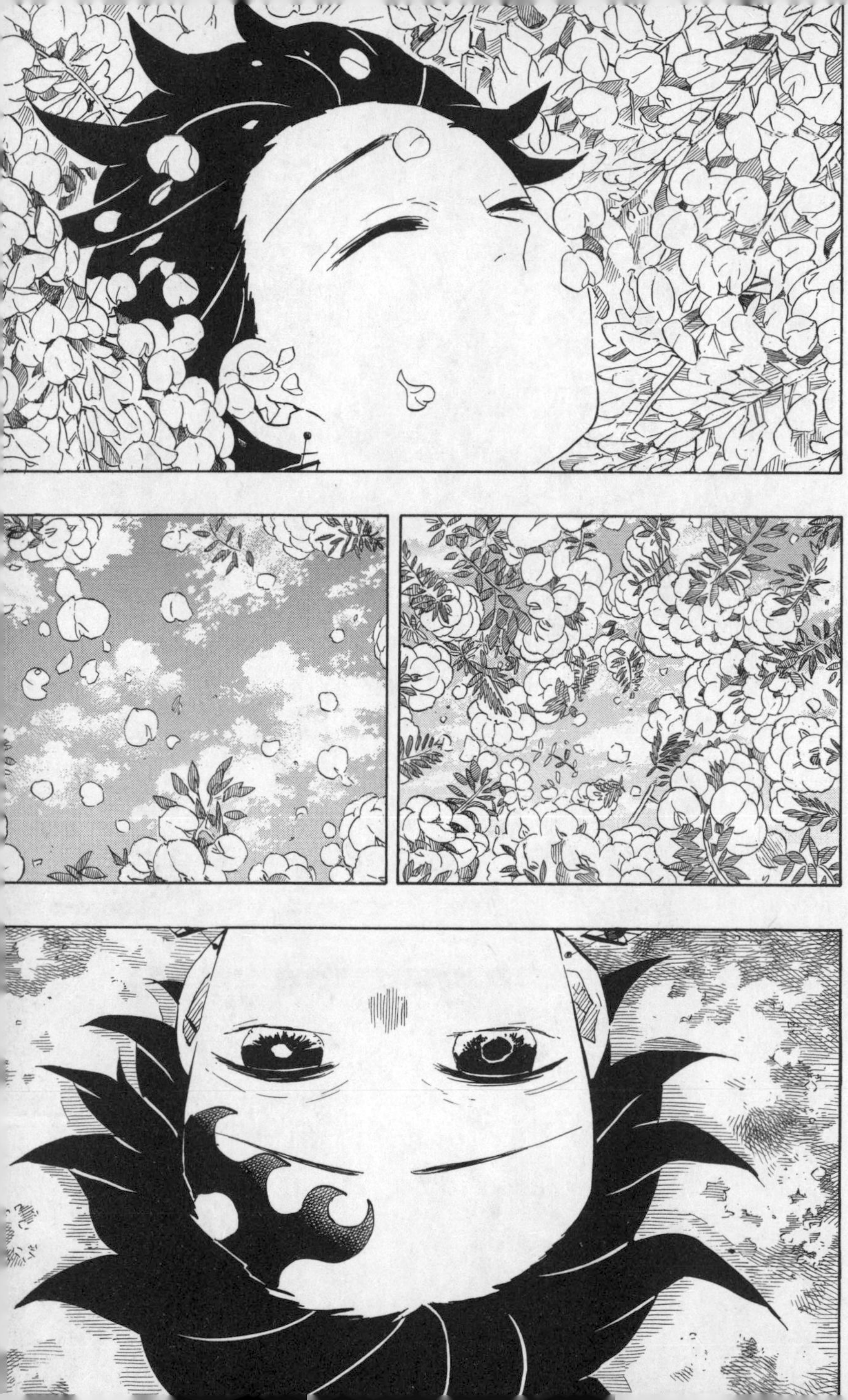

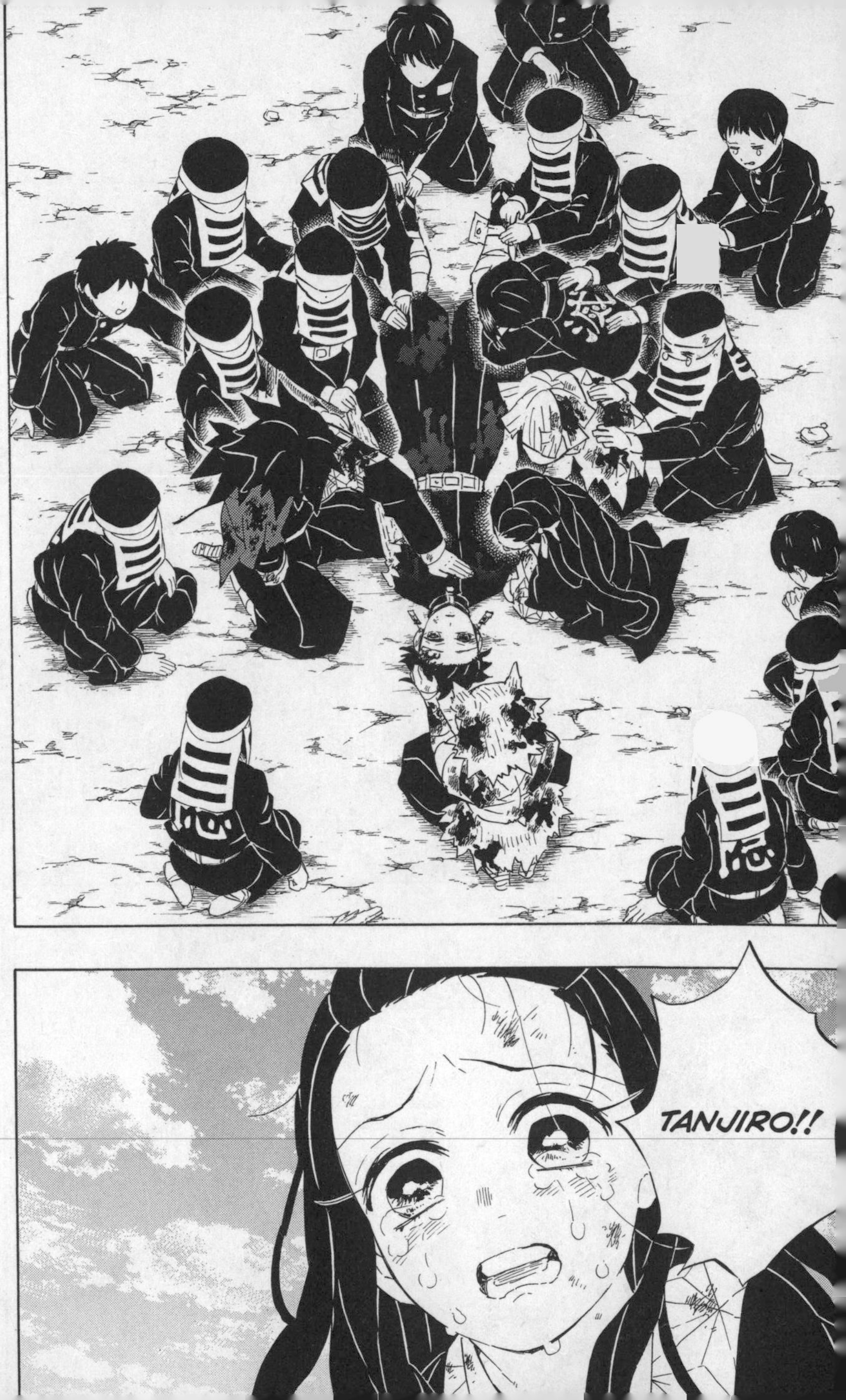
TANJIRO!!

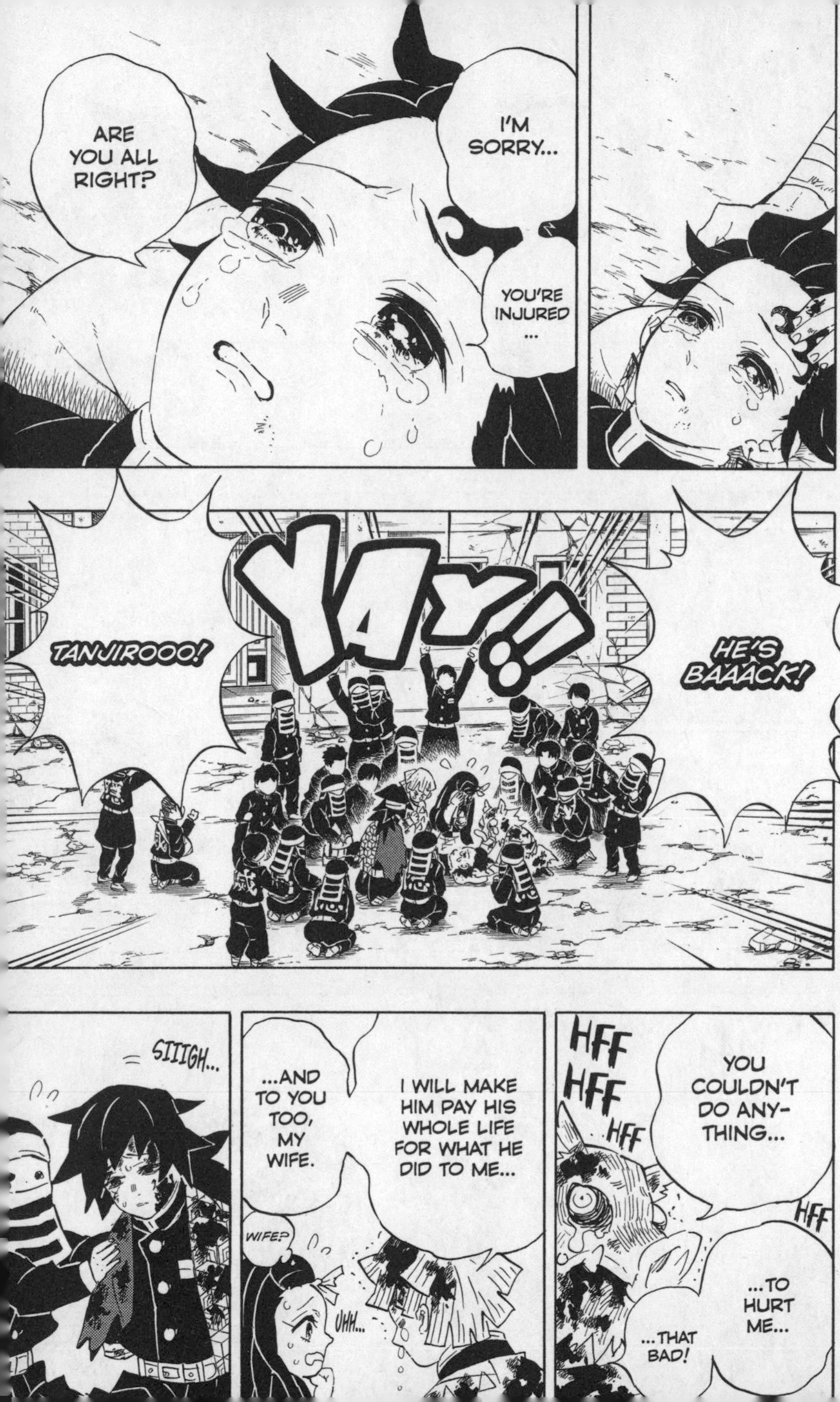

I'M SORRY...
YOU'RE INJURED...
ARE YOU ALL RIGHT?
HE'S BAAACK!
YAY!!
TANJIROOO!
YOU COULDN'T DO ANY-THING...
HFF HFF HFF
HFF
...TO HURT ME...
...THAT BAD!
I WILL MAKE HIM PAY HIS WHOLE LIFE FOR WHAT HE DID TO ME...
...AND TO YOU TOO, MY WIFE.
WIFE?
UHH...
SIIIGH...

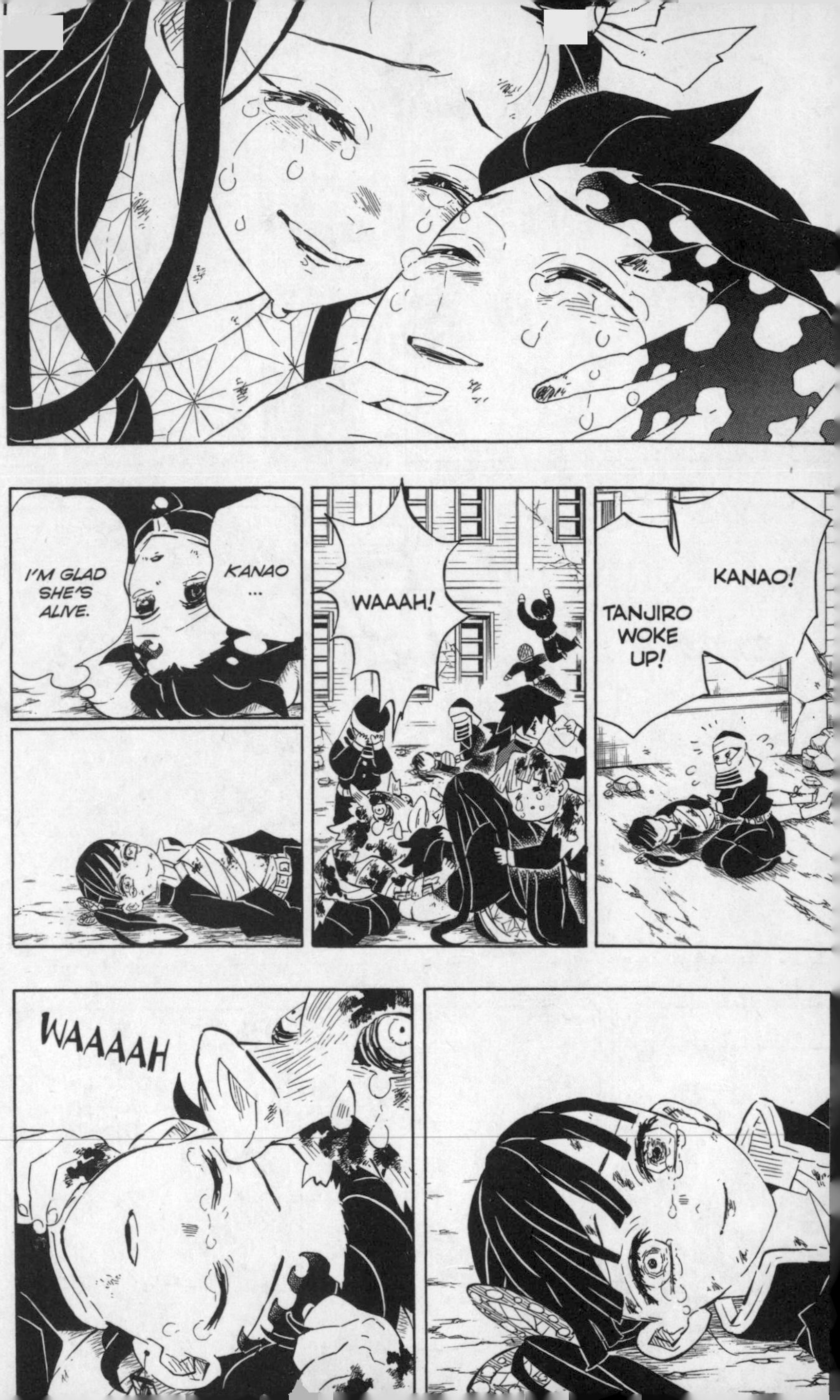
KANAO!
TANJIRO WOKE UP!
WAAAH!
KANAO ...
I'M GLAD SHE'S ALIVE.
WAAAAH

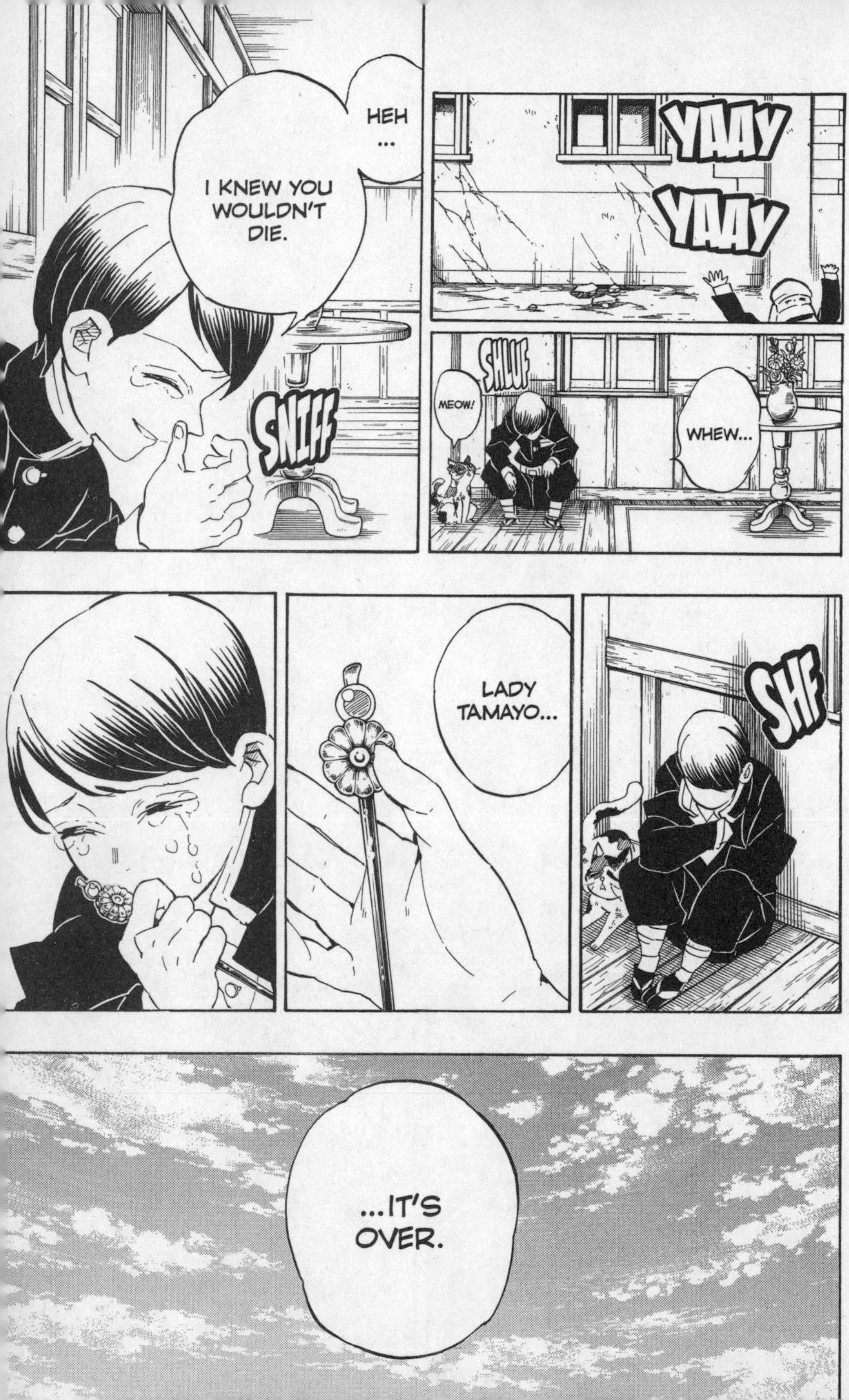
YAAY
YAAY
WHEW...
SHLUF
MEOW!
HEH ...
I KNEW YOU WOULDN'T DIE.
SNIFF
SHF
LADY TAMAYO...
...IT'S OVER.

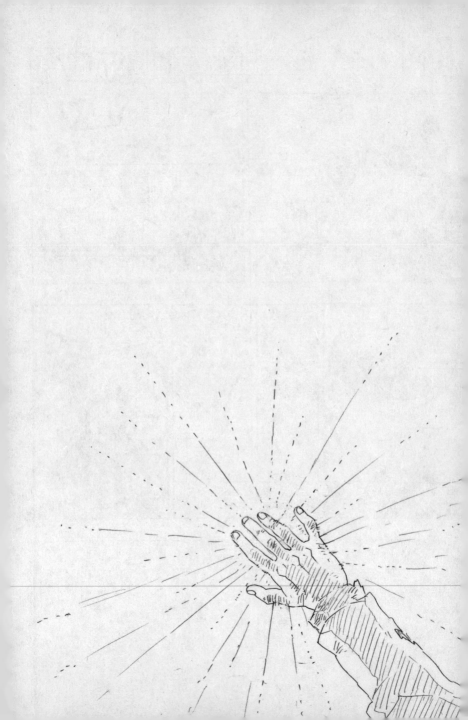

CHAPTER 204: A WORLD WITHOUT DEMONS

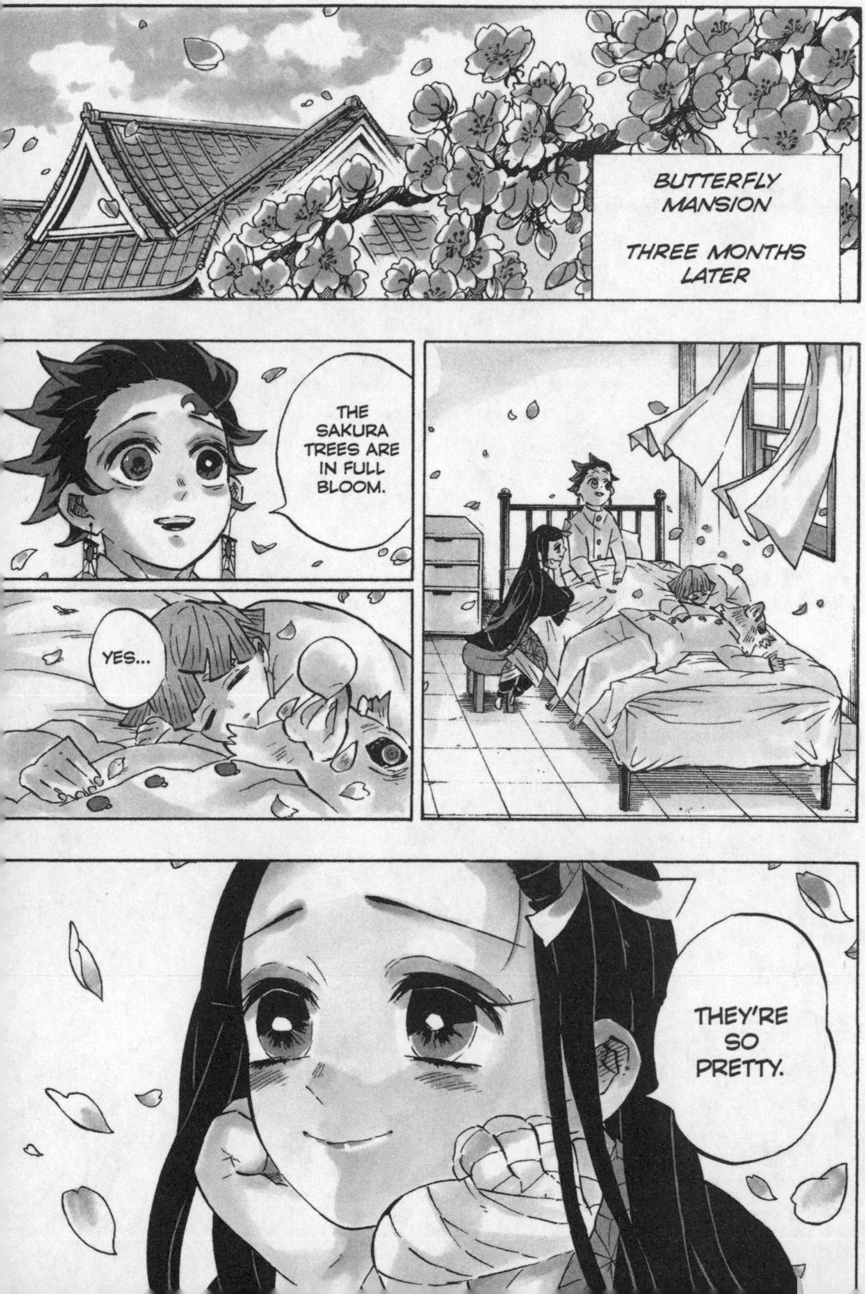
BUTTERFLY MANSION
THREE MONTHS LATER
THE SAKURA TREES ARE IN FULL BLOOM.
YES...
THEY'RE SO PRETTY.

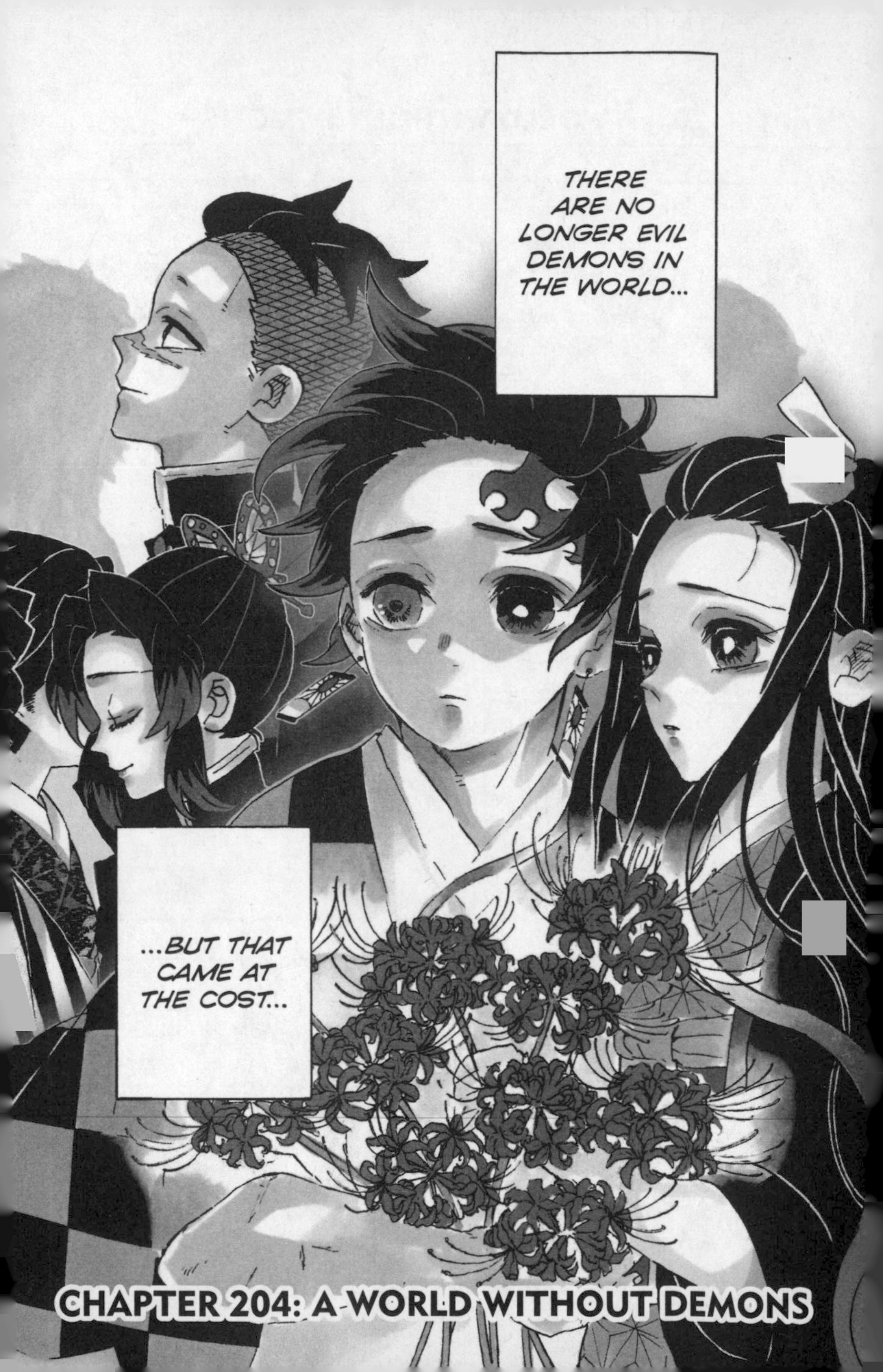
THERE ARE NO LONGER EVIL DEMONS IN THE WORLD...
...BUT THAT CAME AT THE COST...
CHAPTER 204: A WORLD WITHOUT DEMONS

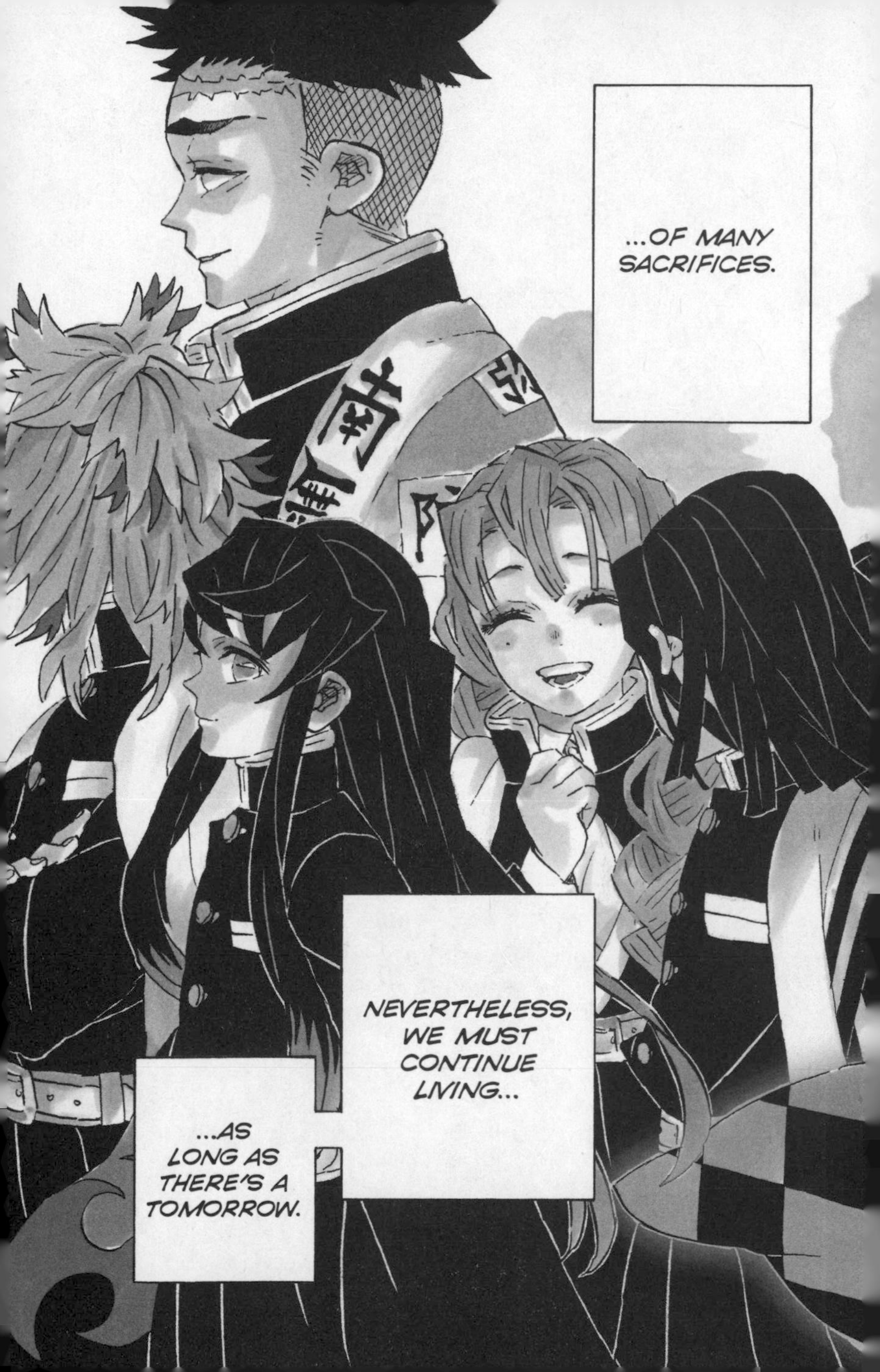
...OF MANY SACRIFICES.
NEVERTHELESS, WE MUST CONTINUE LIVING...
...AS LONG AS THERE'S A TOMORROW.

Wisteria Houses received word of the final battle, so many people spent the night praying for the corps members' safety and success. Exhausted crows went to inform them of victory.

PUFF

WHEEZ

HUFF

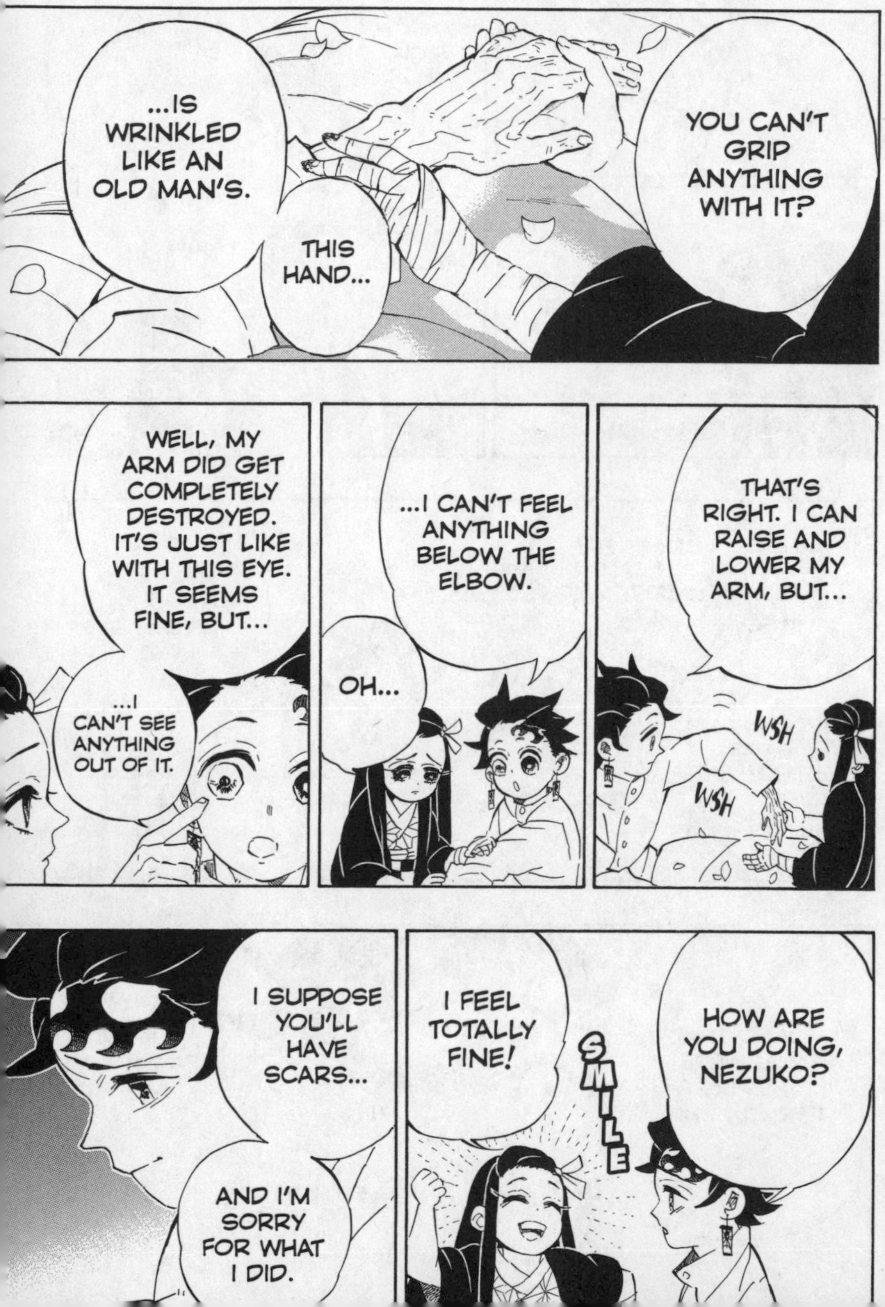
YOU CAN'T GRIP ANYTHING WITH IT?
THIS HAND...
...IS WRINKLED LIKE AN OLD MAN'S.
THAT'S RIGHT. I CAN RAISE AND LOWER MY ARM, BUT...
WSH
WSH
...I CAN'T FEEL ANYTHING BELOW THE ELBOW.
OH...
WELL, MY ARM DID GET COMPLETELY DESTROYED. IT'S JUST LIKE WITH THIS EYE. IT SEEMS FINE, BUT...
...I CAN'T SEE ANYTHING OUT OF IT.
HOW ARE YOU DOING, NEZUKO?
SMILE
I FEEL TOTALLY FINE!
I SUPPOSE YOU'LL HAVE SCARS...
AND I'M SORRY FOR WHAT I DID.

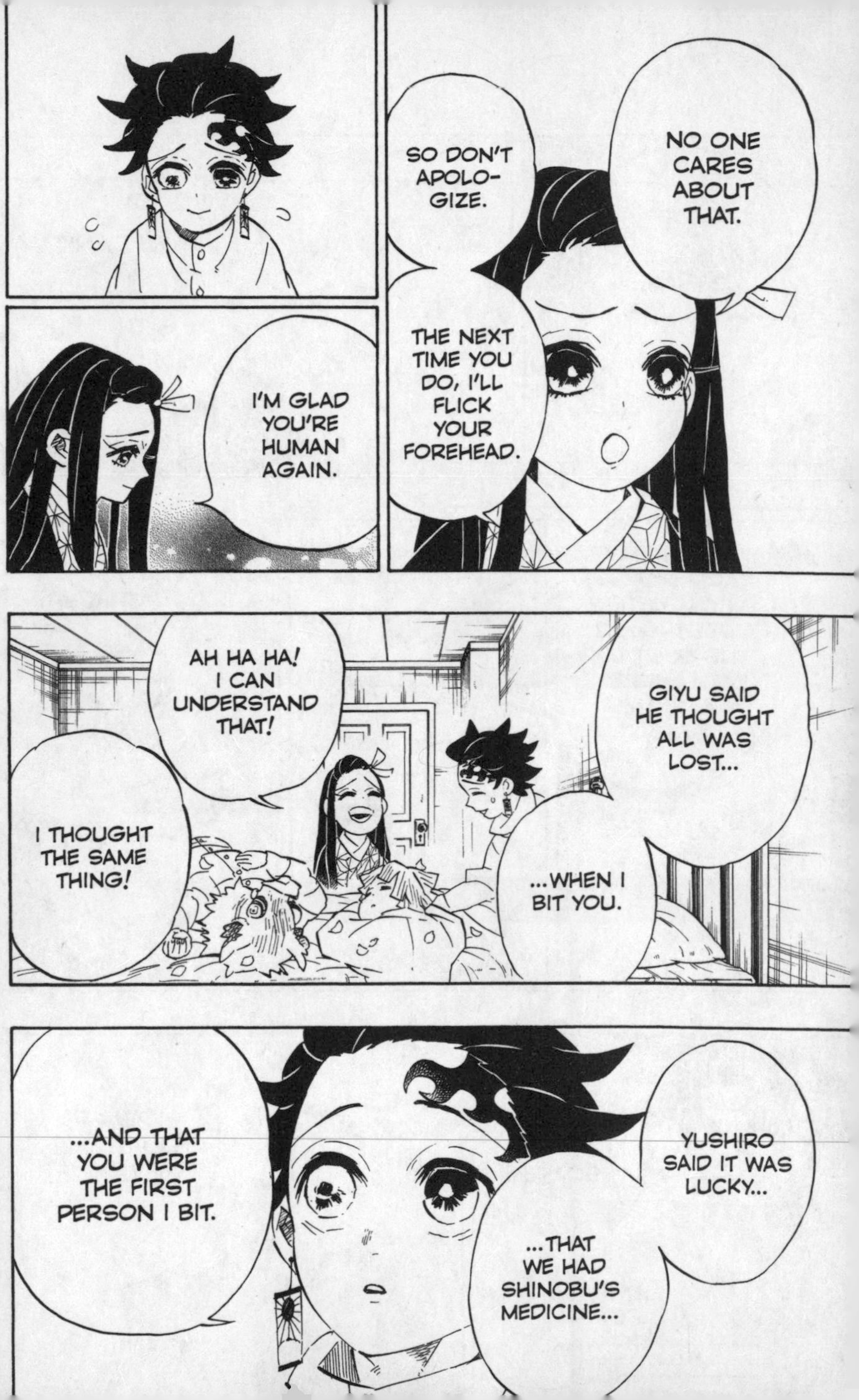
NO ONE CARES ABOUT THAT.
SO DON'T APOLOGIZE.
THE NEXT TIME YOU DO, I'LL FLICK YOUR FOREHEAD.
I'M GLAD YOU'RE HUMAN AGAIN.
GIYU SAID HE THOUGHT ALL WAS LOST...
...WHEN I BIT YOU.
AH HA HA! I CAN UNDERSTAND THAT!
I THOUGHT THE SAME THING!
YUSHIRO SAID IT WAS LUCKY...
...THAT WE HAD SHINOBU'S MEDICINE...
...AND THAT YOU WERE THE FIRST PERSON I BIT.

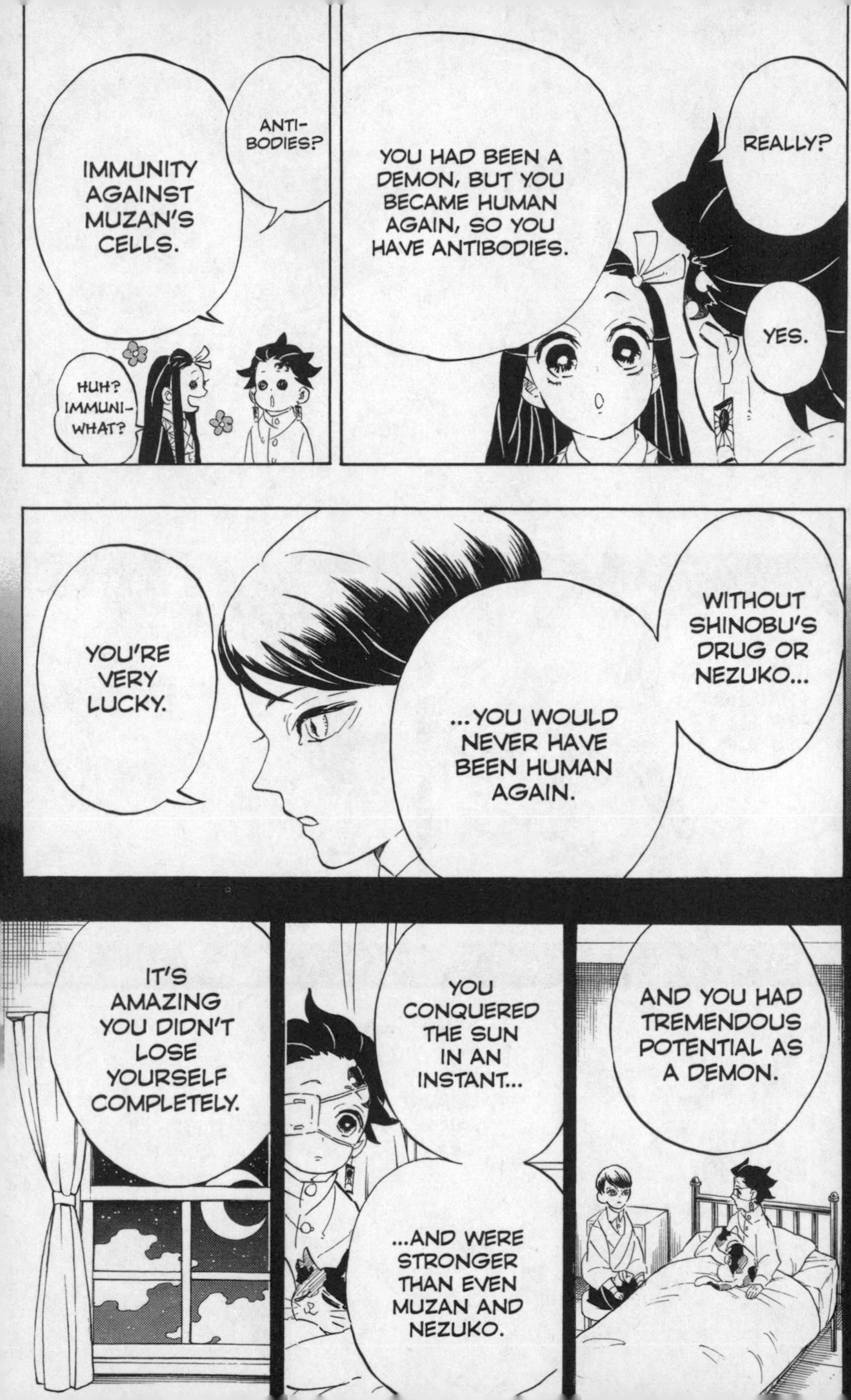
YOU HAD BEEN A DEMON, BUT YOU BECAME HUMAN AGAIN, SO YOU HAVE ANTIBODIES.
REALLY?
YES.
ANTI-BODIES?
IMMUNITY AGAINST MUZAN'S CELLS.
HUH? IMMUNI-WHAT?
WITHOUT SHINOBU'S DRUG OR NEZUKO...
...YOU WOULD NEVER HAVE BEEN HUMAN AGAIN.
YOU'RE VERY LUCKY.
AND YOU HAD TREMENDOUS POTENTIAL AS A DEMON.
YOU CONQUERED THE SUN IN AN INSTANT...
...AND WERE STRONGER THAN EVEN MUZAN AND NEZUKO.
IT'S AMAZING YOU DIDN'T LOSE YOURSELF COMPLETELY.

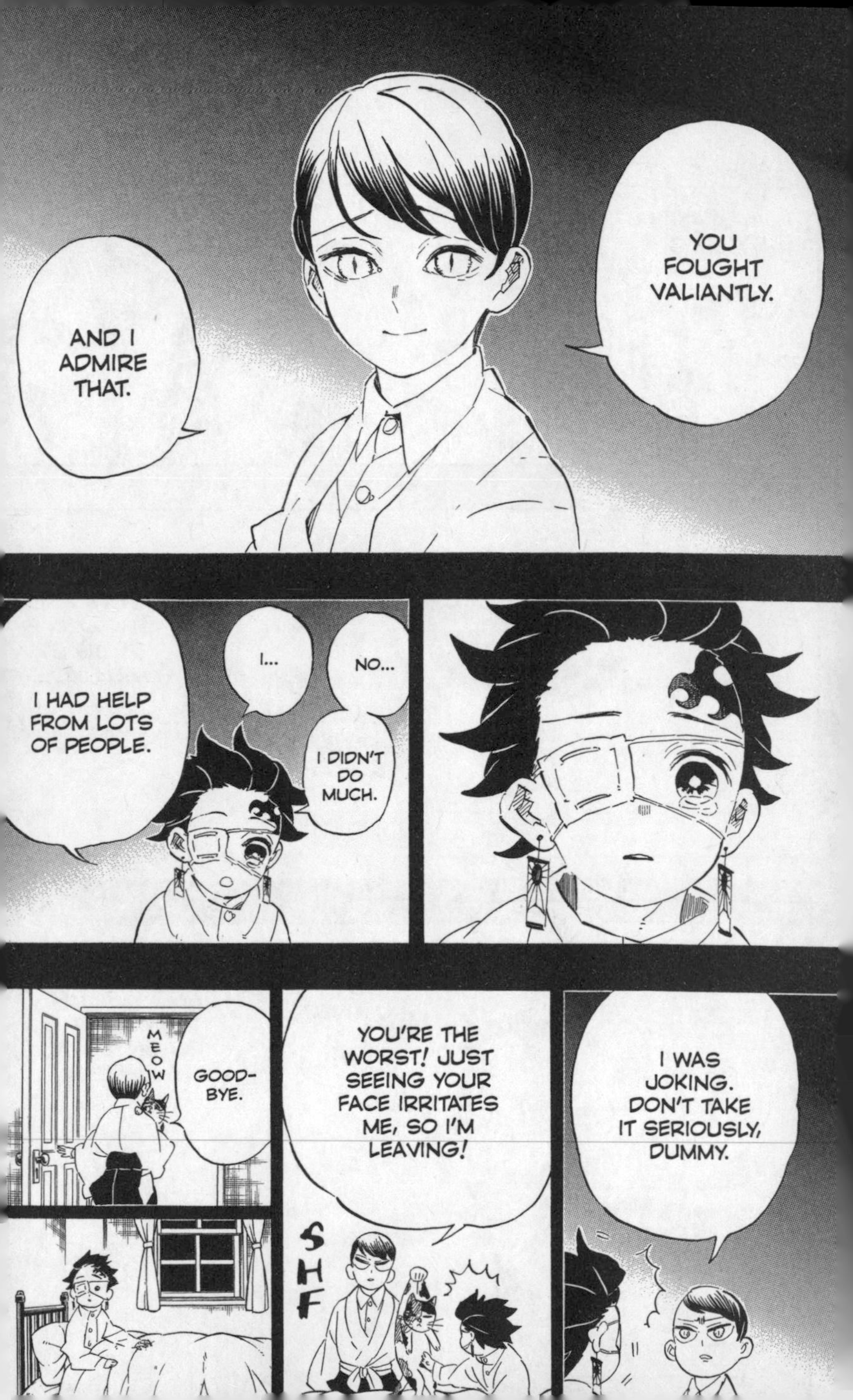
YOU FOUGHT VALIANTLY.
AND I ADMIRE THAT.
NO...
I DIDN'T DO MUCH.
I...
I HAD HELP FROM LOTS OF PEOPLE.
I WAS JOKING. DON'T TAKE IT SERIOUSLY, DUMMY.
YOU'RE THE WORST! JUST SEEING YOUR FACE IRRITATES ME, SO I'M LEAVING!
SHF
GOOD-BYE.
MEOW

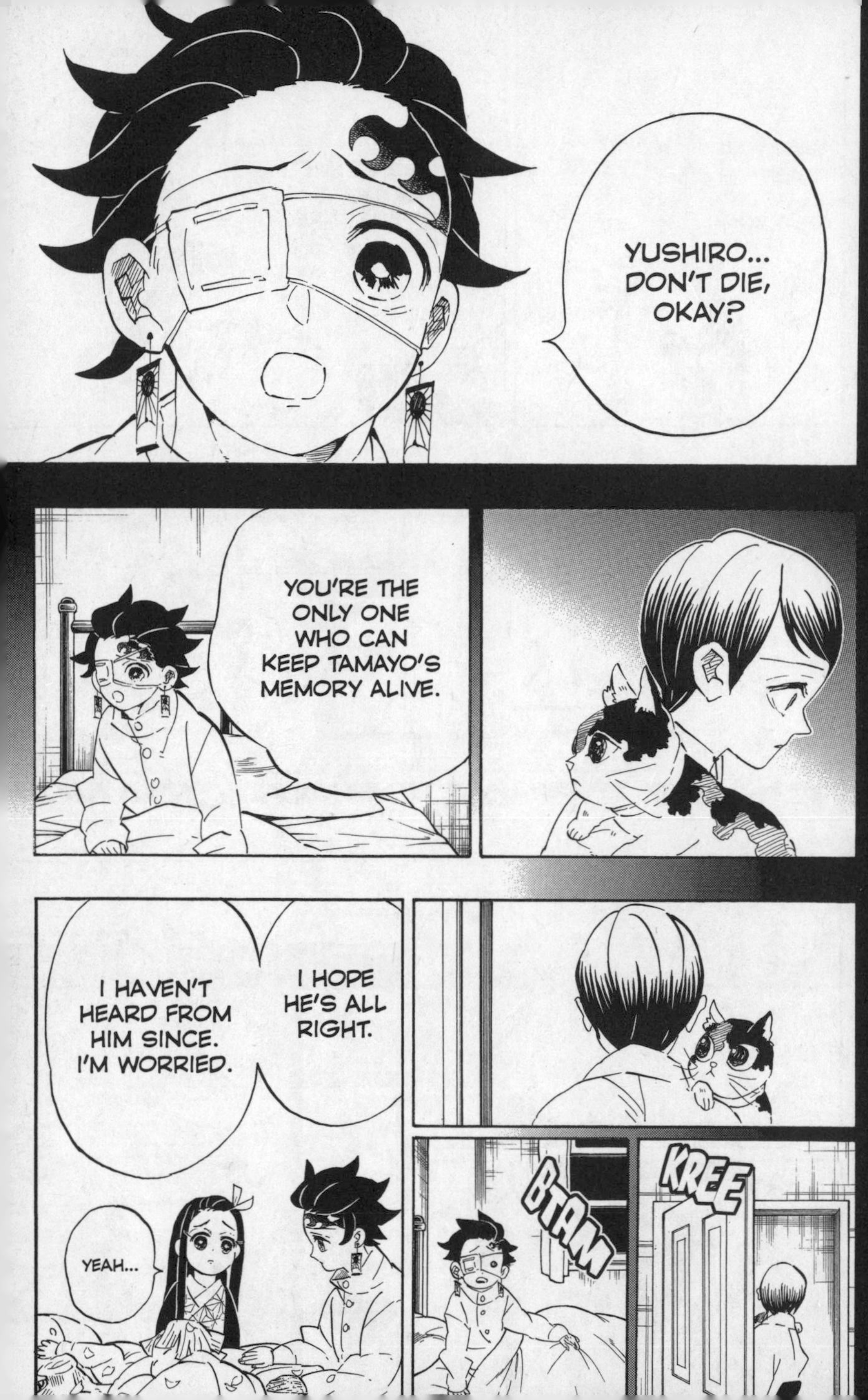
YUSHIRO... DON'T DIE, OKAY?
YOU'RE THE ONLY ONE WHO CAN KEEP TAMAYO'S MEMORY ALIVE.
KREE
BTAM
I HOPE HE'S ALL RIGHT.
I HAVEN'T HEARD FROM HIM SINCE. I'M WORRIED.
YEAH...

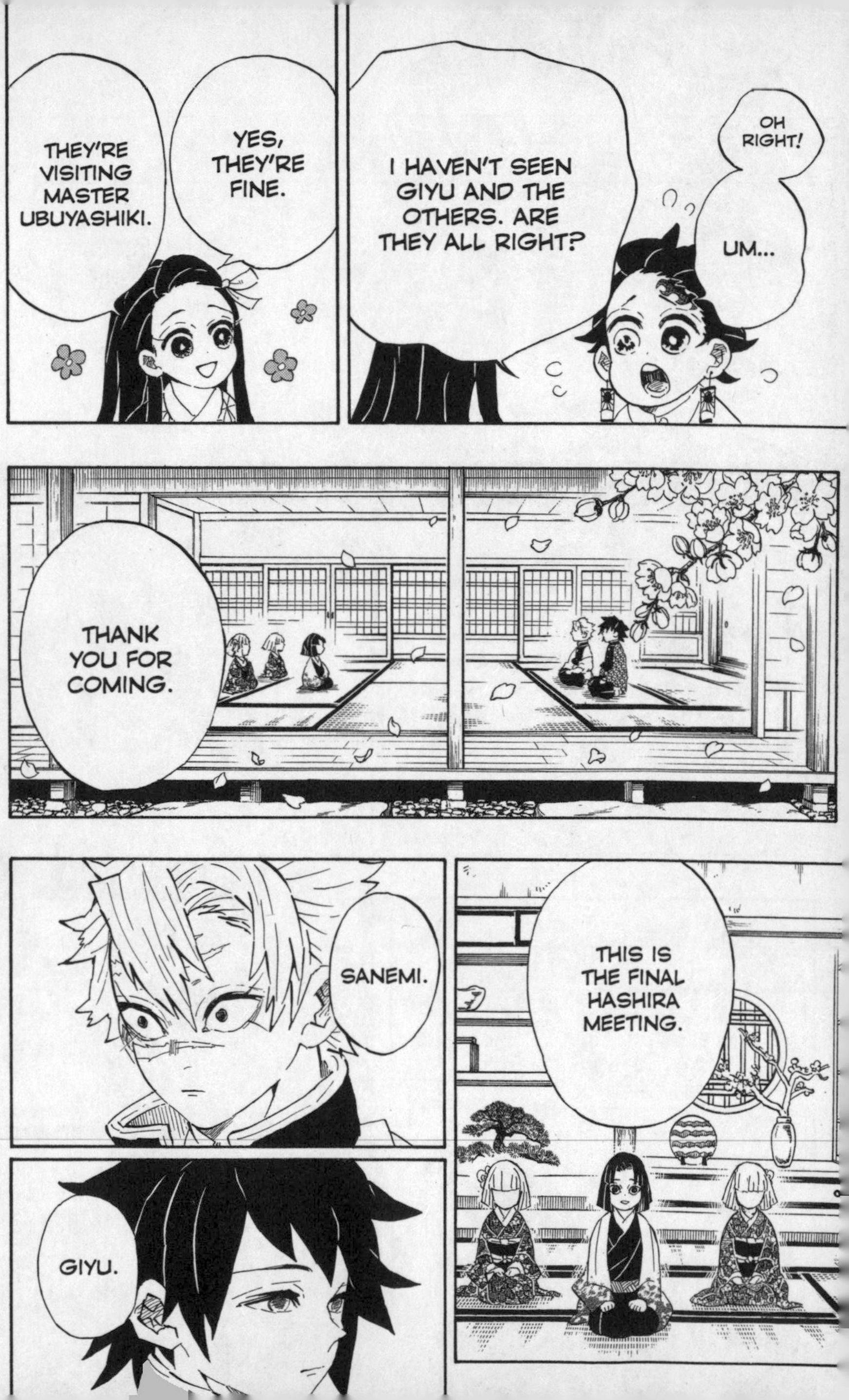
OH RIGHT!
UM...
I HAVEN'T SEEN GIYU AND THE OTHERS. ARE THEY ALL RIGHT?
YES, THEY'RE FINE.
THEY'RE VISITING MASTER UBUYASHIKI.
THANK YOU FOR COMING.
THIS IS THE FINAL HASHIRA MEETING.
SANEMI.
GIYU.

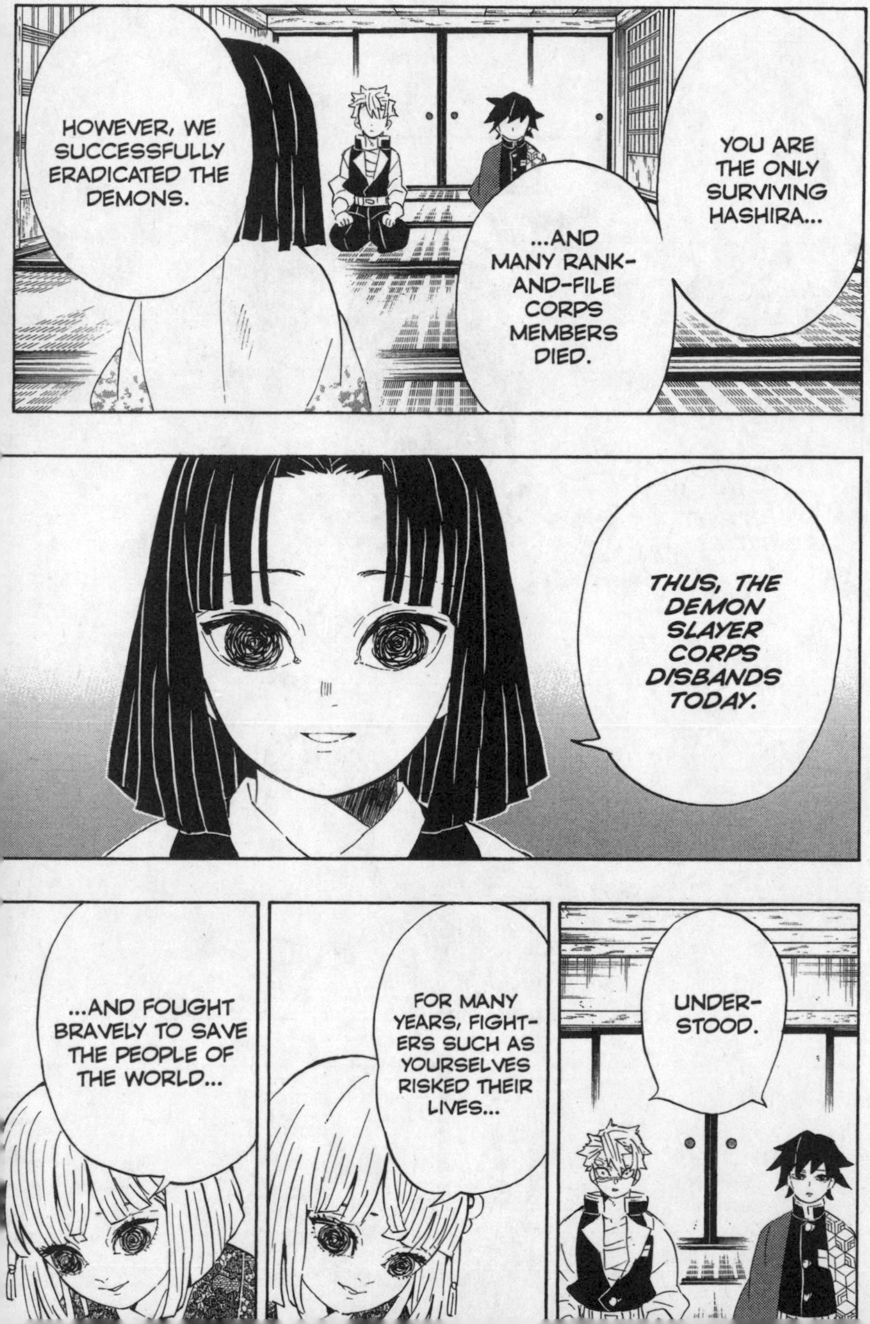
YOU ARE THE ONLY SURVIVING HASHIRA...
...AND MANY RANK-AND-FILE CORPS MEMBERS DIED.
HOWEVER, WE SUCCESSFULLY ERADICATED THE DEMONS.
THUS, THE DEMON SLAYER CORPS DISBANDS TODAY.
UNDER-STOOD.
FOR MANY YEARS, FIGHT-ERS SUCH AS YOURSELVES RISKED THEIR LIVES...
...AND FOUGHT BRAVELY TO SAVE THE PEOPLE OF THE WORLD...

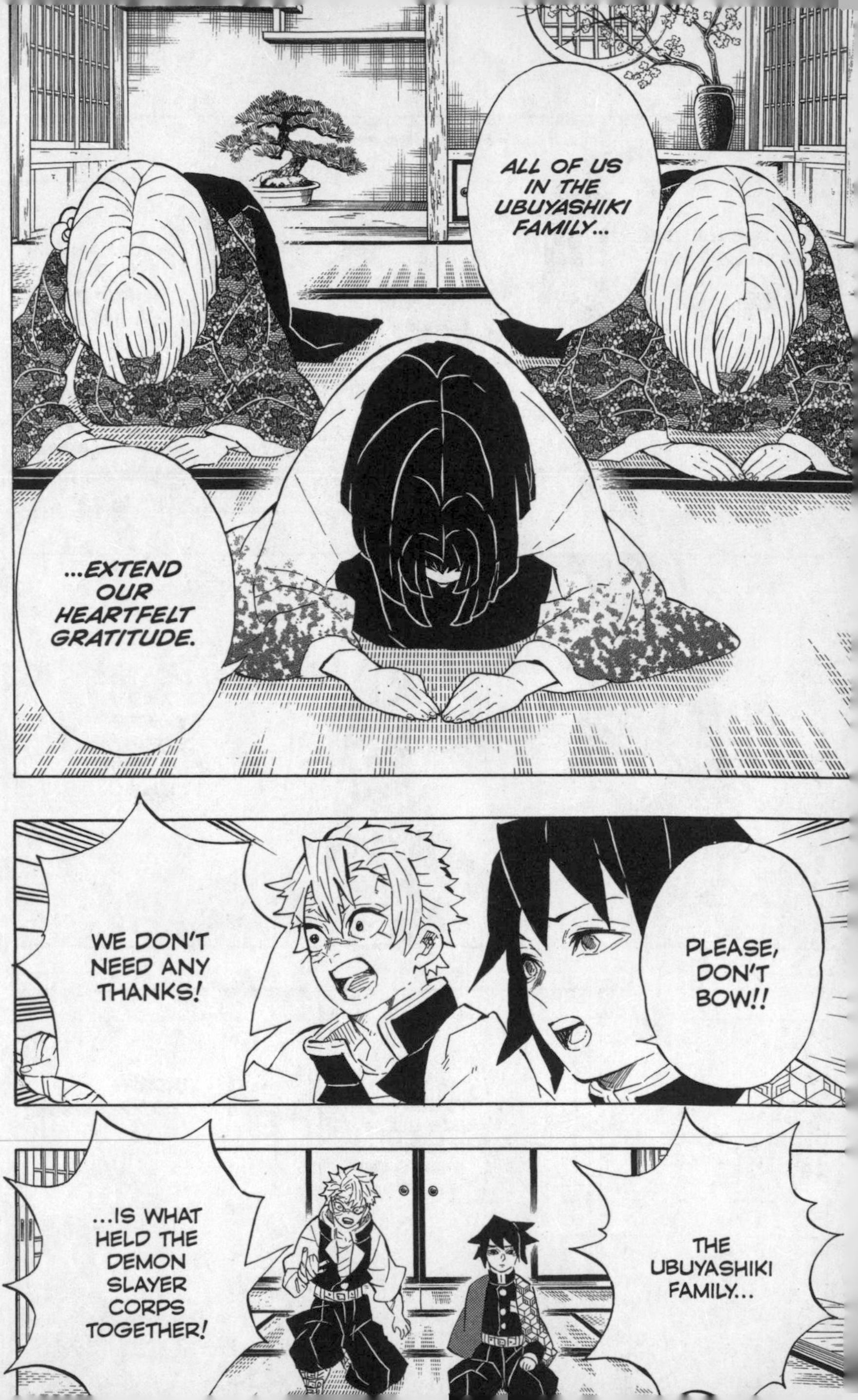
ALL OF US IN THE UBUYASHIKI FAMILY...
...EXTEND OUR HEARTFELT GRATITUDE.
PLEASE, DON'T BOW!!
WE DON'T NEED ANY THANKS!
THE UBUYASHIKI FAMILY...
...IS WHAT HELD THE DEMON SLAYER CORPS TOGETHER!

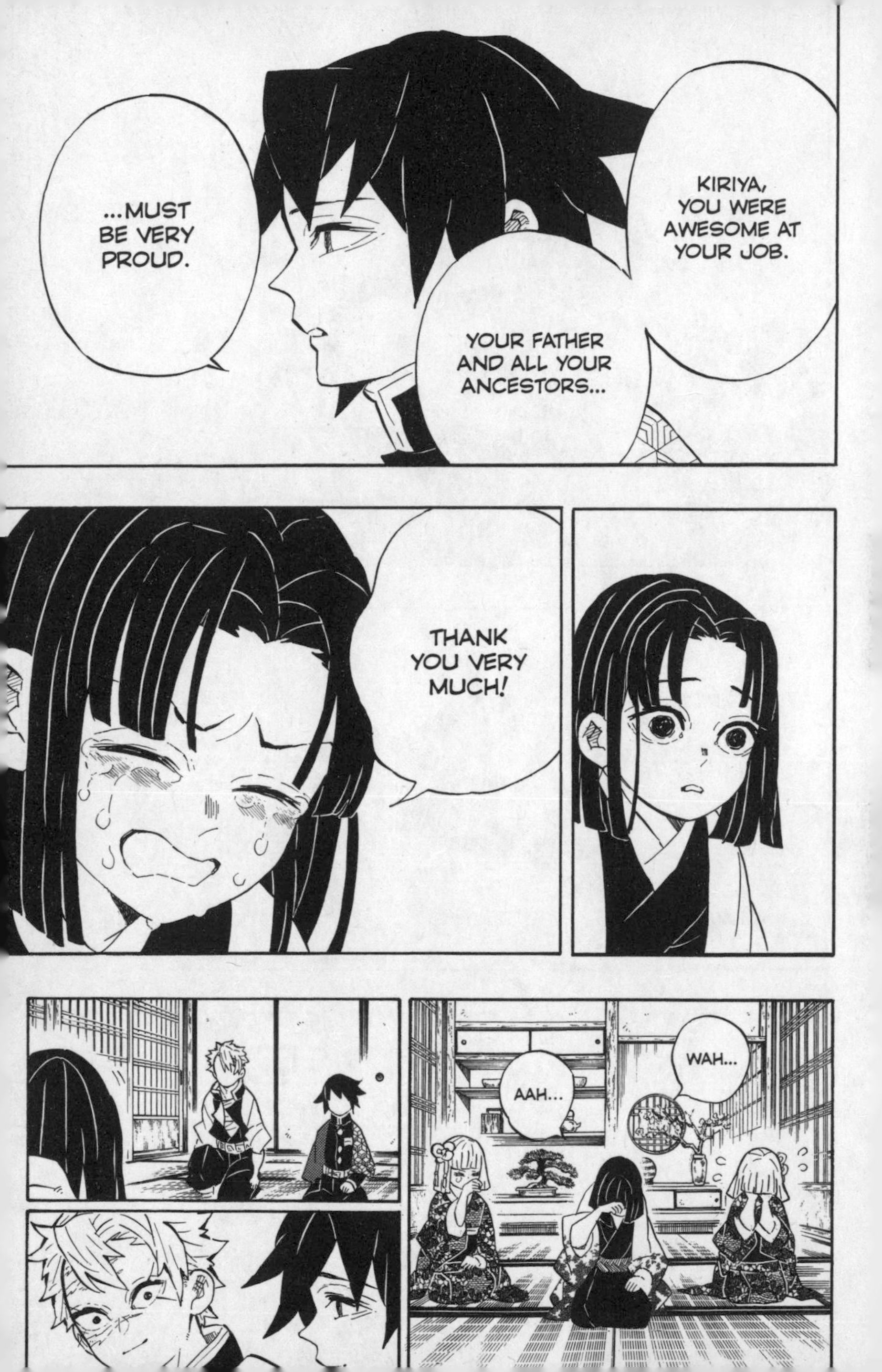
KIRIYA, YOU WERE AWESOME AT YOUR JOB.
YOUR FATHER AND ALL YOUR ANCESTORS...
...MUST BE VERY PROUD.
THANK YOU VERY MUCH!
WAH...
AAH...

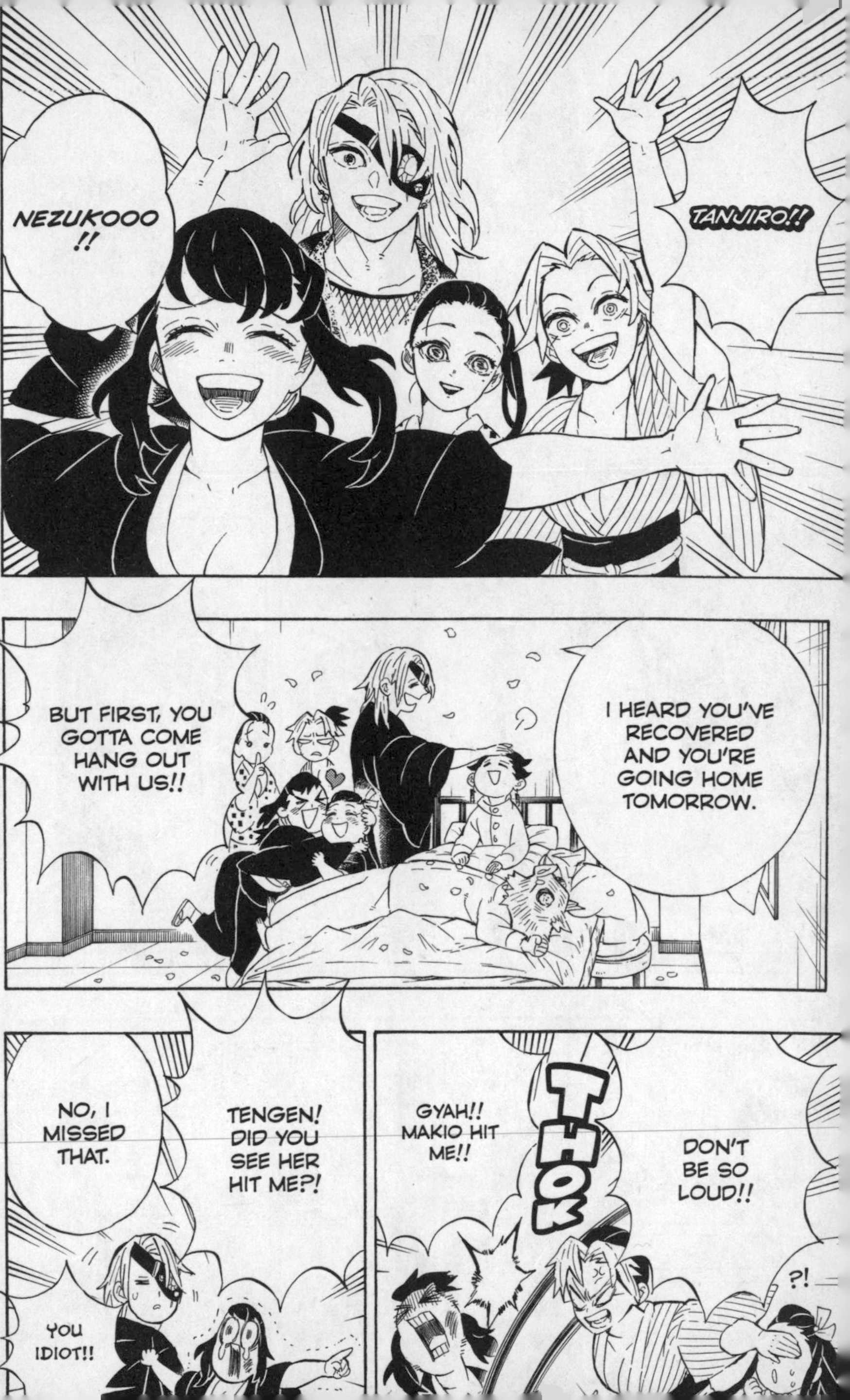
TANJIRO!!
NEZUKOOO !!
I HEARD YOU'VE RECOVERED AND YOU'RE GOING HOME TOMORROW.
BUT FIRST, YOU GOTTA COME HANG OUT WITH US!!
DON'T BE SO LOUD!!
THOK
GYAH!! MAKIO HIT ME!!
?!
TENGEN! DID YOU SEE HER HIT ME?!
NO, I MISSED THAT.
YOU IDIOT!!

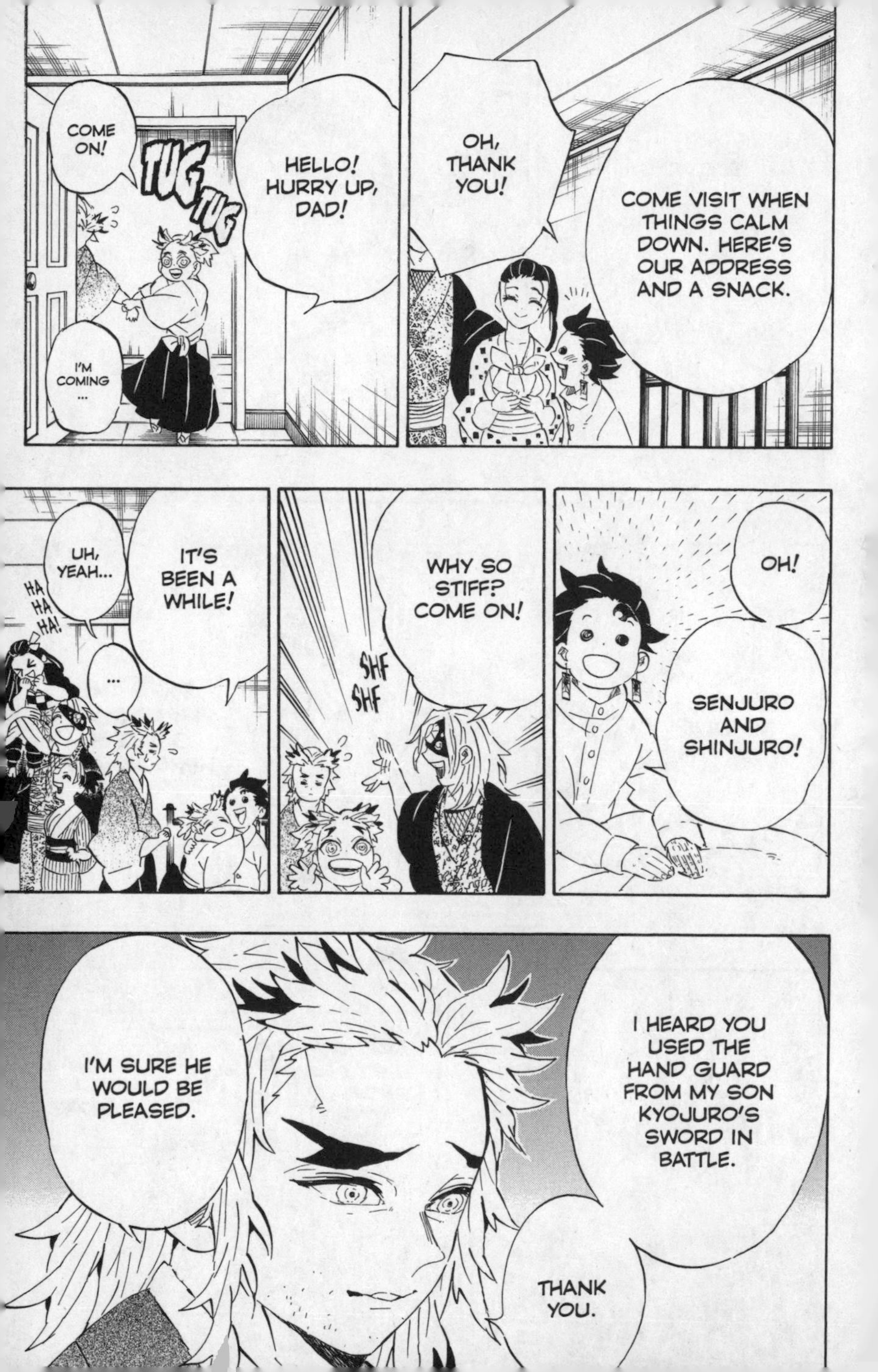
COME VISIT WHEN THINGS CALM DOWN. HERE'S OUR ADDRESS AND A SNACK.
OH, THANK YOU!
HELLO! HURRY UP, DAD!
COME ON!
TUG TUG
I'M COMING ...
OH!
SENJURO AND SHINJURO!
WHY SO STIFF? COME ON!
SHF SHF
IT'S BEEN A WHILE!
UH, YEAH...
HA HA HA!
...
I HEARD YOU USED THE HAND GUARD FROM MY SON KYOJURO'S SWORD IN BATTLE.
THANK YOU.
I'M SURE HE WOULD BE PLEASED.

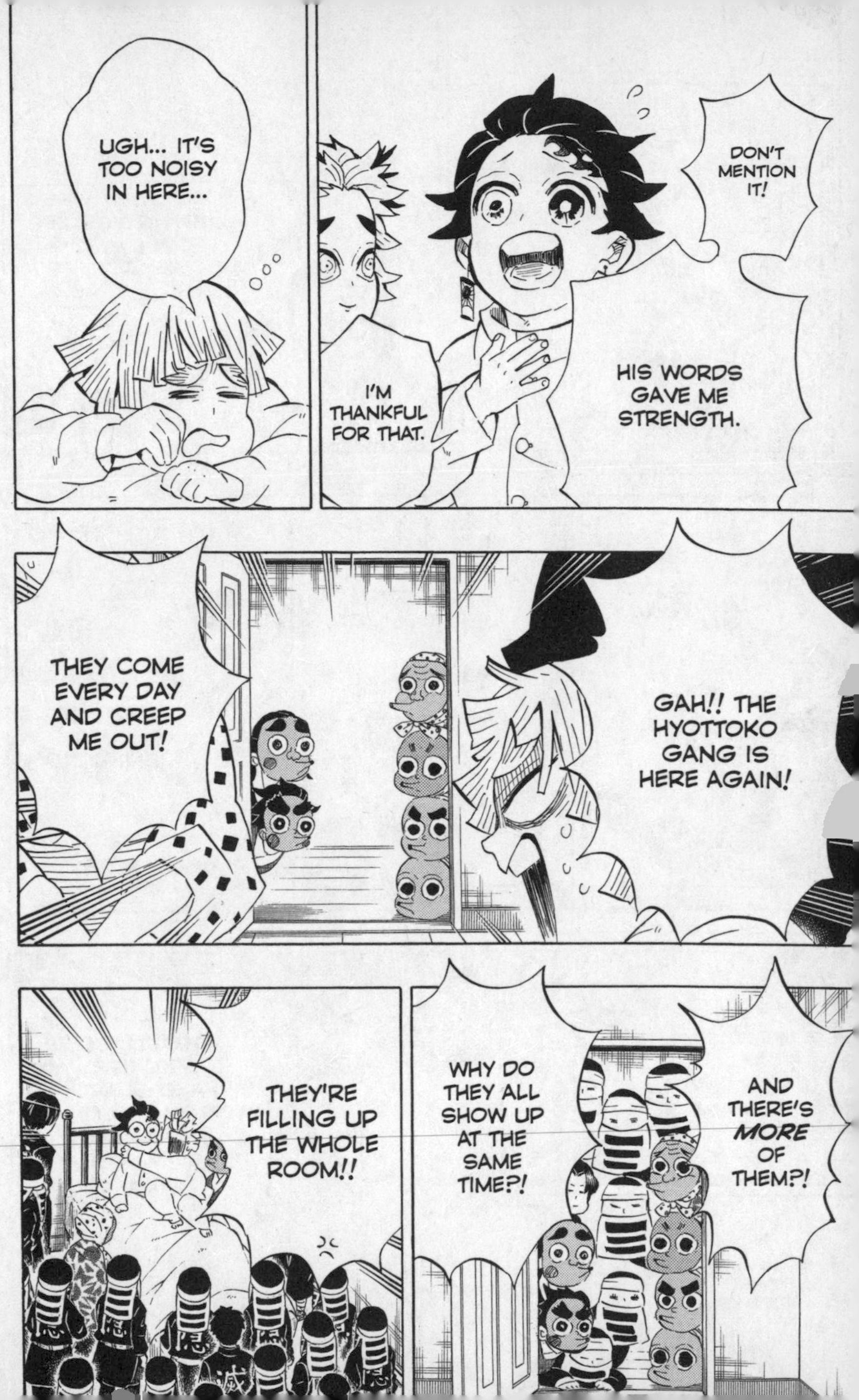
DON'T MENTION IT!
HIS WORDS GAVE ME STRENGTH.
I'M THANKFUL FOR THAT.
UGH... IT'S TOO NOISY IN HERE...
GAH!! THE HYOTTOKO GANG IS HERE AGAIN!
THEY COME EVERY DAY AND CREEP ME OUT!
AND THERE'S *MORE* OF THEM?!
WHY DO THEY ALL SHOW UP AT THE SAME TIME?!
THEY'RE FILLING UP THE WHOLE ROOM!!

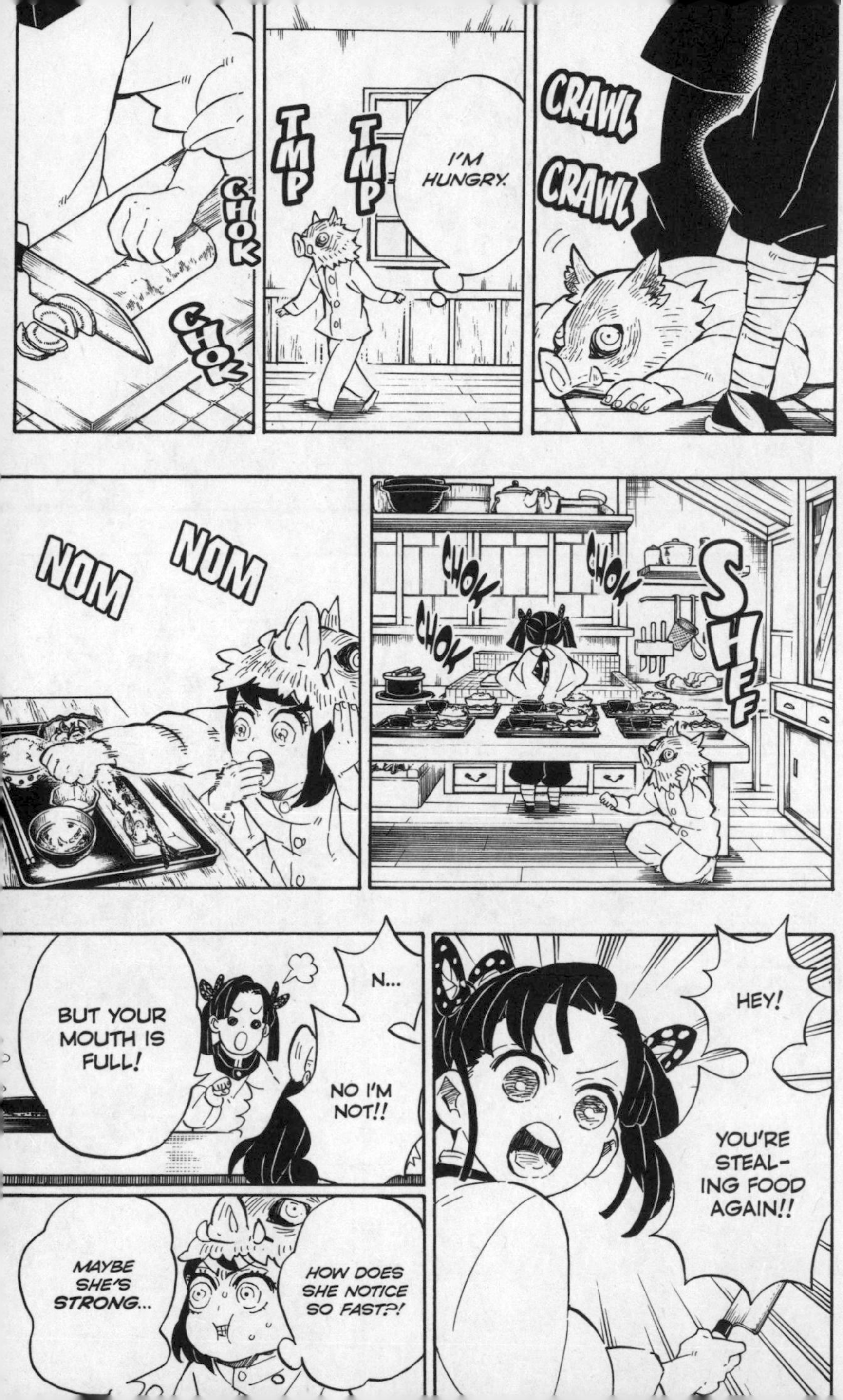
CRAWL
CRAWL
TMP
TMP
I'M HUNGRY.
CHOK
CHOK
SHFF
CHOK
CHOK
CHOK
NOM
NOM
HEY!
YOU'RE STEAL-ING FOOD AGAIN!!
N...
NO I'M NOT!!
BUT YOUR MOUTH IS FULL!
HOW DOES SHE NOTICE SO FAST?!
MAYBE SHE'S STRONG...

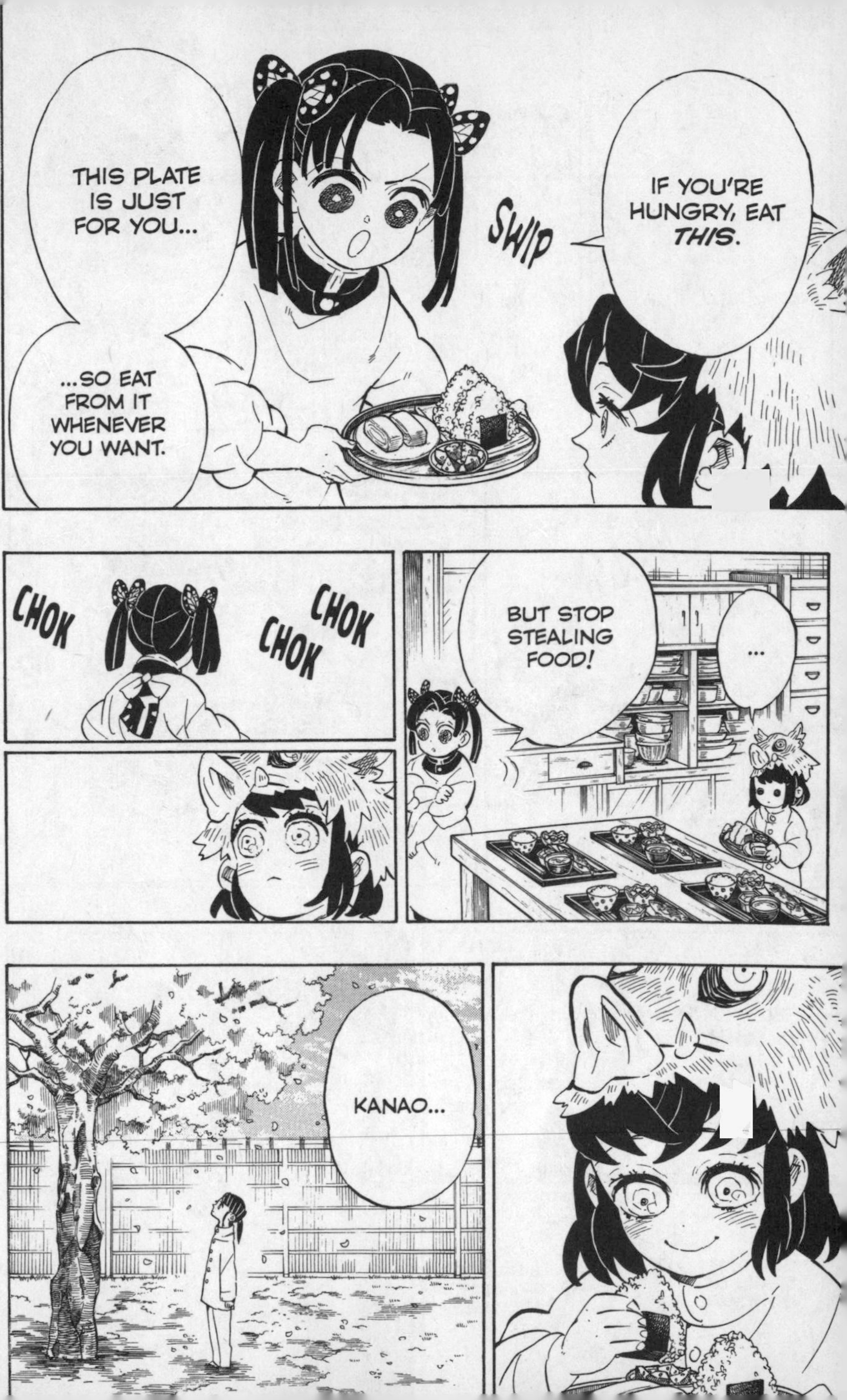
IF YOU'RE HUNGRY, EAT *THIS*.
SWIP
THIS PLATE IS JUST FOR YOU...
...SO EAT FROM IT WHENEVER YOU WANT.
BUT STOP STEALING FOOD!
...
CHOK
CHOK
CHOK
KANAO...

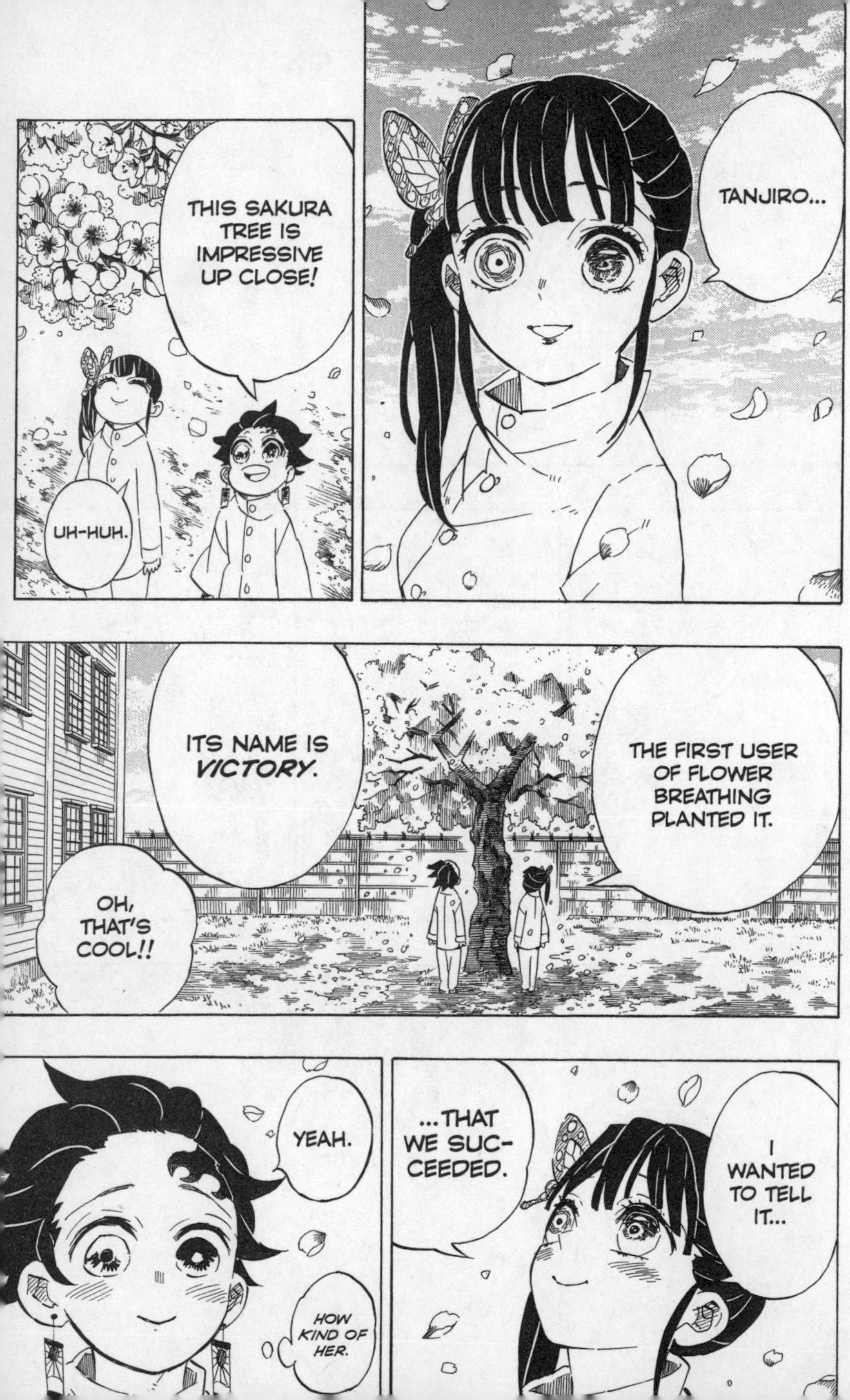
TANJIRO...
THIS SAKURA TREE IS IMPRESSIVE UP CLOSE!
UH-HUH.
THE FIRST USER OF FLOWER BREATHING PLANTED IT.
ITS NAME IS *VICTORY*.
OH, THAT'S COOL!!
I WANTED TO TELL IT...
...THAT WE SUC-CEEDED.
YEAH.
HOW KIND OF HER.

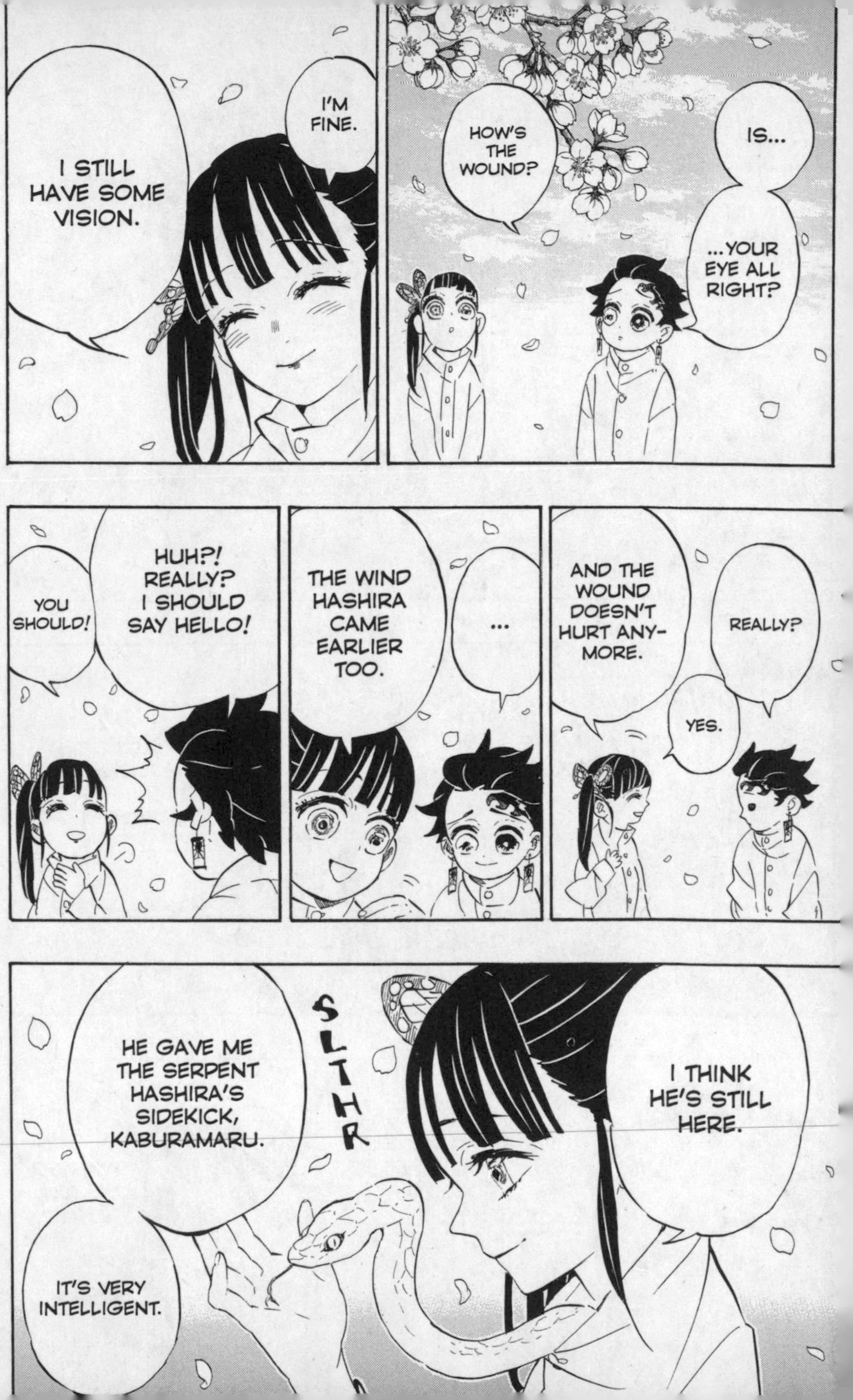
IS...
...YOUR EYE ALL RIGHT?
HOW'S THE WOUND?
I'M FINE.
I STILL HAVE SOME VISION.
REALLY?
YES.
AND THE WOUND DOESN'T HURT ANY-MORE.
...
THE WIND HASHIRA CAME EARLIER TOO.
HUH?! REALLY? I SHOULD SAY HELLO!
YOU SHOULD!
I THINK HE'S STILL HERE.
SLTHR
HE GAVE ME THE SERPENT HASHIRA'S SIDEKICK, KABURAMARU.
IT'S VERY INTELLIGENT.

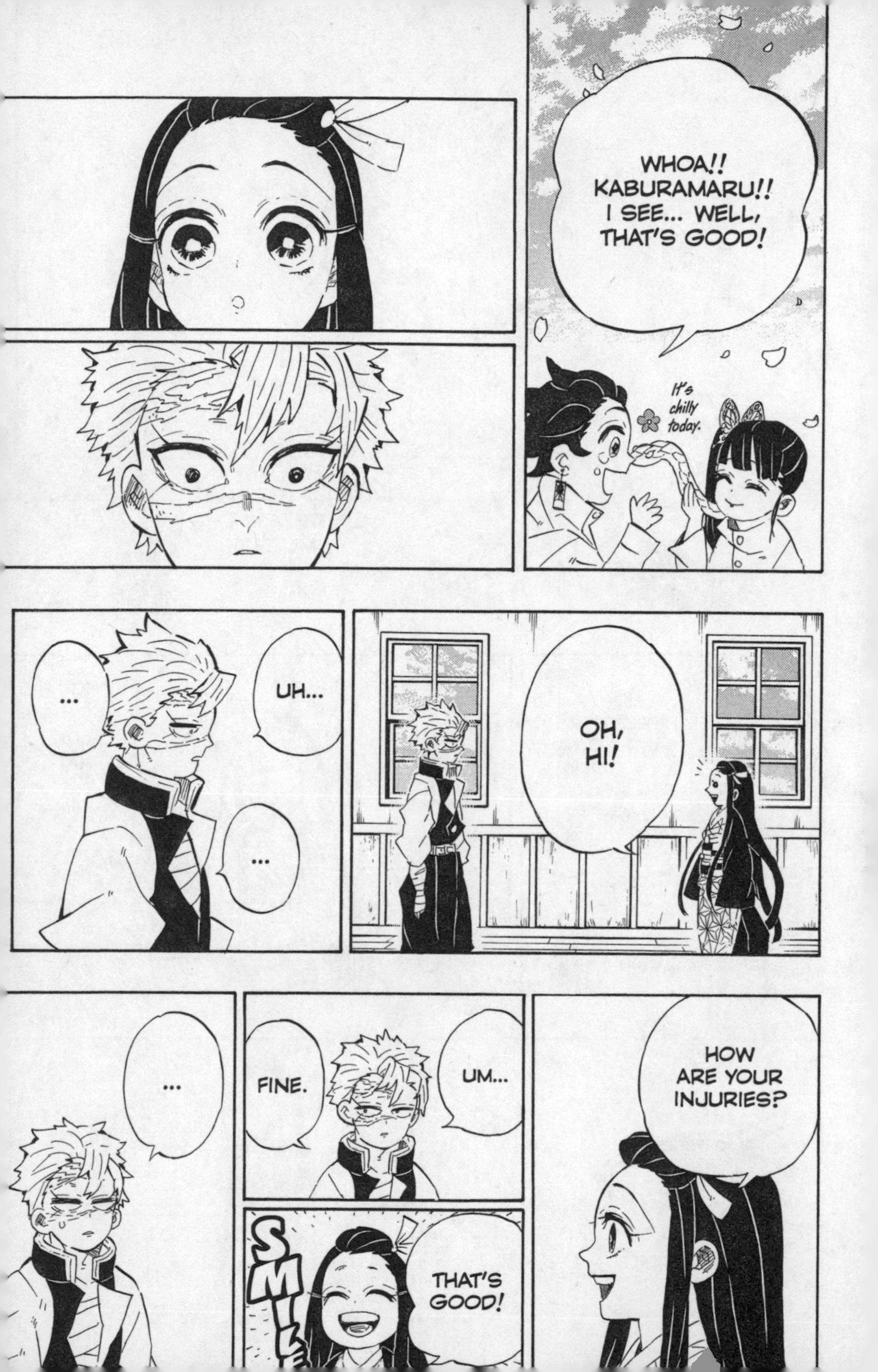
WHOA!! KABURAMARU!! I SEE... WELL, THAT'S GOOD!
It's chilly today.
OH, HI!
UH...
...
...
HOW ARE YOUR INJURIES?
UM...
FINE.
THAT'S GOOD!
SMI
...

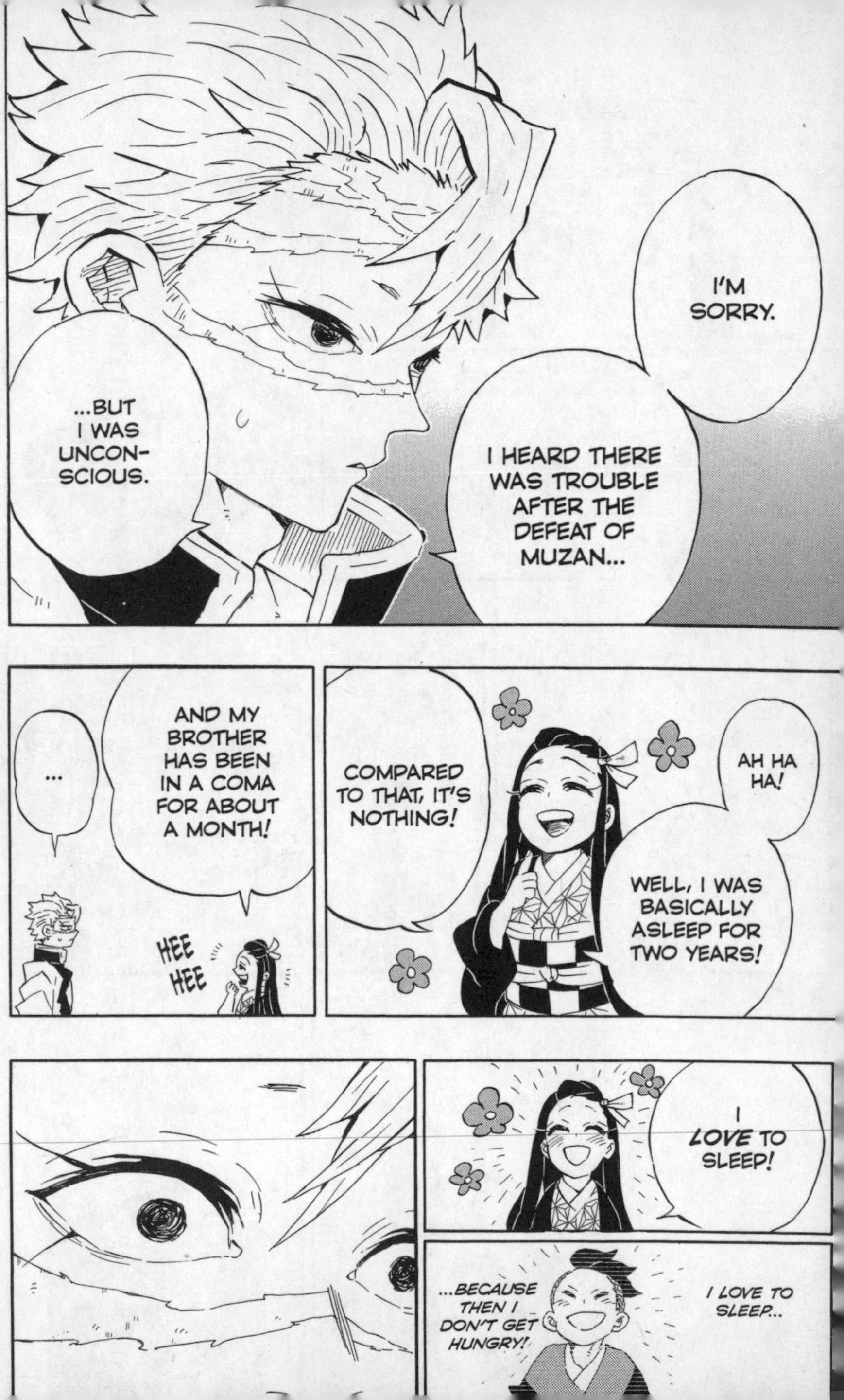
I'M SORRY.
I HEARD THERE WAS TROUBLE AFTER THE DEFEAT OF MUZAN...
...BUT I WAS UNCONSCIOUS.
AH HA HA!
WELL, I WAS BASICALLY ASLEEP FOR TWO YEARS!
COMPARED TO THAT, IT'S NOTHING!
AND MY BROTHER HAS BEEN IN A COMA FOR ABOUT A MONTH!
HEE HEE
...
I *LOVE* TO SLEEP!
I LOVE TO SLEEP...
...BECAUSE THEN I DON'T GET HUNGRY!

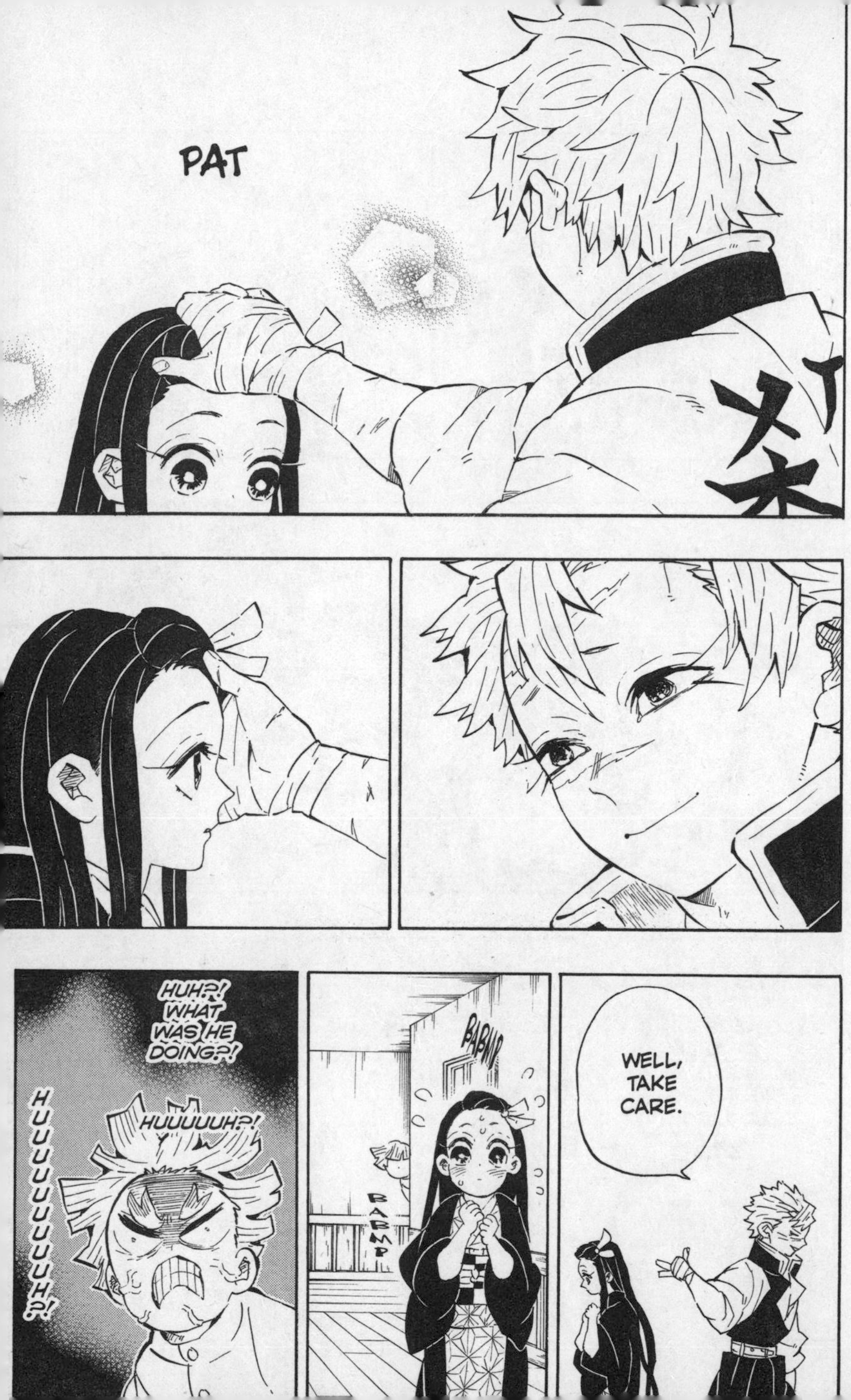
PAT
WELL, TAKE CARE.
BABMP
BABMP
HUH?! WHAT WAS HE DOING?!
HUUUUUUH?!
HUUUUUUUUUUH?!

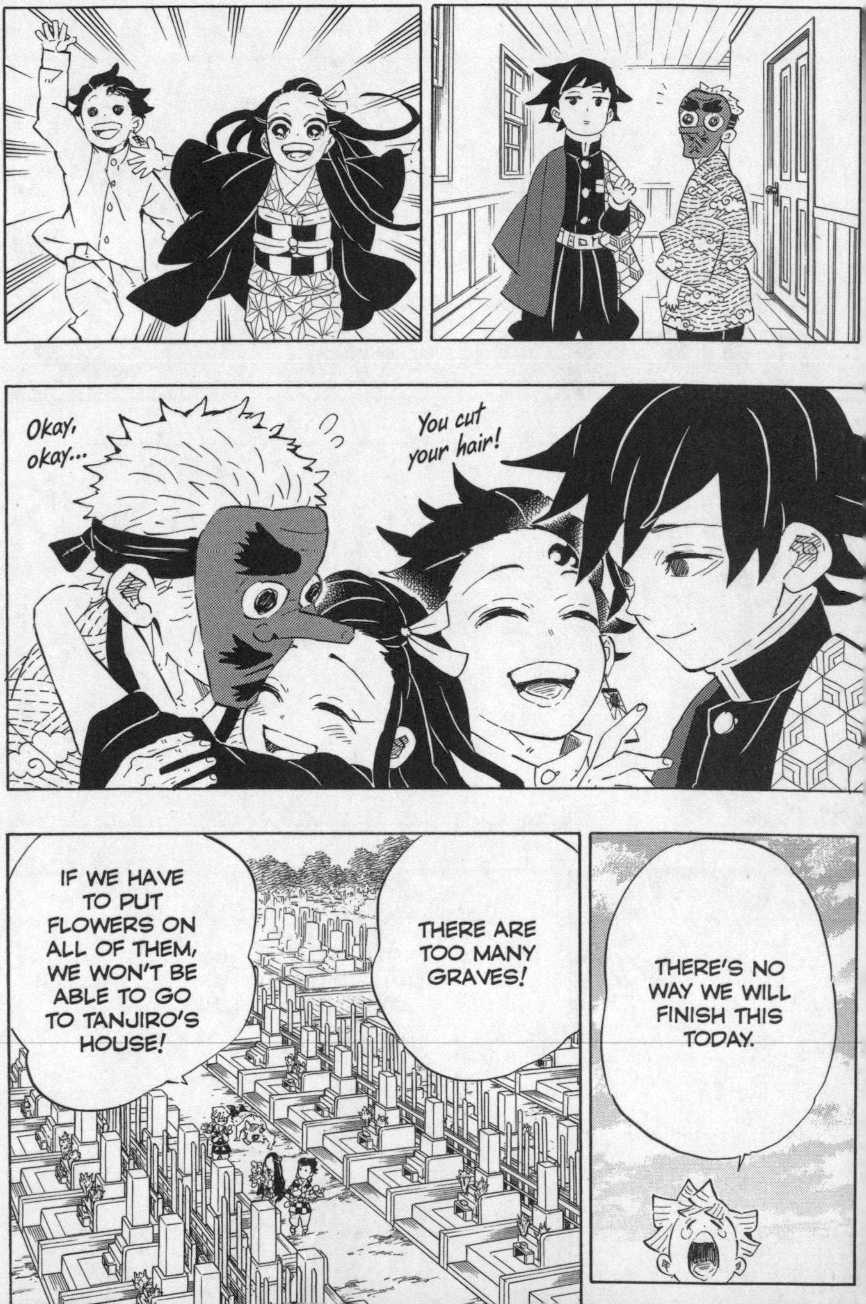
You cut your hair!
Okay, okay...
THERE'S NO WAY WE WILL FINISH THIS TODAY.
THERE ARE TOO MANY GRAVES!
IF WE HAVE TO PUT FLOWERS ON ALL OF THEM, WE WON'T BE ABLE TO GO TO TANJIRO'S HOUSE!

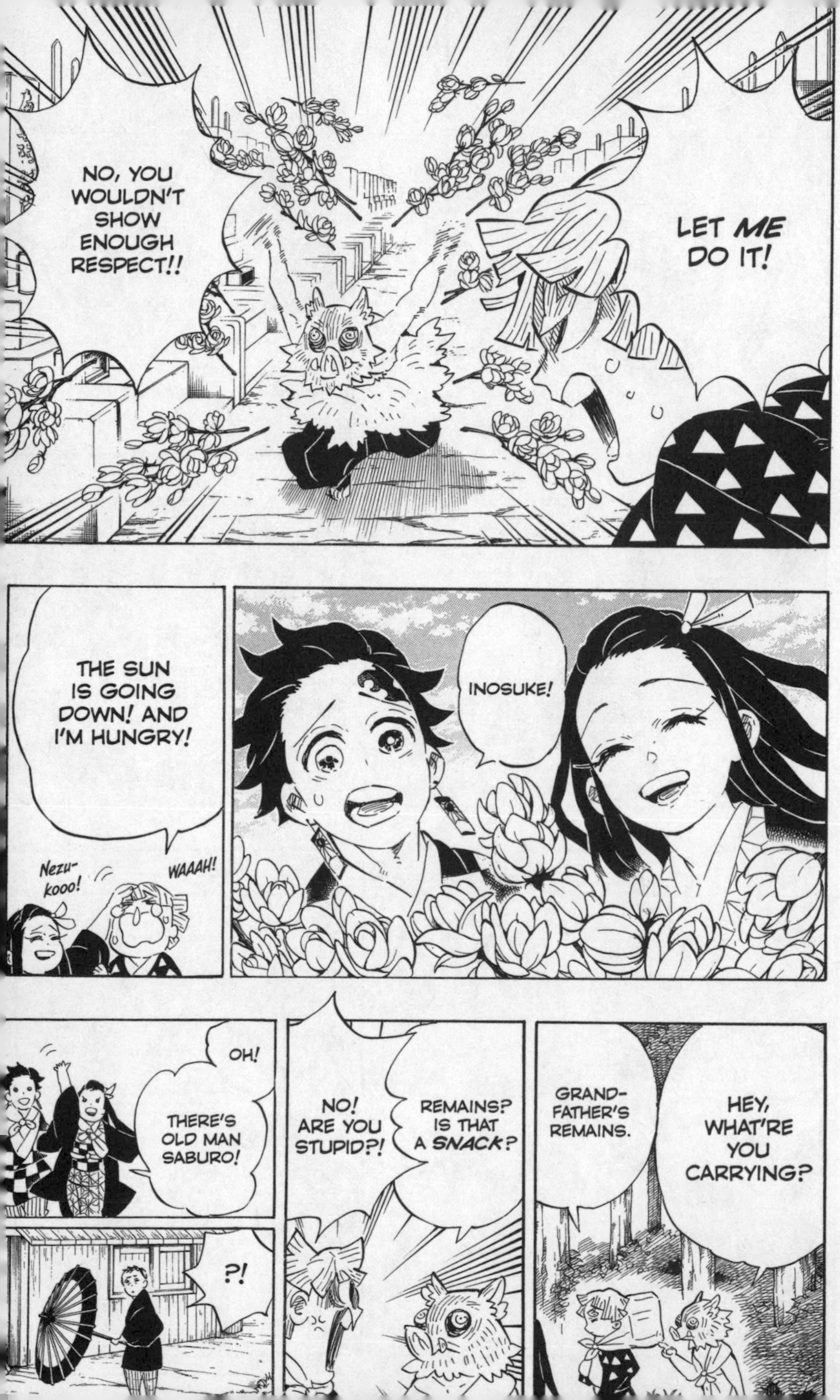
LET *ME* DO IT!
NO, YOU WOULDN'T SHOW ENOUGH RESPECT!!
INOSUKE!
THE SUN IS GOING DOWN! AND I'M HUNGRY!
WAAAH!
Nezu-kooo!
HEY, WHAT'RE YOU CARRYING?
GRAND-FATHER'S REMAINS.
REMAINS? IS THAT A *SNACK*?
NO! ARE YOU STUPID?!
OH!
THERE'S OLD MAN SABURO!
?!

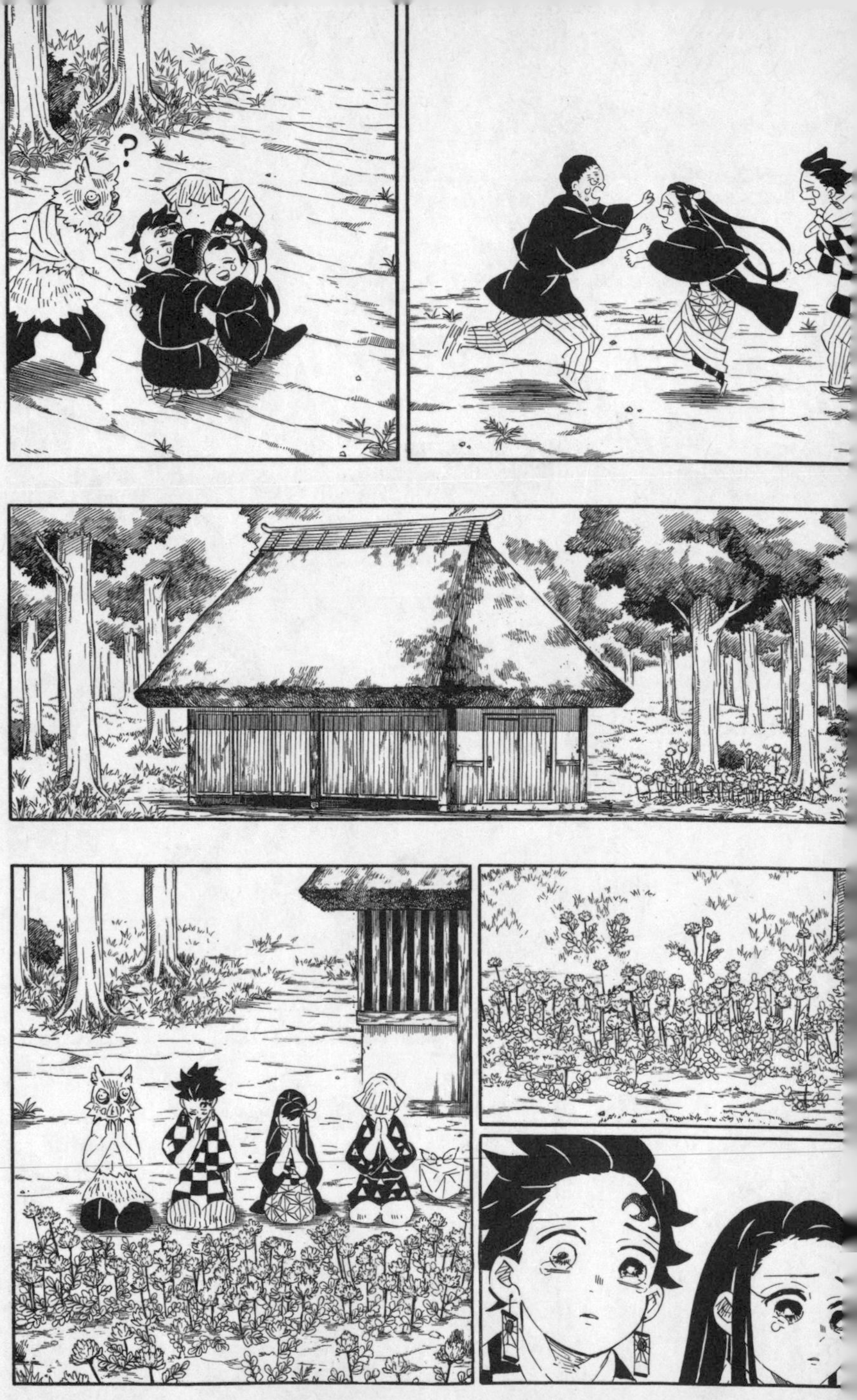

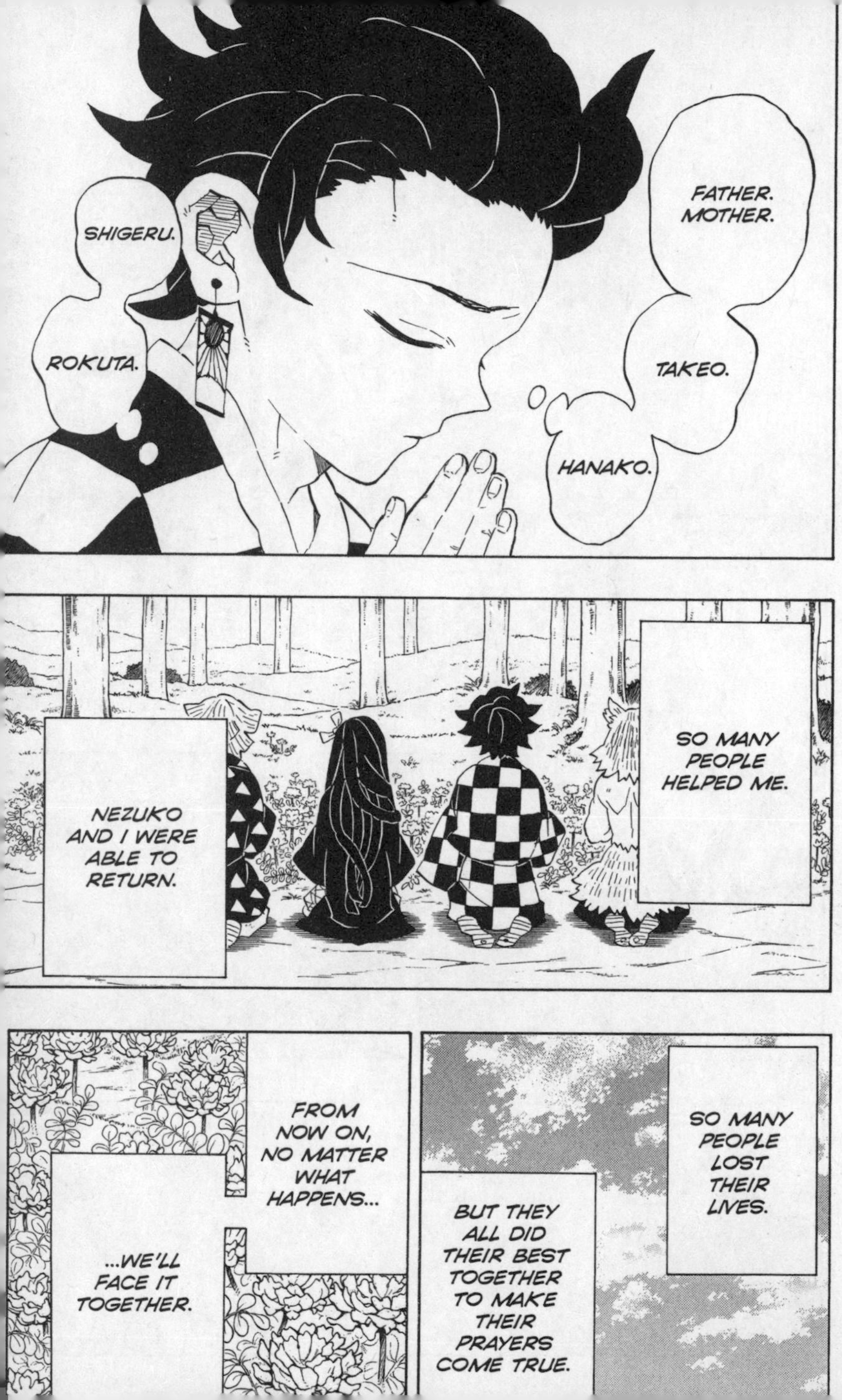
FATHER. MOTHER.
TAKEO.
HANAKO.
SHIGERU.
ROKUTA.
SO MANY PEOPLE HELPED ME.
NEZUKO AND I WERE ABLE TO RETURN.
SO MANY PEOPLE LOST THEIR LIVES.
BUT THEY ALL DID THEIR BEST TOGETHER TO MAKE THEIR PRAYERS COME TRUE.
FROM NOW ON, NO MATTER WHAT HAPPENS...
...WE'LL FACE IT TOGETHER.

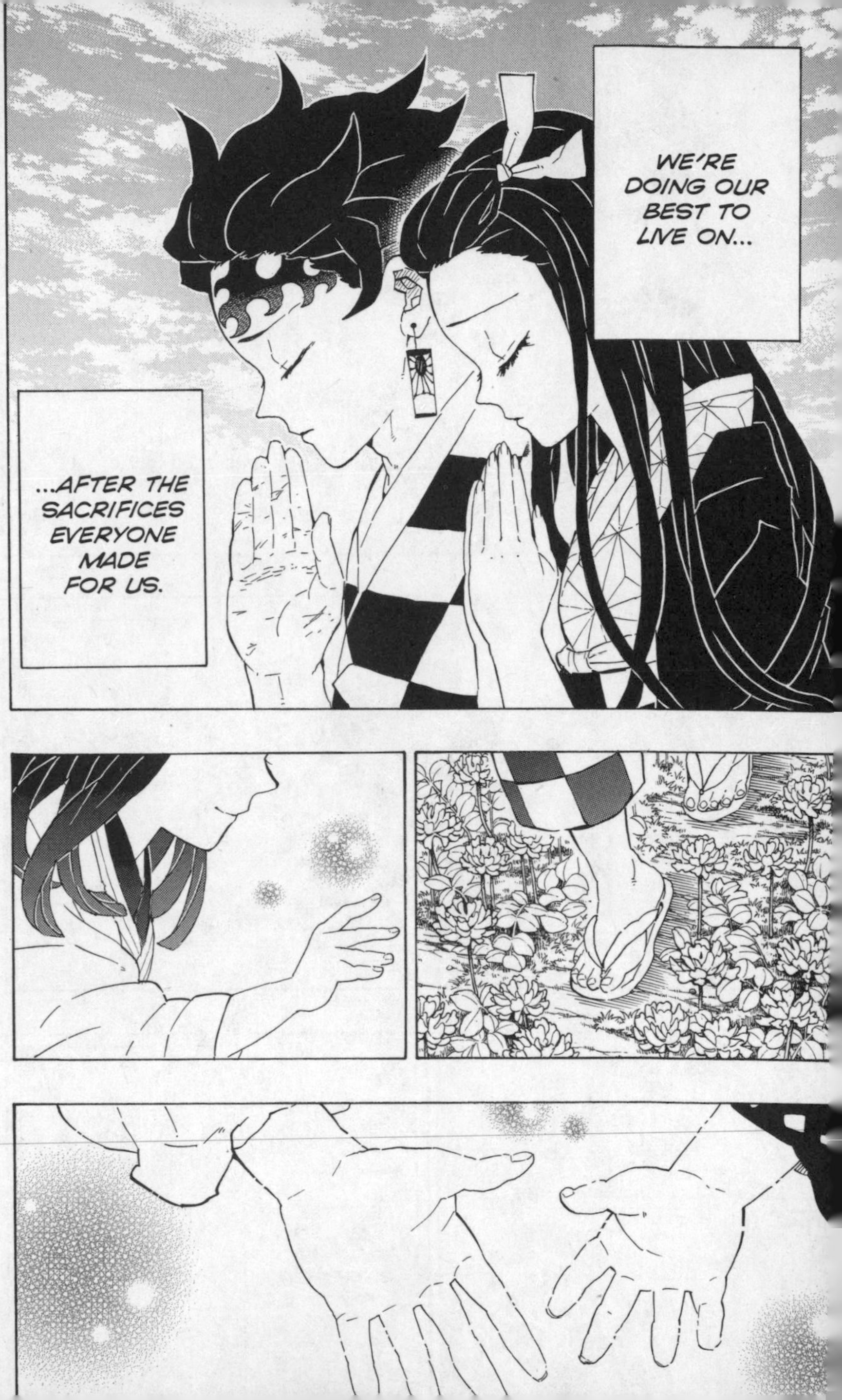
WE'RE DOING OUR BEST TO LIVE ON...
...AFTER THE SACRIFICES EVERYONE MADE FOR US.

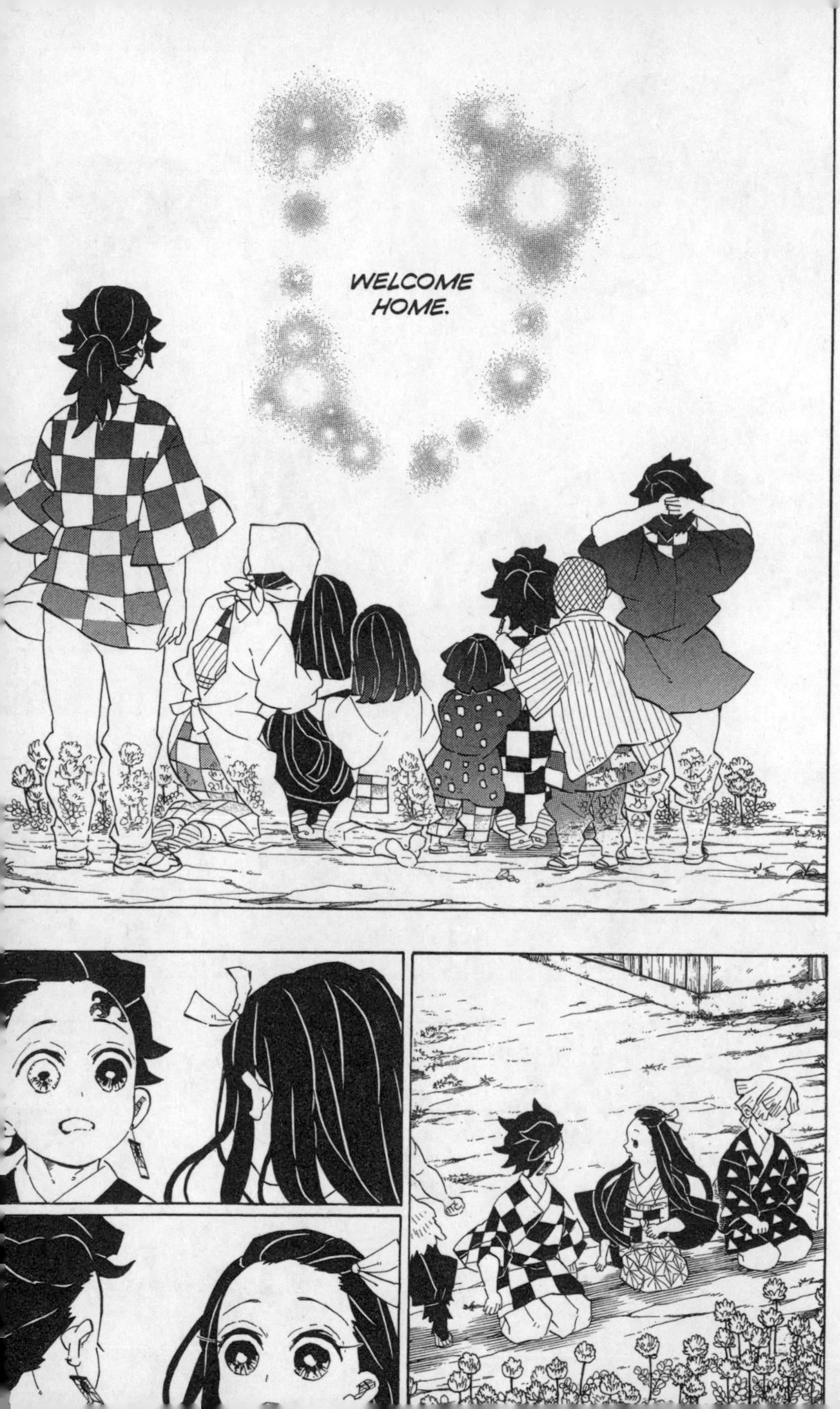
WELCOME HOME.

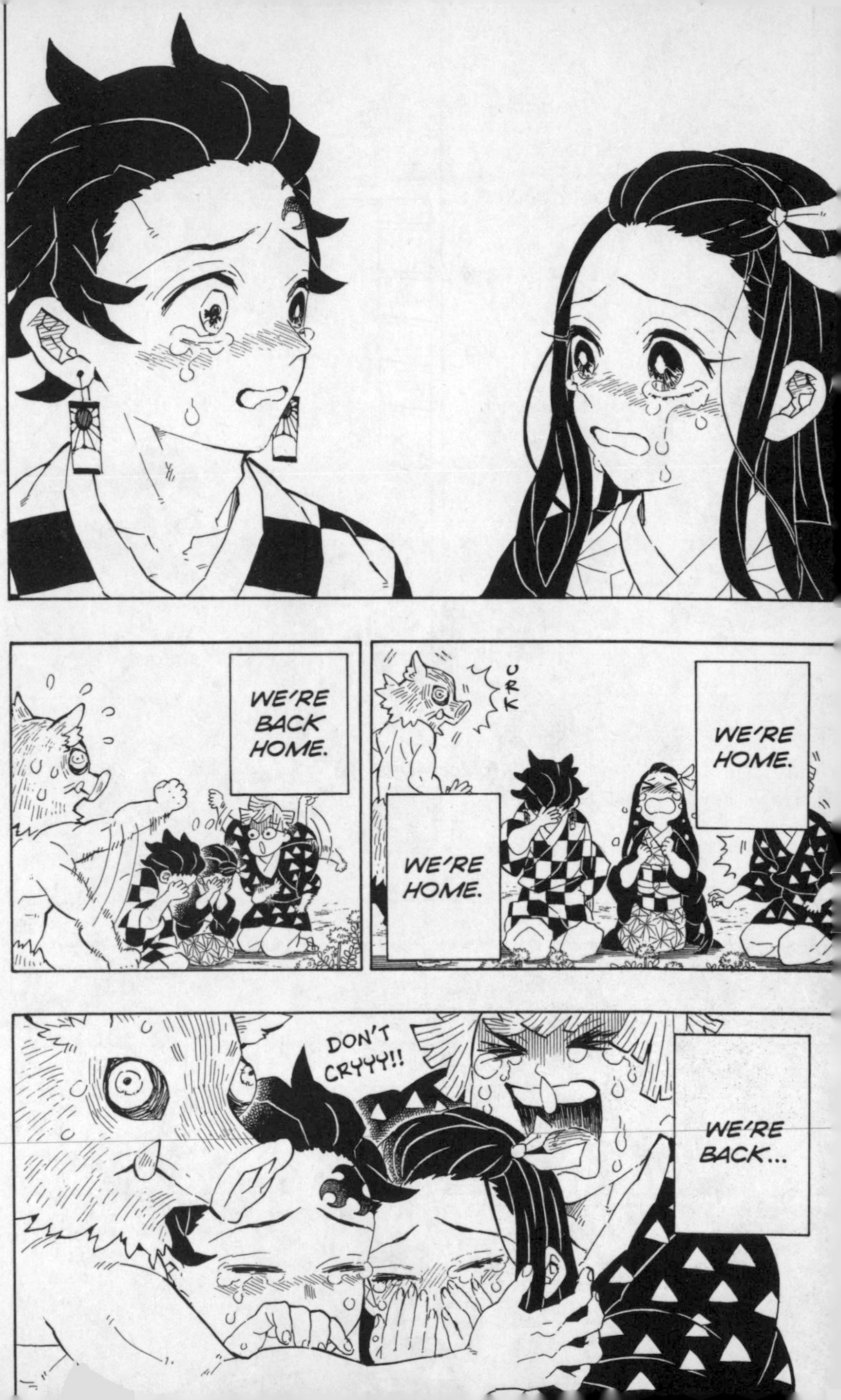
WE'RE HOME.
URK
WE'RE HOME.
WE'RE BACK HOME.
WE'RE BACK...
DON'T CRYYY!!

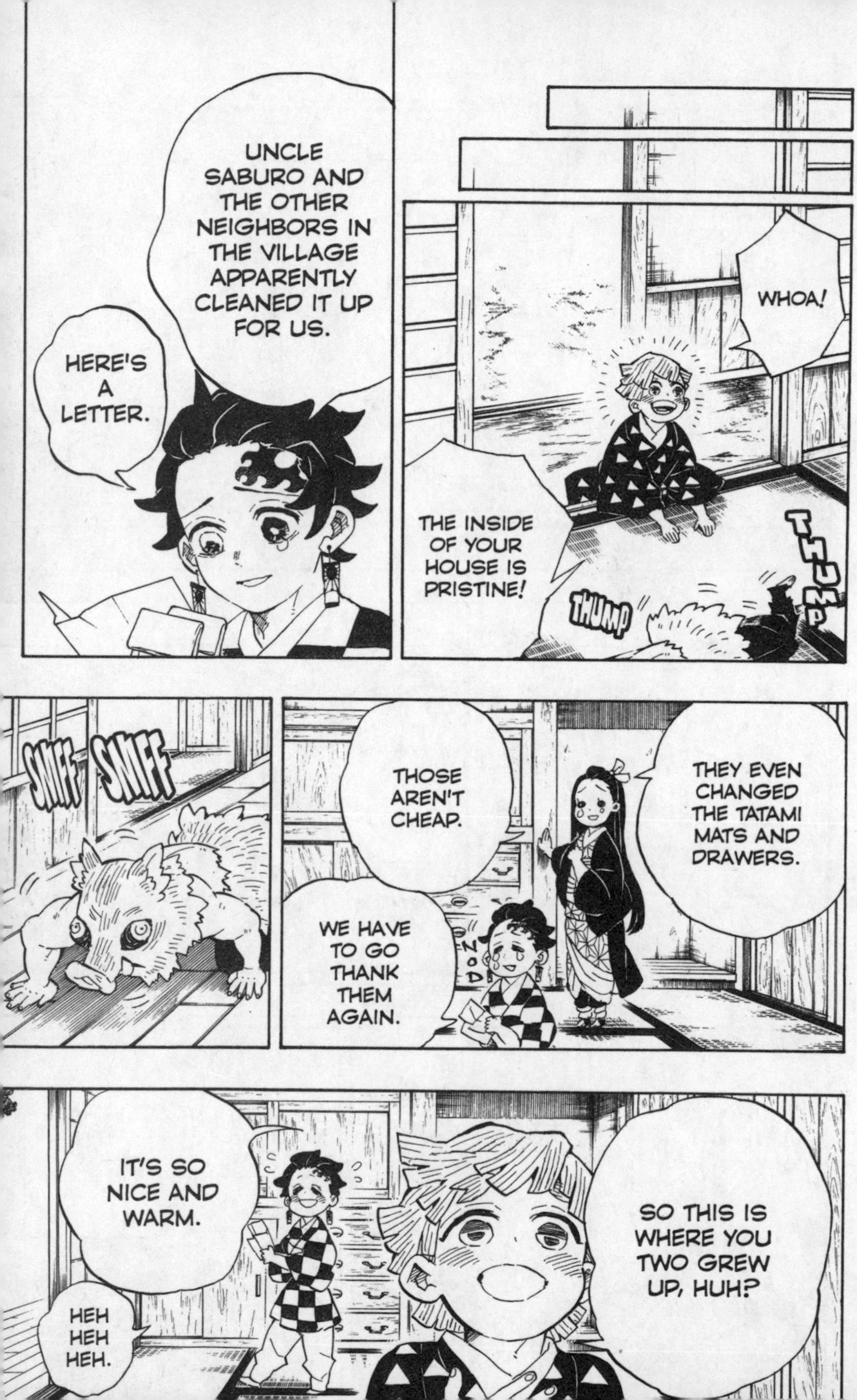
WHOA!
THE INSIDE OF YOUR HOUSE IS PRISTINE!
THUMP
THUMP
UNCLE SABURO AND THE OTHER NEIGHBORS IN THE VILLAGE APPARENTLY CLEANED IT UP FOR US.
HERE'S A LETTER.
THEY EVEN CHANGED THE TATAMI MATS AND DRAWERS.
THOSE AREN'T CHEAP.
NOD
WE HAVE TO GO THANK THEM AGAIN.
SNIFF SNIFF
SO THIS IS WHERE YOU TWO GREW UP, HUH?
IT'S SO NICE AND WARM.
HEH HEH HEH.

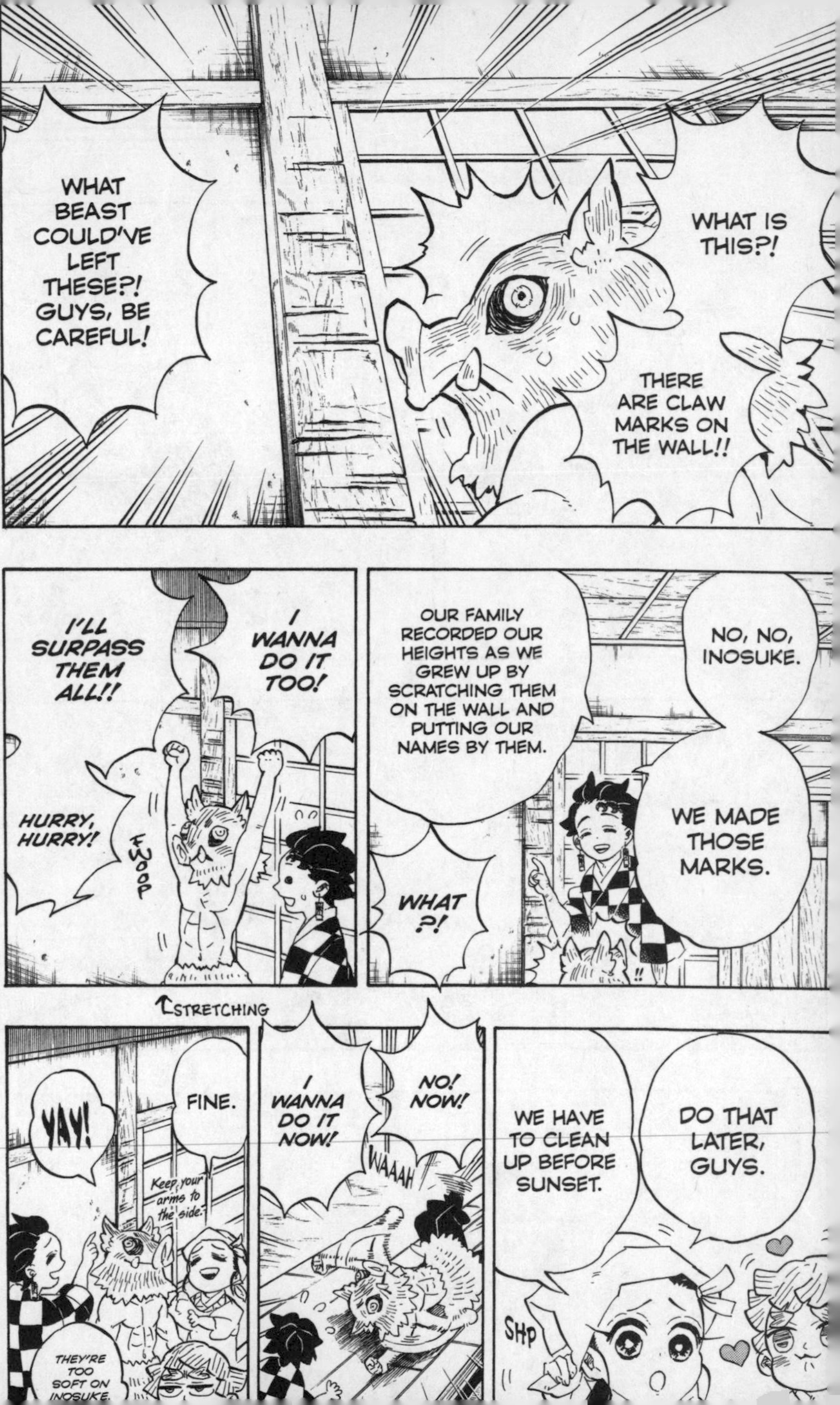
WHAT IS THIS?!
THERE ARE CLAW MARKS ON THE WALL!!
WHAT BEAST COULD'VE LEFT THESE?! GUYS, BE CAREFUL!
NO, NO, INOSUKE.
WE MADE THOSE MARKS.
OUR FAMILY RECORDED OUR HEIGHTS AS WE GREW UP BY SCRATCHING THEM ON THE WALL AND PUTTING OUR NAMES BY THEM.
WHAT ?!
!!
I WANNA DO IT TOO!
I'LL SURPASS THEM ALL!!
HURRY, HURRY!
FWOOP
STRETCHING
DO THAT LATER, GUYS.
WE HAVE TO CLEAN UP BEFORE SUNSET.
SHP
NO! NOW!
I WANNA DO IT NOW!
WAAAH
FINE.
YAY!
Keep your arms to the side.
THEY'RE TOO SOFT ON INOSUKE.

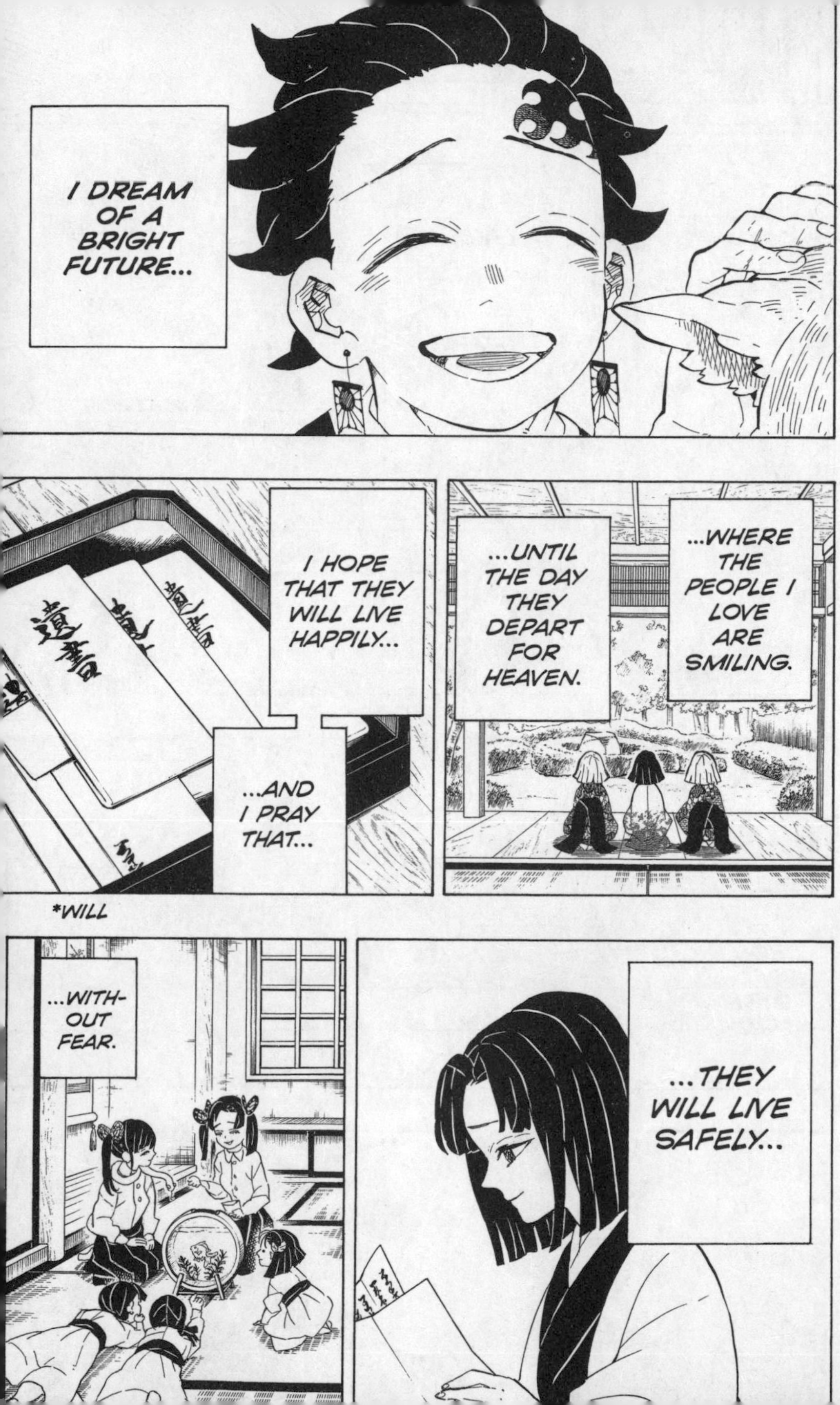
I DREAM OF A BRIGHT FUTURE...
...WHERE THE PEOPLE I LOVE ARE SMILING.
...UNTIL THE DAY THEY DEPART FOR HEAVEN.
I HOPE THAT THEY WILL LIVE HAPPILY...
...AND I PRAY THAT...
遺書
*WILL
...THEY WILL LIVE SAFELY...
...WITH-OUT FEAR.

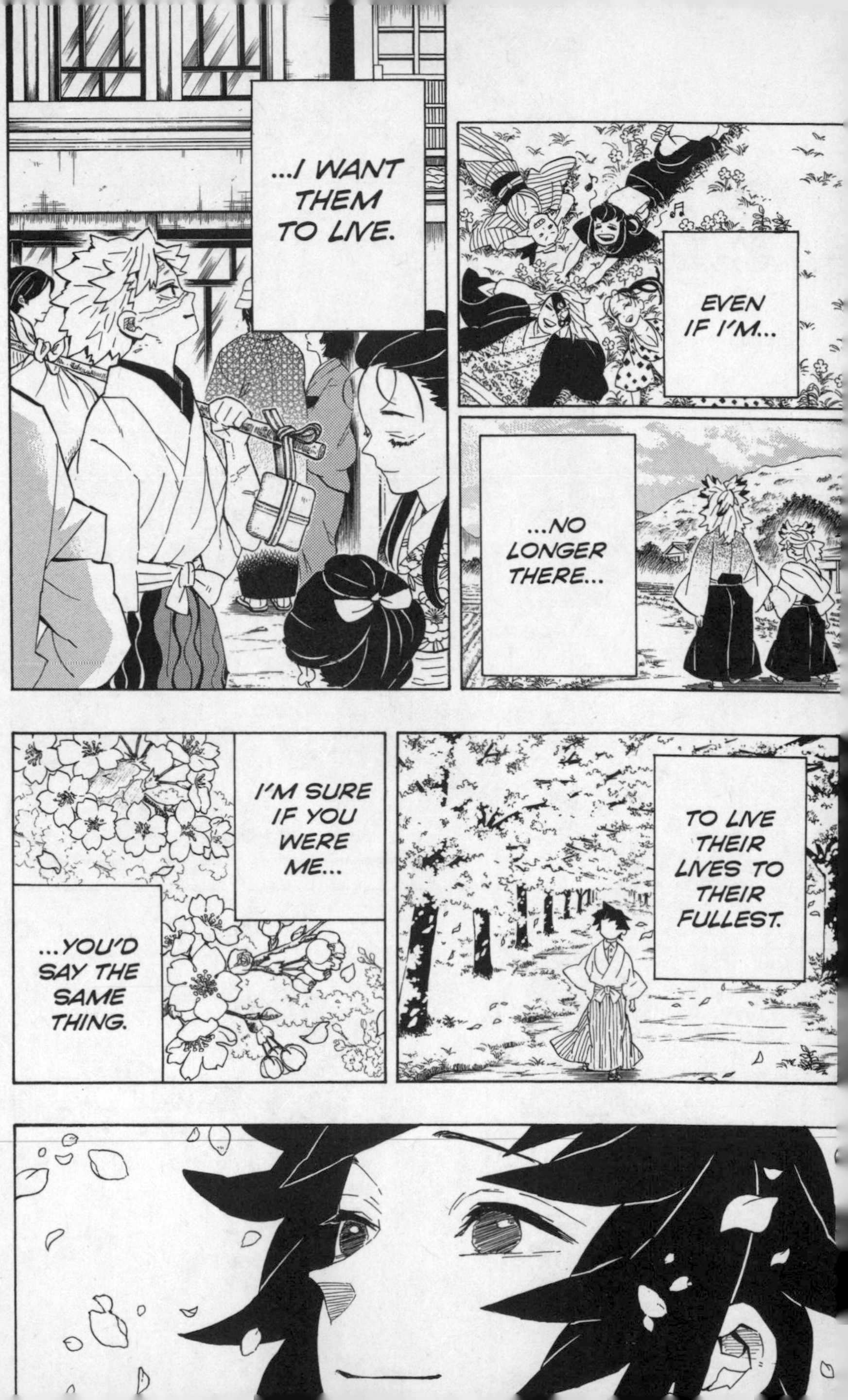
EVEN IF I'M...
...NO LONGER THERE...
...I WANT THEM TO LIVE.
TO LIVE THEIR LIVES TO THEIR FULLEST.
I'M SURE IF YOU WERE ME...
...YOU'D SAY THE SAME THING.

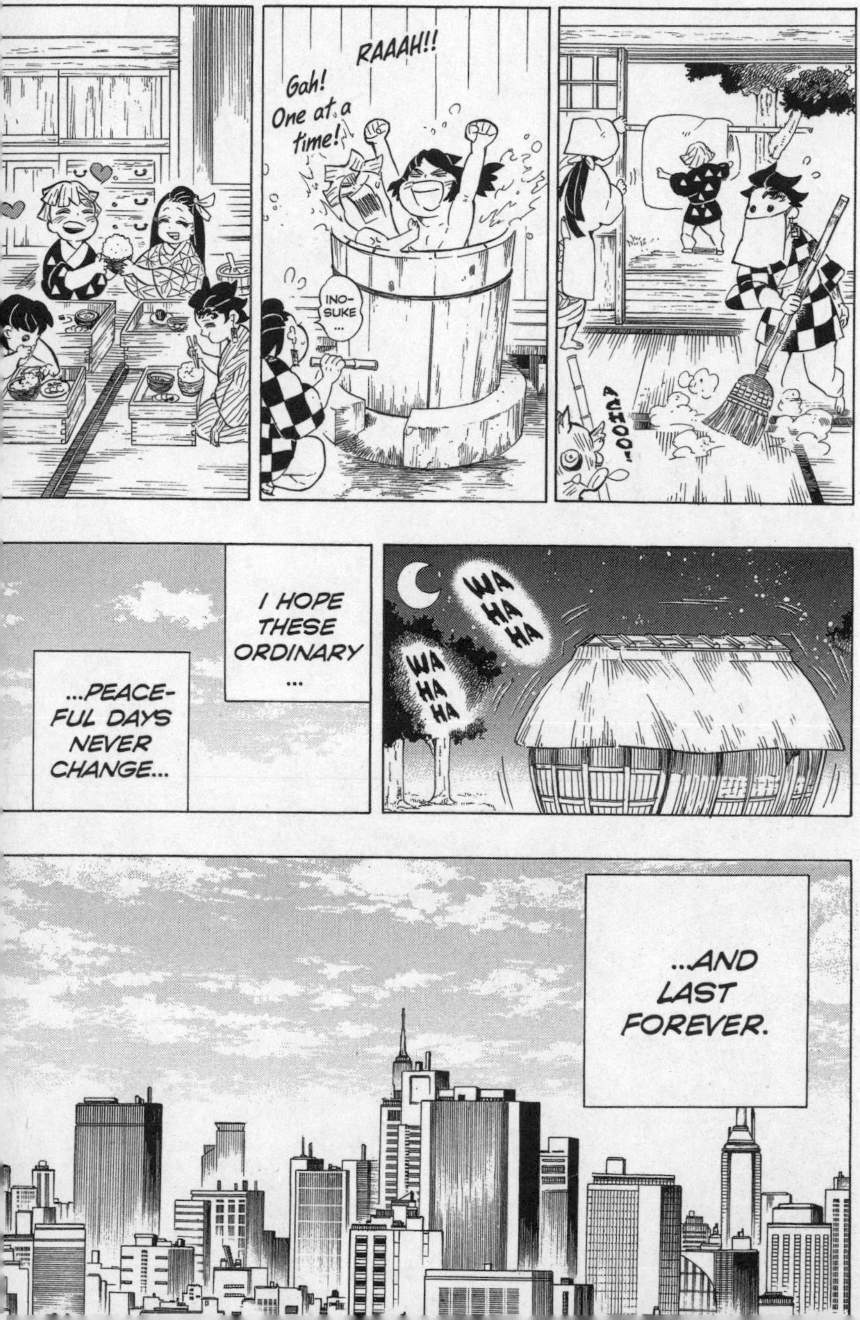
ACHOO!
RAAAH!!
Gah! One at a time!
INO-SUKE ...
WA HA HA
WA HA HA
I HOPE THESE ORDINARY ...
...PEACE-FUL DAYS NEVER CHANGE...
...AND LAST FOREVER.

NEZUKO EXPLAINS GRAVES TO INOSUKE

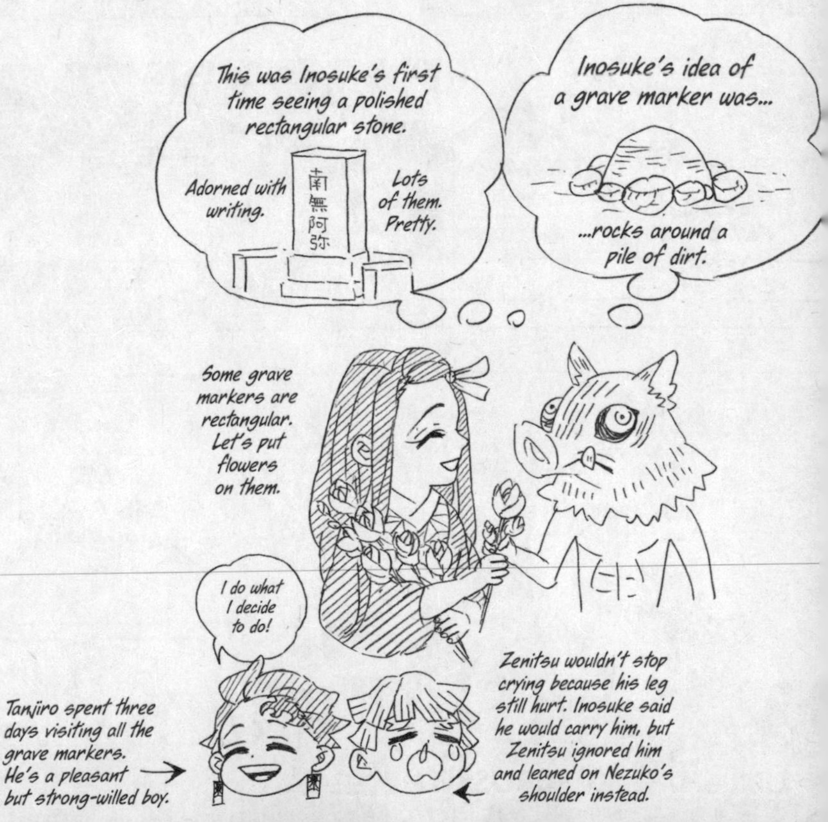
Inosuke's idea of a grave marker was...
...rocks around a pile of dirt.
This was Inosuke's first time seeing a polished rectangular stone.
Lots of them. Pretty.
南無阿弥
Adorned with writing.
Some grave markers are rectangular. Let's put flowers on them.
I do what I decide to do!
Zenitsu wouldn't stop crying because his leg still hurt. Inosuke said he would carry him, but Zenitsu ignored him and leaned on Nezuko's shoulder instead.
Tanjiro spent three days visiting all the grave markers. He's a pleasant but strong-willed boy.

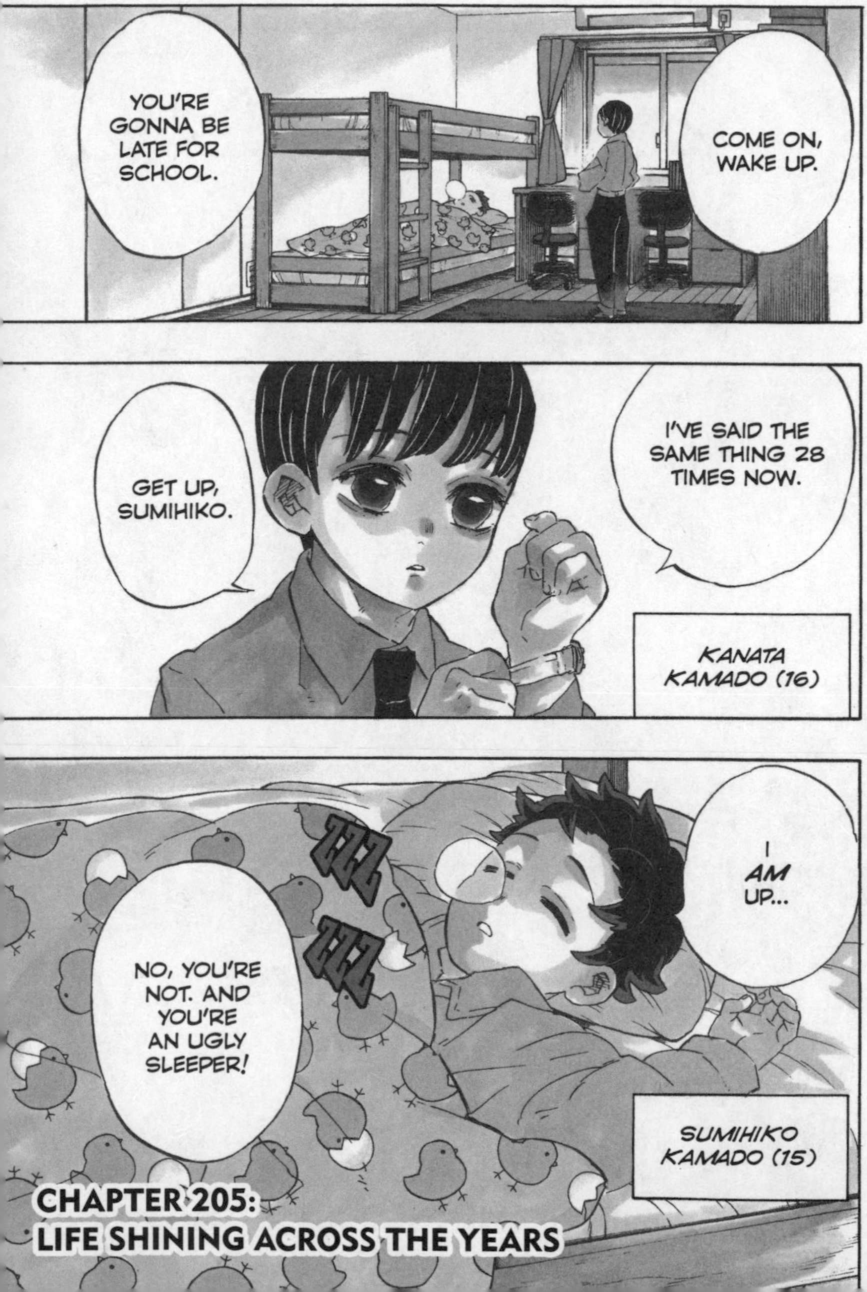
COME ON, WAKE UP.
YOU'RE GONNA BE LATE FOR SCHOOL.
I'VE SAID THE SAME THING 28 TIMES NOW.
GET UP, SUMIHIKO.
KANATA KAMADO (16)
I AM UP...
ZZZ
ZZZ
NO, YOU'RE NOT. AND YOU'RE AN UGLY SLEEPER!
SUMIHIKO KAMADO (15)
CHAPTER 205: LIFE SHINING ACROSS THE YEARS

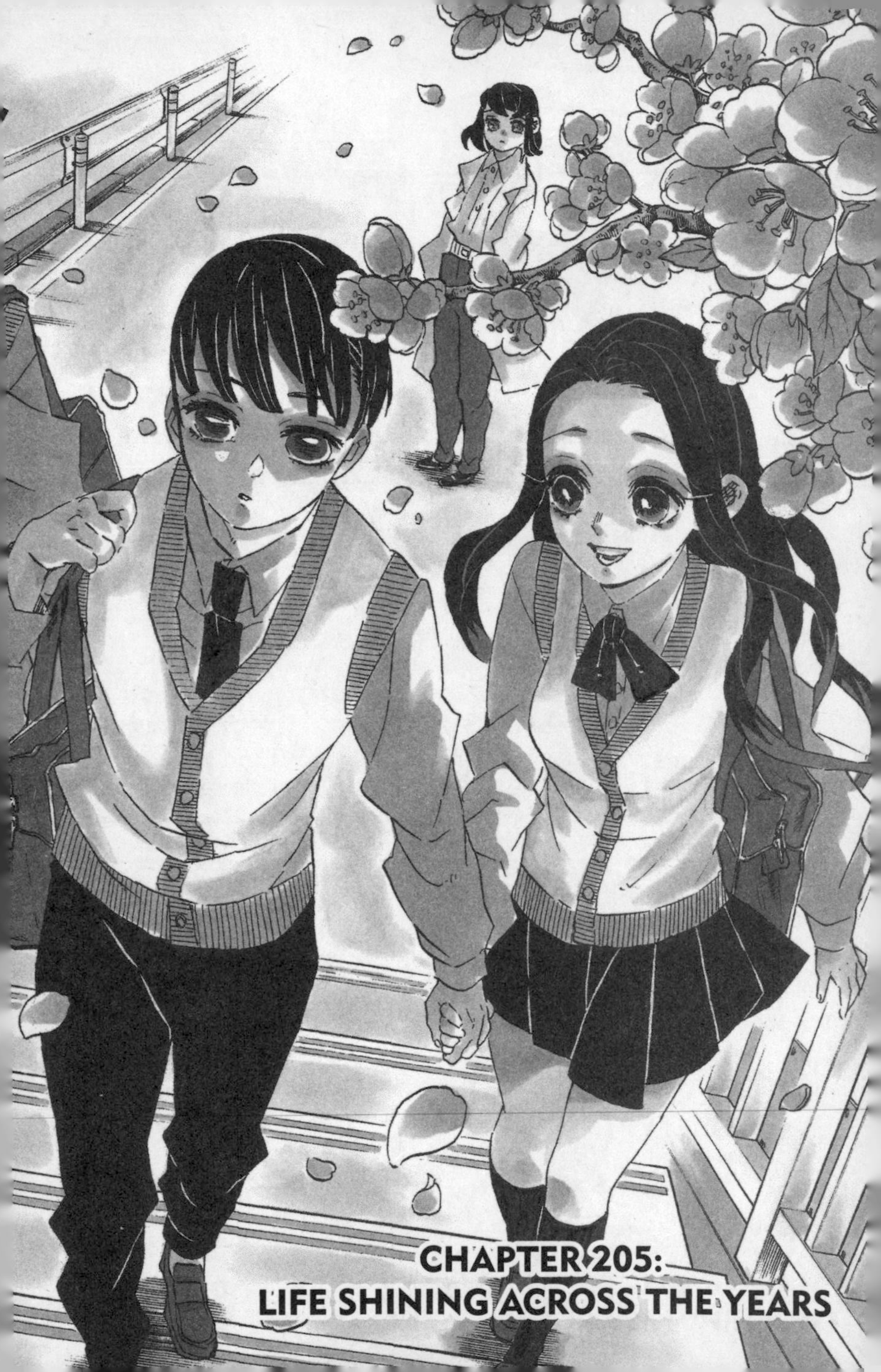
CHAPTER 205:
LIFE SHINING ACROSS THE YEARS

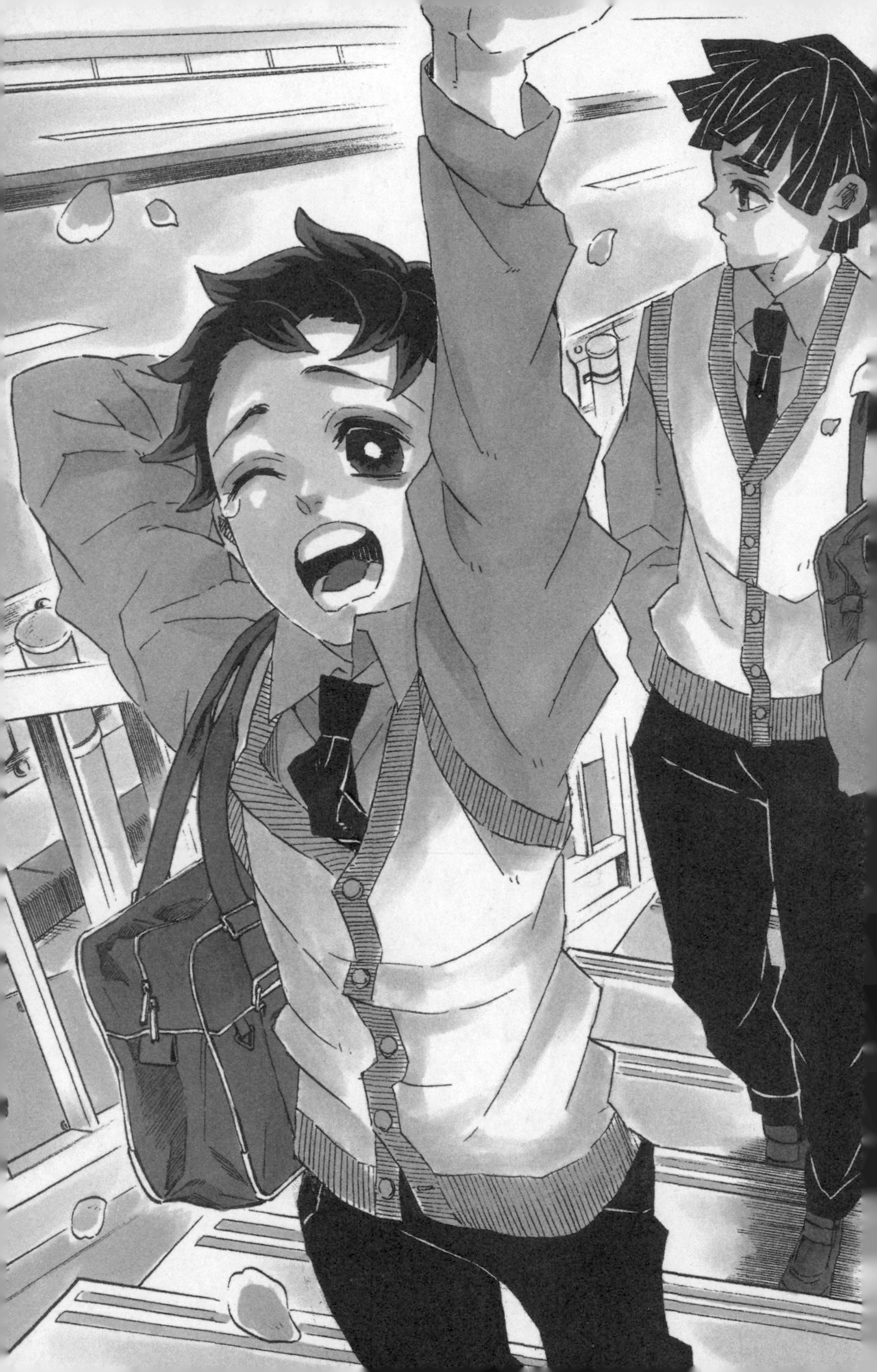

Many of the last wills and testaments left by members of the Demon Slayer Corps contained wishes for Tanjiro and Nezuko's happiness. Kiriya let them read those.

*Will

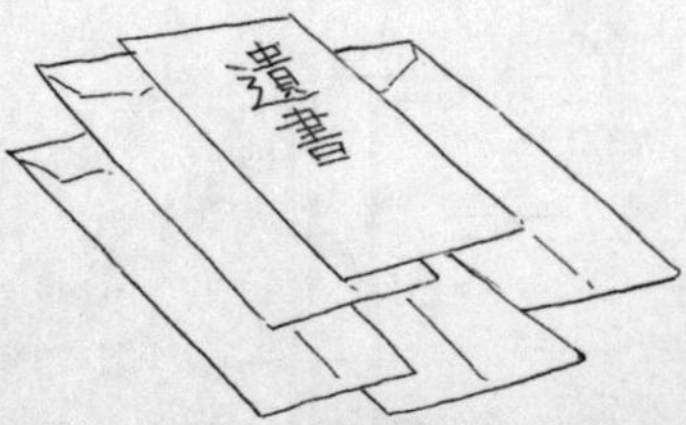
遺書

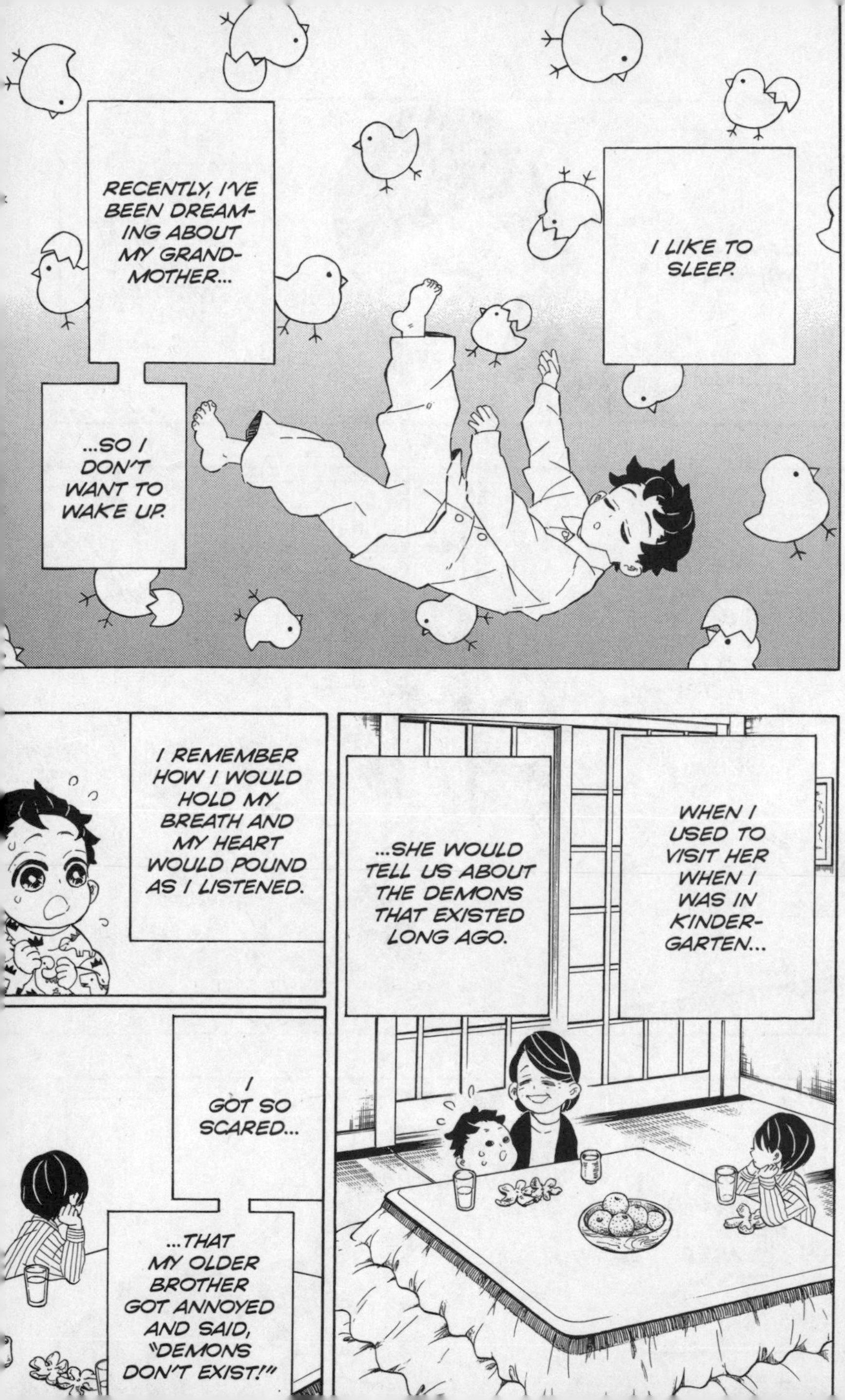
I LIKE TO SLEEP.
RECENTLY, I'VE BEEN DREAMING ABOUT MY GRANDMOTHER...
...SO I DON'T WANT TO WAKE UP.
WHEN I USED TO VISIT HER WHEN I WAS IN KINDERGARTEN...
...SHE WOULD TELL US ABOUT THE DEMONS THAT EXISTED LONG AGO.
I REMEMBER HOW I WOULD HOLD MY BREATH AND MY HEART WOULD POUND AS I LISTENED.
I GOT SO SCARED...
...THAT MY OLDER BROTHER GOT ANNOYED AND SAID, "DEMONS DON'T EXIST!"

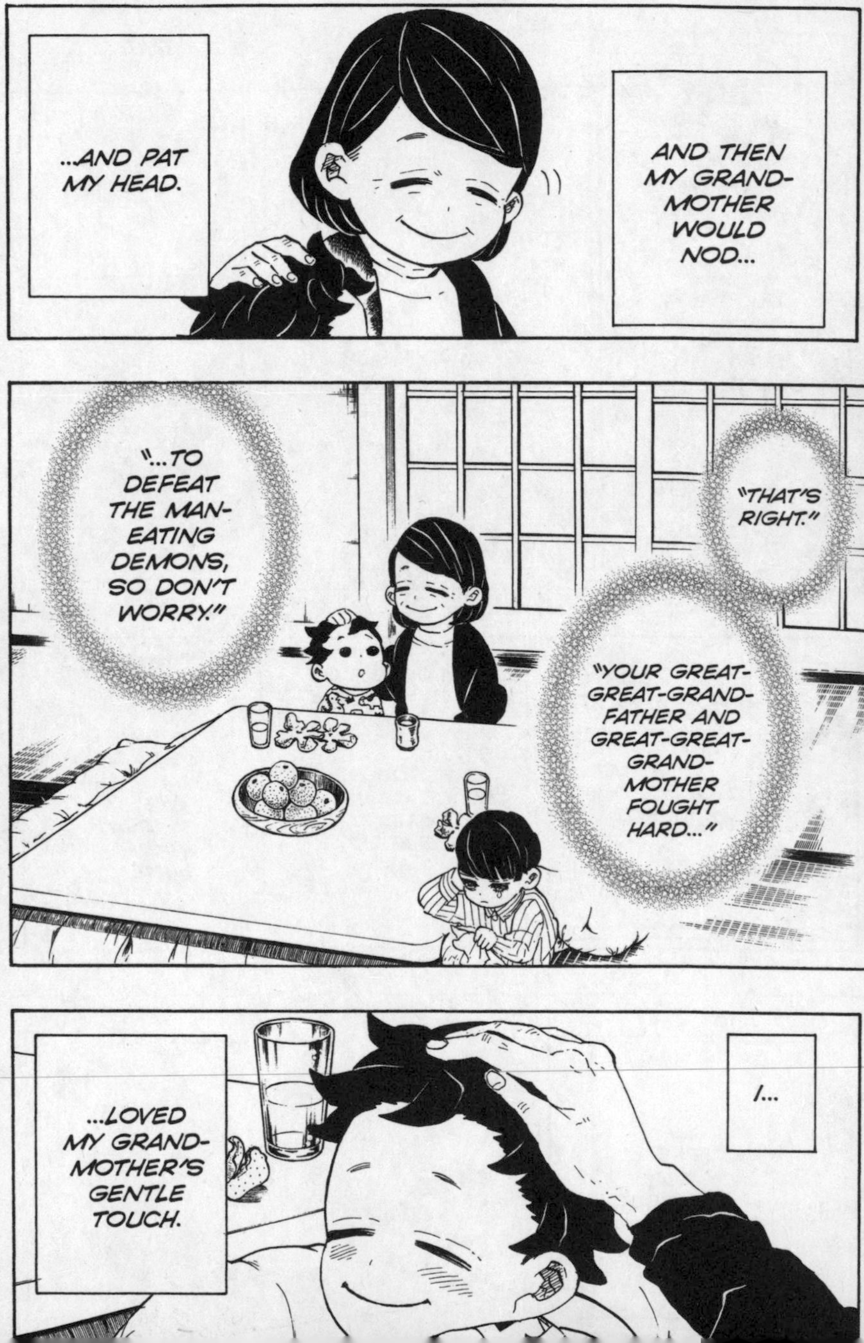
AND THEN MY GRAND-MOTHER WOULD NOD...
...AND PAT MY HEAD.
"THAT'S RIGHT."
"YOUR GREAT-GREAT-GRAND-FATHER AND GREAT-GREAT-GRAND-MOTHER FOUGHT HARD..."
"...TO DEFEAT THE MAN-EATING DEMONS, SO DON'T WORRY."
I...
...LOVED MY GRAND-MOTHER'S GENTLE TOUCH.

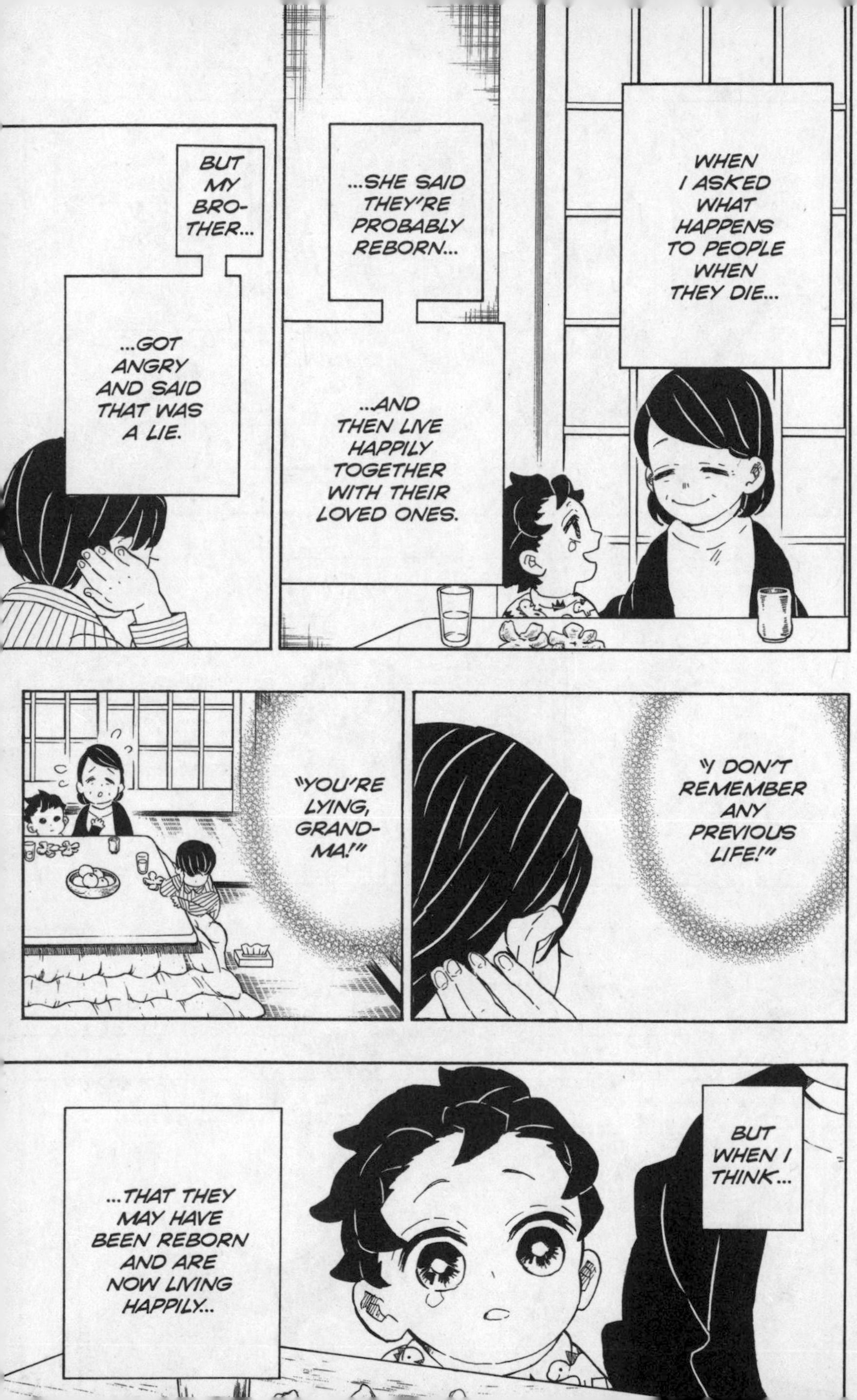
WHEN I ASKED WHAT HAPPENS TO PEOPLE WHEN THEY DIE...
...SHE SAID THEY'RE PROBABLY REBORN...
...AND THEN LIVE HAPPILY TOGETHER WITH THEIR LOVED ONES.
BUT MY BRO-THER...
...GOT ANGRY AND SAID THAT WAS A LIE.
"I DON'T REMEMBER ANY PREVIOUS LIFE!"
"YOU'RE LYING, GRAND-MA!"
BUT WHEN I THINK...
...THAT THEY MAY HAVE BEEN REBORN AND ARE NOW LIVING HAPPILY...

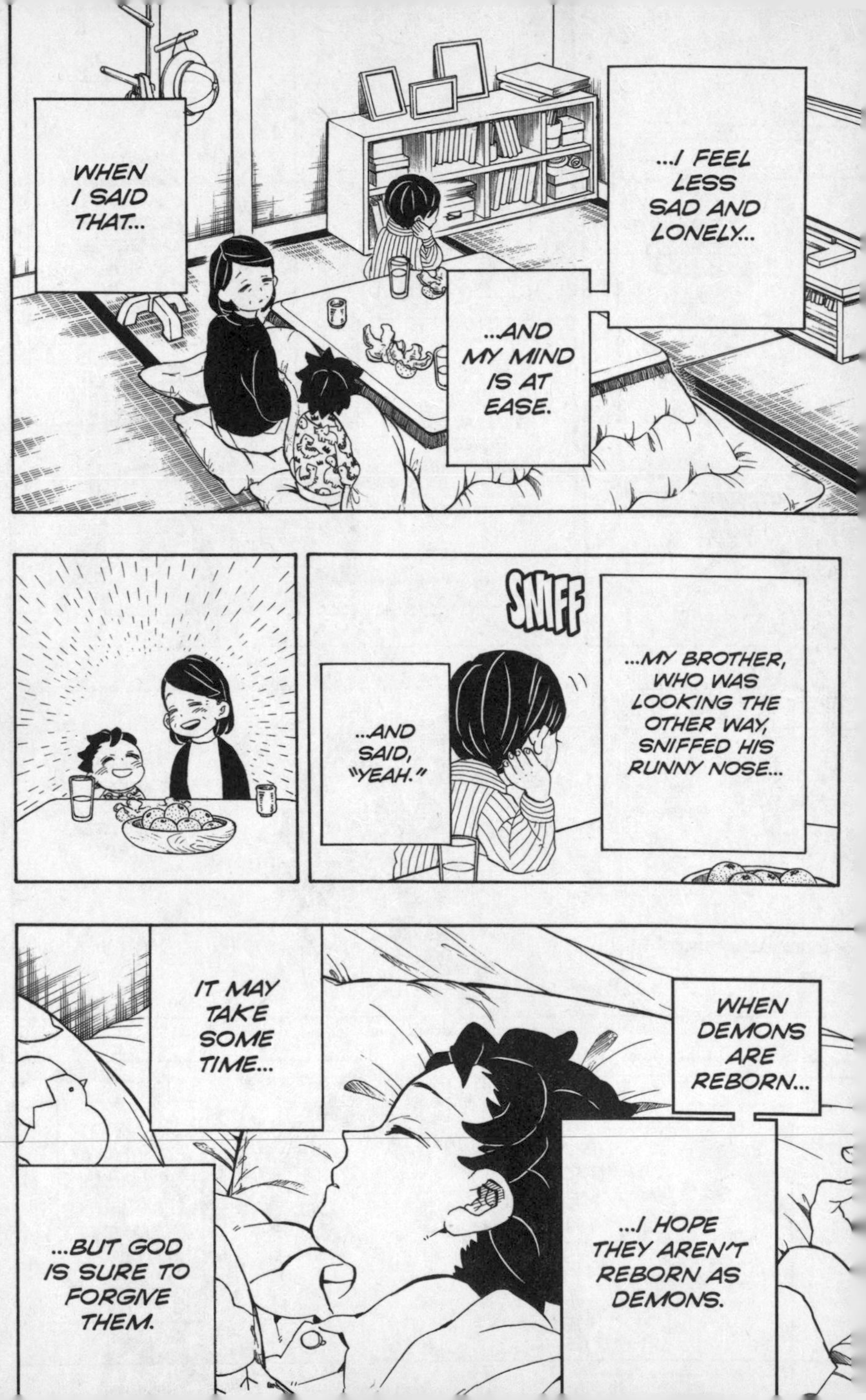
...I FEEL LESS SAD AND LONELY...
...AND MY MIND IS AT EASE.
WHEN I SAID THAT...
SNIFF
...MY BROTHER, WHO WAS LOOKING THE OTHER WAY, SNIFFED HIS RUNNY NOSE...
...AND SAID, "YEAH."
WHEN DEMONS ARE REBORN...
...I HOPE THEY AREN'T REBORN AS DEMONS.
IT MAY TAKE SOME TIME...
...BUT GOD IS SURE TO FORGIVE THEM.

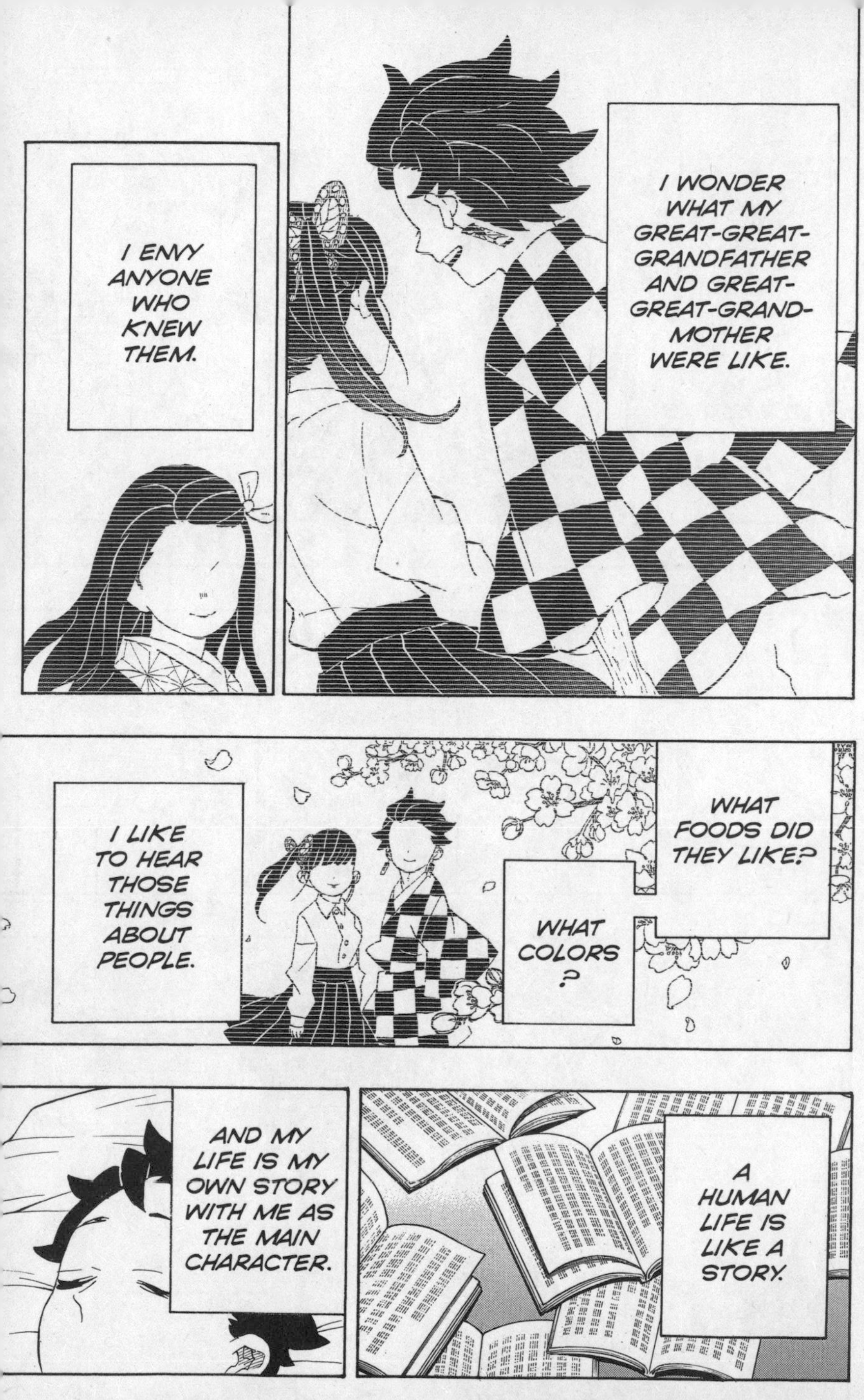
I WONDER WHAT MY GREAT-GREAT-GRANDFATHER AND GREAT-GREAT-GRAND-MOTHER WERE LIKE.
I ENVY ANYONE WHO KNEW THEM.
WHAT FOODS DID THEY LIKE?
WHAT COLORS?
I LIKE TO HEAR THOSE THINGS ABOUT PEOPLE.
A HUMAN LIFE IS LIKE A STORY.
AND MY LIFE IS MY OWN STORY WITH ME AS THE MAIN CHARACTER.

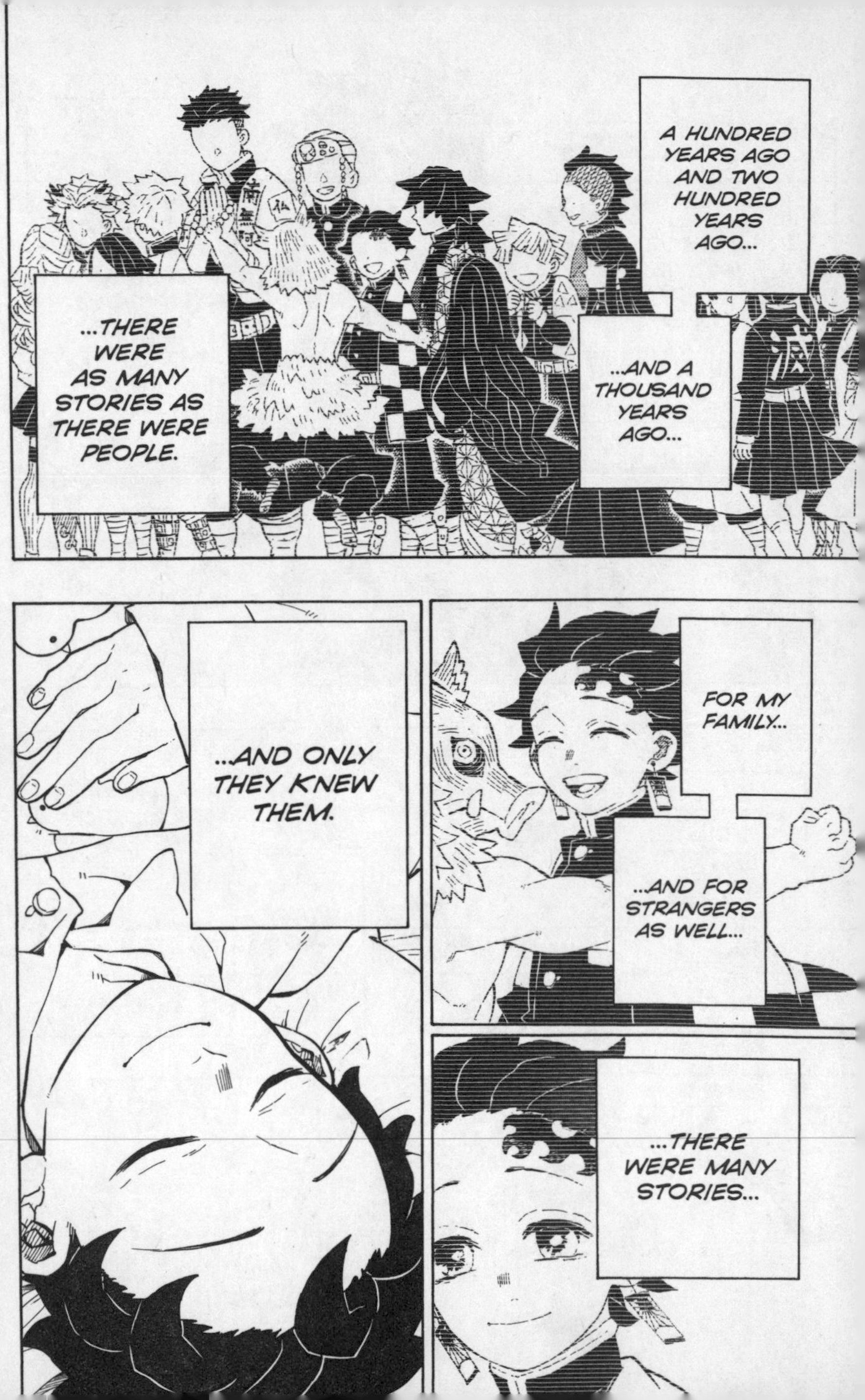
A HUNDRED YEARS AGO AND TWO HUNDRED YEARS AGO...
...AND A THOUSAND YEARS AGO...
...THERE WERE AS MANY STORIES AS THERE WERE PEOPLE.
FOR MY FAMILY...
...AND FOR STRANGERS AS WELL...
...THERE WERE MANY STORIES...
...AND ONLY THEY KNEW THEM.

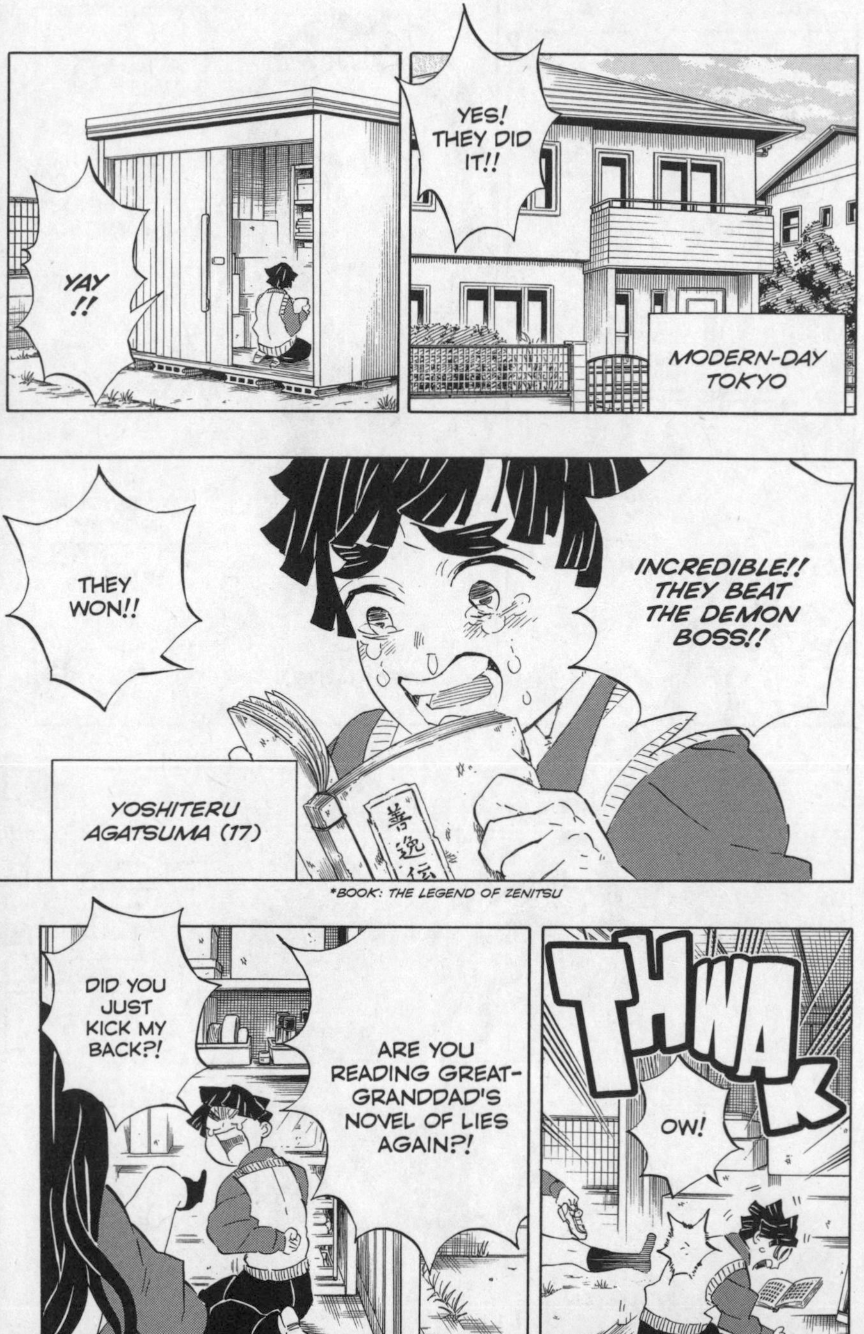
YES! THEY DID IT!!
MODERN-DAY TOKYO
YAY!!
INCREDIBLE!! THEY BEAT THE DEMON BOSS!!
THEY WON!!
YOSHITERU AGATSUMA (17)
善逸伝
*BOOK: THE LEGEND OF ZENITSU
THWAK
OW!
ARE YOU READING GREAT-GRANDDAD'S NOVEL OF LIES AGAIN?!
DID YOU JUST KICK MY BACK?!

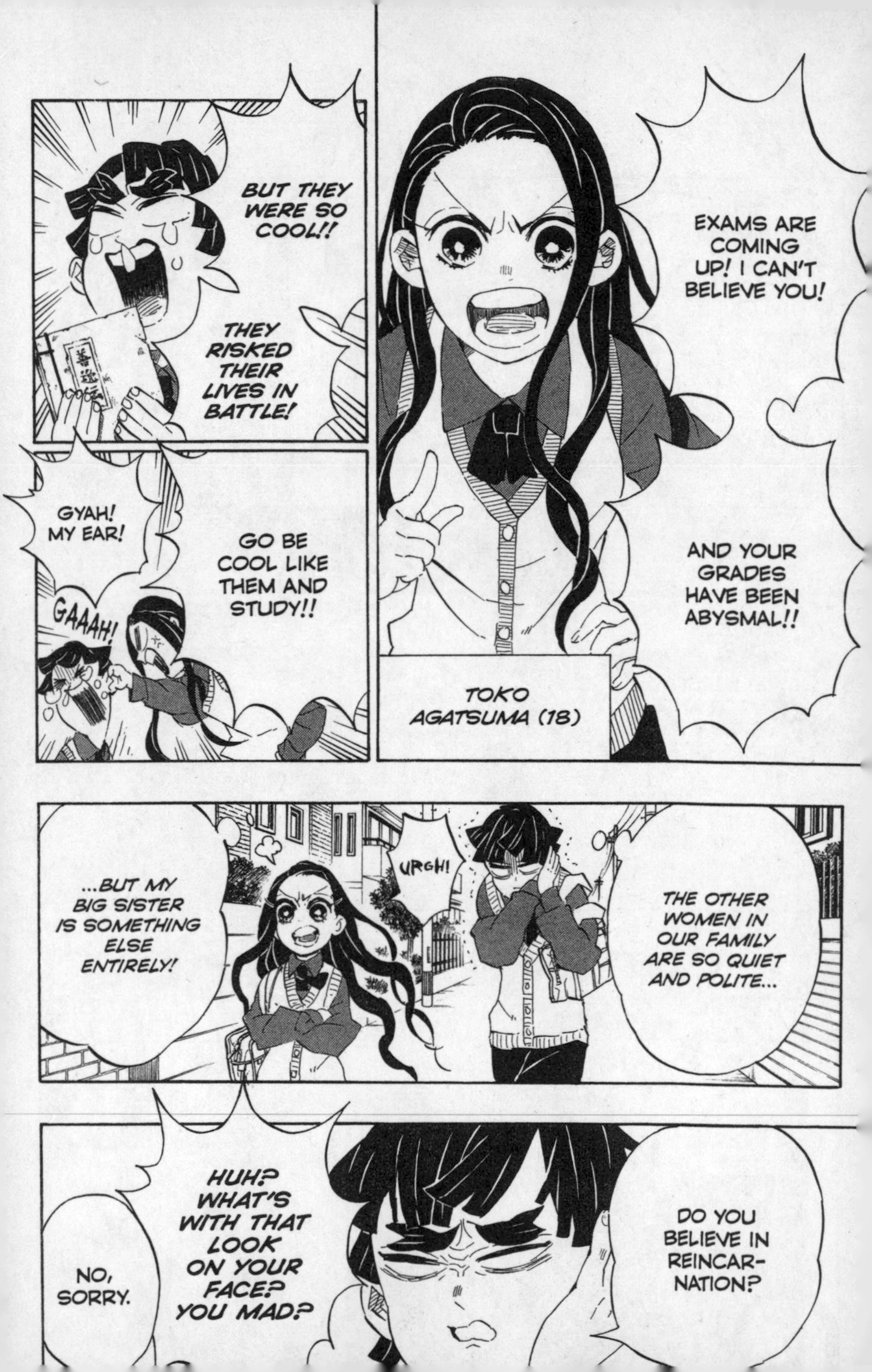
EXAMS ARE COMING UP! I CAN'T BELIEVE YOU!
AND YOUR GRADES HAVE BEEN ABYSMAL!!
TOKO AGATSUMA (18)
BUT THEY WERE SO COOL!!
THEY RISKED THEIR LIVES IN BATTLE!
GO BE COOL LIKE THEM AND STUDY!!
GYAH! MY EAR!
GAAAH!
THE OTHER WOMEN IN OUR FAMILY ARE SO QUIET AND POLITE...
URGH!
...BUT MY BIG SISTER IS SOMETHING ELSE ENTIRELY!
DO YOU BELIEVE IN REINCARNATION?
HUH? WHAT'S WITH THAT LOOK ON YOUR FACE? YOU MAD?
NO, SORRY.

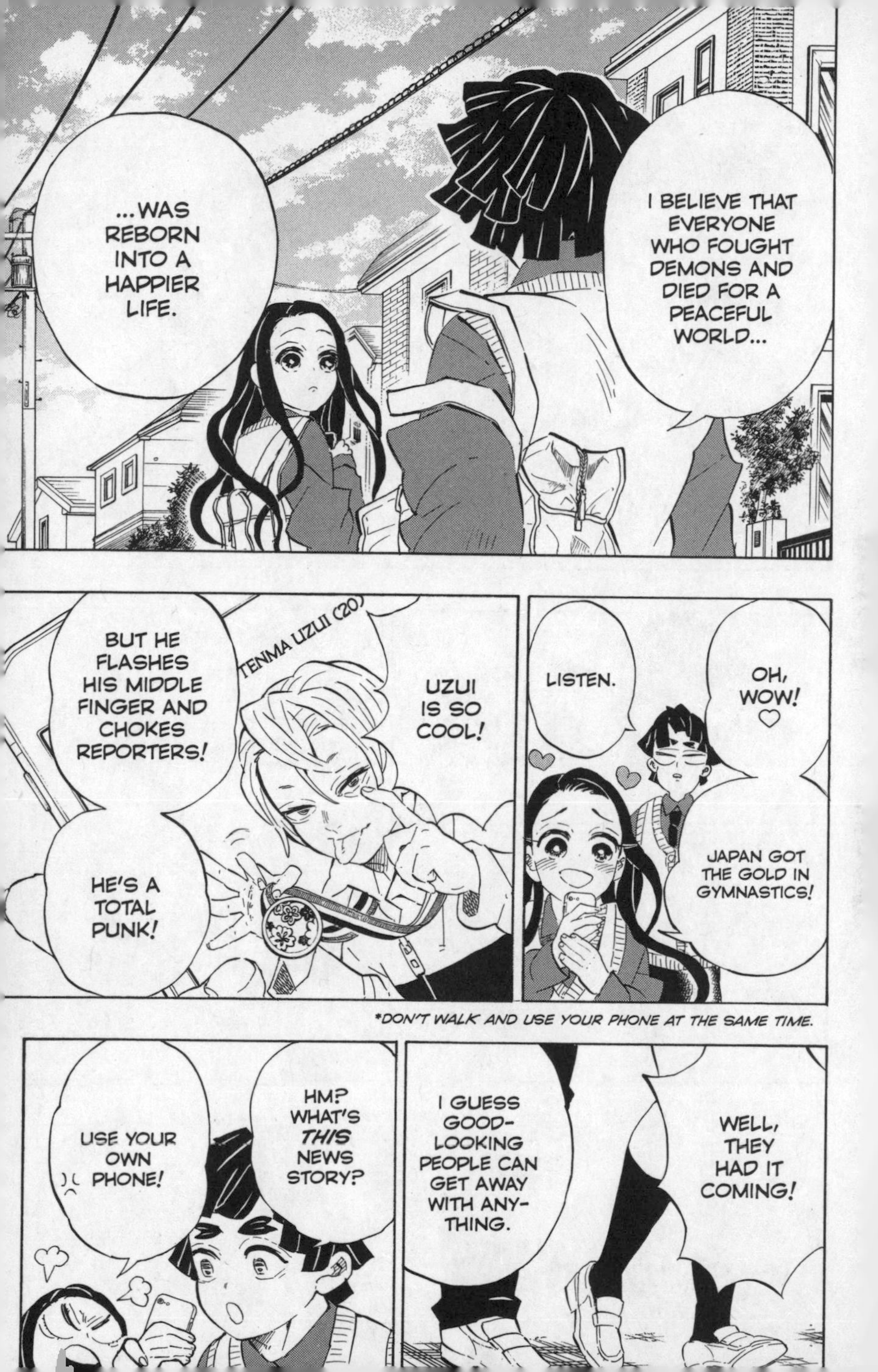
I BELIEVE THAT EVERYONE WHO FOUGHT DEMONS AND DIED FOR A PEACEFUL WORLD...
...WAS REBORN INTO A HAPPIER LIFE.
OH, WOW! ♡
JAPAN GOT THE GOLD IN GYMNASTICS!
LISTEN.
UZUI IS SO COOL!
TENMA UZUI (20)
BUT HE FLASHES HIS MIDDLE FINGER AND CHOKES REPORTERS!
HE'S A TOTAL PUNK!
*DON'T WALK AND USE YOUR PHONE AT THE SAME TIME.
WELL, THEY HAD IT COMING!
I GUESS GOOD-LOOKING PEOPLE CAN GET AWAY WITH ANYTHING.
HM? WHAT'S *THIS* NEWS STORY?
USE YOUR OWN PHONE!

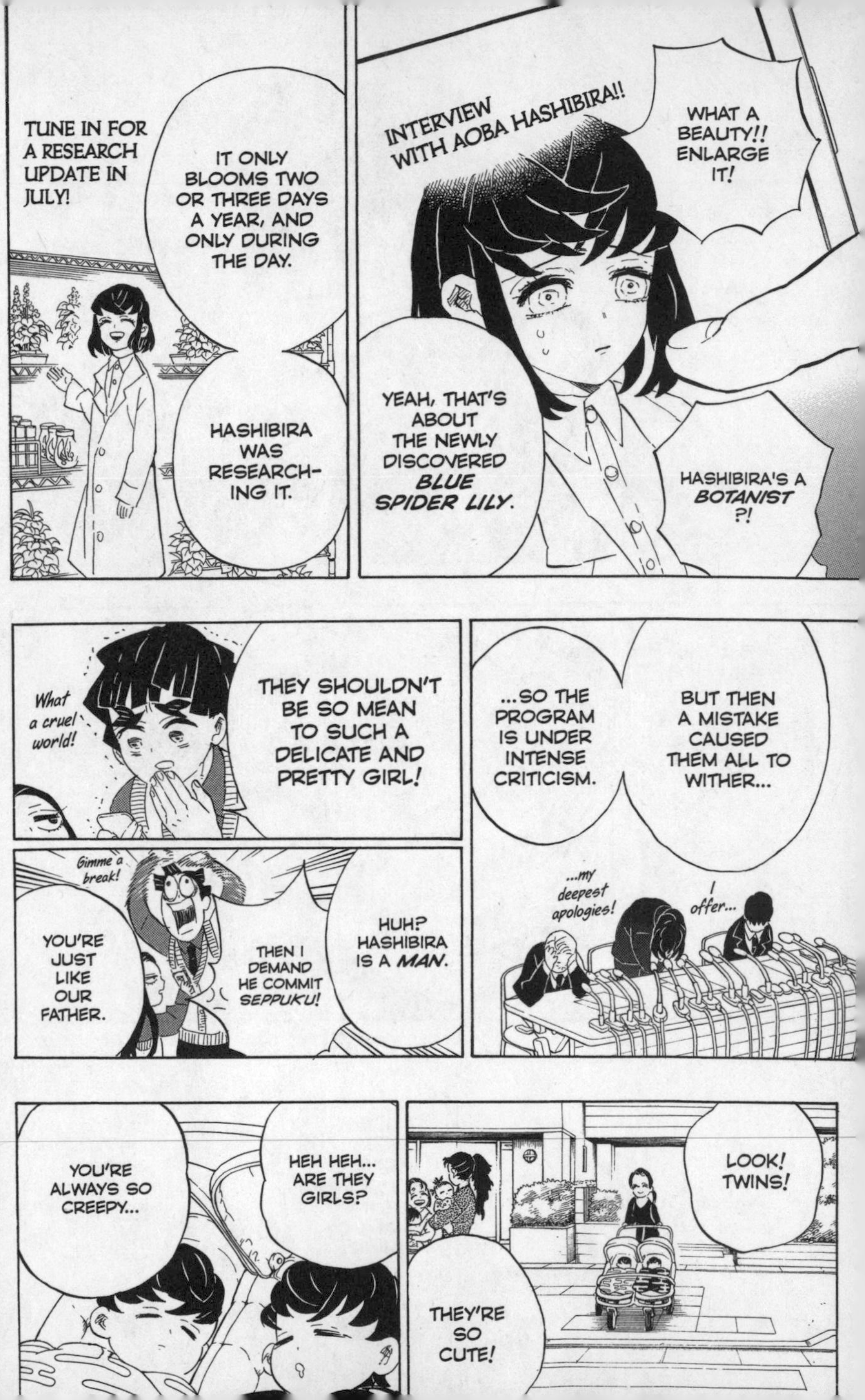
WHAT A BEAUTY!! ENLARGE IT!
INTERVIEW WITH AOBA HASHIBIRA!!
HASHIBIRA'S A *BOTANIST*?!
YEAH, THAT'S ABOUT THE NEWLY DISCOVERED ***BLUE SPIDER LILY***.
IT ONLY BLOOMS TWO OR THREE DAYS A YEAR, AND ONLY DURING THE DAY.
TUNE IN FOR A RESEARCH UPDATE IN JULY!
HASHIBIRA WAS RESEARCHING IT.
BUT THEN A MISTAKE CAUSED THEM ALL TO WITHER...
...SO THE PROGRAM IS UNDER INTENSE CRITICISM.
I offer...
...my deepest apologies!
THEY SHOULDN'T BE SO MEAN TO SUCH A DELICATE AND PRETTY GIRL!
What a cruel world!
HUH? HASHIBIRA IS A ***MAN***.
THEN I DEMAND HE COMMIT *SEPPUKU*!
Gimme a break!
YOU'RE JUST LIKE OUR FATHER.
LOOK! TWINS!
THEY'RE SO CUTE!
HEH HEH... ARE THEY GIRLS?
YOU'RE ALWAYS SO CREEPY...

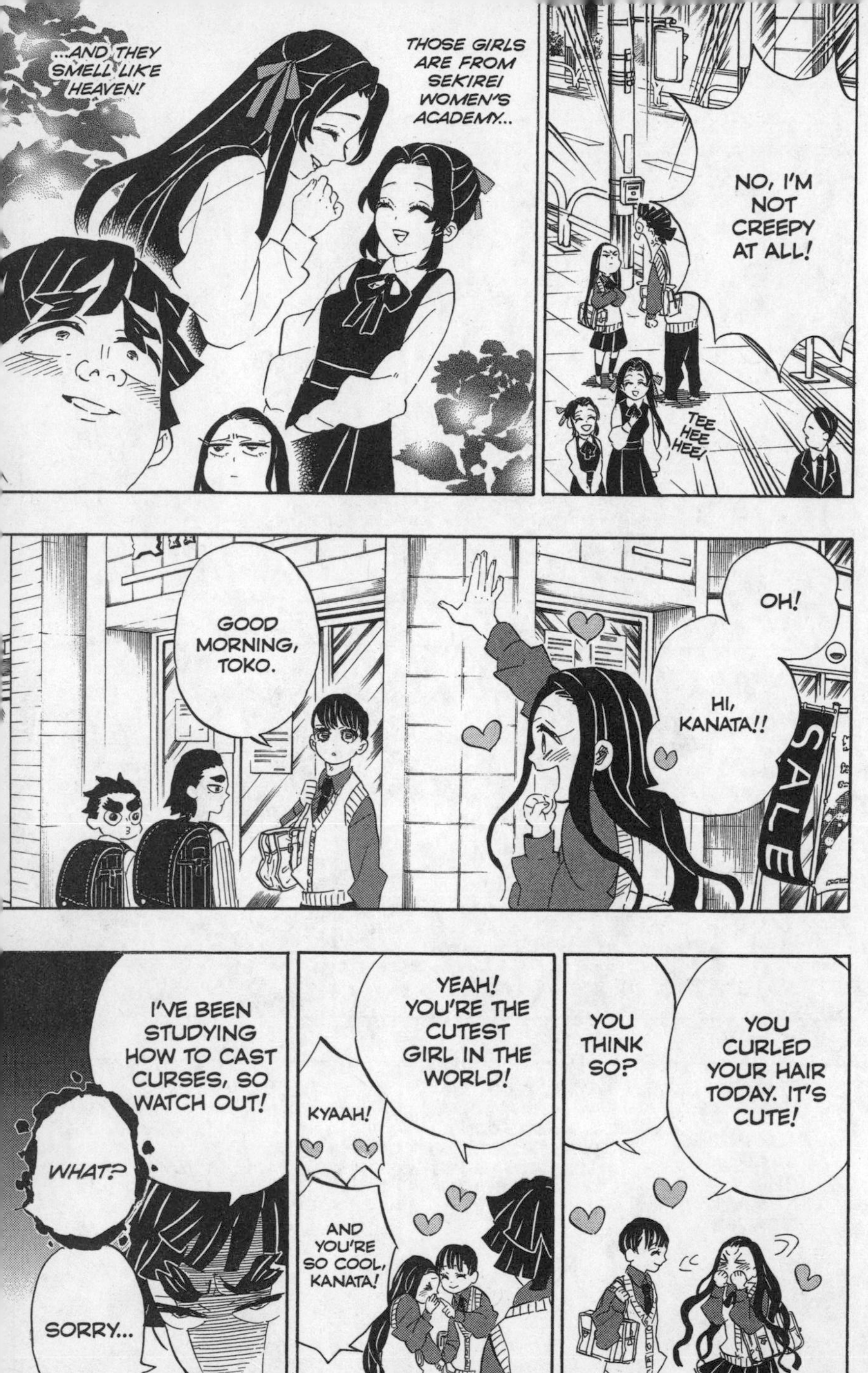
NO, I'M NOT CREEPY AT ALL!
TEE HEE HEE!
THOSE GIRLS ARE FROM SEKIREI WOMEN'S ACADEMY...
...AND THEY SMELL LIKE HEAVEN!
OH!
HI, KANATA!!
SALE
GOOD MORNING, TOKO.
YOU CURLED YOUR HAIR TODAY. IT'S CUTE!
YOU THINK SO?
YEAH! YOU'RE THE CUTEST GIRL IN THE WORLD!
KYAAH!
AND YOU'RE SO COOL, KANATA!
I'VE BEEN STUDYING HOW TO CAST CURSES, SO WATCH OUT!
WHAT?
SORRY...

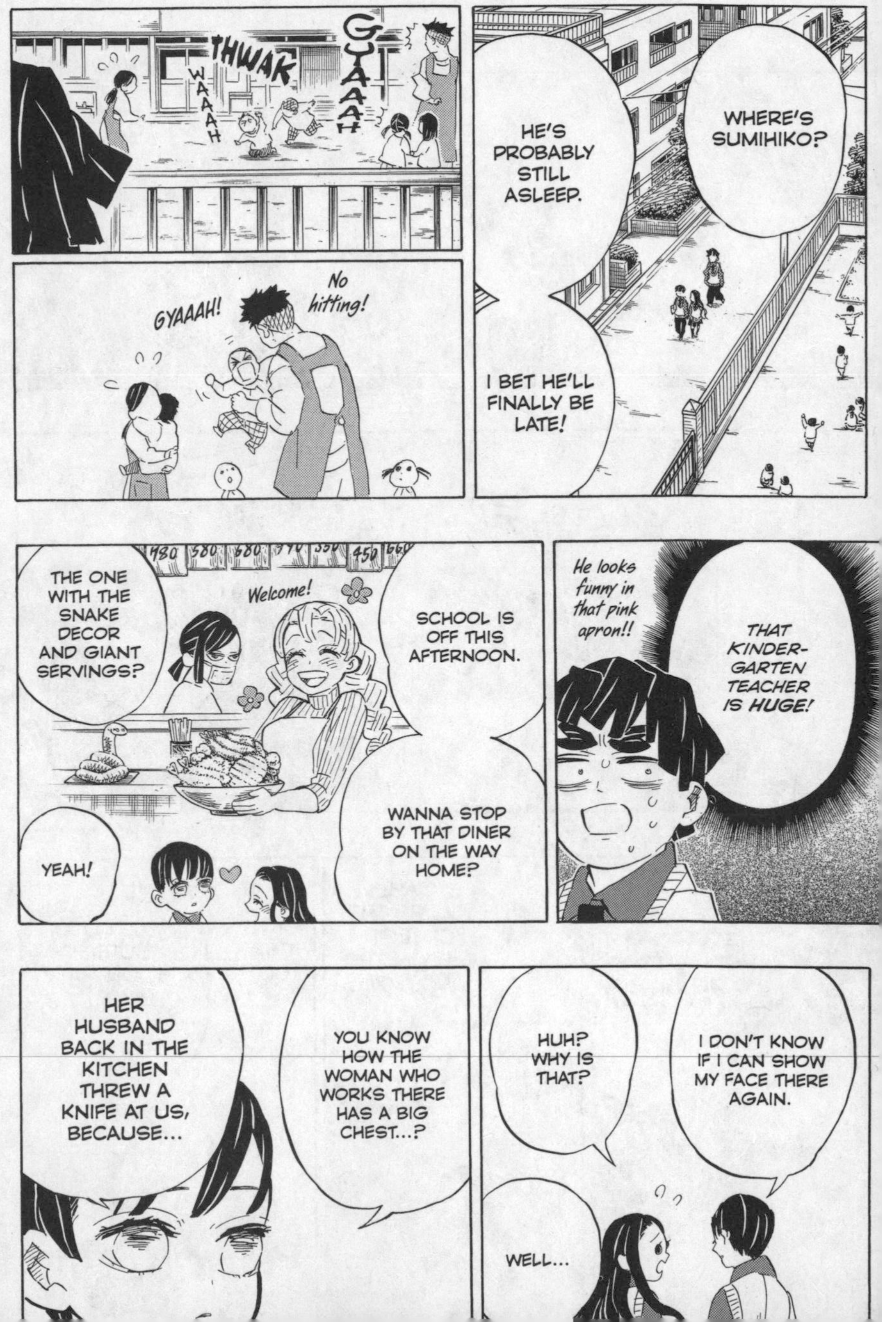
WHERE'S SUMIHIKO?
HE'S PROBABLY STILL ASLEEP.
I BET HE'LL FINALLY BE LATE!
THWAK
WAAAAH
GYAAAAH
No hitting!
GYAAAH!
THAT KINDER-GARTEN TEACHER IS HUGE!
He looks funny in that pink apron!!
SCHOOL IS OFF THIS AFTERNOON.
WANNA STOP BY THAT DINER ON THE WAY HOME?
THE ONE WITH THE SNAKE DECOR AND GIANT SERVINGS?
Welcome!
YEAH!
I DON'T KNOW IF I CAN SHOW MY FACE THERE AGAIN.
HUH? WHY IS THAT?
WELL...
YOU KNOW HOW THE WOMAN WHO WORKS THERE HAS A BIG CHEST...?
HER HUSBAND BACK IN THE KITCHEN THREW A KNIFE AT US, BECAUSE...

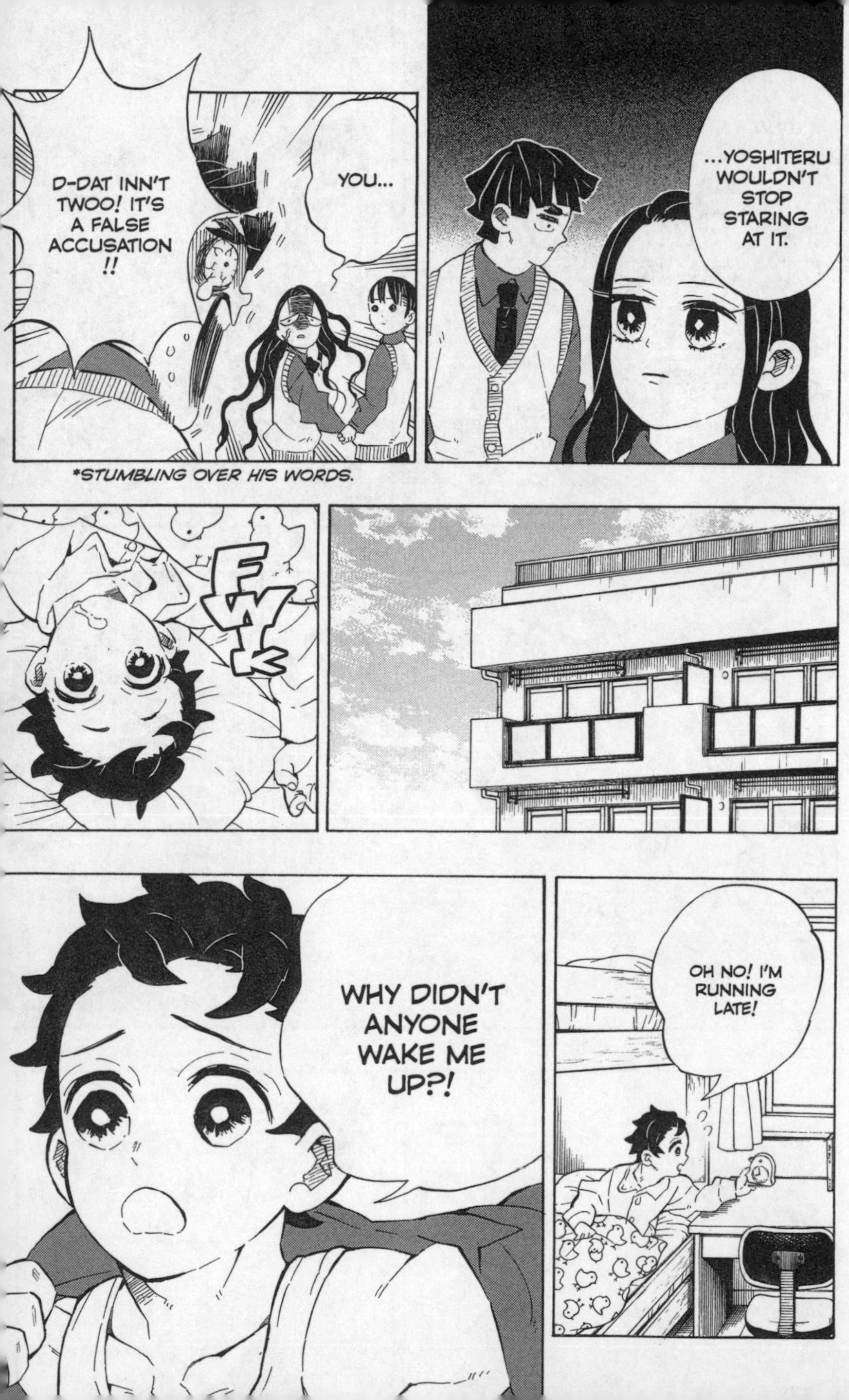
...YOSHITERU WOULDN'T STOP STARING AT IT.
YOU...
D-DAT INN'T TWOO! IT'S A FALSE ACCUSATION!!
*STUMBLING OVER HIS WORDS.
FWK
OH NO! I'M RUNNING LATE!
WHY DIDN'T ANYONE WAKE ME UP?!

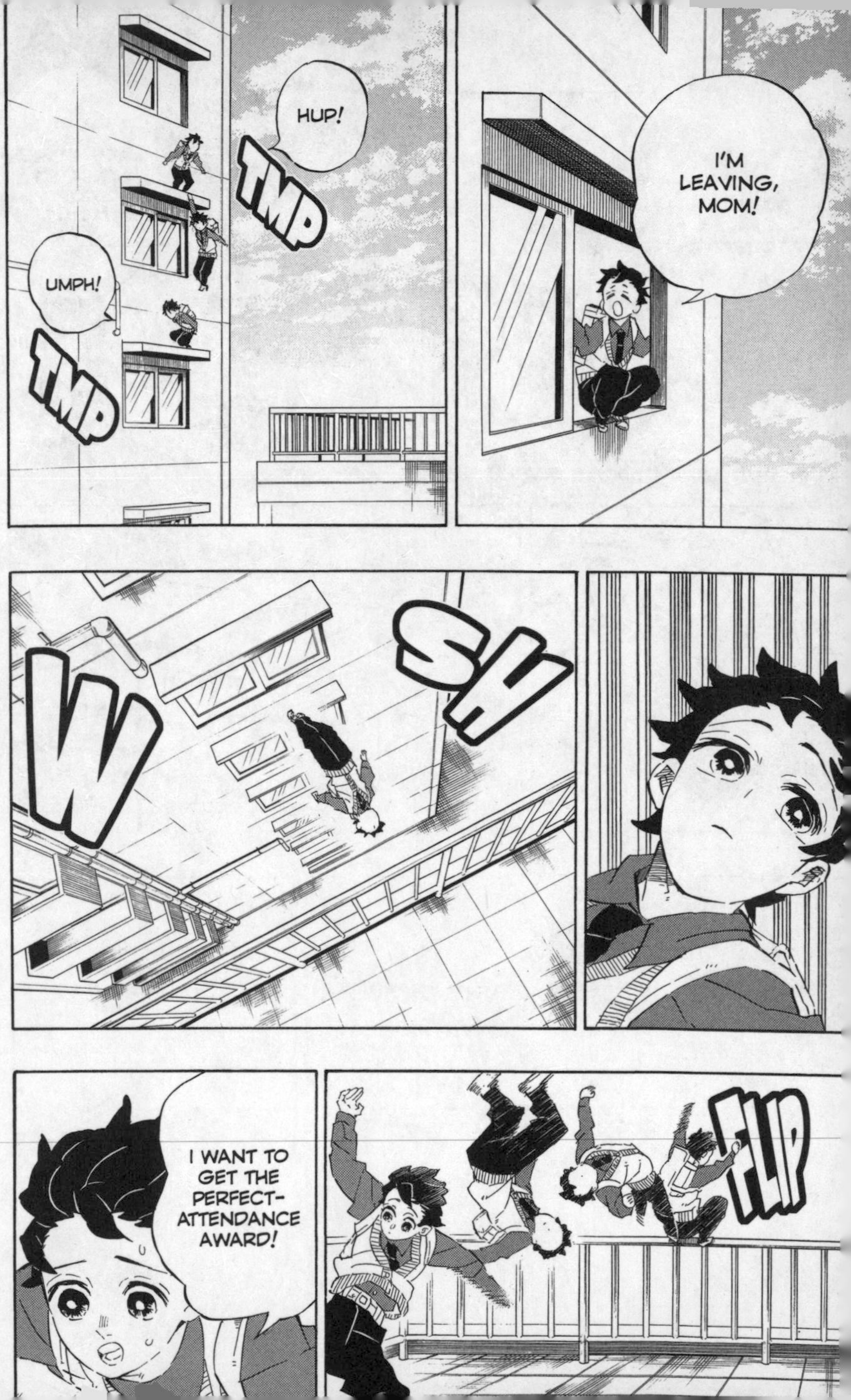
I'M LEAVING, MOM!
HUP!
TMP
UMPH!
TMP
SH
W
FLIP
I WANT TO GET THE PERFECT-ATTENDANCE AWARD!

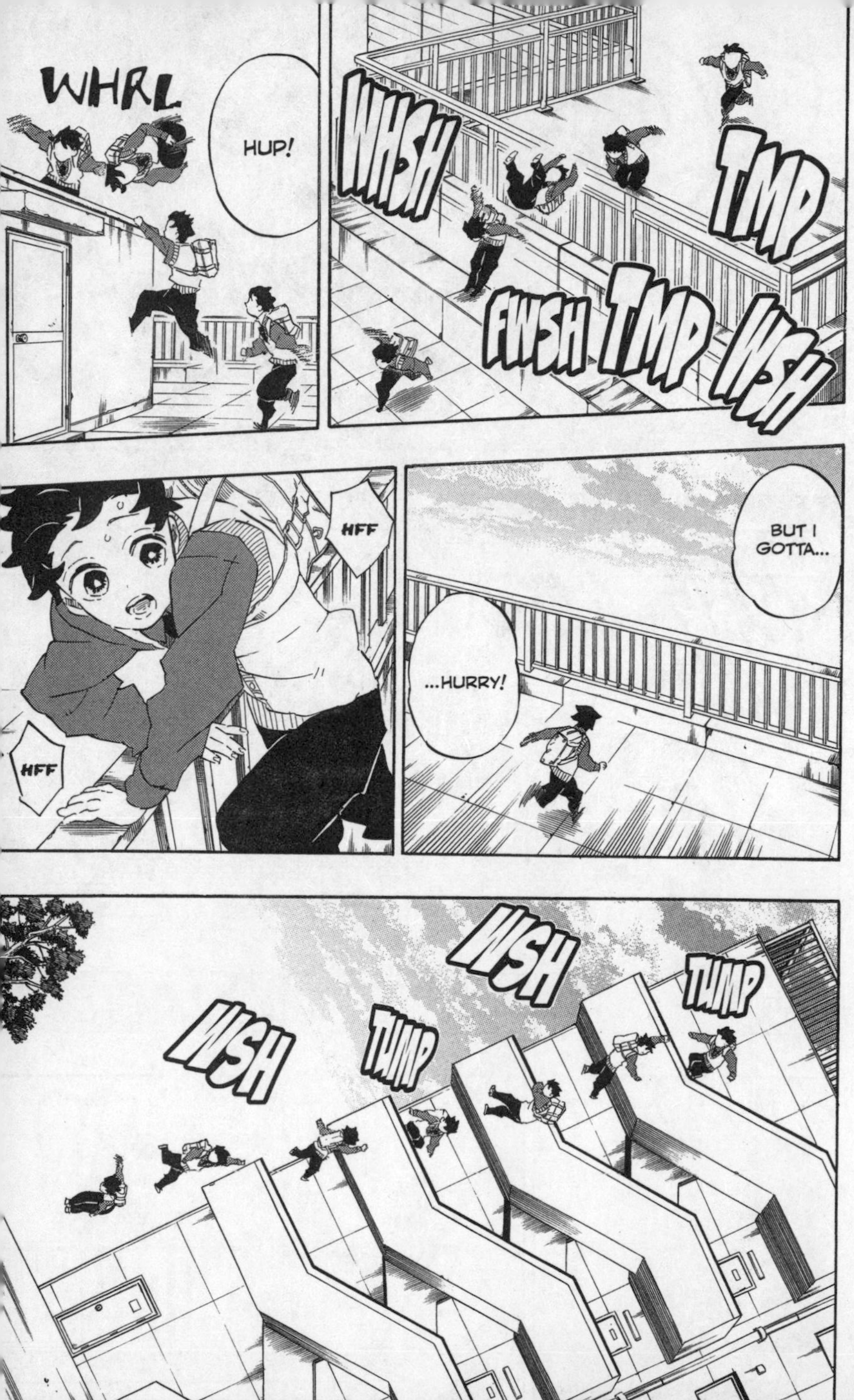
WHSH
TMP
FWSH
TMP
WSH
WHRL
HUP!
BUT I GOTTA...
...HURRY!
HFF
HFF
TUMP
WSH
TUMP
WSH

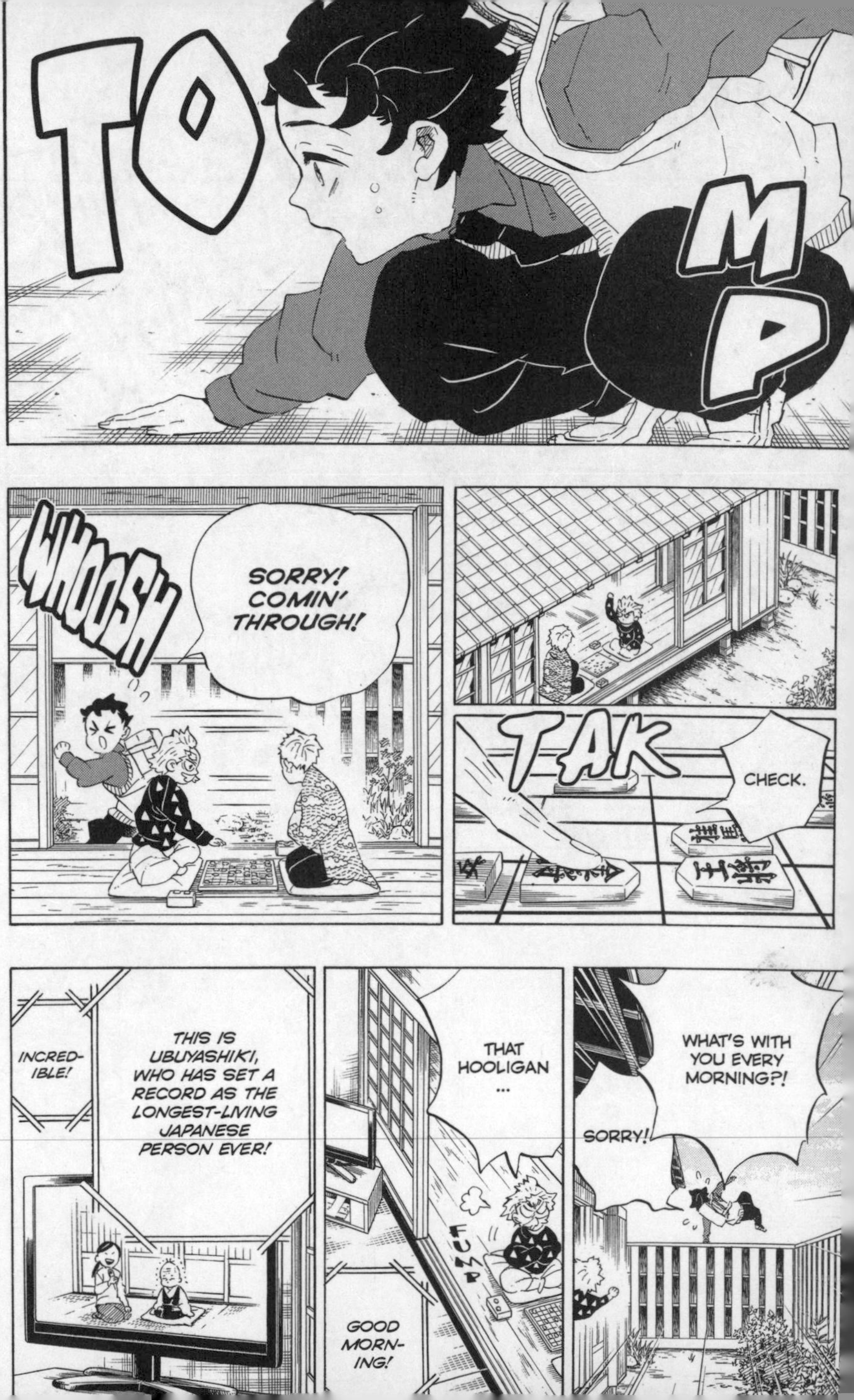
TOMP
CHECK.
TAK
SORRY! COMIN' THROUGH!
WHOOSH
WHAT'S WITH YOU EVERY MORNING?!
SORRY!
THAT HOOLIGAN ...
FUMP
GOOD MORN-ING!
THIS IS UBUYASHIKI, WHO HAS SET A RECORD AS THE LONGEST-LIVING JAPANESE PERSON EVER!
INCREDI-BLE!

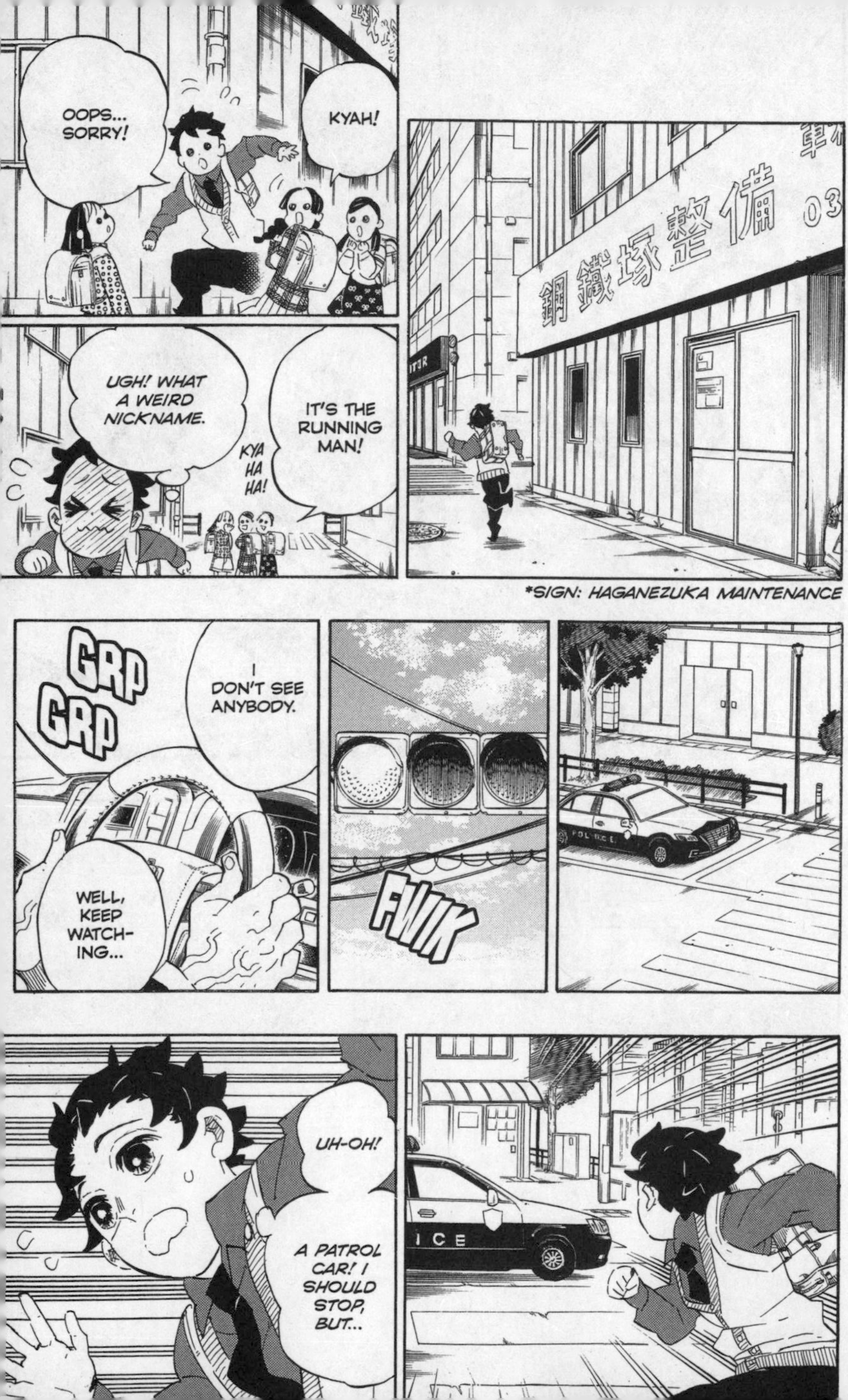
鋼鐵塚整備
03
*SIGN: HAGANEZUKA MAINTENANCE
KYAH!
OOPS... SORRY!
IT'S THE RUNNING MAN!
KYA HA HA!
UGH! WHAT A WEIRD NICKNAME.
POLICE
FWIK
I DON'T SEE ANYBODY.
GRP GRP
WELL, KEEP WATCHING-ING...
ICE
UH-OH!
A PATROL CAR! I SHOULD STOP, BUT...

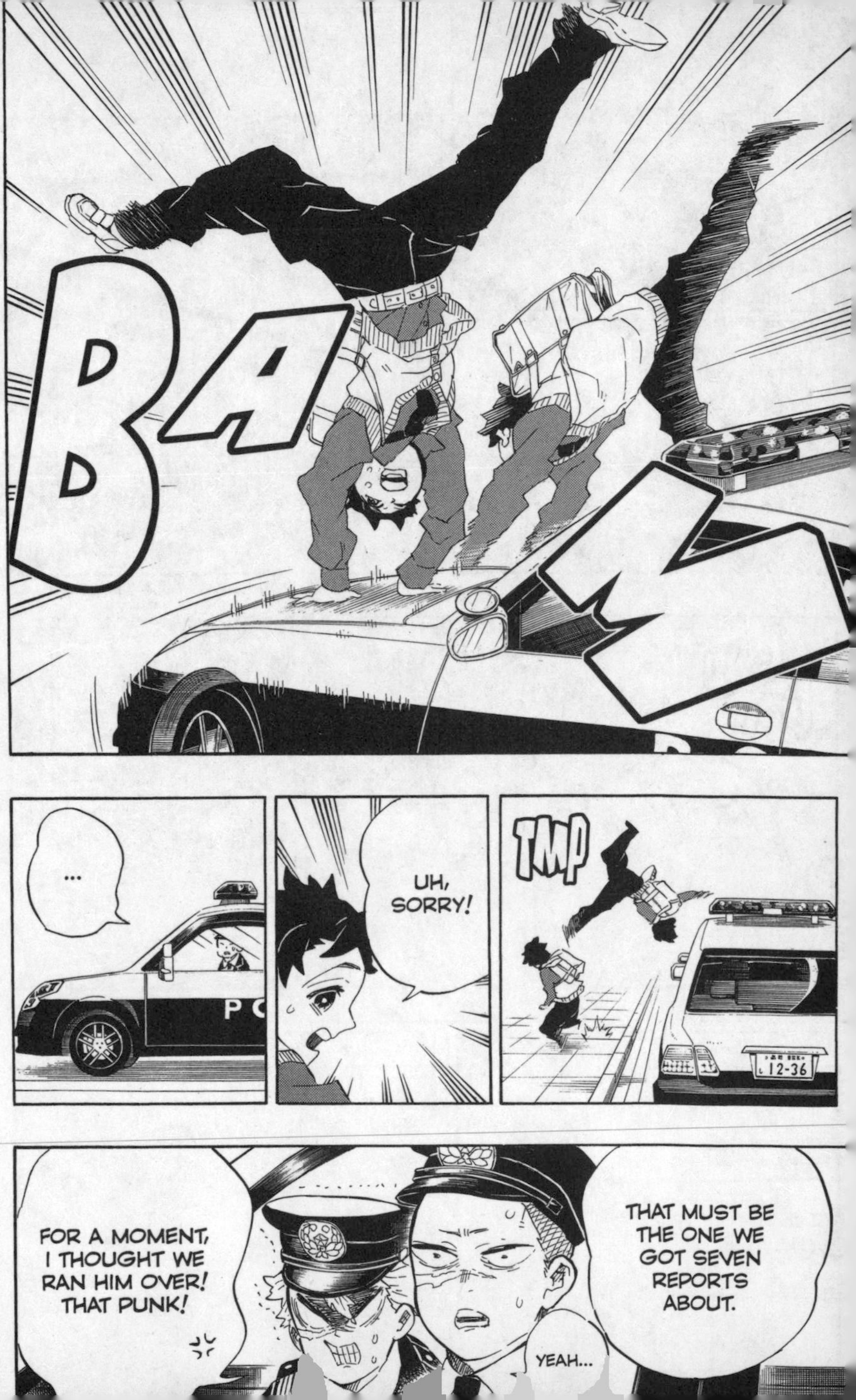
BAM
TMP
UH, SORRY!
...
THAT MUST BE THE ONE WE GOT SEVEN REPORTS ABOUT.
YEAH...
FOR A MOMENT, I THOUGHT WE RAN HIM OVER! THAT PUNK!

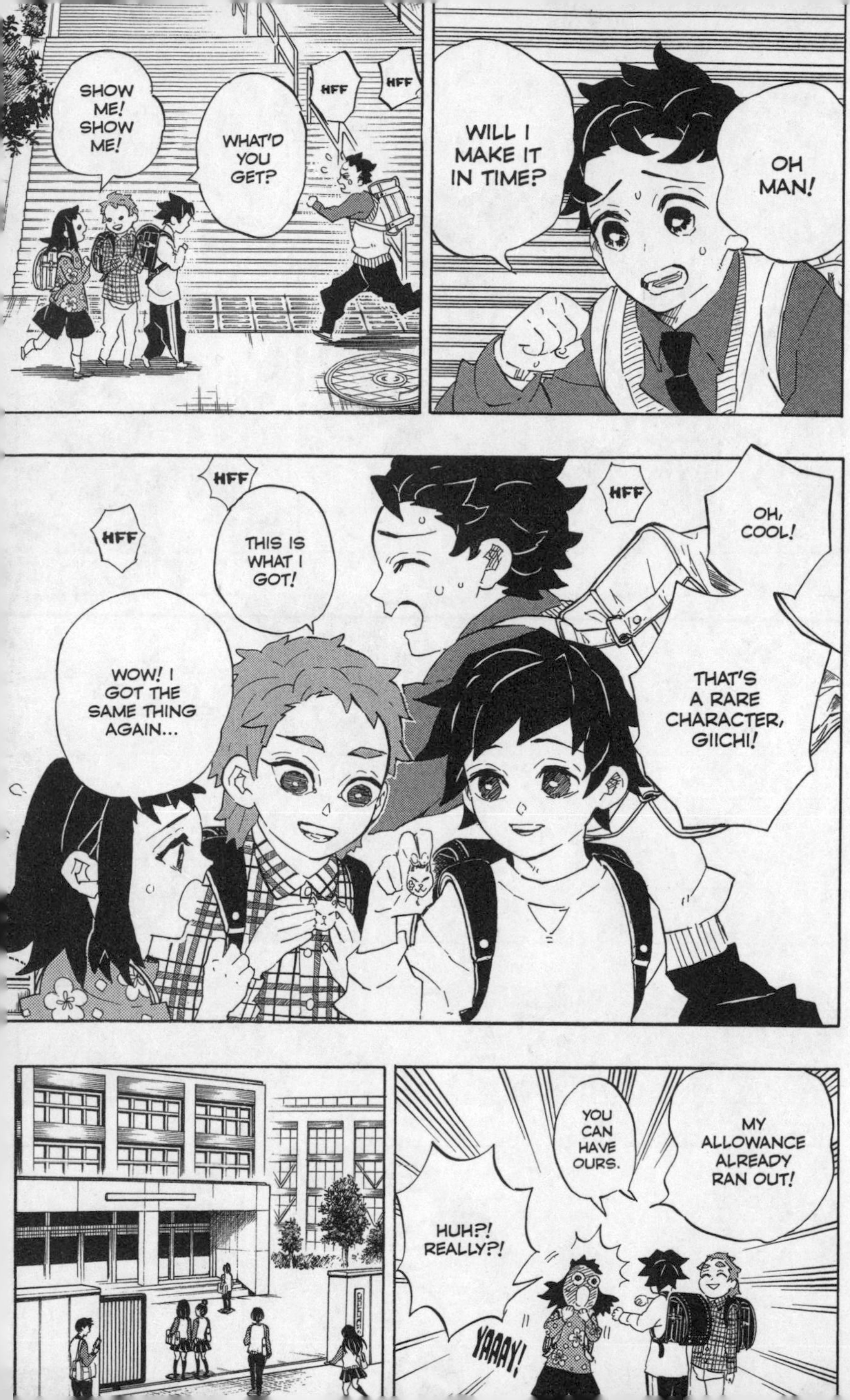
OH MAN!
WILL I MAKE IT IN TIME?
HFF
HFF
WHAT'D YOU GET?
SHOW ME! SHOW ME!
OH, COOL!
HFF
THAT'S A RARE CHARACTER, GIICHI!
HFF
THIS IS WHAT I GOT!
HFF
WOW! I GOT THE SAME THING AGAIN...
MY ALLOWANCE ALREADY RAN OUT!
YOU CAN HAVE OURS.
HUH?! REALLY?!
YAAAY!

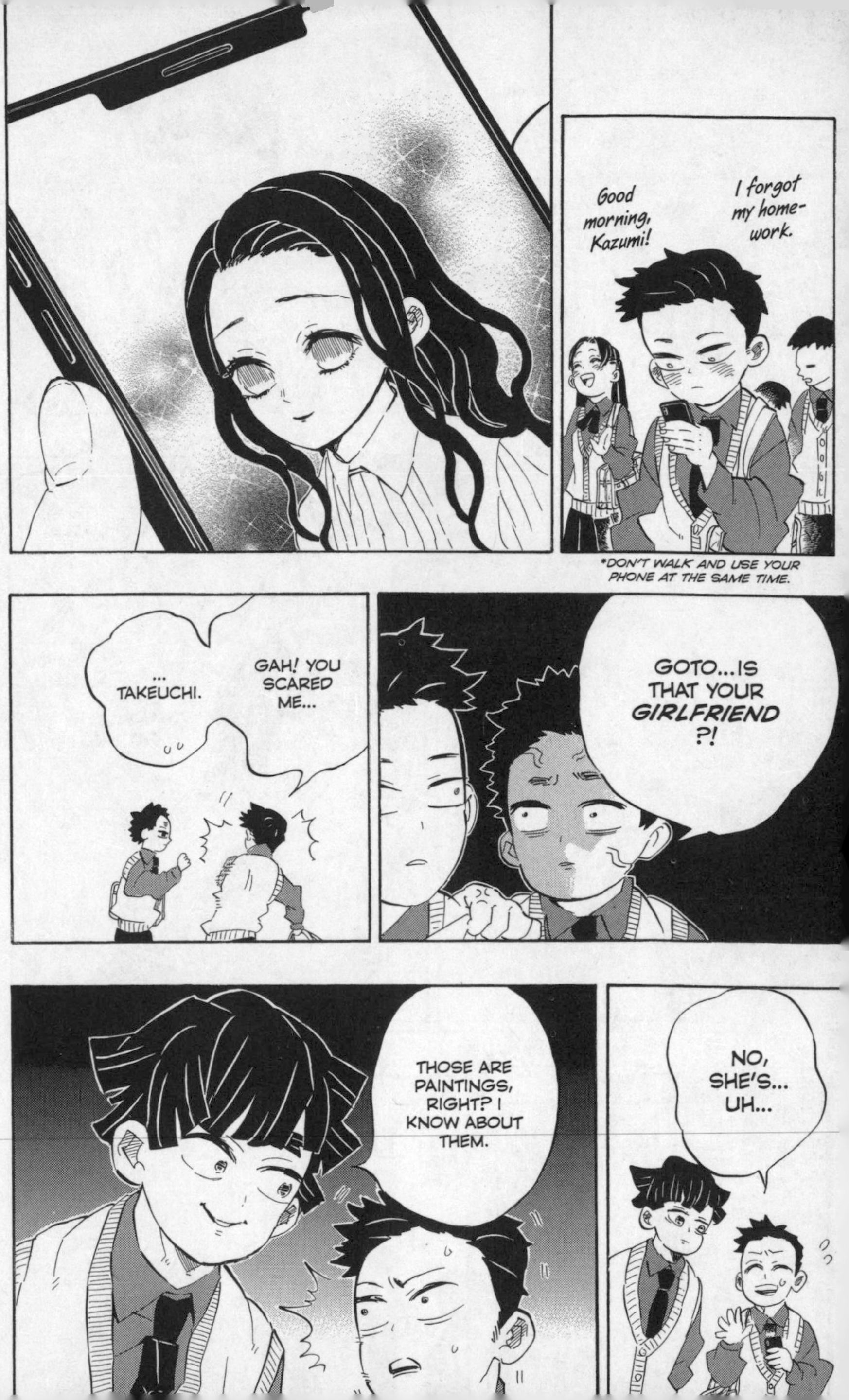
I forgot my home-work.
Good morning, Kazumi!
*DON'T WALK AND USE YOUR PHONE AT THE SAME TIME.
GOTO...IS THAT YOUR GIRLFRIEND?!
GAH! YOU SCARED ME...
... TAKEUCHI.
NO, SHE'S... UH...
THOSE ARE PAINTINGS, RIGHT? I KNOW ABOUT THEM.

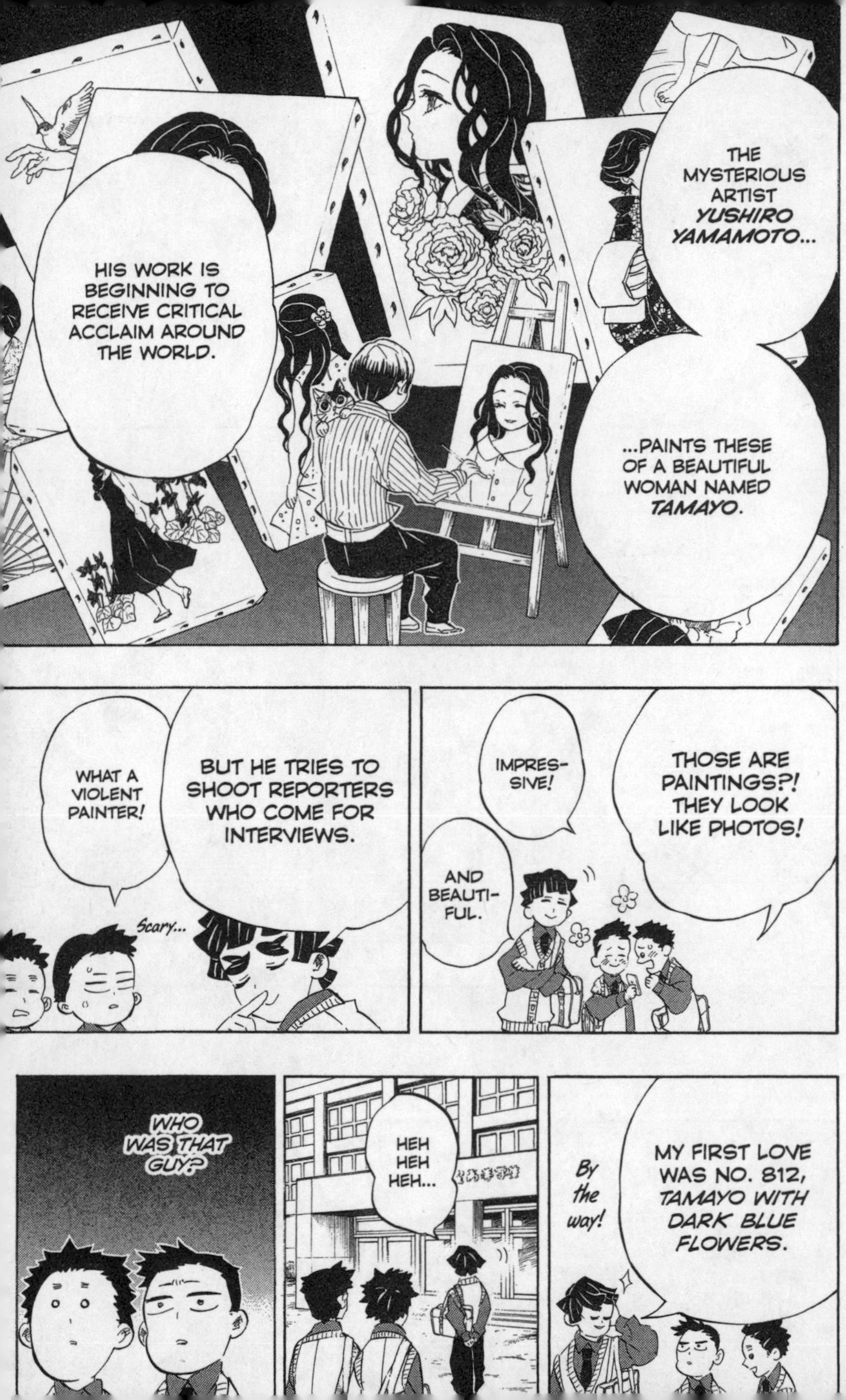
THE MYSTERIOUS ARTIST YUSHIRO YAMAMOTO...
...PAINTS THESE OF A BEAUTIFUL WOMAN NAMED TAMAYO.
HIS WORK IS BEGINNING TO RECEIVE CRITICAL ACCLAIM AROUND THE WORLD.
THOSE ARE PAINTINGS?! THEY LOOK LIKE PHOTOS!
IMPRES-SIVE!
AND BEAUTI-FUL.
BUT HE TRIES TO SHOOT REPORTERS WHO COME FOR INTERVIEWS.
WHAT A VIOLENT PAINTER!
Scary...
MY FIRST LOVE WAS NO. 812, TAMAYO WITH DARK BLUE FLOWERS.
By the way!
HEH HEH HEH...
WHO WAS THAT GUY?

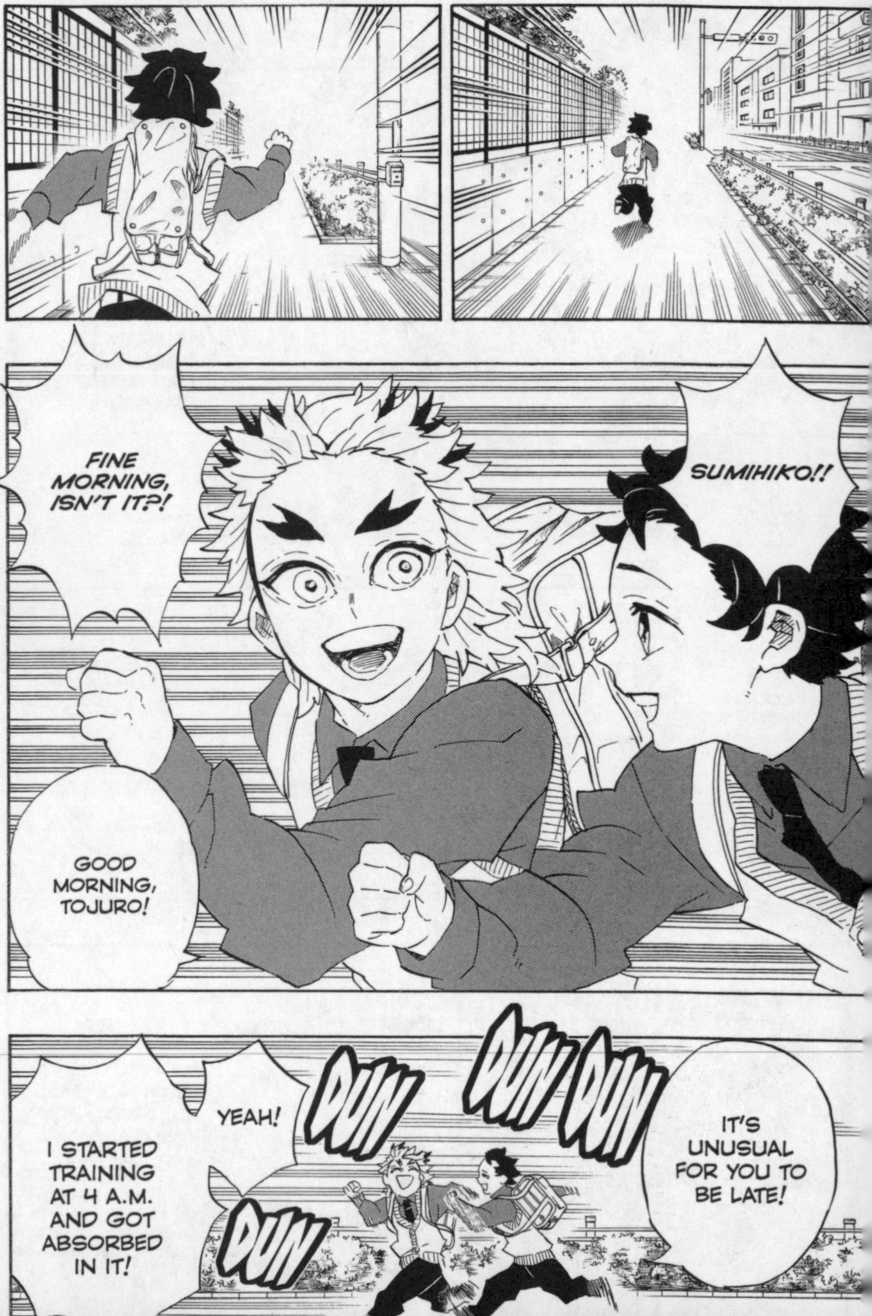
SUMIHIKO!!
FINE MORNING, ISN'T IT?!
GOOD MORNING, TOJURO!
IT'S UNUSUAL FOR YOU TO BE LATE!
DUN DUN
DUN
YEAH!
I STARTED TRAINING AT 4 A.M. AND GOT ABSORBED IN IT!
DUN

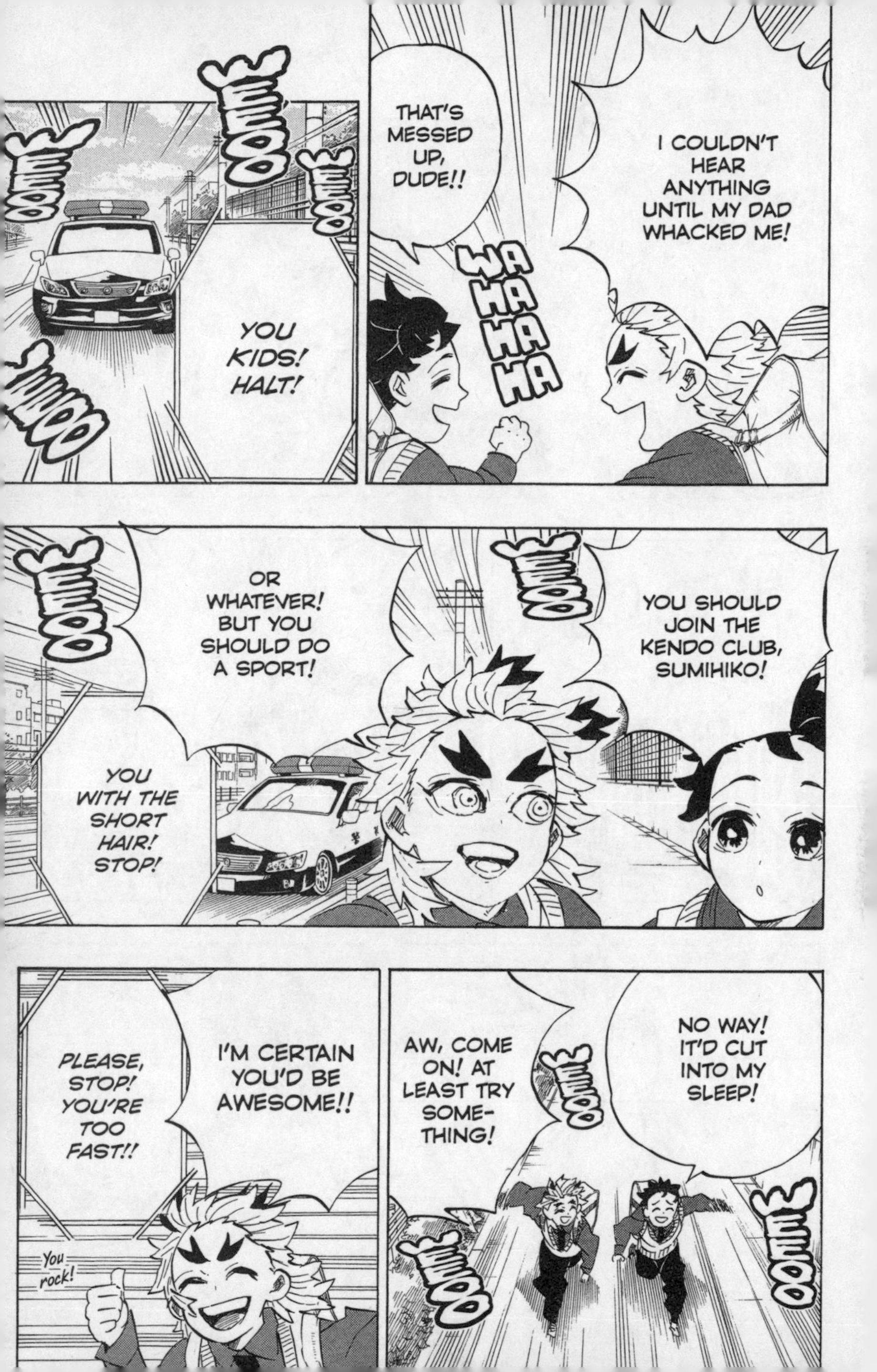
I COULDN'T HEAR ANYTHING UNTIL MY DAD WHACKED ME!
THAT'S MESSED UP, DUDE!!
WA HA HA HA
WEEOO
WEEOO
WEEOO
YOU KIDS! HALT!
WEEOO
YOU SHOULD JOIN THE KENDO CLUB, SUMIHIKO!
WEEOO
OR WHATEVER! BUT YOU SHOULD DO A SPORT!
WEEOO
YOU WITH THE SHORT HAIR! STOP!
NO WAY! IT'D CUT INTO MY SLEEP!
WEEOO
AW, COME ON! AT LEAST TRY SOME-THING!
WEEOO
WEEOO
I'M CERTAIN YOU'D BE AWESOME!!
PLEASE, STOP! YOU'RE TOO FAST!!
You rock!

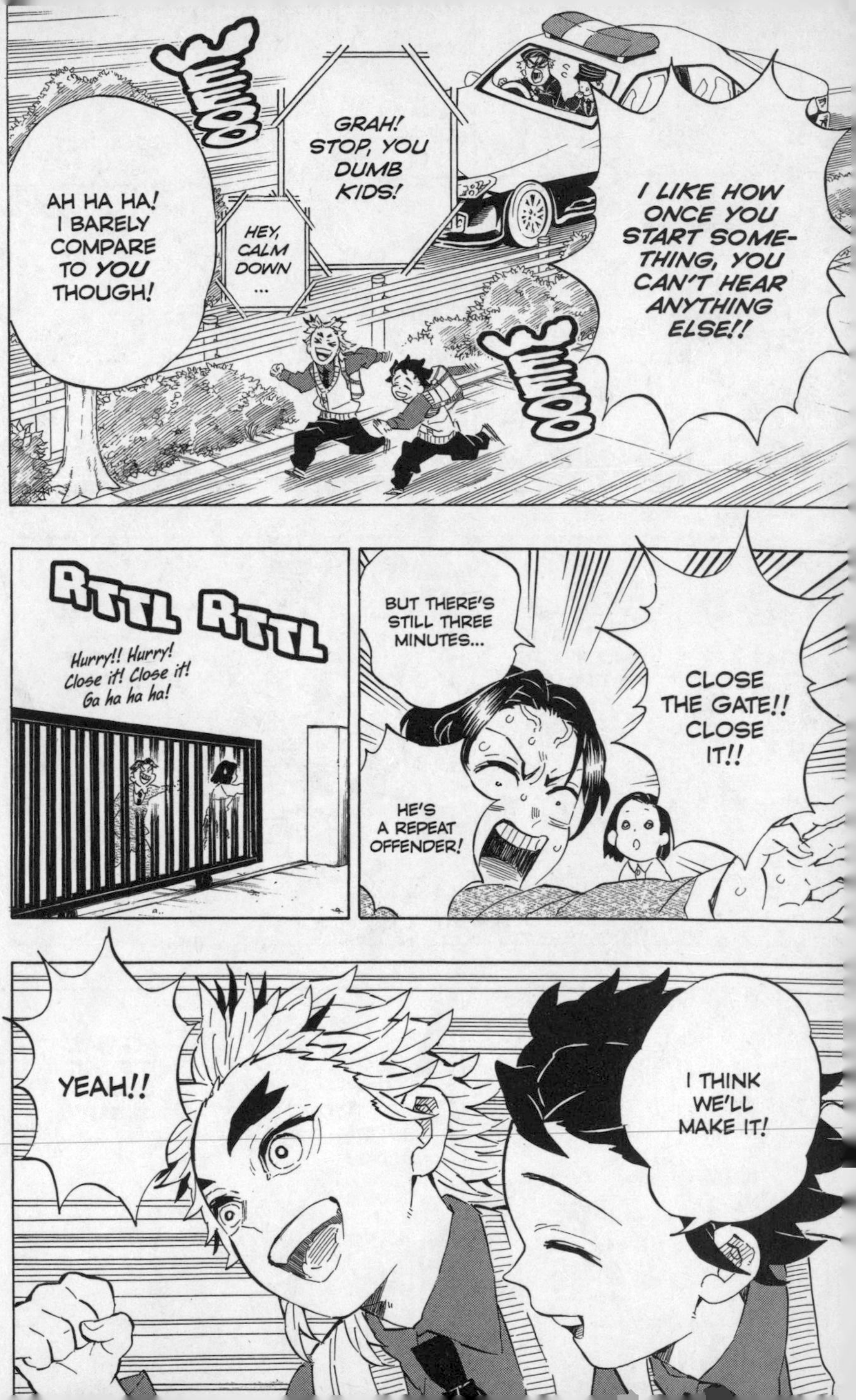
I LIKE HOW ONCE YOU START SOMETHING, YOU CAN'T HEAR ANYTHING ELSE!!
GRAH! STOP, YOU DUMB KIDS!
WHOOO
HEY, CALM DOWN ...
AH HA HA! I BARELY COMPARE TO *YOU* THOUGH!
WHOOO
CLOSE THE GATE!! CLOSE IT!!
BUT THERE'S STILL THREE MINUTES...
HE'S A REPEAT OFFENDER!
RTTL RTTL
Hurry!! Hurry! Close it! Close it! Ga ha ha ha!
I THINK WE'LL MAKE IT!
YEAH!!

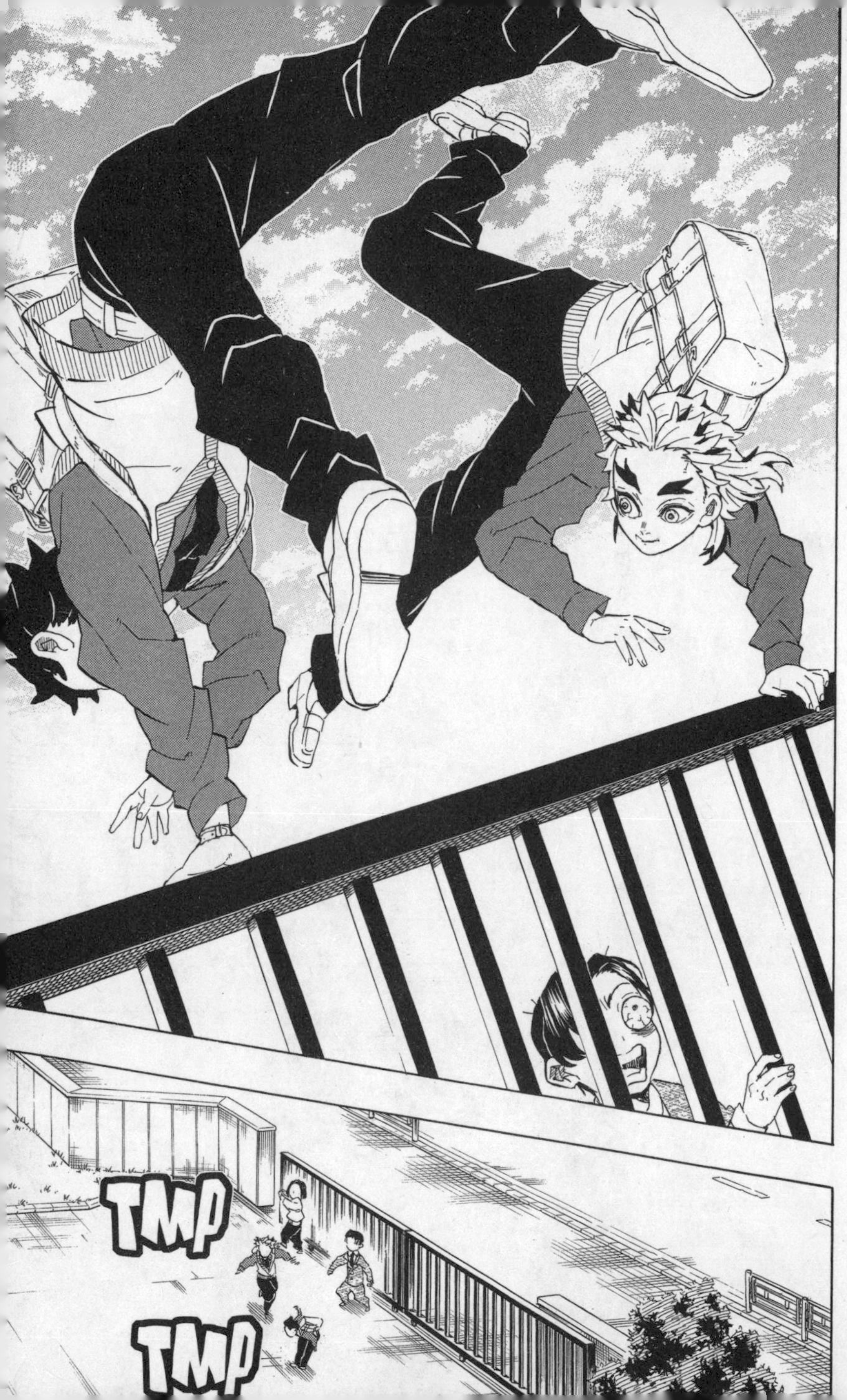
TMP
TMP

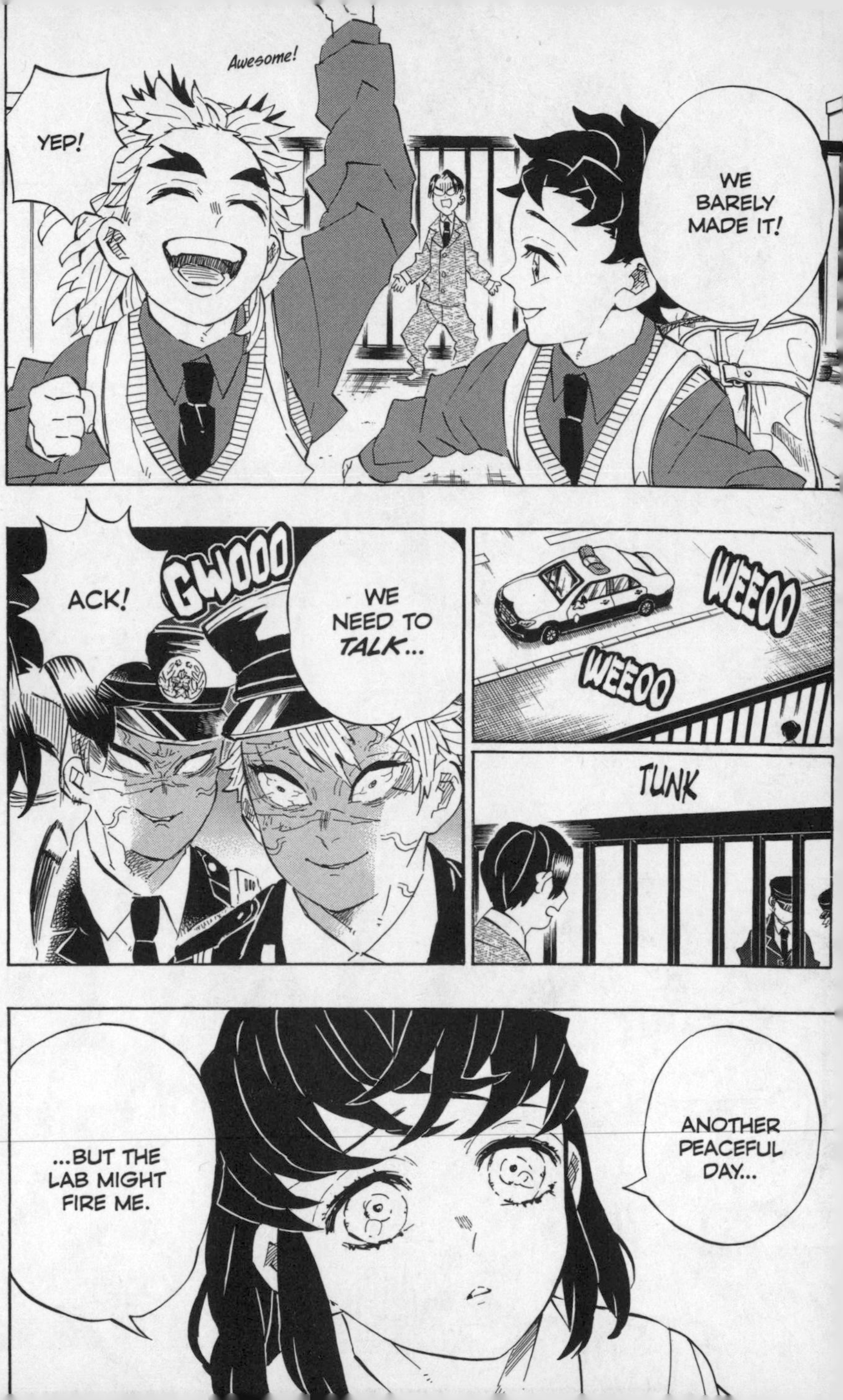
WE BARELY MADE IT!
Awesome!
YEP!
WEEOO
WEEOO
TUNK
WE NEED TO TALK...
GWOOO
ACK!
ANOTHER PEACEFUL DAY...
...BUT THE LAB MIGHT FIRE ME.

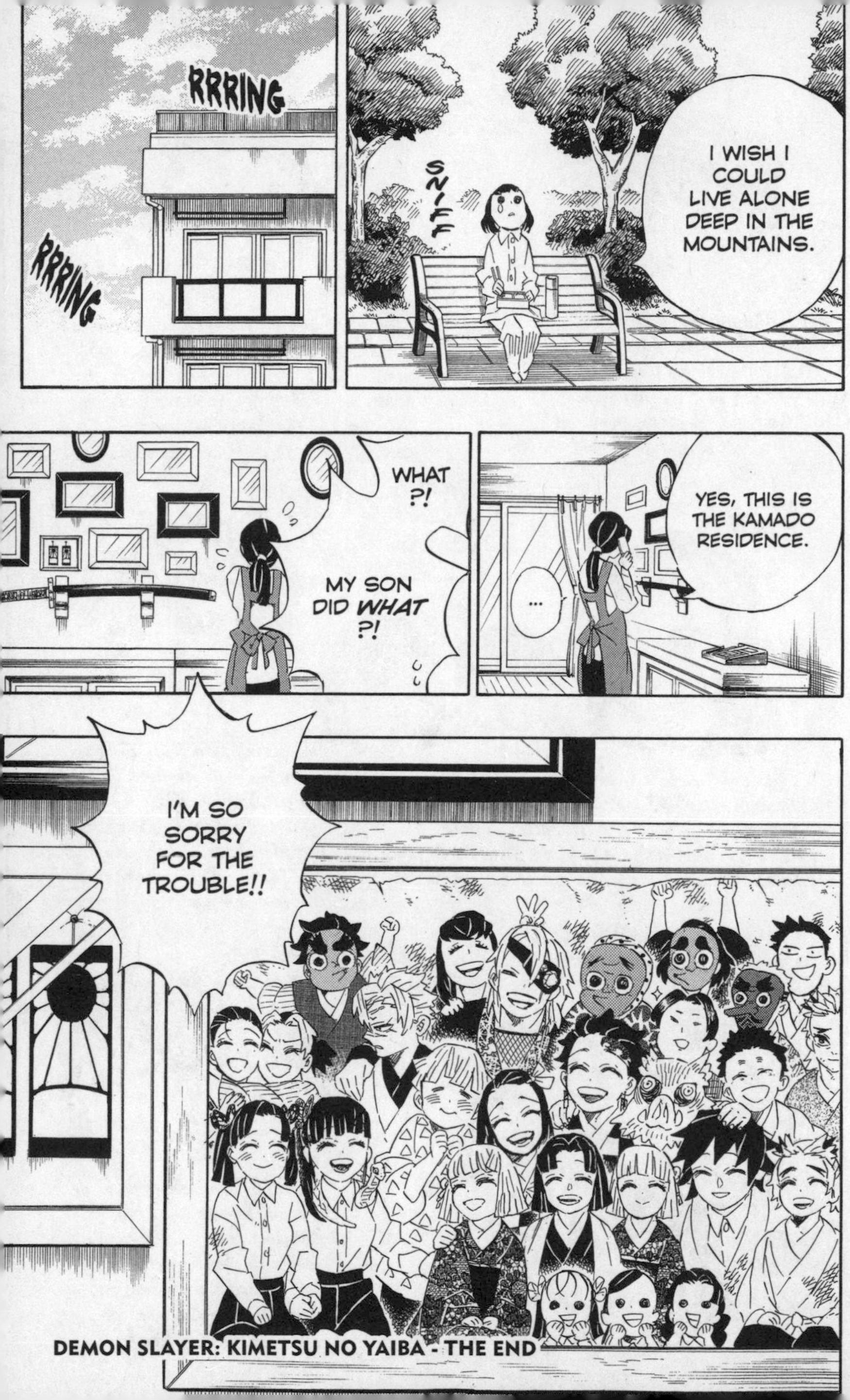
I WISH I COULD LIVE ALONE DEEP IN THE MOUNTAINS.
SNIFF
RRRING
RRRING
YES, THIS IS THE KAMADO RESIDENCE.
...
WHAT?!
MY SON DID WHAT?!
I'M SO SORRY FOR THE TROUBLE!!
DEMON SLAYER: KIMETSU NO YAIBA - THE END

DESCENDANTS OF TANJIRO AND KANAO

SUMIHIKO

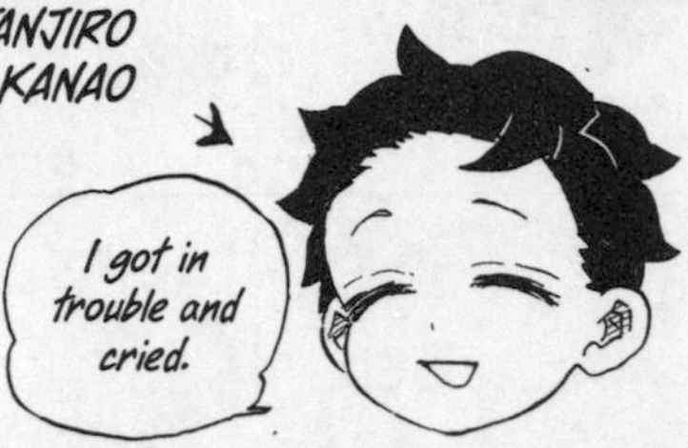
I got in trouble and cried.

The police and his parents lectured him for four hours over his dangerous antics on the way to school. On the way home, he went to the park and cried. His dream for the future is to work at a zoo. His favorite animal is the slow loris.

KANATA

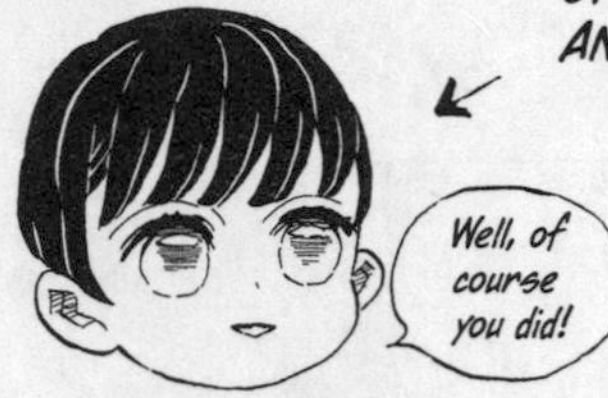
Well, of course you did!

His nickname is "The First-Love Thief." He regrets being sullen toward his grandmother, so now he tries to be open about what's on his mind. He doesn't have a girlfriend.

DESCENDANTS OF NEZUKO AND ZENITSU

YOSHITERU

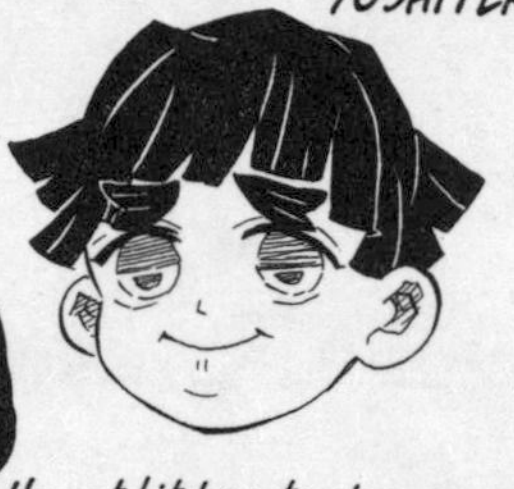

He got hit by a truck once protecting his little sisters. Thanks to first aid from Toko, he recovered without any lasting effects. He's good at heart but he often cheats at things. At the moment, he has marshmallows in his mouth.

TOKO

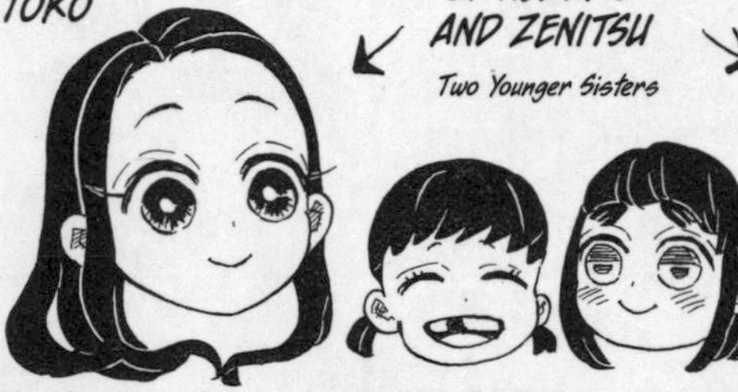
Two Younger Sisters

She thinks Yoshiteru can accomplish anything he wants, so she just wishes he would apply himself. Her dream for the future is to be a prosecutor. Yoshiteru was only able to get into high school because she kept an eye on his studies.

INOSUKE AND AOI'S GREAT-GRANDCHILD

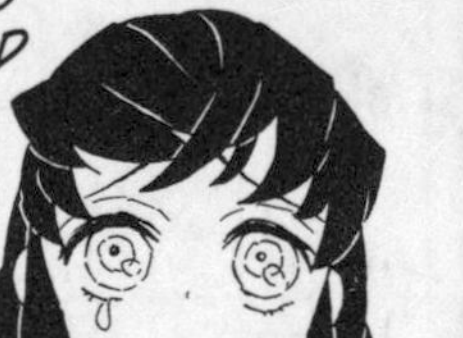
AOBA HASHIBIRA (28)

When he found himself out of work and was crying in the park, he became friends with Sumihiko, who was also there weeping, and they had a good time playing badminton together. He has one younger brother.

SWIMMING SCHOOL CLASSMATES

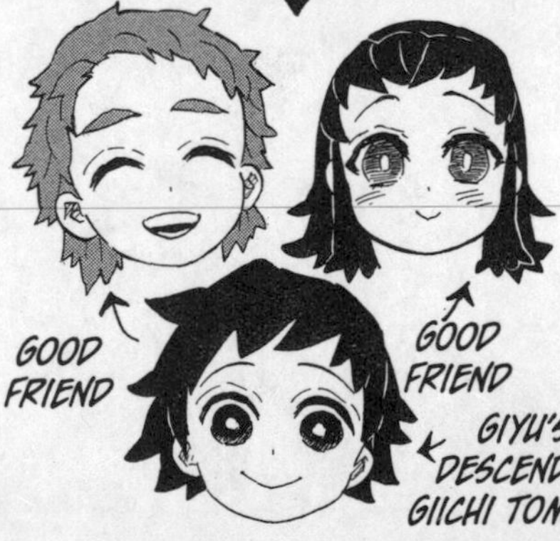
GOOD FRIEND
GOOD FRIEND
GIYU'S DESCENDANT GIICHI TOMIOKA

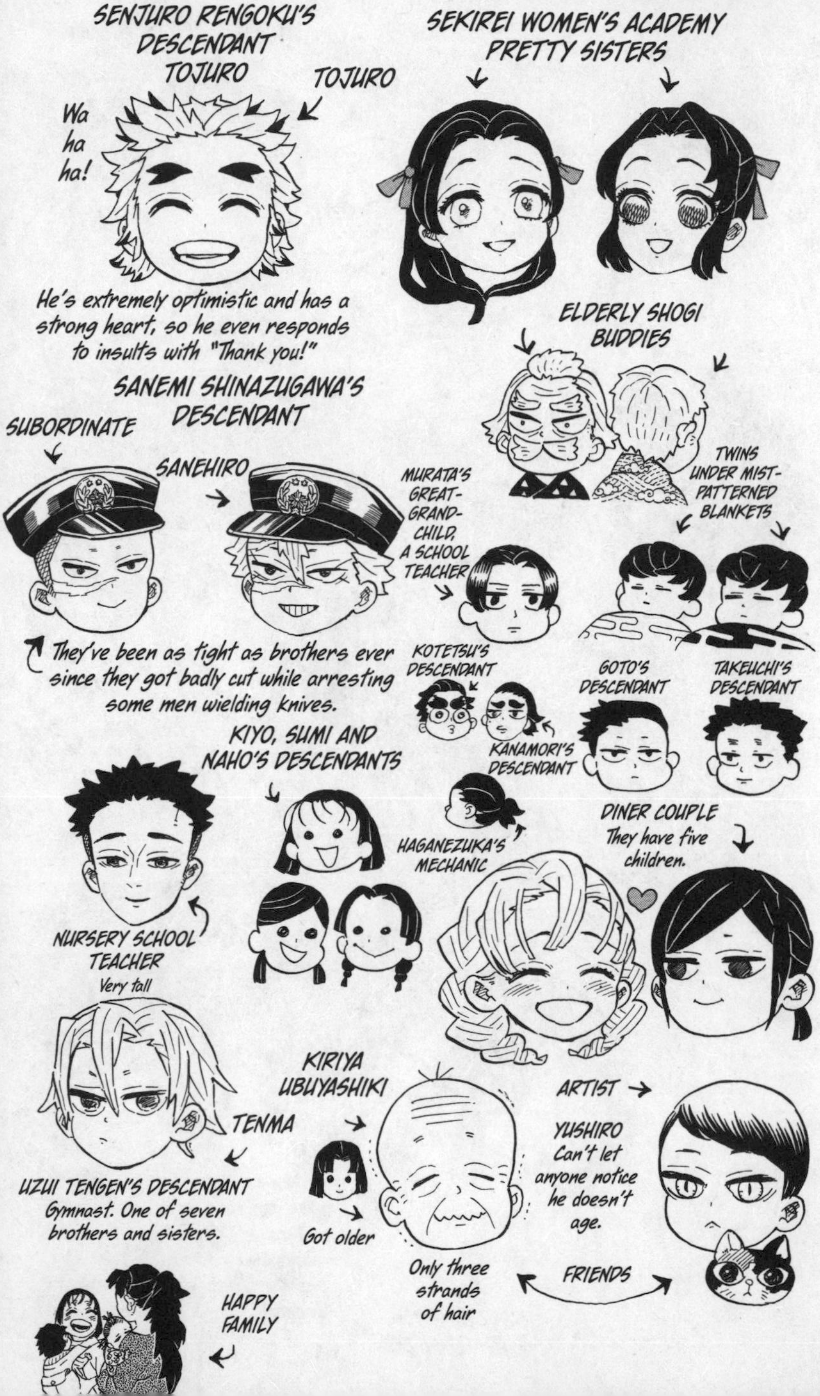
SEKIREI WOMEN'S ACADEMY PRETTY SISTERS
SENJURO RENGOKU'S DESCENDANT TOJURO
TOJURO
Wa ha ha!
He's extremely optimistic and has a strong heart, so he even responds to insults with "Thank you!"
ELDERLY SHOGI BUDDIES
TWINS UNDER MIST-PATTERNED BLANKETS
MURATA'S GREAT-GRANDCHILD, A SCHOOL TEACHER
SANEMI SHINAZUGAWA'S DESCENDANT
SANEHIRO
SUBORDINATE
They've been as tight as brothers ever since they got badly cut while arresting some men wielding knives.
TAKEUCHI'S DESCENDANT
GOTO'S DESCENDANT
KOTETSU'S DESCENDANT
KANAMORI'S DESCENDANT
KIYO, SUMI AND NAHO'S DESCENDANTS
HAGANEZUKA'S MECHANIC
DINER COUPLE
They have five children.
NURSERY SCHOOL TEACHER
Very tall
ARTIST
YUSHIRO
Can't let anyone notice he doesn't age.
KIRIYA UBUYASHIKI
Got older
Only three strands of hair
FRIENDS
TENMA
UZUI TENGEN'S DESCENDANT
Gymnast. One of seven brothers and sisters.
HAPPY FAMILY

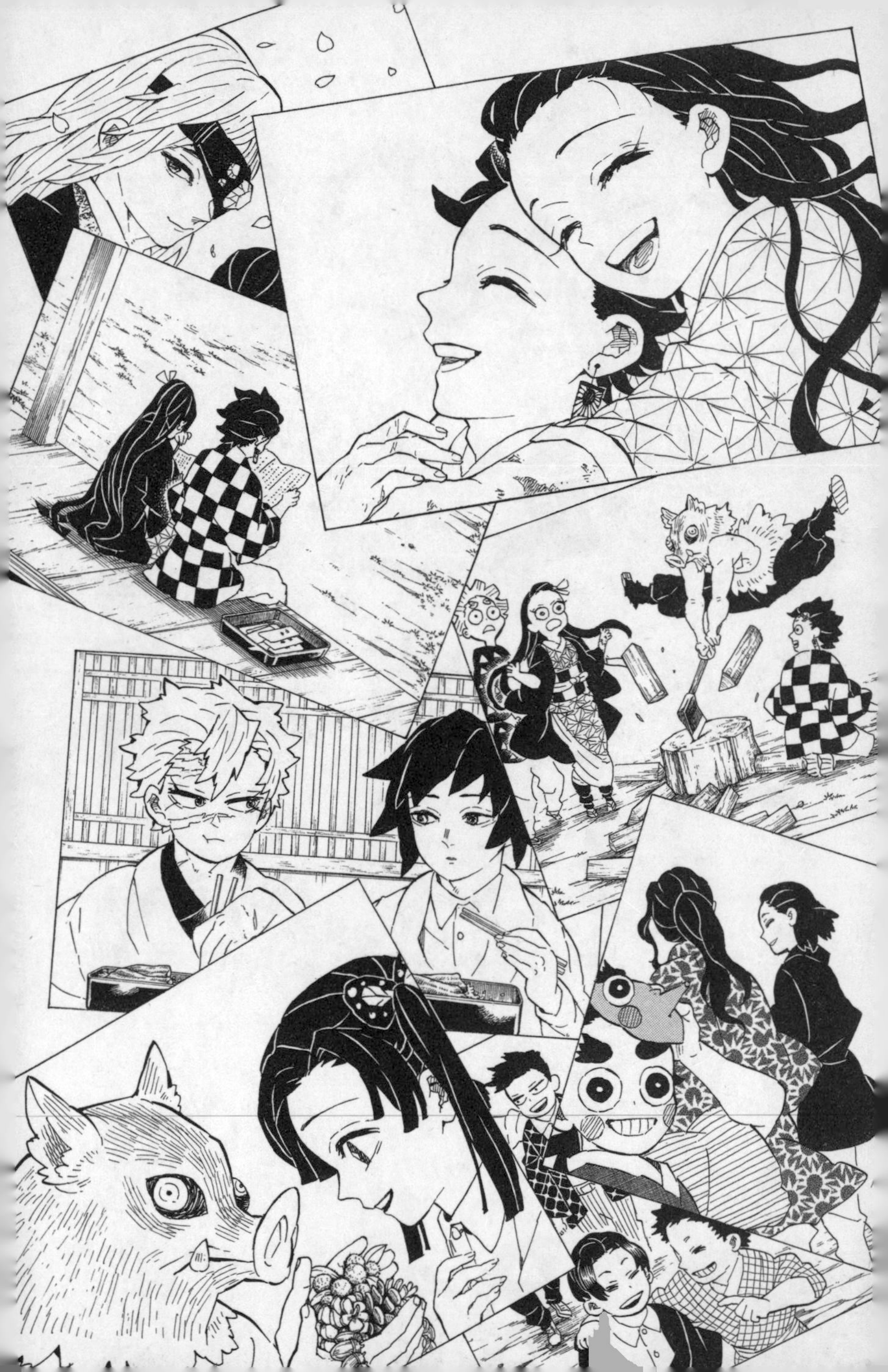

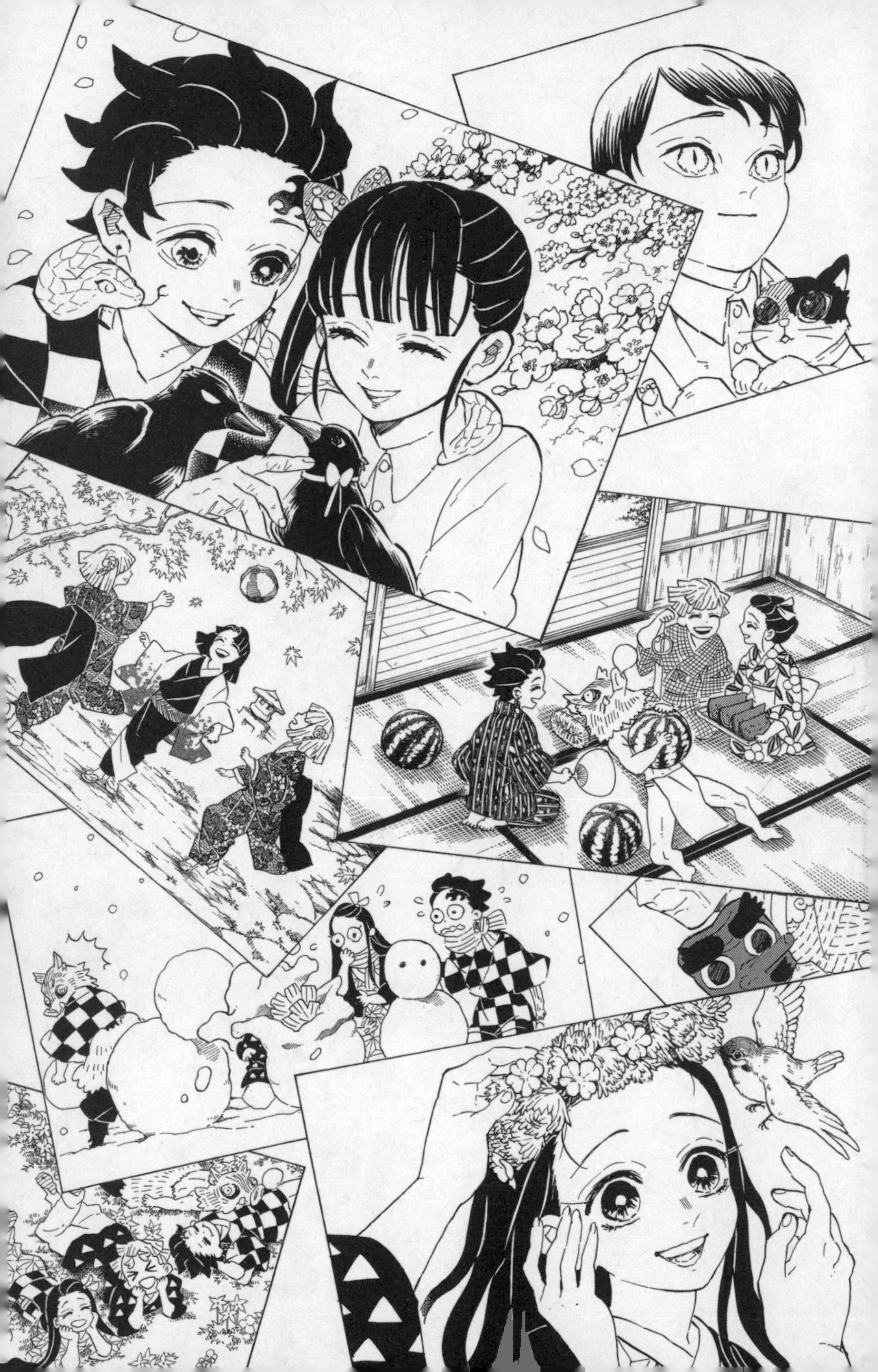

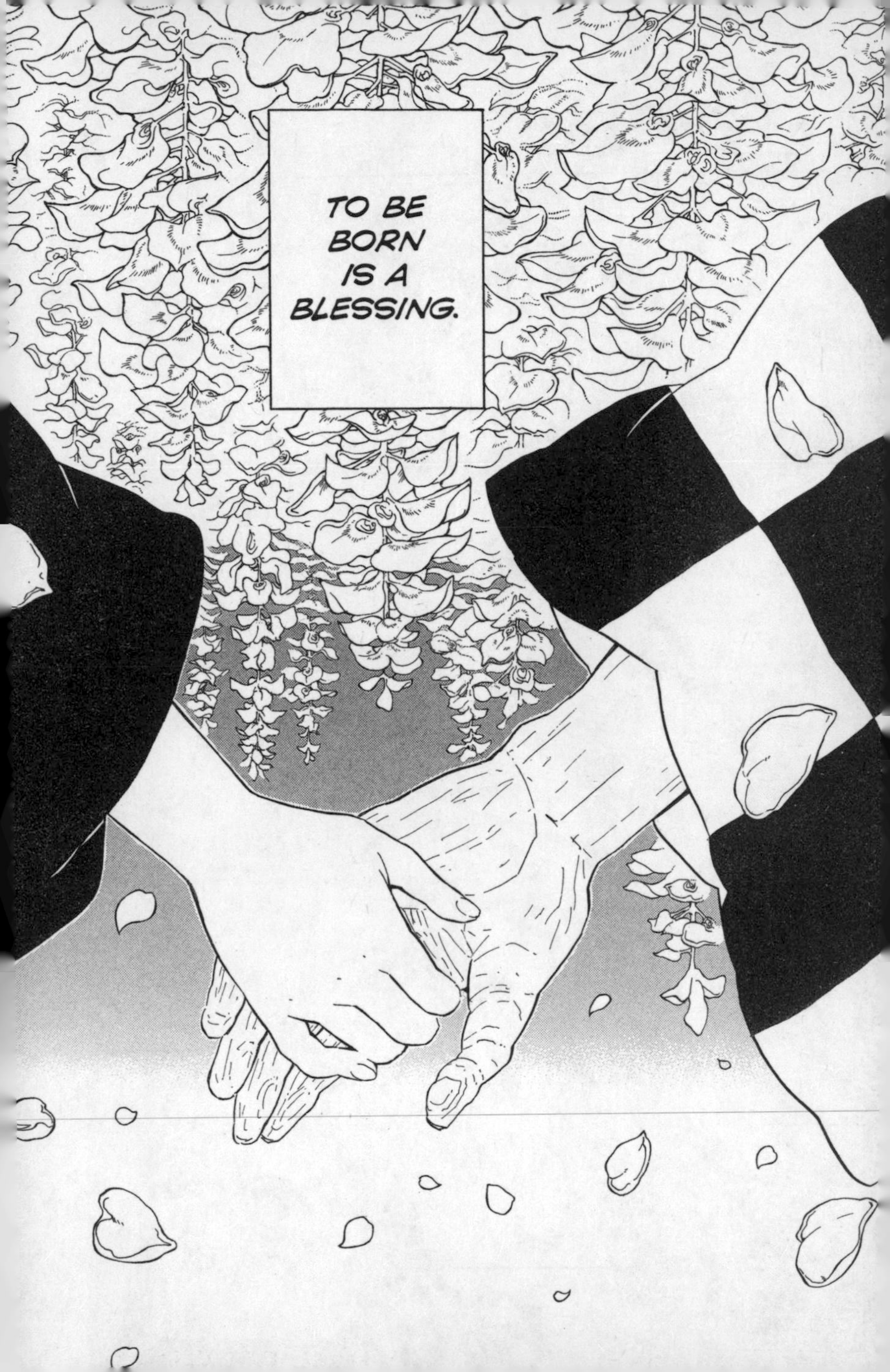
TO BE BORN IS A BLESSING.

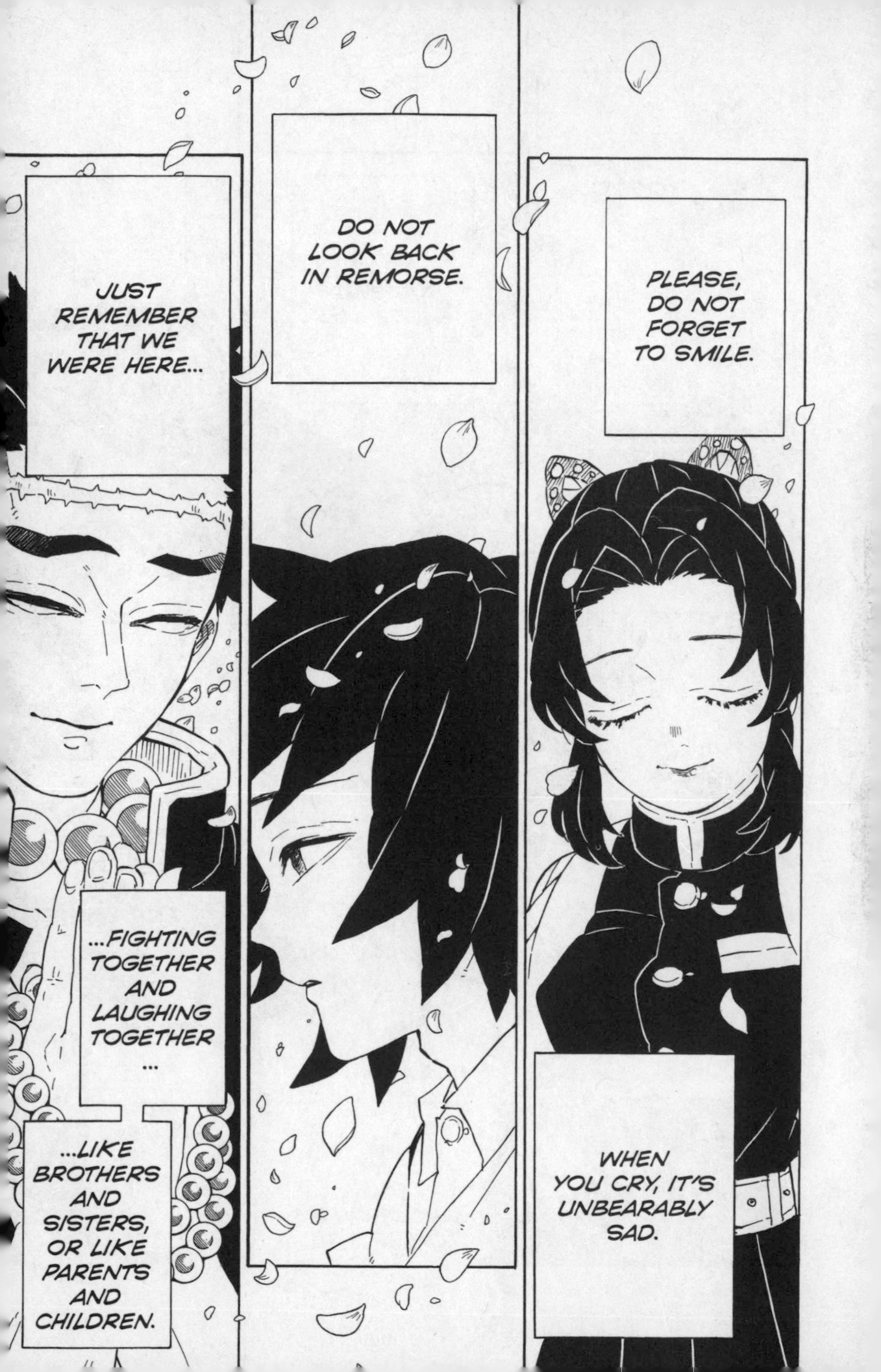
PLEASE, DO NOT FORGET TO SMILE.
WHEN YOU CRY, IT'S UNBEARABLY SAD.
DO NOT LOOK BACK IN REMORSE.
JUST REMEMBER THAT WE WERE HERE...
...FIGHTING TOGETHER AND LAUGHING TOGETHER ...
...LIKE BROTHERS AND SISTERS, OR LIKE PARENTS AND CHILDREN.

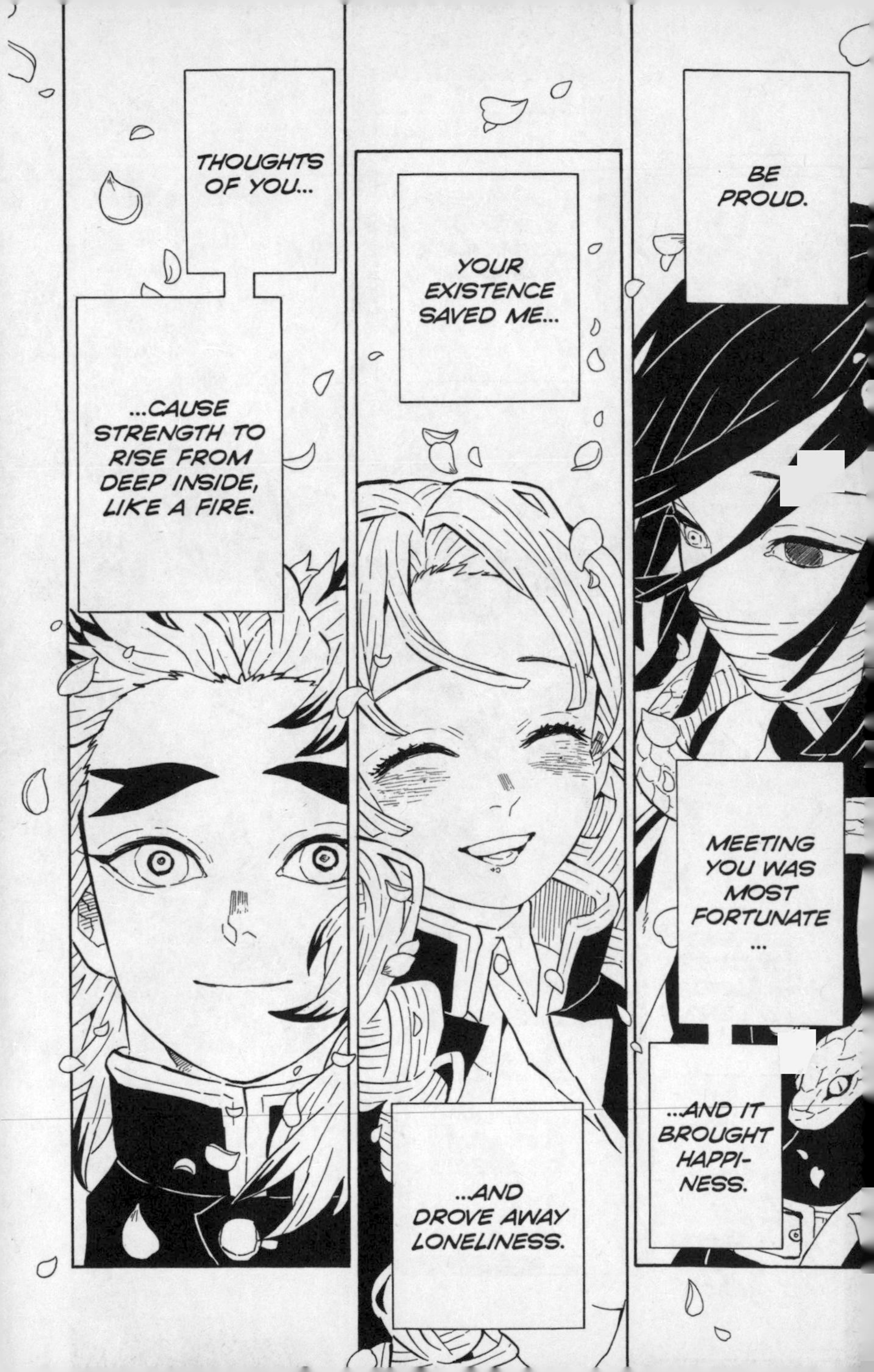
BE PROUD.
MEETING YOU WAS MOST FORTUNATE ...
...AND IT BROUGHT HAPPI-NESS.
YOUR EXISTENCE SAVED ME...
...AND DROVE AWAY LONELINESS.
THOUGHTS OF YOU...
...CAUSE STRENGTH TO RISE FROM DEEP INSIDE, LIKE A FIRE.

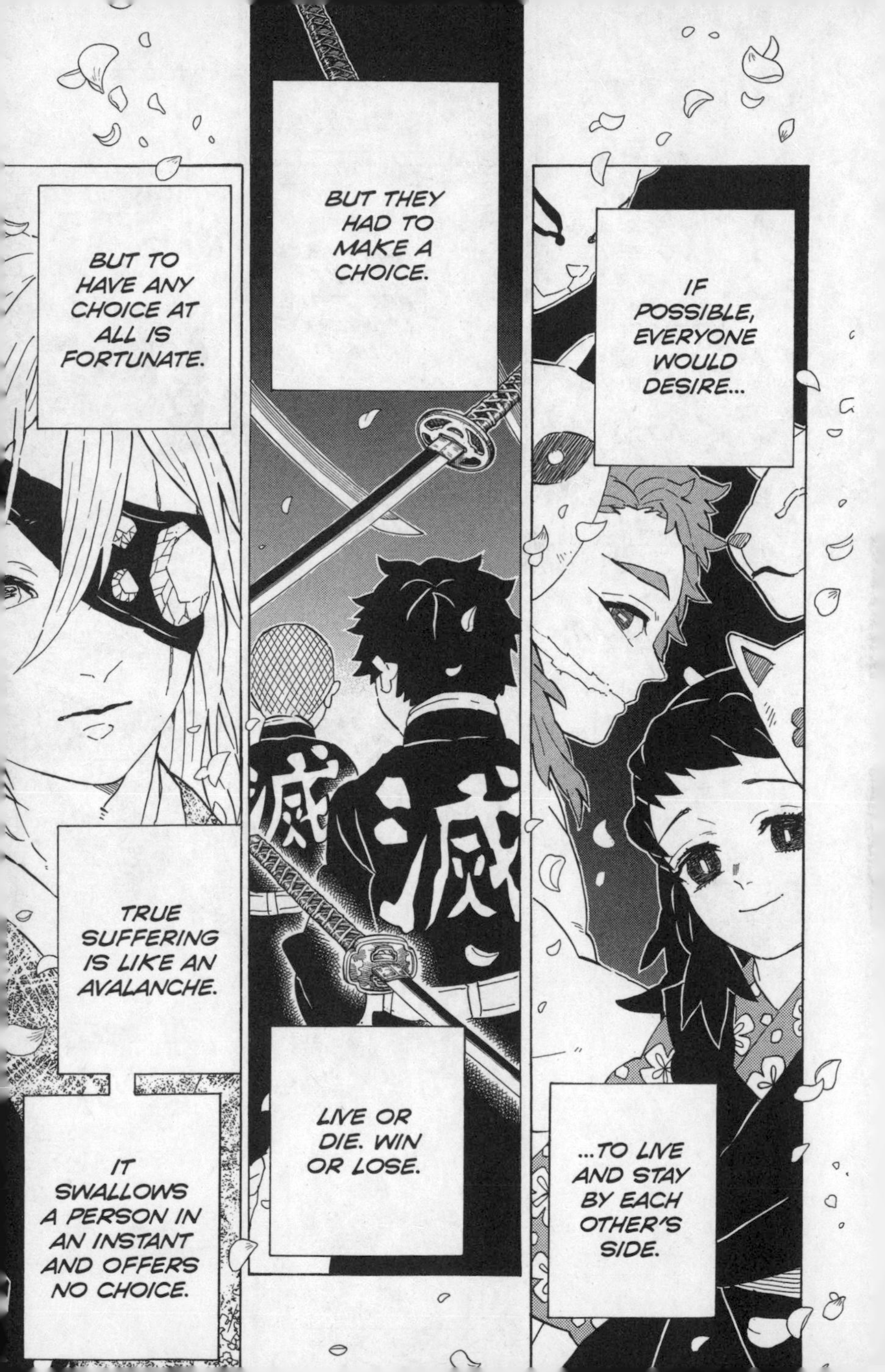
IF POSSIBLE, EVERYONE WOULD DESIRE...
...TO LIVE AND STAY BY EACH OTHER'S SIDE.
BUT THEY HAD TO MAKE A CHOICE.
LIVE OR DIE. WIN OR LOSE.
BUT TO HAVE ANY CHOICE AT ALL IS FORTUNATE.
TRUE SUFFERING IS LIKE AN AVALANCHE.
IT SWALLOWS A PERSON IN AN INSTANT AND OFFERS NO CHOICE.

THEY JUST WANTED TO PROTECT OTHERS.
OTHER LIVES WERE MORE IMPORTANT THAN THEIR OWN.
HAPPINESS ISN'T ABOUT THE LENGTH OF YOUR LIFE.
I WANT YOU TO SEE THE DEPTH OF THIS HAPPINESS I HAVE.
I HAVE NEVER THOUGHT FOR A MOMENT...
...THAT I WAS UNHAPPY.

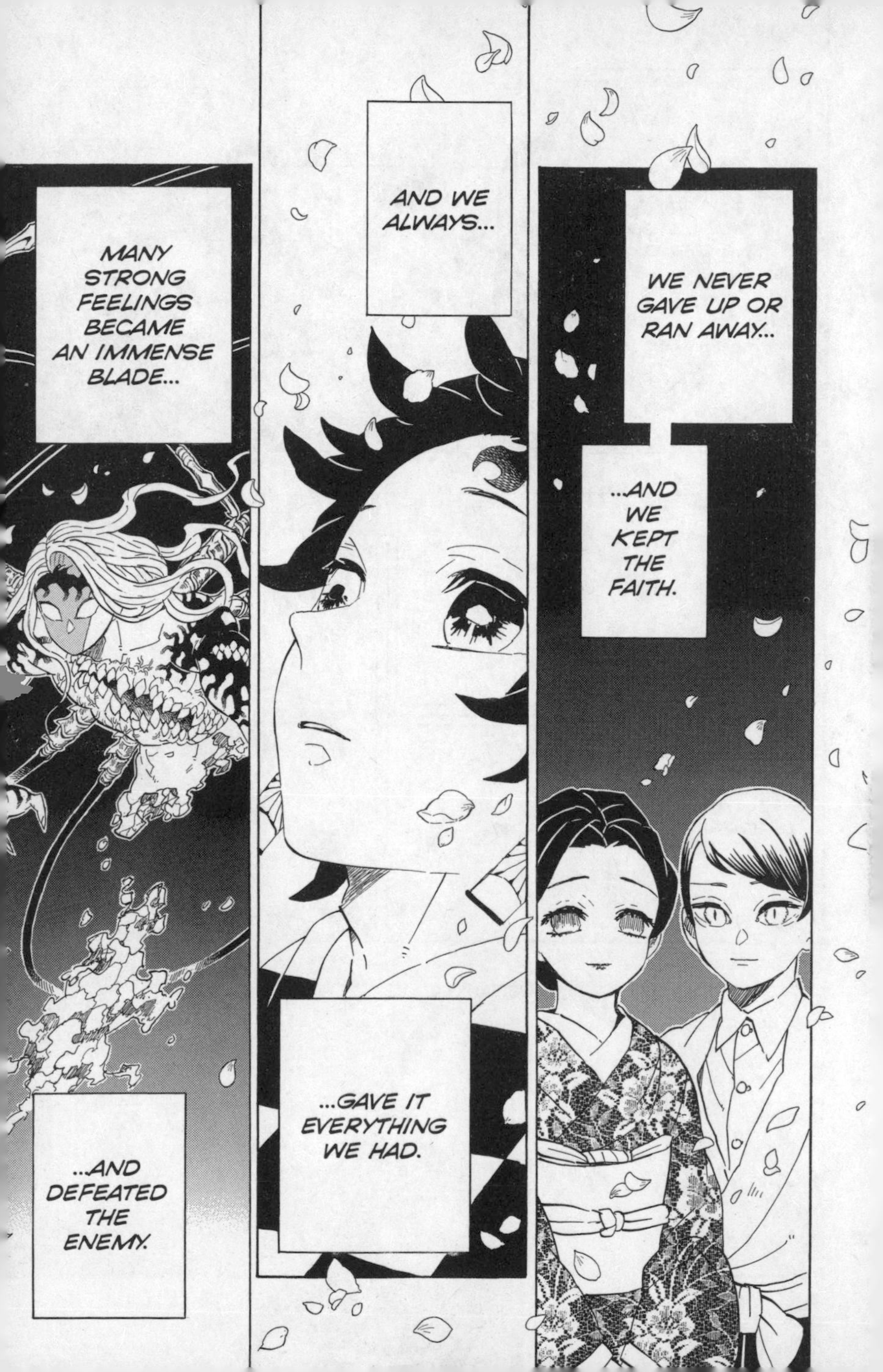
WE NEVER GAVE UP OR RAN AWAY...
...AND WE KEPT THE FAITH.
AND WE ALWAYS...
...GAVE IT EVERYTHING WE HAD.
MANY STRONG FEELINGS BECAME AN IMMENSE BLADE...
...AND DEFEATED THE ENEMY.

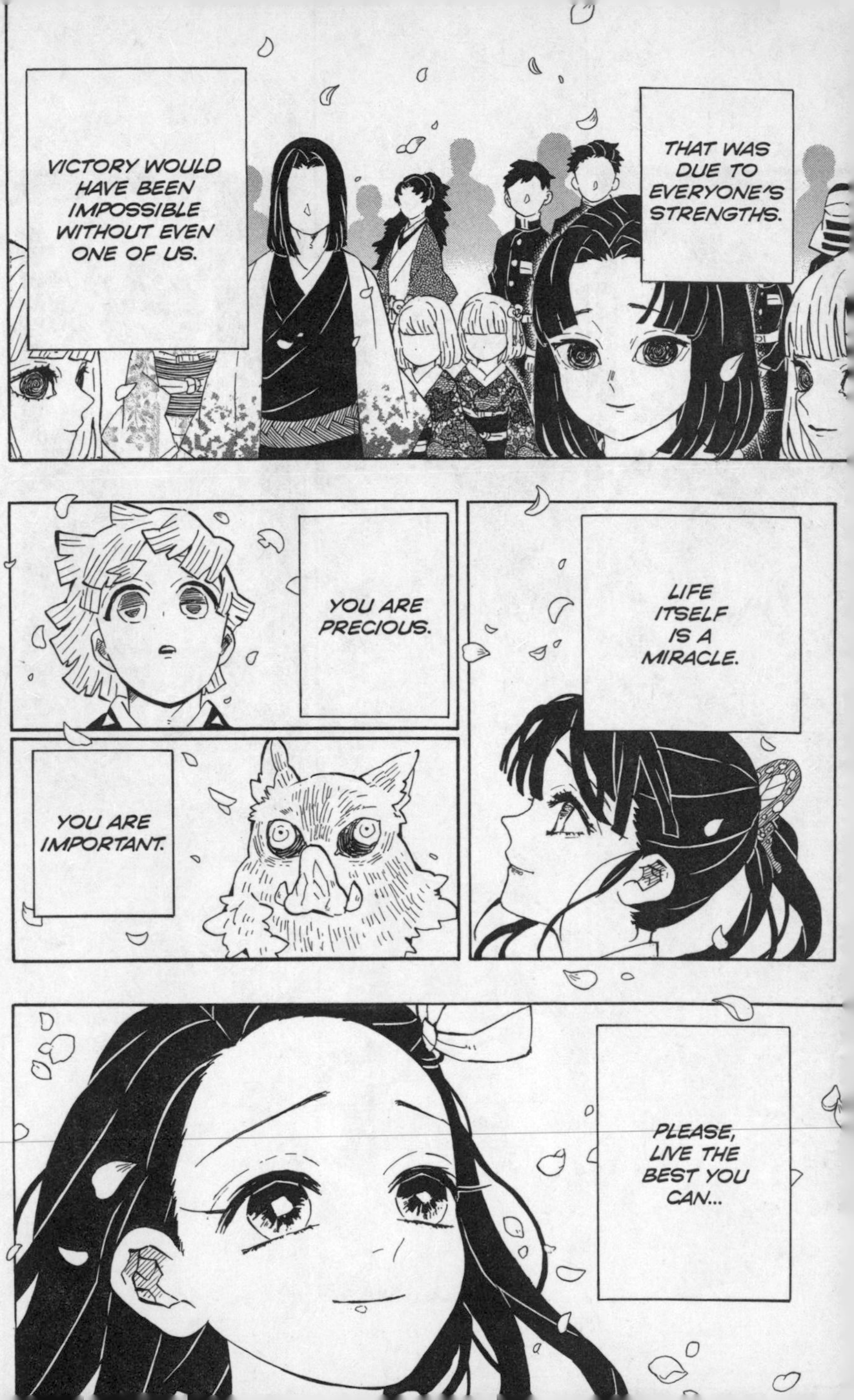
THAT WAS DUE TO EVERYONE'S STRENGTHS.
VICTORY WOULD HAVE BEEN IMPOSSIBLE WITHOUT EVEN ONE OF US.
LIFE ITSELF IS A MIRACLE.
YOU ARE PRECIOUS.
YOU ARE IMPORTANT.
PLEASE, LIVE THE BEST YOU CAN...

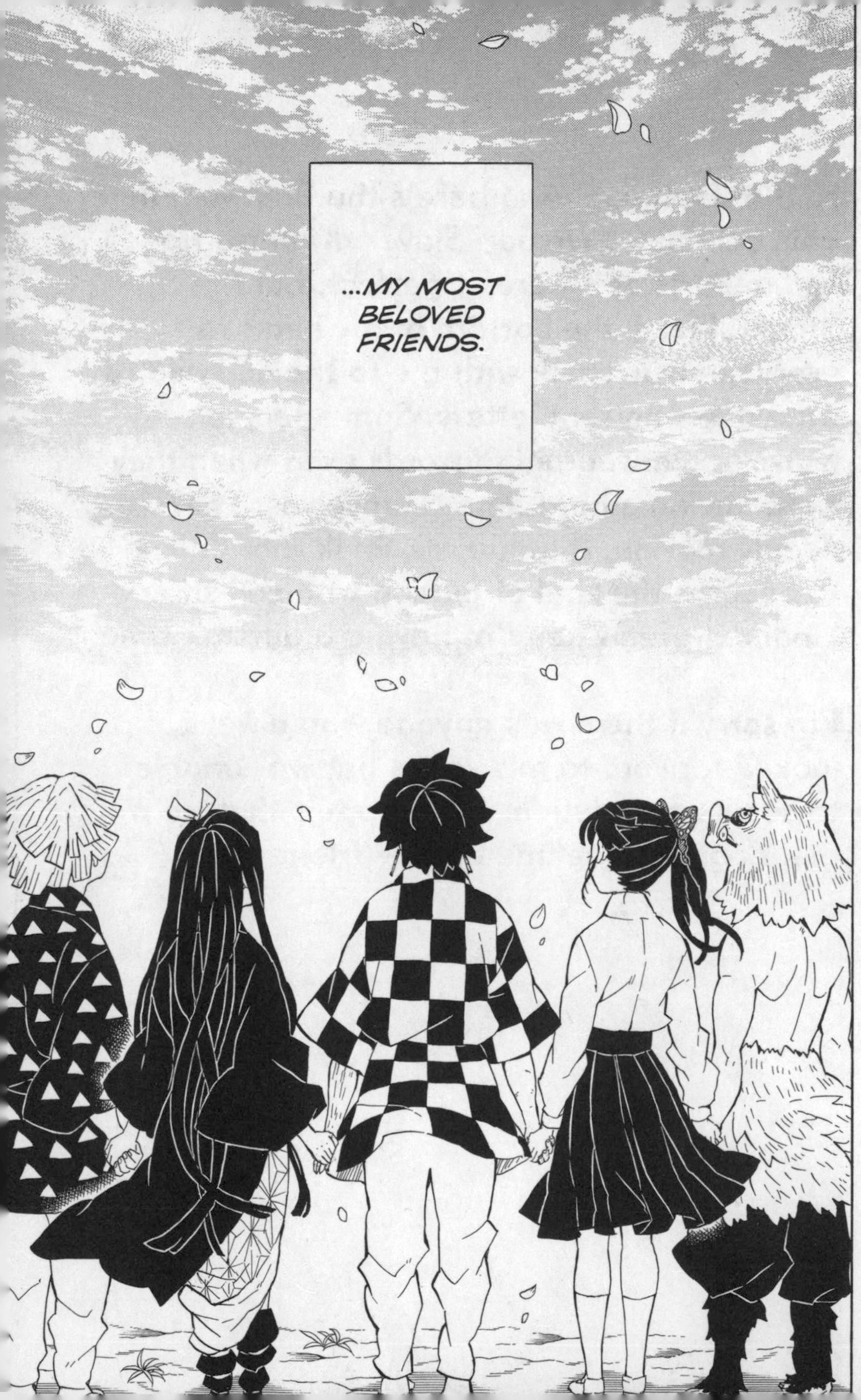
...MY MOST BELOVED FRIENDS.

Hi, I'm Gotouge! And here's the final volume! This completes *Demon Slayer: Kimetsu no Yaiba*. Parts of it weren't perfect, but I'm thankful from the bottom of my heart to everyone who stuck with me to the end and to everyone who sent letters. Some people sent warm and encouraging words even when they were having a hard time themselves. That was deeply moving. It made me think that I'd like to become the kind of person who can spread kindness even when I'm having a difficult time.

I'm sorry if there was anyone who always looked forward to this series but was unable to see its completion. My dream is that we will meet again sometime and be friends.

This series is a story I made with all of you. It's a story that wouldn't exist if you hadn't read it. Thank you for fighting alongside Tanjiro and the other characters, and thank you for your tears and laughter. A lot of people helped me, and I was able to learn and grow a lot. It was a greater honor than I deserve. Thank you so very much. From the bottom of my heart, I wish for the happiness of everyone who provided encouragement, helped out or was involved with the series in some way.

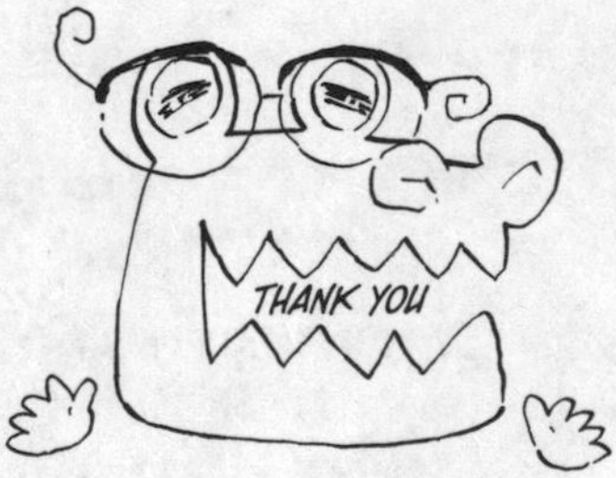
THANK YOU

YOU'RE READING THE
WRONG WAY!

DEMON SLAYER: KIMETSU NO YAIBA
reads from right to left, starting in the
upper-right corner. Japanese is read
from right to left, meaning that action,
sound effects and word-balloon order are
completely reversed from English order.